20 CENTURIES OF
GREAT PREACHING

VOLUME FIVE

MACLAREN

to

TALMAGE

1826–1912

20 CENTURIES OF GREAT PREACHING

An Encyclopedia of Preaching

VOLUME FIVE

MACLAREN

to

TALMAGE

1826–1912

CLYDE E. FANT, JR.
WILLIAM M. PINSON, JR.

DONALD E. HAMMER
Research Associate

WORD BOOKS, Publisher
Waco, Texas

Special Thanks:

We express our deep appreciation to the library at Southern Baptist Theological Seminary for the original photograph of John Broadus and to Jerry Ashby for providing photostats of newspaper transcriptions of sermons by Broadus.

We are grateful to the many who helped obtain material on William Booth: Richard Collier, author of *The General Next to God;* Major Burl Wyatt, of The Salvation Army in Fort Worth, Texas, for his untiring efforts in locating original material by Booth; B. Bernard Booth, grandson of William Booth, for putting us in contact with two recordings by Booth; Colonel J. H. Lewis, Literary Secretary of the International Headquarters for the Salvation Army, London, for putting us in touch with Commissioner Catherine Bramwell-Booth, granddaughter of the founder.

Contents

Illustrations

Abbreviations of the Books of the Bible

Old Testament	Authorized	Douay
Genesis	Gen.	Gen.
Exodus	Exod.	Exod.
Leviticus	Lev.	Lev.
Numbers	Num.	Num.
Deuteronomy	Deut.	Deut.
Joshua	Josh.	Josue
Judges	Judg.	Judges
Ruth	Ruth	Ruth
1 Samuel	1 Sam.	1 Kings
2 Samuel	2 Sam.	2 Kings
1 Kings	1 Kings	3 Kings
2 Kings	2 Kings	4 Kings
1 Chronicles	1 Chron.	1 Par.
2 Chronicles	2 Chron.	2 Par.
Ezra	Ezra	1 Esdras
Nehemiah	Neh.	2 Esdras
Esther	Esther	Esther
Job	Job	Job
Psalms	Ps.	Ps.
Proverbs	Prov.	Prov.
Ecclesiastes	Eccles.	Eccles.
Song of Solomon	Song of Sol.	Cant.
Isaiah	Isa.	Isa.
Jeremiah	Jer.	Jer.
Lamentations	Lam.	Lam.
Ezekiel	Ezek.	Ezech.
Daniel	Dan.	Dan.
Hosea	Hos.	Osee
Joel	Joel	Joel
Amos	Amos	Amos
Obadiah	Obad.	Abdias
Jonah	Jon.	Jon.
Micah	Mic.	Mich.

Old Testament	Authorized	Douay
Nahum	Nah.	Nah.
Habakkuk	Hab.	Hab.
Zephaniah	Zeph.	Soph.
Haggai	Hag.	Aggeus
Zechariah	Zech.	Zach.
Malachi	Mal.	Mal.

New Testament	Authorized and Douay	New Testament	Authorized and Douay
Matthew	Matt.	1 Timothy	1 Tim.
Mark	Mark	2 Timothy	2 Tim.
Luke	Luke	Titus	Titus
John	John	Philemon	Philem.
Acts of the Apostles	Acts	Hebrews	Heb.
Romans	Rom.	James	James
1 Corinthians	1 Cor.	1 Peter	1 Pet.
2 Corinthians	2 Cor.	2 Peter	2 Pet.
Galatians	Gal.	1 John	1 John
Ephesians	Eph.	2 John	2 John
Philippians	Phil.	3 John	3 John
Colossians	Col.	Jude	Jude
1 Thessalonians	1 Thess.	Revelation	Rev. (Apoc.)
2 Thessalonians	2 Thess.		

20 CENTURIES OF
GREAT PREACHING

VOLUME FIVE

MACLAREN

to

TALMAGE

1826–1912

ALEXANDER MACLAREN

1826 - 1910

ALEXANDER MACLAREN, from *A Rosary of Christian Graces* by Alexander Maclaren (London: Horace Marshall & Son, 1899), frontispiece.

ALEXANDER MACLAREN

1826   *Born in Glasgow on February 11*
1842   *Moved with his family to London and entered Step-*
        ney College
1845   *Received a college degree and began theological*
        studies
1846   *Began to preach in Portland Chapel, Southampton;*
        became pastor
1856   *Married Marian McLaren, a cousin*
1858   *Became pastor of Union Chapel, Manchester*
1883   *Journeyed on a preaching mission to Australia*
1903   *Retired as pastor of Union Chapel*
1905   *Elected president of the Baptist World Congregation*
1910   *Died in Manchester*

THOUGH ALEXANDER MACLAREN was a pastor, his primary role was that of scholar and preacher. He was an instructive and profound Bible scholar. His biblical expositions and scholarly commentaries have been treasured by thousands throughout the English-speaking world. Few preachers have had more of their sermons published and distributed than Maclaren. Next to Spurgeon's, Maclaren's sermons perhaps have been the most widely read sermons of their time and are still greatly appreciated. They are a tribute to his single-minded devotion to the task of preaching; nothing else so consumed his life as the preparation and delivery of sermons.

LIFE AND TIMES

Alexander Maclaren was born in Glasgow, Scotland, February 11, 1826. His family surrounded him with a Christian en-

3

vironment. His father was a Glasgow businessman and a lay Baptist preacher. His mother was an intelligent and devout woman. The family attended a Baptist church where the pastor, James Patterson, deeply influenced young Alexander.

Early in life he had significant religious experiences. When he was thirteen years old, he requested baptism. In a letter written many years after his baptism, Maclaren described the inner struggle he had concerning salvation. The doctrine of election troubled him deeply. He felt that if God had already decided for him the destiny of his life, nothing he did would make any difference. His sins weighed heavily on him. During a revival meeting, he found "peace and power in believing that Christ is the Saviour" and gave himself to the Christian life.

As a student in Glasgow, he was shy, hard working, and reflective. His father hoped that he would enter the ministry. He took Alexander to a minister friend and asked whether the boy had the gifts necessary to become a preacher. The clerical friend responded that it might be possible, but he was not enthusiastic about the prospects.

In 1842 Alexander moved with his family to London. He entered Stepney College, a Baptist institution. At Stepney, the tall, silent, shy youth did not appear to be a prospect for ministerial greatness. He gained a respectable education and in 1845 received a degree accredited by the recently established London University. The next year he initiated his long career as a pastor.

In 1846 he began to preach to a small congregation in Portland Chapel in Southampton, England. What was to be a three-month trial period became a twelve-year pastorate. His service at Southampton resulted in enormous increases in the size of the congregation.

Maclaren was never a showy individual. His talent was too great to be hidden, but he shunned publicity. As a result, his fame spread slowly across England. In 1858 the Union Baptist Chapel in Manchester called him as pastor. After ten years, a large building was erected to take the place of the little chapel in which Maclaren had begun his Manchester ministry. His success was met with honor after honor: the University of Edinburgh conferred on him the Doctor of Divinity degree; the University of Glasgow did the same. He was elected president of the Baptist Union twice. He journeyed to Australia on a preaching mission in 1883. He was elected president of the Baptist World Congregation in 1905. Manchester showered him with love and acclaim. His portrait was painted for the Manchester Art Gallery.

Throughout his long ministry in Manchester, his primary concern was with his own church and with his responsibility to preach to the congregation. He spent incredible amounts of time in study and preparation, although his sermons were delivered extemporaneously. He became known as a man of profound scholarship and spiritual insight. His commentaries and biblical expositions were acclaimed throughout the world.

Maclaren's life was placid. His churches prospered and the people responded to his leadership. No serious controversies shattered the peace of his congregations. His marriage added stability to his life. In 1856 he married his cousin, Marian McLaren. They had three children, two daughters and a son. The marriage was extremely happy and blighted only by the early death of his wife.

Maclaren's deep faith remained unshaken amidst the theological storms which raged in England. Liberalism, the impact of evolution, the rising tide of the critical approach to the Bible, the wrestling with the complexities of modern life as it related to the Christian faith—all of these washed across Maclaren's life with the effect of a wave upon a mighty granite boulder—he was unmoved in his conservative evangelical position.

New ideas concerning social reform affected him little. He was concerned about moral and social issues, but he put little stock in the concept of changing men through the changing of social institutions. He believed that social rightness was merely the projection of personal rightness; if individuals could be made right, then society would be right. If Christians would only do what the gospel demanded of them, social evils would disappear. If Christians did not fight, there would be no war; if Christians were just in their economic dealings, there would be no economic injustice. Socialist theory had little appeal to him, which is especially interesting in light of the fact that his father had strong liberal leanings.

Although Maclaren's concept of social reform was centered on the individual, he believed nevertheless in attacking social ills and applying the gospel to them. In a sermon entitled "The Christian Attitude to Social Sins" he said:

What was it that kept slavery alive for centuries? Largely, that Christian men solemnly declared that it was a Divine institution. What is it that has kept war alive for all these centuries? Largely, that bishops and preachers have always been ready to bless colors, and to read a christening service over a man-of-war — and, I suppose, to ask God that an eighty-ton gun might be blessed to smash our enemies to pieces, and not to blow our sailors to bits.

And what is it that preserves the crying evils of our community, the immoralities, the drunkenness, the trade dishonesty, and all the other things that I do not need to remind you of in the pulpit? Largely this, that professing Christians are mixed up with them. If only the whole body of those who profess and call themselves Christians would shake their hands clear of all complicity with such things, they could not last.[1]

Maclaren was not naïve enough to believe that Christian abstinence alone from evil was enough to eradicate evil from society. He called for direct action by Christians against social problems. In the same sermon he declared:

This task is laid on the shoulders of all professing Christians. A silent abstinence is not enough. . . . If Christian people think that they have done all their duty, in regard of clamant and common iniquities, by simply abstaining from them and presenting a noble example, they have yet to learn one very important chapter of their duty. A dumb church is a dying church, and it ought to be. For Christ has sent us here in order, amongst other things, that we may bring Christian principles to bear upon the actions of the community, and not be afraid to speak when we are called upon by conscience to do so.[2]

Maclaren realized that evangelism and social concern must go together. He built his preaching upon the solid rock of biblical revelation and applied it to the deeds of his hearers both as persons and as members of the social order. Though Maclaren did not become involved in social and political activities as did

---

1. Gaius Glenn Atkins, ed., *The Best of Alexander Maclaren* (New York: Harper & Bros., 1949), p. 90. Used by permission.
2. Ibid.

other preachers of his day—such as Robert Dale—he did not ignore these evils from the pulpit.

After a long and significant pastorate, Maclaren retired as pastor of Union Chapel in 1903. He remained active in Baptist work in England. He continued to preach and to serve his denomination. In 1910, after almost sixty-five years in the ministry, he died in Manchester.

His sermons had made him famous; his travels throughout Great Britain, on the Continent, in Australia, and in America had made him the object of affection by many. A humble and modest man, he became famous in spite of his retiring character.

After his body was cremated, a cross was placed above his ashes which bears an inscription he himself had chosen: *"In Christo, in pace, in spes"* — "In Christ, in peace, in hope." The phrase well summarizes his life.

PREACHING AND SERMONS

Alexander Maclaren has always been regarded as a model of expository preaching. Joseph Parker preferred him to Spurgeon: "He always says something to his people, something that sticks. In this respect he is much superior to Spurgeon. He thinks more and better." No doubt a good many people would disagree with that evaluation, but there can be no argument that Maclaren was superior in his exposition of Scripture.

Expository preachers generally believe in long hours of Bible study, and Maclaren was no exception. It comes as no surprise to learn that he spent two hours a day studying the Bible in its original languages, poring over texts and meditating upon their meanings. He wrote, "The preacher who has steeped himself in the Bible will have a clearness of outlook which will illuminate many dark things, and a firmness of touch which will breed confidence in him among his hearers. He will have the secret of perpetual freshness, for he cannot exhaust the Bible. . . . Our sufficiency is in God, and God's sufficiency will be ours in the measure in which we steadfastly follow out the purpose of making our preaching truly biblical."

But it may be more surprising to discover that Maclaren never wrote manuscripts of his sermons; he preached entirely without notes:

> I began my ministry with the resolution that I would not write my sermons, *but would think and feel them,*

and I have stuck to it ever since. It costs quite as much time in preparation as writing, and a far greater expenditure of nervous energy in delivery, but I am sure that it is best for me, and equally sure that everybody has to find out his own way.[3]

A contemporary of Maclaren's said that he "so saturated his mind with his subject that facing his congregation, looking into their eyes, his thoughts clothed themselves in suitable words." Maclaren did not write his sermons in full, but he did write parts of his sermons:

I write my sermons in part. The amount of written matter varies. When I can, I like to write a couple of sentences or so of introduction, in order to get a fair start, and for the rest I content myself with jottings, fragmentary hints of a word or two each, interspersed here and there with a fully written sentence. Illustrations and metaphors I never write; a word suffices for them. If I have *heads,* I word these carefully and I like to write the closing sentences.

I do not adhere to what is written, as there is very little of it that is sufficiently consecutive. I make no attempt to reproduce more than the general course of thought and constantly find that the best bits of my sermon make themselves in preaching. *I do adhere to* my *introductory* sentences, which serve to shove me off into deep water; beyond that I let the moment shape the thing. Expressions I do not prepare; if I can get the fire alight, that is what I care for most.

This is my ideal, a sufficiently scrappy one you will think, but I am frequently obliged to preach with much less preparation. The amount written varies from about six or seven pages of ordinary note paper to the barest skeleton that would go in half a page.[4]

Even though Maclaren did not spend a great deal of time in written preparation, he devoted hours and hours to his sermons, thinking and rethinking the words that he would say when he entered the pulpit, and he never lacked the right word to express

---

3. From *The Life of Alexander McLaren* by Elizabeth Teague McLaren (London: Hodder & Stoughton) as quoted in Albert H. Currier, *Nine Great Preachers* (Boston: Pilgrim Press, 1912), p. 289.
4. Currier, pp. 289–90.

his thoughts. Maclaren was so completely immersed in the teachings of the Scripture which he had studied and his mental outline that his exposition flowed naturally and smoothly.

Because of his method of preparation, few people realized what an expenditure of energy his preaching cost him. Early in his ministry he spoke of each Sunday service as a "woe." His biographer, Miss E. T. McLaren, who was both a cousin and his sister-in-law, wrote:

> This feeling continued through his life, and only those who were with him when he was anticipating, not only his special services, but his weekly preparation for his own pulpit, can know the tear and wear of spirit which that preparation involved. . . . In retrospect, it seems little short of a miracle that his life of strenuous preparation for each sermon preached was continued for nearly sixty years.[5]

The best source for understanding Maclaren's philosophy of preaching is an address entitled "An Old Preacher on Preaching" delivered in 1901 at the City Temple in London at a joint meeting of the Baptist and Congregational Unions. It was one of the few times when Maclaren spoke from a complete manuscript. The audience considered it as a great success; Nicoll said of it, "Considering its design and its speaker and its audience, it was simply perfect and will never be forgotten by those who heard it." But Maclaren was frustrated: "A failure because I read it. Again and again I was tempted to fling the paper from me and *let myself go*." Nevertheless, the manuscript has preserved the philosophy of Maclaren's preaching.

The first principle Maclaren enunciated in that address was a dedication to the exposition of the Scripture. He had stated that principle in 1896 at a "Complimentary Breakfast" in London celebrating his "Ministerial Jubilee," the completion of his fiftieth year in the ministry:

> I have tried to make my ministry a ministry of exposition of scripture. I know that it has failed in many respects; but I will say that I have endeavored from the beginning to the end to make that a characteristic of my public work. I have tried to preach Jesus Christ, and

---

5. Ibid., p. 313.

the Jesus Christ not of the gospels only, but the Christ of the gospels and the epistles. He is the same.[6]

In his address at City Temple Maclaren condemned those who "get their opinions" of Christian truth from others instead of forming them for themselves:

> The opinions do not grow, are not shaped by patient labor, but are imported into the new owner's mind, ready-made, "in Germany" or elsewhere, but certainly not in his own workshop. . . . We have need to remember the woes pronounced on two classes of prophets; those who stole the word, every man from his neighbor, and those who prophesied out of their own hearts, having seen nothing and heard no voice from on high. So we have to be sure that we stand on our own feet and see with our own eyes; . . . and on the other hand we have to see that the Word, which is in that sense our own, is in a deeper sense not our own but God's. We have to deal at first hand with Him and to suppress self that He may speak.[7]

Maclaren explained that he believed in "brooding" over a text or passage of Scripture in a devout spirit:

> We need for the prophet's office much secluded fellow-ship with God. . . .
> No man will ever be the Lord's prophet, however eloquent or learned he may be, unless he knows what it is to sit silent before God and in the silence to hear the still, small, most mighty Voice that penetrates the soul. . . .[8]

Maclaren believed that "the preacher has need of the personal element in his message." Unlike many expository preachers of the modern period whose discourses are dry, filled with tedious meanderings and irrelevant discussions of meaningless facts of grammar or background, Maclaren filled his messages with personal applications to real people. He believed in preaching with a note of urgency to the people who sat before him, but

6. Remarks quoted in the *London Baptist Magazine* cited in William Cleaver Wilkinson, *Modern Masters of Pulpit Discourse* (New York: Funk & Wagnalls Co., 1905), p. 118.
7. Alexander Maclaren, "An Old Preacher on Preaching," *The Baptist Handbook for 1902* (London: Veale, Chifferiel & Co., 1901), pp. 100, 107–8.
8. Ibid., pp. 106–8.

always marked by tenderness: "The evangelist has also need of tenderness. . . . Are we not too little accustomed to preach with our hearts?"

Several accounts have been left of Maclaren's appearance in the pulpit. One of the best of these was by Charles H. Parkhurst, himself a distinguished preacher:

> The Union Chapel was a brick building seating fifteen hundred people. Two thousand were packed into it that day, the people crowding in chairs close up to and back of the pulpit. The preacher then was in his sixty-first year. In personal appearance he was thin, tall, spare, with an attractive face. When young he must have been a handsome man. He did not look clerical. He wore no pulpit gown, not even the ministerial white cravat.
>
> In preaching he had no manuscript or note before him. In the introduction he clearly announced his subject, and told his hearers how . . . he proposed to present it. Soon his subject possesses him and he takes fire. His thought transforms him. His voice becomes resonant, tender, impressive. It seems as if God was speaking to you. Every person in the house is held in solemn and impressive awe of the truth. "That is preaching," I said, "and we have not heard the like of it in Europe."[9]

Harwood Pattison said, "He has a face which in its profile at times suggests that of Dante; eyes of wonderful lustre and depth; a tall lithe figure; appropriate and effective gestures; and a varied voice, which, while retaining enough of the Scottish accent to make it pathetic, is more remarkable for its power to give a sharp and crisp accentuation to certain words."

An Australian journalist described his preaching when Maclaren visited that continent: "A wonderously pathetic little bit in the sermon about Abraham and Isaac going up Moriah will not soon be forgotten. Here the voice changed, softened, and seemed to linger over the words: 'Where is the lamb?' While the answer, 'My son, God will provide Himself a lamb,' was like the wail of a breaking heart."

Another contemporary described his appearance in 1889:

9. Quoted in Harry C. Howard, *Princes of the Christian Pulpit and Pastorate* (Nashville: Cokesbury Press, 1927), pp. 321–22.

Maclaren wears no Geneva gown and not even a clerical white necktie. He does not look old for a man of five-and-sixty; his face is thin and sharp; he has an eye like a hawk; his iron grey hair is brushed back from an ample forehead; and even long study has not brought him to the need of using glasses. . . .

He then announced his text from the fourteenth chapter of John, . . . and for forty minutes, without a line of manuscript, he poured forth a bright, pure, clear stream of devout and quickening thought, like one of the crystal rivulets of his own Scottish highlands. . . .

He never preaches but once on the Sabbath, and into that single sermon he puts his whole concentrated strength.[10]

Maclaren was a master of illustration as well as exposition. His sermons were filled with analogies and stories. He was particularly fond of Tennyson and Thomas Carlyle. He said of Carlyle, "No man of our times stirs me like him." Maclaren used illustrations from nature, history, art, and human experience.

Many notable evaluations of Maclaren have been given by famous men but the best, and the most fittingly conclusive, was spoken by a plain farmer's wife. Nine years after she had heard him preach, she said: "I can hear him now; and the strange thing was I never at the time thought about its being Dr. Maclaren that we all knew and liked: it just seemed listening to a message from God."

---

10. Quoted in John Edwards, *Nineteenth Century Preachers and Their Methods* (London: Charles H. Kelley, 1902), p. 77.

Sermons

THE GUIDING PILLAR

"So it was alway; the cloud covered [the tabernacle] by day, and the appearance of fire by night" (Numbers 9:16).

THE CHILDREN OF ISRAEL in the wilderness, surrounded by miracle, had nothing which we do not possess. They had some things in an inferior form; their sustenance came by manna; ours comes by God's blessing on our daily work, which is better. Their guidance came by this supernatural pillar; ours comes by the reality of which that pillar was nothing but a picture. And so, instead of fancying that men thus led were in advance of us, we should learn that these, the supernatural manifestations, visible and palpable, of God's presence and guidance were the beggarly elements: "God having provided some better thing for us, that they without us should not be made perfect."

With this explanation of the relation between the miracle and symbol of the old, and the reality and standing miracle of the new covenants, let us look at the eternal truths, which are set before us in a transitory form, in this cloud by day and fiery pillar by night.

I. Note, first, the double form of the guiding pillar.

The fire was the center; the cloud was wrapped around it. The former was the symbol, making visible to a generation who had to be taught through their senses the inaccessible holiness, and flashing brightness, and purity of the Divine nature; the latter tempered and veiled the too great brightness for feeble eyes.

The same double element is found in all God's manifestations of Himself to men. In every form of revelation are present both the heart and core of light, which no eye can look upon, and the merciful veil which, because it veils, unveils; because it hides, reveals; makes visible because it conceals; and shows God because it is the hiding of His power. So, through all the history of His dealings with men, there has ever been what is called in Scripture language the "face," or the "name of God"; the aspect of the Divine nature on which eye can look; and

---

Reprinted from *The Best of Alexander Maclaren*, ed. Gaius Glenn Atkins (New York: Harper & Bros., 1949), pp. 111–17, from *The Unchanging Christ* (London: Alexander & Shepheard, 1889).

13

manifested through it there has always been the depth and inaccessible abyss of that infinite Being. We have to be thankful that in the cloud is the fire, and that round the fire is the cloud. For only so can our eyes behold and our hands grasp the else invisible and remote central Sun of the universe. God hides to make better known the glories of His character. His revelation is the flashing of the uncreated and intolerable light of His infinite Being through the encircling clouds of human conceptions and words, or of deeds which each show forth, in forms fitted to our apprehension, some fragment of His luster. After all revelation, He remains unrevealed. After ages of showing forth His glory He is still the King invisible, whom no man hath seen at any time nor can see. The revelation which He makes of Himself is "truth, and is no lie." The recognition of the presence in it of both the fire and the cloud does not cast any doubt on the reality of our imperfect knowledge, or the authentic participation in the nature of the central light, of the sparkles of it which reach us. We know with a real knowledge what we know of Him. What He shows us is Himself, though not His whole self.

This double aspect of all possible revelation of God, which was symbolized in comparatively gross external form in the pillar that led Israel on its march, and lay stretched out and quiescent, a guarding covering above the tabernacle when the weary march was still, recurs all through the history of Old Testament revelation by type, and prophecy, and ceremony, in which the encompassing cloud was comparatively dense, and the light which pierced it relatively faint. It reappears in both elements, but combined in new proportions, so as that "the veil — that is to say, His flesh" is thinned to transparency and all aglow with the indwelling luster of manifest Deity. So a light, set in some fair alabaster vase, shines through its translucent walls, bringing out every delicate tint and meandering vein of color, while itself diffused and softened by the enwrapping medium which it beautifies by passing through its pure walls. Both are made visible and attractive to dull eyes by the conjunction. He that hath seen Christ hath seen the Father, and he that hath seen the Father in Christ hath seen the man Christ as none see Him who are blind to the incarnate Deity which illuminates the manhood in which it dwells.

But we have to note also the varying appearance of the pillar according to need. There was a double change in the pillar according to the hour, and according as the congregation was on the march or encamped. By day it was a cloud; by night it glowed in the darkness. On the march it moved before them, an upright pillar, as gathered together for energetic movement; when the camp rested it "returned to the many thousands of Israel" and lay quietly stretched above the tabernacle like one of the long-drawn motionless clouds above the setting summer's sun, glowing through all its substance with unflashing radiance reflected from unseen light, and "on all the glory" (shrined in the Holy Place beneath) was "a defense."

But these changes of aspect symbolize for us the reality of the Protean capacity of change according to our ever-varying needs, which for our blessing we may find in that ever-changing, unchanging Divine presence which will be our companion, if we will.

It was not only by a natural process that, as daylight declined, what had seemed but a column of smoke, in the fervid desert sunlight, brightened into a column of fire, blazing amid the clear stars. But we may well believe in an actual admeasurement of the degree of light correspondent to the darkness and to the need for certitude and cheering sense of God's protection which the defenseless camp would feel as they lay down to rest.

When the deceitful brightness of earth glistens and dazzles around me, my vision of Him may be "a cloudy screen to temper the deceitful ray"; and when "there stoops on our path, in storm and shade, the frequent night," as earth grows darker, and life becomes grayer and more somber, and verges to its even, the pillar blazes brighter before the weeping eye, and draws near to the lonely heart. We have a God that manifests Himself in the pillar of cloud by day, and in the flaming fire by night.

II. Note the guidance of the pillar.

When it lifts the camp marches; when it glides down and lies motionless the march is stopped and the tents are pitched. The main thing which is dwelt upon in this description of the God-guided pilgrimage of the wandering people is the absolute uncertainty in which they were kept as to the duration of their encampment, and as to the time and circumstances of their march. Sometimes the cloud tarried upon the tabernacle many days; sometimes for a night only; sometimes it lifted in the night. "Whether it was by day or by night that the cloud was taken up, they journeyed. Or whether it were two days, or a month, or a year, that the cloud tarried upon the tabernacle, remaining thereon, the children of Israel abode in their tents, and journeyed not: but when it was taken up, they journeyed." So never, from moment to moment, did they know when the moving cloud might settle, or the resting cloud might soar. Therefore, absolute uncertainty as to the next stage was visibly represented before them by that hovering guide which determined everything, and concerning whose next movement they knew absolutely nothing.

Is not that all true about us? We have no guiding cloud like this. So much the better. Have we not a more real guide? God guides us by circumstances; God guides us by His word; God guides us by His Spirit, speaking through our common sense and in our understanding; and, most of all, God guides us by that dear Son of His, in whom is the fire and round whom is the cloud. And perhaps we may even suppose that our Lord implies some allusion to this very symbol in His own great words, "I am the light of the world; he that followeth me shall not walk in darkness, but shall have the sight of life." For the conception of "following" the light seems to make it plain that our Lord's image is not that of the sun in the heavens, or any such supernal light, but of some light that comes near enough to a man to move before him, and behind which he can march.

So, I think that Christ Himself laid His hand upon this ancient symbol, and in these great words said in effect, "I am that which it only shadowed and foretold." At all events, whether in them He was pointing to our text or no, we must feel that He is the reality which was expressed by this outward symbol. And no man who can say, "Jesus Christ is the Captain of my salvation, and after His pattern I march; at the pointing of His guiding finger I move; and in His footsteps, He being my helper, I want to tread," need feel or fancy that any possible pillar, floating before the dullest eye, was a better, surer, and Diviner guide than he possesses. They whom Christ guides want none other for leader, pattern, counselor, companion, reward. This Christ is our Christ forever and ever; He will be our guide, even unto death, and beyond it. The pillar that we follow, which will glow with the ruddy flame of love in the darkest hours of life – blessed be His name – will glide in front of us through the valley of the shadow of death, brightest then when the murky midnight is blackest. Nor will the pillar which guides us cease to blaze as did the guide of the desert march, when Jordon has been crossed. It will still move before us on paths of continuous and ever-increasing approach to infinite perfection. They who follow Christ afar off and with faltering steps here shall there "follow the Lamb whithersoever he goeth."

In like manner, the same absolute uncertainty which was intended to keep the Israelites (though it failed often) in the attitude of constant dependence, is the condition in which we all have to live, though we mask it from ourselves. That we do not know what lies before us is a commonplace. The same long tracks of monotonous continuance in the same place and doing the same duties, befall us that befell these men. Years pass, and the pillar spreads itself out, a defense above the unmoving sanctuary. And then, all of a flash, when we are least thinking of change, it gathers itself together, is a pillar again, shoots upwards, and moves forwards; and it is for us to go after it. And so our lives are shuttle-cocked between uniform sameness which may become mechanical monotony, and agitation by change which may make us lose our hold of fixed principles and calm faith, unless we recognize that the continuance and the change are alike the will of the guiding God whose will is signified by the stationary or moving pillar.

III. That leads me to the last thing that I would note – viz., the docile following of the Guide.

In the context the writer does not seem to be able to get away from the thought that whatever the pillar did, that moment prompt obedience follows. He says it over and over and over again. "As long as the cloud abode . . . they rested. . . . And when the cloud tarried long . . . [they] journeyed not"; and "when the cloud was a few days on the tabernacle . . . they abode"; and "according to the commandment they journeyed"; and "when the cloud abode until the morning . . . they journeyed"; and "whether it were two days, or a month, or a year, that the cloud tarried . . . [they] journeyed not, but abode in their tents." So, after he has reiterated the thing half a dozen times or more, he finishes by putting it all again in one verse, as the last impression which he would leave from the whole narrative—"at the commandment of the Lord they rested in their tents, and at the commandment of the Lord they journeyed." Obedience was prompt; whensoever and for whatsoever the signal was given the men were ready. In the night, after they had had their tents pitched for a long period, somewhere or other, in the night, when only the watchers' eyes were open, the pillar lifts, and in an instant the alarm is given, and all the camp is in a bustle. That is what we have to set before us as the type of our lives—that we shall be as ready for every indication of God's will as they were. The peace and blessedness of our lives largely depend on our being eager to obey, and therefore quick to perceive the slightest sign of motion in the resting or of rest in the moving pillar which regulates our march and our encamping.

What do we want in order to cultivate and keep such a disposition? We need perpetual watchfulness lest the pillar should lift unnoticed. When Nelson was second in command at Copenhagen, the admiral in command of the fleet hoisted the signal for recall, and Nelson put his telescope to his blind eye and said, "I do not see it." That is very like what we are tempted to do; the signal for unpleasant duties that we want to get out of is hoisted; we are very apt to put the telescope to the blind eye and pretend to ourselves that we do not see the fluttering flags.

We need still more to keep our wills in absolute suspense, if His will has not declared itself. Do not let us be in a hurry to run before God. When the Israelites were crossing the Jordan they were told to leave a great space between themselves and the guiding ark, that they might know how to go, because "they had not passed that way heretofore." Impatient hurrying at God's heels is apt to lead us astray. Let Him get well in front, that you may be quite sure which way He wants you to go, before you go. And if you are not sure which way He wants you to go, be sure that He does not at that moment want you to go anywhere.

We need to hold the present with a slack hand, so as to be ready to fold our tents and take to the road if God will. We must not reckon on continuance, nor strike our roots so deep that it needs a hurricane to remove us. To those who set their gaze on Christ, no present from which He wishes them to remove can be so good for them as the new conditions into which He would have them pass. It is hard to leave the spot, though it be in the desert, where we have so long encamped that it has come to look like home. We may look with regret on the circle of black ashes on the sand where our little fire glinted cheerily, and our feet may ache and our hearts ache more as we begin our tramp once again, but we must set ourselves to meet the God-appointed change cheerfully, in the confidence that nothing will be left behind which it is not good to lose, nor anything met which does not bring a blessing, however its first aspect may be — harsh or sad.

We need, too, to cultivate the habit of prompt obedience. "I made haste and delayed not to keep Thy commandments" is the only safe motto. It is reluctance which usually puts the drag on. Slow obedience is often the germ of incipient disobedience. In matters of prudence and of intellect second thoughts are better than first, and third thoughts, which often come back to first ones, better than second; but, in matters of duty, first thoughts are generally best. They are the instructive response of conscience to the voice of God, while second thoughts are too often the objections of disinclination, or sloth, or cowardice. It is easiest to do our duty when we are first sure of it. It then comes with an impelling power which carries us over obstacles on the crest of a wave, while hesitation and delay leave us stranded in shoal water. If we would follow the pillar, we must follow it at once.

A heart that waits and watches for God's direction, that uses common sense as well as faith to unravel small and great perplexities, and is willing to sit loose to the present, however pleasant, in order that it may not miss the indications which say "Arise! this is not your rest" — fulfills the conditions on which, if we keep them, we may be sure that He will guide us by the right way, and bring us at last to the city of habitation.

ZION'S JOY AND GOD'S

"Sing, O daughter of Zion; shout, O Israel; be glad and rejoice with all the heart, O daughter of Jerusalem. . . . He will rejoice over thee with joy; He will rest in His love, He will joy over thee with singing" (Zephaniah 3:14,17).

WHAT A WONDERFUL RUSH of exuberant gladness there is in these words! The swift, short clauses, the triple invocation in the former verse, the triple promise in the latter, the heaped together synonyms, all help the impression. The very words seem to dance with joy. But more remarkable than this is the parallelism between the two verses. Zion is called to rejoice in God because God rejoices in her. She is to shout for joy and sing because God's joy too has a voice, and breaks out into singing. For every throb of joy in man's heart, there is a wave of gladness in God's. The notes of our praise are at once the echoes and the occasions of His. We are to be glad because He is glad: He is glad because we are so. We sing for joy, and He joys over us with singing because we do.

I. God's joy over Zion.

It is to be noticed that the former verse of our text is followed by the assurance: "The Lord is in the midst of thee"; and that the latter verse is preceded by the same assurance. So, then, intimate fellowship and communion between God and Israel lies at the root both of God's joy in man and man's joy in God.

We are solemnly warned by "profound thinkers" of letting the shadow of our emotions fall upon God. No doubt there is a real danger there; but there is a worse danger, that of conceiving of a God who has no life and heart; and it is better to hold fast by this — that in Him is that which corresponds to what in us is gladness. We are often told, too, that the Jehovah of the Old Testament is a stern and repellent God, and the religion of the Old Testament is gloomy and servile. But such a misconception is hard to maintain in the face of such words as these. Zephaniah, of whom we know little, and whose words are mainly forecasts of judgments and woes pronounced against Zion that was rebellious and polluted, ends his prophecy with these companion pictures, like a gleam of sunshine which often streams out at the close of a dark winter's day. To him the judgments which he prophesied were no contradiction of the love and gladness of God. The thought of a glad God might be a very awful thought; such an insight as this prophet had gives a blessed meaning to it. We may think of the joy that

Reprinted with permission of Wm. B. Eerdmans Publishing Co. from *Maclaren's Expositions of Holy Scripture*, by Alexander Maclaren, vol. 4 (Grand Rapids: 1959), pp. 245–48.

belongs to the divine nature as coming from the completeness of His being, which is raised far above all that makes of sorrow. But it is not in Himself alone that He is glad; but it is because He loves. The exercise of love is ever blessedness. His joy is in self-impartation; His delights are in the sons of men: "As the bridegroom rejoiceth over the bride, so shall thy God rejoice over thee." His gladness is in His children when they let Him love them, and do not throw back His love on itself. As in man's physical frame it is pain to have secretions dammed up, so when God's love is forced back upon itself and prevented from flowing out in blessing, some shadow of suffering cannot but pass across that calm sky. He is glad when His face is mirrored in ours, and the rays from Him are reflected from us.

But there is another wonderfully bold and beautiful thought in this representation of the gladness of God. Note the double form which it assumes: "He will rest" — literally, be silent — "in His love; He will joy over thee with singing." As to the former, loving hearts on earth know that the deepest love knows no utterance, and can find none. A heart full of love rests as having attained its desire and accomplished its purpose. It keeps a perpetual Sabbath, and is content to be silent.

But side by side with this picture of the repose of God's joy is set with great poetic insight the precisely opposite image of a love which delights in expression, and rejoices over its object with singing. The combination of the two helps to express the depth and intensity of the one love, which like a song-bird rises with quivering delight and pours out as it rises an ever louder and more joyous note, and then drops, composed and still, to its nest upon the dewy ground.

II. Zion's joy in God.

To the Prophet, the fact that "the Lord is in the midst of thee" was the guarantee for the confident assurance "Thou shalt not fear any more"; and this assurance was to be the occasion of exuberant gladness, which ripples over in the very words of our first text. That great thought of "God dwelling in the midst" is rightly a pain and a terror to rebellious wills and alienated hearts. It needs some preparation of mind and spirit to be glad because God is near; and they who find their satisfaction in earthly sources, and those who seek for it in these, see no word of good news, but rather a "fearful looking for of judgment" in the thought that God is in their midst. The word rendered "rejoices" in the first verse of our text is not the same as that so translated in the second. The latter means literally, to move in a circle; while the former literally means, to leap for joy. Thus the gladness of God is thought of as expressing itself in dignified, calm movements, whilst Zion's joy is likened in its expression to the more violent movements of the dance. True human joy is like God's, in that He delights in us and we in Him, and in that both He and we delight in the exercise of love. But we are never to forget that the differences are real as the resemblances, and that it is reserved for the higher form of our experiences in a future life to "enter into the joy of the Lord."

It becomes us to see to it that our religion is a religion of joy. Our text is an authoritative command as well as a joyful exhortation, and we do not fairly represent the facts of Christian faith if we do not "rejoice in the Lord always." In all the sadness and troubles which necessarily accompany us, as they do all men, we ought by the effort of faith to set the Lord always before us that we be not moved. The secret of stable and perpetual joy still lies where Zephaniah found it — in the assurance that the Lord is with us, and in the vision of His love resting upon us, and rejoicing over us with singing. If thus our love clasps His, and His joy finds its way into our hearts, it will remain with us that our "joy may be full"; and being guarded by Him whilst still there is fear of stumbling, He will set us at last "before the presence of His glory without blemish in exceeding joy."

GRACE, MERCY, AND PEACE

"Grace be with you, mercy, and peace, from God the Father, and from the Lord Jesus Christ, the Son of the Father, in truth and love" (2 John 3).

WE HAVE here a very unusual form of the Apostolic salutation. "Grace, mercy, and peace" are put together in this fashion only in Paul's two Epistles to Timothy, and in this the present instance; and all reference to the Holy Spirit as an agent in the benediction is, as there, omitted.

The three main words, "Grace, mercy, and peace," stand related to each other in a very interesting manner. If you will think for a moment you will see, I presume, that the Apostle starts, as it were, from the fountain-head, and slowly traces the course of the blessing down to its lodgment in the heart of man. There is the fountain, and the stream, and, if I may so say, the great still lake in the soul, into which its waters

Reprinted with permission of Wm. B. Eerdmans Publishing Co. from *Maclaren's Expositions of Holy Scripture*, by Alexander Maclaren, vol. 2 (Grand Rapids: 1959), pp. 47–53.

flow, and which the flowing waters make. There is the sun, and the beam, and the brightness grows deep in the heart of man. Grace, referring solely to the Divine attitude and thought: mercy, the manifestation of grace in act, referring to the workings of that great Godhead in its relation to humanity: and peace, which is the issue in the soul of the fluttering down upon it of the mercy which is the activity of the grace. So these three come down, as it were, a great, solemn, marble staircase from the heights of the Divine mind, one step at a time, down to the level of earth; and the blessings which are shed along the earth. Such is the order. All begins with grace; and the end and purpose of grace, when it flashes into deed, and becomes mercy, is to fill my soul with quiet repose, and shed across all the turbulent sea of human love a great calm, a beam of sunshine that gilds, and miraculously stills while it gilds, the waves.

If that be, then, the account of the relation of these three to one another, let me just dwell for a moment upon their respective characteristics, that we may get more fully the large significance and wide scope of this blessing. Let us begin at what may be regarded either as the highest point from which all the stream descends, or as the foundation upon which all the structure rests. "Grace from God the Father and from the Lord Jesus Christ, the Son of the Father." These two, blended and yet separate, to either of whom a Christian man has a distinct relation, these two are the sources, equally, of the whole of the grace.

The Scriptural idea of grace is love that stoops, and that pardons, and that communicates. I say nothing about that last characteristic, but I would like to dwell for a moment or two upon the other phases of this great word, a key-word to the understanding of so much of Scripture.

The first thing then that strikes me in it is how it exults in that great thought that there is no reason whatsoever for God's love except God's will. The very foundation and notion of the word "grace" is a free, undeserved, unsolicited, self-prompted, and altogether gratuitous bestowment, a love that is its own reason, as indeed the whole of the Divine acts are, just as we say of Him that He draws His being from Himself, so the whole motive for His action and the whole reason for His heart of tenderness to us lies in Himself. We have no power. We love one another because we apprehend something deserving of love, or fancy that we do. We love one another because there is something in the object on which our love falls; which, either by kindred or by character, or by visible form, draws it out. We are influenced so, and love a thing because the thing or the person is perceived by us as being worthy, for some reason or other, of the love. God loves because He cannot help it; God loves because He is God. Our love is drawn out — I was going to say pumped out — by an application of external causes. God's love is like an artesian well, whensoever you strike, up comes, self-impelled, gushing into light because there is such a central store of it beneath everything, the bright and flashing waters. Grace is love that is not drawn out, but that bursts out, self-originated, undeserved. "Not for your sakes, be it known unto you, O house of Israel, but for Mine own name's sake, do I this." The grace of God is above that, comes spontaneously, driven by its own fulness, and welling up unasked, unprompted, undeserved, and therefore never to be turned away by our evil, never to be wearied by our indifference, never to be brushed aside by our negligence, never to be provoked by our transgression, the fixed, eternal, unalterable centre of the Divine nature. His love is grace.

And then, in like manner, let me remind you that there lies in this great word, which in itself is a gospel, the preaching that God's love, though it be not turned away by, is made tender by our sin. Grace is love extended to a person that might reasonably expect, because he deserves, something very different; and when there is laid, as the foundation of everything, "the grace of our Father and of the Son of the Father," it is but packing into one word that great truth which we all of us, saints and sinners, need—a sign that God's love is love that deals with our transgressions and shortcomings, flows forth perfectly conscious of them, and manifests itself in taking them away, both in their guilt, punishment, and peril. "The grace of our Father" is a love to which sin-convinced consciences may certainly appeal; a love to which all sin-tyrannised souls may turn for emancipation and deliverance. Then, if we turn for a moment from that deep fountain, "Love's ever-springing well," as one of our old hymns has it, to the stream, we get other blessed thoughts. The love, the grace, breaks into mercy. The fountain gathers itself into a river, the infinite, Divine love concentrates itself in act, and that act is described by this one word, mercy. As grace is love which forgives, so mercy is love which pities and helps. Mercy regards men, its object, as full of sorrows and miseries, and so robes itself in garb of compassion, and takes wine and oil into its hands to pour into the wound, and lays often a healing hand, very carefully and very gently, upon the creature, lest, like a clumsy surgeon, it should pain instead of heal, and hurt where it desires to console. God's grace softens itself into mercy, and all His dealings with us men must be on the footing that we are not only sinful, but that we are weak and wretched, and so fit subjects for a compassion which is the strangest paradox of a perfect and divine heart. The mercy of God is the outcome of His grace.

And as is the fountain and the stream, so is the great lake into which it spreads itself when it is received into a human heart. Peace comes, the all-sufficient summing up of everything that God can give, and that men can need, from His loving-kindness, and from their needs. The world is too wide to be narrowed to any single aspect of the various discords and disharmonies which trouble men. Peace with God; peace in this anarchic kingdom within me, where conscience and will, hopes and fears, duty and passion, sorrows and joys, cares and confidence, are ever fighting one another; where we are torn asunder by conflicting aims and rival claims, and wherever any part of our nature asserting itself against another leads to intestine warfare, and troubles the poor soul. All that is harmonised and quieted down, and made concordant and co-operative to one great end, when the grace and the mercy have flowed silently into our spirits and harmonised aims and desires.

There is peace that comes from submission; tranquillity of spirit, which is the crown and reward of obedience; repose, which is the very smile upon the face of faith, and all these things are given unto us along with the grace and mercy of our God. And as the man that possesses this is at peace with God, and at peace with himself, so he may bear in his heart that singular blessing of a perfect tranquillity and quiet amidst the distractions of duty, of sorrows, of losses, and of cares. "In everything by prayer and supplication with thanksgiving let your requests be known unto God; and the peace of God which passeth all understanding shall keep your hearts and minds in Christ Jesus." And he who is thus at friendship with God, and in harmony with himself, and at rest from sorrows and cares, will surely find no enemies amongst men with whom he must needs be at war, but will be a son of peace, and walk the world, meeting in them all a friend and a brother. So all discords may be quieted; even though still we have to fight the good fight of faith, we may do, like Gideon of old, build an altar to "Jehovah-shalom," the God of peace.

And now one word, as to what this great text tells us are the conditions for a Christian man, of preserving, vivid and full, these great gifts, "Grace, mercy, and peace be unto you," or, as the Revised Version more accurately reads, "shall be with us in truth and love." Truth and love are, as it were, the space within which the river flows, if I may so say, the banks of the stream. Or, to get away from the metaphor, these are set forth as being the conditions abiding in which for our parts, we shall receive this benediction—"In truth and in love."

I have no time to enlarge upon the great thoughts that these two words, thus looked at, suggest; let me put it into a sentence. To "abide in the truth" is to keep ourselves conscientiously and habitually under the influence of the Gospel of Jesus Christ, and of the Christ who is Himself the Truth. They who, keeping in Him, realising His presence, believing His word, founding their thinking about the unseen, about their relations to God, about sin and forgiveness, about righteousness and duty, and about a thousand other things, upon Christ and the revelation that He makes, these are those who shall receive "Grace, mercy, and peace." Keep yourselves in Christ, and Christ coming to you, brings in His hands, and *is*, the "grace and the mercy and the peace" of which my text speaks. And in love, if we want these blessings, we must keep ourselves consciously in the possession of, and in the grateful response of our hearts to, the great love, the incarnate Love, which is given in Jesus Christ.

Here is, so to speak, the line of direction which these great mercies take. The man who stands in their path, they will come to him and fill his heart; the man that steps aside, they will run past him and not touch him. You keep yourselves in the love of God, by communion, by the exercise of mind and heart and faith upon Him; and then be sure—for my text is not only a wish, but a confident affirmation—be sure that the fountain of all blessing itself, and the stream of petty benedictions which flow from it, will open themselves out in your hearts into a quiet, deep sea, on whose calm surface no tempests shall ever rave, and on whose unruffled bosom God Himself will manifest and mirror His face.

GROWTH

"But grow in grace, and in the knowledge of our Lord and Saviour Jesus Christ" (2 Peter 3:18).

THESE ARE THE LAST WORDS of an old man, written down as his legacy to us. He was himself a striking example of his own precept. It would be interesting study to examine these two letters of the Apostle Peter, in order to construct from them a picture of what he became, and to contrast it with his own earlier self when full of self-confidence, rashness, and instability. It took a lifetime for Simon, the son of Jonas, to grow into Peter; but it was done. And the very faults of the character became strength. What he had proved possible in his own case he commands and commends to us, and from the height to which he has reached, he looks upwards to the infinite ascent which he knows he will attain when he puts off this tabernacle; and then downwards to his brethren, bidding them, too, climb and aspire. His last word is like that of the great Roman Catholic apostle to the East Indies: "Forward!" He is like some trumpeter on the battlefield who spends his

Reprinted with permission of Wm. B. Eerdmans Publishing Co. from *Maclaren's Expositions of Holy Scripture*, by Alexander Maclaren, vol. 2 (Grand Rapids: 1959), pp. 234–46.

last breath in sounding an advance. Immortal hope animates his dying injunction: "Grow! grow in grace, and in the knowledge of our Lord and Saviour."

So I think we may take these words, dear friends, as the starting-point for some very plain remarks about what I am afraid is a neglected duty of growth in Christian character.

I. I begin, first, with a word or two about the direction which Christian growth ought to take.

Now those of you who use the Revised Version will see in it a very slight, but very valuable alteration. It reads there: "Grow in the grace and knowledge of our Lord and Saviour." The effect of that alteration being to bring out more clearly that whilst the direction of the growth is twofold, the process is one. And to bring out more clearly, also, that both the grace and the knowledge have connection with Jesus Christ.

He is the Giver and the Author of the grace. He is the Object of the knowledge. The one is more moral and spiritual; the other, if we may so say, more intellectual; but both are realised by one act of progress, and both inhere in, and refer to, and are occupied with, and are derived from, Jesus Christ Himself.

Let us look a little more closely at this double direction, this bifurcation, as it were, of Christian growth. The tree, like some of our forest trees, in its normal progress, diverges into two main branches at a short distance upwards from the root.

First, we have growth in the "grace" of Christ. Grace, of course, means, first, the undeserved love and favour which God in Jesus Christ bears to us sinful and inferior creatures; and then it means the consequence of that love and favour in the manifold spiritual endowments which in us become "graces," beauties, and excellences of Christian character. So then, if you are a Christian, you ought to be continually realising a deeper and more blessed consciousness of Christ's love and favour as yours. You ought to be, if I may so say, nestling every day nearer and nearer to His heart, and getting more and more sure, and more and more happily sure, of more and more of His mercy and love to you.

And if you are a Christian you ought not only thus to be realising daily, with increasing certitude and power, the fact of His love, but you ought to be drinking in and deriving more and more every day of the consequences of that love, of the spiritual gifts of which His hands are full. There is open for each of us in Him an inexhaustible store of abundance. And if our Christian life is real and vigorous there ought to be in us a daily increasing capacity, and therefore a daily increasing possession of the gifts of His grace. There ought to be, in other words, also a daily progressive transformation into His likeness. It is "the grace of our Lord Jesus," not only in the sense that He is the Author and the Bestower of it to each of us, but also in the sense that He Himself possesses and exemplifies it. So that there is nothing mystical and remote from the experience of daily life in this exhortation: "Grow in grace"; and it is not growth in some occult theological virtue, or transcendent experience, but a very plain, practical thing, a daily transformation, with growing completeness and precision of resemblance, into the likeness of Jesus Christ; the grace that was in Him being transferred to me, and my character being growingly irradiated and refined, softened and ennobled by the reflection of the lustre of His.

This it is to "grow into the grace of our Lord and Saviour"; a deeper consciousness of His love creeping round the roots of my heart every day, and fuller possession of His gifts placed in my opening hand every day; and a continual approximation to the beauty of His likeness, which never halts nor ceases.

"Grow in the knowledge of our Lord and Saviour." The knowledge of a person is not the same as the knowledge of a creed or of a thought or of a book. We are to grow in the knowledge of Christ, which includes but is more than the intellectual apprehension of the truths concerning Him. He might turn the injunction into—"Increase your acquaintance with your Saviour." Many Christians never get to be any more intimate with Him than they were when they were first introduced to Him. They are on a kind of bowing acquaintance with their Master, and have little more than that. We sometimes begin an acquaintance which we think promises to ripen into a friendship, but are disappointed. Circumstances or some want of congeniality which is discovered prevent its growth. So with not a few professing Christians. They have got no nearer Jesus Christ than when they first knew Him. Their friendship has not grown. It has never reached the stage where all restraints are laid aside and there is perfect confidence. "Grow in the knowledge of your Lord and Saviour Jesus Christ." Get more and more intimate with Him, nearer to Him, and franker and more cordial with Him day by day.

But there is another side to the injunction besides that. We are to grow in the grasp, the intellectual grasp and realisation of the truths which lie wrapped up and enfolded in Him. The first truths that a man learns when he becomes a Christian are the most important. The lesson that the little child learns contains the Omega as well as the Alpha of all truth. There is no word in all the gospel that is an advance on that initial word, the faith of which saves the most ignorant who trusts to it. We begin with the end, if I may say so, and the highest truth is the first truth that we learn. But the aspect which that truth bears to the man when, first of all, it dawns upon him, and he sees in it the end of his fears, the cleansing of his heart, the pardoning of his sins, his acceptance with God, is a very different thing from the aspect that it ought to wear to him, after, say forty years of pondering, of growing up to it, after years of experience have taught him. Life is the best commentary upon the truths of the gospel, and the experience teaches their depths and their power, their far-reaching applications and harmonies. So our growth in the knowledge of Jesus Christ is not a growing away from the earliest lessons, or a leaving them behind, but a growing up to and into them. So as to learn more fully and clearly all their infinite contents of grace and truth. The treasure put into our hands at first is discovered in its true preciousness as life and trial test its metal and its inexhaustibleness. The child's lesson is the man's lesson. All our Christian progress in knowledge consists in bringing to light the deep meaning, the far-reaching consequences of the fact of Christ's incarnation, death, and glory. "God so loved the world that He gave His only begotten Son that whosoever believeth in Him should not perish, but have everlasting life." The same truth which shone at first a star in a far-off sky, through a sinful man's night of fear and agony, grows in brilliance as we draw nearer to it, until at last it blazes, the central Sun of the Universe, the hearth for all vital warmth, the fountain of all guiding light, the centre of all energy. Christ in His manhood, in His divinity, Christ in His cross, resurrection, and glory, is the object of all knowledge, and we grow in the knowledge of Him by penetrating more deeply into the truths which we have long ago learned, as well as by following them as they lead us into new fields, and disclose unsuspected issues in creed and practice.

That growth will not be one-sided; for grace and knowledge will advance side by side — the moral and spiritual keeping step with the intellectual, the practical with the theoretical. And that growth will have no term. It is growth towards an infinite object of our aspiration, imitation, and affection. So we shall ever approach and never surpass Jesus Christ. Such endless progress is the very salt of life. It keeps us young when physical strength decays. It flames, an immortal hope, to light the darkness of the grave when all other hopes are quenched in night.

II. Now, for a moment, look at another thought, viz., the obligation.

It is a command, that is to say, the will is involved. Growth is to be done by effort, and the fact that it is a command teaches us this, that we are not to take this one metaphor as if it exhausted the whole of the facts of the case in reference to Christian progress.

You would never think of telling a child to grow any more than you would think of telling a plant to grow, but Peter does tell Christian men and women to grow. Why? Because they are not plants, but men with wills, which can resist, and can either further or hinder their progress.

> Lo! in the middle of the wood,
> The folded leaf is wooed from out the bud,
> .   .   .   .   .   and there
> Grows green and broad, and takes no care.

But that is not how we grow. "In the sweat of thy brow," with pain and peril, with effort and toil, and not otherwise, do men grow in everything but stature. And especially is it so in the Christian character. There are other metaphors that need to be taken into consideration as well as this of growth, with all its sweet suggestions of continuous, effortless, spontaneous advance.

The Christian progress is not only growth, it is warfare. The Christian progress is not only growth, it is a race. The Christian progress is not only growth, it is mortifying the old man. The Christian progress is not only growth, it is putting off the old man with his deeds and putting on the new! "First the blade, then the ear, after that the full corn in the ear," was never meant for a complete account of how the Christian life is perfected.

We are bidden to grow, and that command points to hindrances and resistance, to the need for effort and the governing action of our own wills.

The command is one sorely needed in the present state of our average Christianity. Our churches are full of monsters, specimens of arrested growth, dwarfs, who have scarcely grown since they were babes, infants all their lives. I come to you with a very plain question: Have you any more of Christ's beauty in your characters, any more of His grace in your hearts, any more of His truth in your minds than you had a year ago, ten years ago, or at that far-off period when some of you grey-headed men first professed to be Christians? Have you experienced so many things in vain? Have the years taught you nothing? Ah, brethren! for how many of us is it true: "When for the time ye ought to be teachers ye have need that one teach you which be the first principles of the oracles of God"? "Grow in grace, and in the knowledge of our Lord and Saviour."

And we need the command because all about us there are hindrances. There is the hindrance of an abuse of the evangelical doctrine of conversion, and the idea that springs up in many hearts that if once a man has "passed from death unto life," and has managed to get inside the door of the banqueting-hall, that is enough. And there are numbers of people in our Nonconformist communities especially, where that doctrine of conversion is most distinctly preached, whose growth is stopped by the abuse that they make of it in fancying if they have once exercised faith in Jesus Christ they may safely and sinlessly stand still. "Conversion" is turning round. What do we turn round for? Surely, in order that we may travel on in the new direction, not that we may stay where we are. There is also the hindrance of mere indolence, and there is the hindrance arising from absorption in the world and its concerns.

If all your strength is going thither, there is none left to grow with. Many professing Christians take such deep draughts of the intoxicating cup of this world's pleasures that it stunts their growth. People sometimes give children gin in order to keep them from growing. Some of you do that for your Christian character by the deep draughts that you take of the Circean cup of this world's pleasures and cares.

And not unfrequently, some one favourite evil, some lust or passion, or weakness, or desire, which you have not the strength to cast out, will kill all aspirations and destroy all possibilities of growth; and will be like an iron band round a little sapling, which will confine it and utterly prevent all expansion. Is that the case with any of us? We all need—and I pray you suffer—the word of exhortation.

III. Now, again, consider the method of growth.

There are two things essential to the growth of animal life. One is food, the other is exercise; and your Christian character will grow by no other means.

Now as to the first. The true means by which we shall grow in Christain grace is by holding continual intercourse and communion with Jesus Christ. It is from Him that all come. He is the Fountain of Life; He gives the life, He nourishes the life, He increases the life. And whilst I have been saying, in an earlier part of this discourse, that we are not to expect an effortless growth, I must here say that we shall very much mistake what Christian progress requires if we suppose that the effort is most profitably directed to the cultivation of specific and single acts of goodness and purity. Our efforts are best when directed to keeping ourselves in union with our Lord. The heart united to Him will certainly be advancing in all things fair and lovely and of good report. Keep yourselves in touch with Christ; and Christ will make you grow. That is to say, occupy heart and mind with Him, let your thoughts go to Him. Do you ever, from morning to night, on a week-day, think about your Master, about His truth, about the principles of His Gospel, about His great love to you? Keep your heart in union with Him, in the midst of the rush and hurry of your daily life. Are your desires turning to Him? Do they go out towards Him and feel after Him? It will take an effort to keep up the union with Him, but without the effort there will be no contact, and without the contact there will be no growth. As soon may you expect a plant, wrenched from the soil and shut out from the sunshine to grow, as expect any Christian progress in the hearts which are disjoined from Jesus Christ. But rooted in that soil, smiled upon by that sun, watered by the perpetual dew from His Heaven, we shall "grow like the lily, and cast forth our roots like Lebanon." The secret of real Christian progress and the direction in which the effort of Christian progress can most profitably and effectually be made, is simply in keeping close to our Lord and Master. He is the food of the Spirit. "I am come that they might have life, and that they might have it more abundantly."

Communion with Christ includes prayer. Desire to grow will help our growth. We tend to become what we long to be. Desire which impels to effort will not be in vain if it likewise impels to prayer. We may have the answer to our petition for growth in set ways; we may be but partially conscious of the answer, nor know that our faces shine when we go among men. But certainly if we pray for what is in such accordance with His will as "growth in grace" is, we shall have the petition that we desire. That longing to know Him better and to possess more of His grace, like the tendrils of some climbing plant, will always find the support round which it may twine, and by which it may ascend.

The other condition of growth is exercise. Use the grace which you have, and it increases. Practice the truth which you know, and many things will become clearer. The blacksmith's muscles are strengthened by wielding the forge-hammer, but unused they waste. The child grows by exercise. To him that hath — truly possesses with the possession which only use secures — shall be given.

Communion with Christ, including prayer, and exercise are the means of growth.

IV. Lastly, observe the solemn alternative to growth.

It is not a question of either growing or not growing, and there an end; but if you will look at the context you will see that the exhortation of my text comes in in a very significant connection. "Behold! beware, lest being led away . . . ye fall from your own steadfastness." "But grow in grace." That is to say, the only preventive of falling away from steadfastness is continual progress. The alternative of advance is retrogression. There is no standing still upon the inclined plane. If you are not going up, gravity begins to act, and down you go. There must either be continual advance or there will be certain decay and corruption. As soon as growth ceases in this physiology *disintegration* commences. Just as the graces exercised are strengthened, so the graces unexercised decay. The slothful servant wraps his talent in a napkin, and buries it in the ground. He may try to persuade his Master and himself with "There Thou hast that is Thine"; but He will not take up what you buried. Rust and verdigris will have done their work upon the coin; the inscription will be obliterated and the image will be marred. You cannot bury your Christian grace in indolence without diminishing it. It will be like a bit of ice wrapped in a cloth and left in the sun, it will all have gone into water when you come to take it out. And the truth that you do *not* live by, whose relations and large harmonies and controlling power are not being increasingly realised in your lives; that truth is becoming less and less real, more and more shadowy and ghostlike to you. Truth which is not growing is becoming fossilised. "The things most surely believed" are often the things which have least power. Unquestioned truth too often lies "bedridden in the dormitory of the soul side by side with exploded error." The sure way to reduce your knowledge of Jesus Christ to that inert condition is to neglect increasing it and applying it to your daily life. There are men, in all churches, and there are some whole communions whose creeds are the most orthodox, and also utterly useless, and as near as possible nonentities, simply because the creed is accepted and shelved. If your belief is to be of any use to you, or to be held by you in the face of temptations to abandon it, you must keep it fresh, and oxygenated, so to say, by continual fresh apprehension of it and closer application of it to conduct. As soon as the stream stands, it stagnates; and the very manna from God will breed worms and stink. And Christian truth unpractised by those who hold it, corrupts itself and corrupts them.

So Peter tells us that the alternative is growth or apostasy. This decay may be most real and unsuspected. There are many, many professing Christians all ignorant that, like the Jewish giant of old, their strength is gone from them, and the Spirit of God departed. My brother, I beseech you, rouse yourself from your contented slothfulness. Do not be satisfied with merely having come within the Temple. Count nothing as won whilst anything remains to be won. There is a whole ocean of boundless grace and truth rolling shoreless there before you. Do not content yourselves with picking up a few shells on the beach, but launch out into the deep, and learn to know more and more of the grace and truth and beauty of your Saviour and your God.

But remember dead things do not grow. You cannot grow unless you are alive, and you are not alive unless you have Jesus Christ.

Have you given yourselves to Him? have you taken Him as yours? given yourselves to Him as His servants, subjects, soldiers? taken Him for yours as your Saviour, Sacrifice, Pattern, Inspirer, Friend? If you have, then you have life which will grow if you keep it in union with Him. Joined to Him, men are like a "tree that is planted by the rivers of water," which spreads its foliage and bears its fruit, and year after year flings a wider shadow upon the grass, and lifts a sturdier bole to the heavens. Separated from Him they are like the chaff, which has neither root nor life, and which cannot grow.

Which, my friend, are you?

GOD'S PEACEMAKERS

"Blessed are the Peacemakers: for they shall be called the children of God" (Matthew 5:9).

THIS IS THE LAST BEATITUDE DESCRIPTIVE of the character of the Christian. There follows one more, which describes his reception by the world. But this one sets the top stone, the shining apex, upon the whole temple-structure which the previous Beatitudes had been gradually building up. You may remember that I have pointed out in previous sermons how all these various traits of the Christian life are deduced from the root of poverty of spirit. You may also remember how I have had occasion to show that if we consider that first Beatitude, "Blessed are the poor in spirit," as the root and mother of all the rest, the remainder are so arranged as that we have alternately a grace which regards mainly the man himself and his relations to God, and one which also includes his relations to man.

Now there are three of these which look out into the world, and these three are consummated by this one of my text. These are "the meek," which describes a man's attitude to opposition and hatred; "the merciful," which describes his indulgence in judgment and his pitifulness in action; and "the peacemakers." For Christian people are not merely to bear injuries and to recompense them with pity and with love, but they are actively to try to bring about a wholesomer and purer state of humanity, and to breathe the peace of god, which passes understanding, over all the janglings and struggles of this world.

So, I think, if we give a due depth of significance to that name "peacemaker," we shall find that this grace worthily completes the whole linked series, and is the very jewel which clasps the whole chain of Christian and Christlike characteristics.

I. HOW ARE CHRIST'S PEACEMAKERS MADE?

Now there are certain people whose natural disposition has in it a fine element, which diffuses soothing and concord all around them. I dare say we all have known such — perhaps some good woman, without any very shining gifts of intellect, who yet dwelt in such peace of heart herself that conflict and jangling were rebuked in her presence. And there are other people who love peace, and seek after it in the cowardly fashion of letting things alone; whose "peace-making" has no nobler source than hatred of trouble, and a wish to let sleeping dogs lie. These, instead of being peacemakers, are war-makers, for they are laying up materials for a tremendous explosion some day.

Reprinted with permission of Wm. B. Eerdmans Publishing Co. from *A Garland of Gladness*, by Alexander Maclaren (Grand Rapids: 1945), pp. 109–20.

But it is a very different temper that Jesus Christ has in view here, and I need only ask you to do again what we have had occasion to do in the previous sermons of this series — to link this characteristic with those that go before it, of which it is regarded as being the bright and consummate flower and final outcome. No man can bring to others that which he does not possess. Vainly will he whose own heart is torn by contending passions, whose own life is full of animosities and unreconciled outstanding causes of alienation and divergence between him and God, between him and duty, between him and himself, ever seek to shed any deep or real peace amongst men. He may superficially solder some external quarrels, but that is not all that Jesus Christ means. His peacemakers are created by having passed through all the previous experiences which the preceding verses bring out. They have learned the poverty of their own spirits. They have wept tears, if not real and literal, yet those which are far more agonizing — tears of spirit and conscience — when they have thought of their own demerits and foulness. They have bowed in humble submission to the will of God, and even to that will as expressed by the antagonisms of man. They have yearned after the possession of a fuller and nobler righteousness than they have attained. They have learned to judge others with a gentle judgment because they know how much they themselves need it, and to extend to others a helping hand because they are aware of their own impotence and need of succour. They have been led through all these, often painful, experiences into a purity of heart which has been blessed by some measure of vision of God; and, having thus been equipped and prepared, they are fit to go out into the world and say, in the presence of all its tempests, "Peace! be still." Something of the miracle-working energy of the Master whom they serve will be shed upon those who serve Him.

Brethren, the peacemaker who is worthy of the name must have gone through these deep spiritual experiences. I do not say that they are to come in regular stages, separable from each other. That is not the way in which a character mounts towards God. It does so not by a flight of steps, at distinctly different elevations, but rather by an ascending slope. And, although these various Christian graces which precede that of my text are separable in thought, and are linked in the fashion that our Lord sets forth in experience, they may be, and often are, contemporaneous.

But whether separated from one another in time or not, this life-preparation, of which the previous verses give us the outline in some fashion or other it must precede our being the sort of peacemakers that Christ desires and blesses.

There is only one more point that I would make here before I go on, and that is, that it is well to notice that the climax of Christian character, according to Jesus Christ Himself, is found in our relations to men, and not in our relation to God. Worship of heart and spirit, devout emotions of the sacredest, sweetest, most hallowed and hallowing sort, are absolutely indispensable, as I have tried to show you. But equally, if not more, important is it for us to remember that the purest communion with God, and the selectest emotional experiences of the Christian life, are meant to be the bases of active service; and that, if such service does not follow these, there is good reason for supposing that these are spurious, and worth very little. The service of man is the outcome of the love of God. He who begins with poverty of spirit is perfected when, forgetting himself, and coming down from the mountain-top, where the Shekinah cloud of the Glory and the audible voice are, he plunges into the struggles of the multitude below, and frees the devil-ridden boy from the demon that possesses him. Begin by all means with poverty of spirit, or you will never get to this—"Blessed are the peacemakers." But see to it that poverty of spirit leads to the meekness, the mercifulness, the peace-bringing influence which Christ has pronounced blessed.

II. WHAT IS THE PEACE?

This is a very favorite text with people that know very little of the depths of Christianity. They fancy that it appeals to common sense and men's natural consciences, apart altogether from minutenesses of doctrine or of Christian experience. They are very much mistaken. No doubt there is a surface of truth, but only a surface, in the application that is generally given to these words of our text, as if it meant nothing more than "he is a good man that goes about and tries to make contending people give up their quarrels, and produces a healing atmosphere of tranquillity wherever he goes." That is perfectly true, but there is a great deal more in the text than that. If we consider the Scriptural usage of this great word "peace," and all the ground that it covers in human experience; if we remember that it enters as an element into Christ's own name, the "Peace-Bringer," the "Prince of Peace"; and if we notice, as I have already done, the place which this Beatitude occupies in the series, we shall be obliged to look for some far deeper meaning before we can understand the sweep of our Lord's intention here.

I do not think that I am going one inch too far, or forcing meanings into His words which they are not intended to bear, when I say that the first characteristic of the peace, which His disciples have been passed through their apprenticeship in order to fit them to bring, is the peace of reconciliation with God. The cause of all the other fightings in the world is that men's relation to the Father in heaven is disturbed, and that, whilst there flow out from Him only amity and love, these are met by us with antagonism often, with opposition of will often, with alienation of heart often, and with indifference and forgetfulness almost uniformly. So the first thing to be done to make men at peace with one another and with themselves is to rectify their relation to God, and bring peace there.

We often hear in these days complaints of Christian Churches and Christian people because they do not fling themselves, with sufficient energy to please the censors, into movements which are intended to bring about happier relations in society. The longest way round is sometimes the shortest way home. It does not belong to all of us Christians, and I doubt whether it belongs to the Christian Church as such at all, to fling itself into the movements to which I have referred. But if a man go and carry to men the great message of a reconciled and a reconciling God manifest in Jesus Christ, and bringing peace between men and God, he will have done more to sweeten society and put an end to hostility than I think he will be likely to do by any other method. Christian men and women, whatever else you and I are here for, we are here mainly that we may preach, by lip and life, the great message that in Christ is our peace, and that God "was in Christ reconciling the world to Himself."

We are not to leave out, of course, that which is so often taken as being the sole meaning of the great word of my text. There is much that we are all bound to do to carry the tranquilizing and soothing influences of Gospel principles and of Christ's example into the littlenesses of daily life. Any fool can stick a lucifer match into a haystack and make a blaze. It is easy to promote strife. There is a malicious love of it in us all; and ill-natured gossip has a great deal to do in bringing it about. But it takes something more to put the fire out than it did to light it, and there is no nobler office for Christians than to seek to damp down all these devil's flames of envy and jealousy and mutual animosity. We have to do it, first, by making very sure that we do not answer scorn with scorn, gibes with gibes, hate with hate, but "seek to overcome evil with good." It takes two to make a quarrel, and your most hostile antagonist cannot break the peace unless you help him. If you are resolved to keep it, kept it will be.

May I say another word? I think that our text, though it goes a good deal deeper, does also very plainly tell us Christian folk what is our duty in relation to literal warfare. There is no need for me to discuss here the question as to whether actual fighting with armies and swords is ever legitimate or not. It is a curious kind of Christian duty certainly, if it ever gets to be one. And when one thinks of the militarism that is crushing Europe and driving her ignorant classes to wild schemes of revolution; and when one thinks of the hell of battlefields, of the miseries of the wounded, of mourning widows, of ruined peaceful peasants, of the devil's passions that war sets loose, some of us find it extremely hard to believe that all that is ever in accordance with the mind of Christ. But whether you agree with me in that or no, surely my text points to the duty of the Christian Church to take up a very much more decisive position in reference to the military spirit

$$369.50 \div$$
$$4. =$$
$$92.38 *$$

$$369.50 \div$$
$$12. =$$
$$30.79 *$$

ne. Certainly it does seem to be not very obviously in accordance with Christ's teachings that men-of-war should be sung because thousands religious service, or that *Te Deums* should be sung because thousands have been killed. It certainly does seem to be something like a satire on European Christianity that one of the chief lessons we have taught the East is that we have instructed the Japanese in Western weapons to fight their enemies. Surely, surely, if Christian churches laid to heart as they ought these plain words of the Master they would bring their united influence to bear against the system of war, and that pinchbeck, spurious glory which is connected with it. "Blessed are the peacemakers"; let us try to earn the benediction.

III. The Reward of Peacemakers

"They shall be called the sons of God." Called? By whom? Christ does not say, but it should not be difficult to ascertain. It seems to me that to suppose that it is by men degrades this promise, instead of making it the climax of the whole series. Besides, it is not true that if a Christian man lives as I have been trying to describe, protesting against certain evils, trying to diffuse an atmosphere of peace round about him; and, above all, seeking to make known the Name of the great Peacemaker, men will generally call him a "son of God." The next verse but one tells us what they will call him. "Blessed are ye when men shall revile you, and persecute you, and say all manner of evil against you falsely for my sake." They are a great deal more likely to have stones and rotten eggs flung at them than to be pelted with bouquets of scented roses of popular approval. No! no! it is not man's judgment that is meant here. It matters very little what men call us. It matters everything what God calls us. It is He who will call them "sons of God." So the Apostle John thought that Christ meant, for he very beautifully and touchingly quotes this passage when he says, "Beloved! behold what manner of love the Father hath bestowed upon us, that we should be called the sons of God."

God's calling is a recognition of men for what they are. God owns the man that lives in the fashion that we have been trying to outline — God owns him for His child; manifestly a son, because he has the Father's likeness. "Be ye therefore imitators of God as beloved children, and walk in love." God in Christ is the first Peacemaker, and they who go about the world proclaiming His peace and making peace, bear the image of the heavenly, and are owned by God as His sons.

What does that owning mean? Well, it means a great deal which has yet to be disclosed, but it means this, too, that the whisper of the Voice which owns us for children will be heard by ourselves. The Spirit which cries, "Abba, Father!" will open our ears to hear Him say, "Thou art My beloved Son." Or, to put it into plain English, there is no surer

way by which we can come to the calm, happy, continual consciousness of being the children of God than by this living like Him, to spread
the peace of God over all hearts.

I have said in former sermons that all these promises, which are but
the natural outcome of the characteristics to which they are attached,
have a double reference, being fulfilled in germ here, and in maturity
hereafter. Like the rest, this one has that double reference. For the
consciousness, here and now, that we are the children of God is but,
as it were, the morning twilight of what shall hereafter be an un-
setting meridian sunshine. What depths of divine assimilation, what
mysteries of calm, peaceful, filial fellowship, what riches beyond
count of divine inheritance, lie in the name of son, the possession
of these alone can tell. For the same Apostle, whose comment upon
these words we have already quoted, goes on to say, "It doth not yet
appear what we shall be."

Only we have one assurance, wide enough for all anticipation, and
firm enough for solid hope: "If children, then heirs; heirs of God, and
joint-heirs with Christ." He must make us sons before we can be
called sons of God. He must give us peace with God, with ourselves,
with men, with circumstances, before we can go forth effectually to
bring peace to others. If He has given us these good things, He has
bound us to spread them. Let us do so. And if our peace ever is spoken
in vain as regards others, it will come back to us again; and we shall be
kept in perfect peace, even in the midst of strife, until we enter at last
into the city of peace and serve the King of Peace forever.

FOR ADDITIONAL INFORMATION ABOUT ALEXANDER MACLAREN:

Atkins, Gaius Glenn, ed. *The Best of Alexander Maclaren*. New York:
    Harper & Bros., 1949.
Carlile, John C. *Alexander Maclaren, D.D.: The Man and His Mes-
    sage*. New York: Funk & Wagnalls Co., 1902.
Currier, Albert H. "Alexander McLaren." *Nine Great Preachers*.
    New York: Pilgrim Press, 1912.
Edwards, John. "Dr. Alexander Maclaren." *Nineteenth Century
    Preachers and Their Methods*. London: Charles H. Kelly, 1902.
Insko, Chester Arthur. "The Biblical Preaching of Alexander Mac-

laren." Th.D. dissertation, Southern Baptist Theological Seminary, 1950.

Jeffs, Ernest H. "Dr. Alexander Maclaren." *Princes of the Modern Pulpit*. London: Sampson Low, Marston & Co., 1931.

McLaren, Elizabeth Teague. *Dr. McLaren: A Sketch*. 2d ed. London: Hodder & Stoughton, 1911.

Wilkinson, William Cleaver. "Alexander McLaren." *Modern Masters of Pulpit Discourse*. New York: Funk & Wagnalls Co., 1905.

FOR OTHER SERMONS BY ALEXANDER MACLAREN:

Christ in the Heart, and Other Sermons. New York: Funk & Wagnalls Co., 1905.

Maclaren's Expositions of Holy Scripture. 11 vols. Grand Rapids: Wm. B. Eerdmans Publishing Co., 1952.

Also: *A Garland of Gladness* (1945), *The Best of Alexander Maclaren* (1949).

JOHN A. BROADUS

1827-1895

JOHN A. BROADUS, original photograph, courtesy of the
library at Southern Baptist Theological Seminary.

JOHN ALBERT BROADUS

1827	*Born January 24, Culpeper County, Virginia*
1844	*Schoolteacher in Clarke County, Virginia*
1850	*Graduated from the University of Virginia; ordained; married; accepted private teaching position*
1851	*Became pastor of Charlottesville Baptist Church, Charlottesville, Virginia; accepted position as an assistant professor, University of Virginia*
1853	*Resigned his teaching position to pastor full time*
1855	*Became chaplain, University of Virginia; resigned pastorate*
1857	*Resumed pastorate in Charlottesville; wife died October 21*
1859	*Married Charlotte E. Sinclair January 4; started career as a professor of Greek and homiletics, Baptist Seminary, Greenville, South Carolina*
1862	*Seminary closed because of war; served as pastor, Cedar Grove and Williamston Baptist Churches, South Carolina, until 1864; preached in Confederate Army camps*
1865	*Began teaching again when seminary reopened; also preached in rural churches*
1877	*Helped move the seminary to Louisville, Kentucky*
1886	*Published Sermons and Addresses*
1889	*Delivered the Lyman Beecher Lectures; became president of Southern Baptist Theological Seminary*
1895	*Died, March 16*

JOHN A. BROADUS wrote a book on homiletics—perhaps the most widely used text on the subject—*On the Preparation and Delivery of Sermons*, which has remained in print for more

43

than a hundred years. He was also a noted and effective preacher, but even so, the central focus of his life was not on preaching. The task which consumed his life's energy was the building of a strong Baptist seminary in the South, and preaching was one of the principal tools he used to accomplish that task.

LIFE AND TIMES

John A. Broadus was born January 24, 1827, in Culpeper County, Virginia. His father, Major Edmund Broadus, was widely known as a Christian politician and a firm advocate of missions, temperance, and ministerial education. He farmed, taught school, and served in the legislature; but in spite of his busy life, he was a devoted father. Broadus's mother led her children to love books, music, and flowers. She did not make a profession of faith in Christ and become a church member until late in life, although her husband and children were active Baptist church members.

As a boy Broadus worked and played in the midst of southern culture. Slavery was an accepted way of life. Education was valued but schools were scarce. The economy was centered in agriculture. John played with Negro slave children, studied in small schools and at home, and grew up in a world dominated by farming. As a young man he was exceptionally bright and friendly, but somewhat shy.

In 1843, when Broadus was sixteen, he became a professing Christian during a revival meeting. He was baptized in Mountain Run Stream and joined Mount Poney Baptist Church. In a church meeting a few months later, the preacher urged the people to move about the auditorium and encourage the unconverted to become Christians. Broadus spoke to a mentally retarded man named Sandy, who promptly made a profession of faith. Thereafter, whenever Sandy saw Broadus he would say, "Howdy, John? Thankee, John." Later in life Broadus often told of this experience and would add: "And if ever I reach the heavenly home and walk the golden streets, I know the first person to meet me will be Sandy, coming and saying again: 'Howdy, John? Thankee, John.' "

At the age of seventeen Broadus did not know which career he would enter. Since he wanted a college education but had no money, he began teaching school to gather funds for college and to explore possible vocations. For two years the young teacher continued his own study, participated in the life of the local Baptist church, and explored several vocations – among them medicine, politics, law, and the ministry. Then in August, 1846, after hearing a sermon on the work of the minister, he sought out his pastor and said, "Brother Grimsley, the question is decided; I must try to be a preacher."

The later success of Broadus in his vocation emphasizes the importance of home and education for a preacher. The Christian home out of which Broadus came was a decided asset to him. In addition to the nurture of his family, he received the benefits of an excellent education; both his elementary and high school teachers were among the best in the area.

Broadus entered the University of Virginia in 1846. The school played a particularly important part in his life. At that time the University of Virginia was one of the finest educational institutions in the United States. An elective system was in effect whereby a student could choose many of his courses along the lines of his own particular needs and interests. (Later Broadus established this system at the Southern Baptist Theological Seminary.) The Jefferson Society, a debating club at the University of Virginia, offered young Broadus an opportunity to develop his speaking ability. He was considered the best debater in the society and developed a skill with words which he later put to good use.

In 1850 he graduated from the university, was ordained, married Marie Harrison, and accepted a private teaching position in Virginia. He became pastor of the Charlottesville Baptist Church in Charlottesville, Virginia, in 1852. In that same year he also was appointed an assistant professor in the University of Virginia. Later, in 1855, he became chaplain to the university. The cast of his life was set: he would be a professor who was also a preacher. For many years Broadus was both professor in a school and pastor of a church.

In 1859 he became a professor at the newly founded Baptist Seminary in Greenville, South Carolina. The school closed during the Civil War and Broadus spent his time writing, pastoring rural churches, and preaching to the Confederate troops. In 1865 the seminary reopened and Broadus resumed his teaching. The struggling school survived and in 1877 moved to Louisville, Kentucky. Broadus assumed the presidency in 1889 and served until 1895, when death took him from his post. During the years that Broadus was a professor in the school at Greenville and Louisville, he continued to preach. He was a noted and sought-after preacher throughout much of the nation, particularly in the South.

Great crowds attended the preaching of Broadus. For example, he spent the month of August, 1890, in Detroit, Michigan, supplying the pulpit at Woodward Avenue Church in the absence of the pastor, Dr. Henderson, who was vacationing in Europe. On August 7, 1890, the *Christian Herald* in Detroit wrote, "Dr. Broadus was greeted by large audiences last Sunday. His family, wife, three daughters and son, arrived yesterday from Louisville, Ky., and proceeded to Algonac, where they will spend August." On August 21, 1890, this article appeared:

> *Woodward Av.* church was closed last Sunday evening for the first time since its dedication. Rev. Dr. Broadus, who is supplying the pulpit, had been indisposed during the previous week, and did not feel able to preach in the evening. By concurrence with the deacons it was announced that the house would be closed. Notwithstanding special request was made for all present to give notice of suspension of services, more than enough to twice fill the house gathered at time of evening service, and greatly disappointed, returned to their homes or went to other churches. Dr. Broadus has two more Sundays to supply the pulpit before the return of Pastor Henderson, and he expects to be able to respond in person at each of the four remaining services.

The *Christian Herald* reported on August 29, "Dr. J. A. Broadus preached to a great throng last Sunday morning and evening. It was estimated that one thousand people were unable to gain admittance in the evening." On September 4, this final entry: "Hundreds were unable to find seats last Sunday to listen to Dr. Broadus' farewell discourses. Pastor Henderson will resume his work next Sunday."

Many similar statements could be cited as evidence of the popularity of the preaching of Broadus, not only with lay audiences, but with ministers as well. When Broadus preached the commencement sermon at Richmond College, the *Religious Herald* for June 19, 1890, said, "The audience was very large, filling the spacious room to overflowing. . . . It is not necessary to say that the sermon was one of great ability and power. . . . One of the Richmond pastors said he felt, after hearing Dr.

Broadus, that he must go right to work to make better sermons. Another said he could not preach any more."

Nevertheless, Broadus was as diligent a pastor as preacher. His thorough pastoral journal reveals his involvement with his church. This note appears in longhand, as were all of his entries: "From Oct. 1, 1857 to Sept. 1, 1859. Pastoral visits paid 1013. This list does not include visits of ceremony or mere sociality, apart from my relation as pastor."

He records many baptisms, including that of the famous Baptist missionary to China, Miss Lottie Moon, on December 22, 1858. It is also interesting to notice that on July 3, 1859, his Day Book records "14 colored persons" baptized. Broadus wrote, "From the beginning of my pastoral work to August 21, 1859, I have baptized Whites 129 Colored 112 Total 241."

As to the number of sermons preached, "From Oct. 1, 1851 to this date [Aug. 28, 1859] Sermons 761 Wed. night Lectures 49 Discourses 810. Of the 761 sermons, 122 were at the University, 218 at other places, leaving 421 at Charlottesville." Later he wrote, "No list for 1869. Preached very rarely that year, from bad health."

Broadus lived in a time filled with many disrupting events. The conflict over the question of slavery, the political chaos which led to the Civil War, the occupation of the South by Federal troops, the ordeal of reconstruction, and the general poverty of the South were all factors which deeply affected his life.

The attitude of Broadus toward these controversial issues is particularly interesting. Apparently he was a slave owner. In a letter written from England he referred to himself in these terms: "Mrs. M＿＿＿ had never before seen a slaveholder, and talked quite innocently about having thought they were all fierce-looking, and I had much fun joking her." Although a part of the slaveholding tradition of the South, he was no stern defender of slavery. His evaluation of *Uncle Tom's Cabin* in a letter to his wife is remarkably balanced: "I have finished 'Uncle Tom's Cabin.' It is exceedingly well written, having some passages of rarely equaled power, and being altogether, so far as I can judge, a very remarkable book."[1]

He was also opposed to the dissolution of the Union. After South Carolina seceded, he wrote from that state, "I have at

---

1. A. T. Robertson, *Life and Letters of John Albert Broadus* (Philadelphia: Judson Press, 1901), p. 102.

this hour no sympathy with secession, though of course it would be worse than idle to speak against it now, and though, equally of course, I mean to do my duty as a citizen here."[2]

During the war he preached to the Confederate troops. Upon hearing that Broadus was coming to his camp, General Stonewall Jackson said, "That is good; very good. I am so glad of that. And when Doctor Broadus comes you must bring him to see me. I want him to preach at my headquarters, and I wish to help him in his work all I can."[3] Although he frequently preached to the Confederate troops, he was never a chaplain. On his war tour in 1863, his journal lists 61 sermons, 48 of which were specifically preached to army units in the field. On August 28, 1863, he wrote:

> If my health were vigorous and my "Commentary" work had never been undertaken, I should have no hesitation in thinking it my duty to labor in the army permanently. I could, with God's blessing, do much good, though there are numerous brethren who could do more, for I greatly lack some important requisites for such work . . . I could, perhaps, stand a soldier's life as a soldier, but with all the anxiety and nervous exhaustion attendant upon a preacher's work, which even before I went to Greenville used often to bring me into great prostration, I could not stand it. This is my chief reason, but I do feel that my commentary work is of more importance, and that even at home I should not be living merely for myself. . . .[4]

After the war Broadus helped reopen the Baptist Seminary which had been closed by the war. He was a gifted speaker, an able administrator, and a man of great intelligence and kindness. In one class he had only a single student—and he was blind; yet Broadus thoroughly prepared his lectures and delivered them as if he were speaking to a multitude. The careful preparation of these lectures led to the writing of his famous book on sermon preparation and delivery.

In 1870 he published *On the Preparation and Delivery of Sermons,* which became the best-known and most widely used

---

2. Ibid., p. 181.
3. Ibid., p. 198.
4. Ibid., p. 206.

book on homiletics written by an American. The book has gone through many editions and is still extensively used. In 1944 Jesse Burton Weatherspoon revised it, and this revised edition has also enjoyed wide acceptance. The preaching of many outstanding ministers has been influenced by John A. Broadus. Thousands of seminarians have studied his book on homiletics and read his sermons.

Broadus was no narrow sectarian, no provincial Southerner. Through travel and correspondence Broadus developed wide acquaintances. In England he visited with Spurgeon, heard Liddon preach, discussed theology with Bishop Ellicott, and chatted with professors Lightfoot, Westcott, and Hort. In the North he won many friends, among them John D. Rockefeller (Rockefeller once financed a trip to Europe by Broadus for some much needed rest). New York churches heard him gladly and the Calvary Church, New York City, attempted to call him as pastor. He dined as a guest in the home of Dwight L. Moody and there chatted with Henry Drummond and others. He preached and lectured in many northern cities, among them Boston, New Haven, Rochester, and Northfield, Moody's Bible study center. With Philip Schaff he worked on a translation of the writings of early Christian leaders; Broadus wrote the section on Chrysostom in *A Select Library of the Nicene and Post-Nicene Fathers of the Christian Church*. Lew Wallace, author of *Ben Hur*, once corresponded with him concerning a book review.

In 1889 Broadus was asked to deliver the Lyman Beecher Lectures at Yale. His topic was *Preaching and Ministerial Life*. The lectures were delivered from notes, not written out in full. The subjects of the eight lectures were "The Young Preacher's Outfit," "Freshness in Preaching," "Sensational Preaching," "Freedom in Preaching," "The Ministers' General Meeting," "The Minister and His Hymnbook," "The Minister and His Bible," and "The Minister's Private Life."

Broadus did not deal extensively with social issues, but whatever he did on the subject was well done. Once while attending a social gathering with friends, he heard a group of young men delighting in the activities of the Ku Klux Klan. Broadus was incensed. Professor H. P. Griffith described the scene:

Just after the war when the Ku Klux were committing great atrocities and terrorizing the upper part of South

Carolina, I was with Doctor Broadus at a place where
a small party of six or eight young men were present.
They were all strangers to him and some of them were
to me. One of the young men introduced the subject
of the Ku Klux and several of them put verbal endorse-
ment on the organization, or expressed their approval
of it, as many good men did.

Dr. Broadus was solemn for some time, but finally
he spoke, and I never heard a more scathing rebuke
administered than he gave the young men of the Ku
Klux. He grew eloquent over the woes already inflicted
by the organization, and spoke with withering power
of the criminality of lawlessness and of the just retribution that was sure to come.

After we had left, I said, "Doctor you were pretty
hard on those young men." He replied, "Yes, I saw
that two or three of them were Ku Klux, and I felt it my
duty to reprimand them in strong terms."[5]

On September 27, 1886, Broadus published an article in the
Louisville Courier Journal on the race situation which greatly
helped to prevent a riot and lynching in Louisville. Under the
circumstances it was a courageous article, and well indicates
the forthrightness of Broadus upon unpopular subjects:

I write as a Southern man, having spent my life
successively in Virginia, South Carolina, and Kentucky. . . . We must not forget that the Negroes differ
widely among themselves, having come from different
races in Africa, and having had very different relations
to the white people while held in slavery. Many of
them are greatly superior to others in character. . . .
There is a goodly number of intelligent Negroes who
really take sound and wholesome views of the situation.
If we continue to tolerate lynching we lead these better
Negroes to think that we are the enemies of all their
race. We alienate the better class from the support of
justice and government and civilization.

Now, then, I appeal to thoughtful men wherever
the "Courier Journal" is read, will you not come out and
condemn this business of lynching? Will you not openly
discourage and oppose and stop it? We can stop it. Is
not this our duty? Is it not high time? . . . Men and

5. Ibid., pp. 221–22.

women, the thing is wrong, and getting worse and tending to be ruinous; I pray you, think, speak out, act in such way as you deem wisest.

I will not apologize for publishing this respectful appeal. As a minister of religion, I take no part in the manipulations of party politics, though careful to vote at every election, since voting is surely one of the highest duties of an American citizen. But this is in no sense a question of party politics. It is a question of justice, of fundamental right, of essential civilization, of human welfare.[6]

The entire article is fascinating, particularly since Broadus argues that Southerners must obey the law no matter what the circumstance. In any event, it was a courageous action and one that no doubt certainly netted him much opposition as well as appreciation.

The qualities displayed by Broadus will serve any preacher well; kindness, urbanity, understanding, and sympathy abounded in this Virginia gentleman. He once said, "If I were asked what is the first thing in effective preaching, I should say sympathy; and what is the second thing, I should say sympathy; and what is the third thing, I should say sympathy." His deep awareness of the needs of people led him to meet the immediate, personal needs of others and to call for an end to social injustice.

PREACHING AND SERMONS

Among the men who delivered the Yale lectures, John A. Broadus is one of the best-known writers on homiletics and one of the least-known preachers. His historic volume on homiletics, *On the Preparation and Delivery of Sermons,* has been in continuous use for more than a hundred years. Few other writings on homiletics have ever compiled such a record. Broadus never expected such success for his book. In a letter written from Greenville, South Carolina, on January 11, 1870, he said:

Last summer I went to work at a treatise on the "Preparation and Delivery of Sermons," hoping to make

---

6. Ibid., pp. 353–54.

a text-book for Manly, and at the same time meet the
wants of young ministers who have no course of instruction in homiletics, and give some useful hints
to older ministers.

I worked at it all summer, but have not yet completed
it. Such books do not get a wide sale, and no publisher
is willing to take one from an unknown Southern
author. So I am arranging to publish at my own expense,
through Smith and English. A generous contribution
from unknown persons in Richmond, lately received
through Wm. B. Isaacs & Co., came when I was quite
despondent about the prospect of commanding the
means to publish, and will be a very important help to
me. . . . [7]

Broadus was a brilliant thinker; the depth of his learning
has not been generally appreciated. He was an excellent critical scholar: in addition to his significant work for Philip Schaff
in the *Nicene and Post-Nicene Fathers* on Chrysostom, he was
also asked to write the Pastoral Epistles for the *International
Critical Commentary.* He declined because of a planned work
on interbiblical history. His commentary on Matthew, still in
print in the *American Commentary on the New Testament,*
is a model of exposition.

His Yale lectures on preaching in January, 1889, created
great excitement. A. T. Robertson said that they created more
enthusiasm than any lectures since the days of Henry Ward
Beecher. The theological faculty of Yale expressed "their high
appreciation of the suggestive and stimulating series of lectures," together with the hope that they would be published.
But as usual, Broadus had not written them out in full, preferring to speak from notes according to his custom when lec-
turing. He also expected to incorporate some of them into his
Preparation and Delivery of Sermons. Broadus did not live
to accomplish this task, but his successor at Southern Baptist
Theological Seminary, E. C. Dargan, did integrate these lectures into a revised edition of the work.

His lectures abroad were also attended with considerable
interest. While in London in 1870, Broadus delivered some
lectures at the London Baptist Association which were attended by Charles Haddon Spurgeon. Broadus wrote:

---

7. Ibid., pp. 233–34.

Dr. Davies invited me to attend today a quarterly meeting of the London Baptist Association, which I did. They received me most cordially, introducing me to the body. An excellent essay was read, followed by a capital address from Mr. Spurgeon, and then I was invited to speak. I was in the mood and succeeded pretty well.[8]

On another occasion Broadus lectured in New York before a group of distinguished ministers, including Edward Beecher. He delivered many other notable lectures, including the Newton Lectures, the Rochester Lectures, lectures on the Chautauqua circuit, and repeated Bible lectures at Northfield for Moody.

Broadus often lectured at Northfield for the students gathered around Dwight Moody. A visitor to Northfield in the days of Moody was told that no one had ever made such an impression in those Bible lectures as Broadus had made. Moody himself, in his meeting at Louisville in the winter of 1887–1888, made extensive reference to his appreciation for the work of Broadus at Northfield.

Because of his fame as a lecturer, many institutions clamored for Broadus's services. He was offered the presidency of the University of Chicago, Brown University, and Crozer Theological Seminary, among others. But his dedication to Southern Baptist Seminary and his determination to see theological education advanced in the South kept him at his post.

For all of the attention devoted to Broadus as a lecturer on homiletics, little attention has been given to his own personal preaching. Broadus was a superbly gifted preacher who might have attracted international fame by his preaching alone had he been a native of London or Edinburgh, or even New York, instead of a Southern Baptist professor of homiletics. Nevertheless, he was in great demand in the North as well as in the South. He not only lectured repeatedly in New York, but he preached during the summers at Yonkers, New York (where he was offered the pastorate of the church), at North Orange, New Jersey, and at Baltimore, as well as frequently preaching abroad. Although the original source for Spurgeon's statement cannot be determined, Professor J. H. Farmer, in the *McMaster University Monthly* for May, 1895, said that "Spurgeon himself pronounced him the greatest of living preachers."

---

8. Ibid., p. 247.

He preached in Detroit to great crowds, and afterward the
Christian Herald of Detroit published a report of the sermons.
This paper for August 8, 1890, says:

> The exalted esteem in which Dr. Broadus is held
> arises not only from his eminent scholarly attainments
> and rare gifts in the capacity of author, teacher, and
> preacher, but from a singular transparency of nature . . .
> which never fails to impress all with whom he comes in
> contact.
> As a preacher, his style is so easy and conversational,
> the language so crystal clear a medium for the thought,
> that one may fail at first hearing to appreciate the won-
> derful freshness of his Scriptural expositions, and the
> wealth of knowledge and of spiritual power which are
> being unfolded, but his words are found to linger in the
> mind like strains of noble music. . . .
> Dr. Broadus' sermons are pre-eminently sermons,
> not essays, not orations, not anything for the display of
> the preacher's erudition, but symmetrical growths from
> a life devoted to studious thinking and noble living.[9]

Unlike many notable preachers whose first sermons were
miserable failures, Broadus began with great poise. His first
sermon was delivered at the Mount Eagle Presbyterian Church
in Albemarle County, Virginia. The text was from Psalms 62:8,
"God is a refuge for us." One who heard that sermon wrote:

> Dr. William McGuffey, professor of moral philosophy
> in the University of Virginia, had charge of the church.
> Being sick on this particular Sunday, he sent down one
> of his students "to fill his place." And well did he fill
> it. The doctor was dry and logical and preached more
> to the head than to the heart.
> On this day, which I well remember, there stood up in
> his place a slightly built, dark haired youth, scarcely
> twenty years of age, who spoke as I never heard man
> speak before of our gracious Saviour. There was some-
> thing in his manner very entreating, very touching,
> very convincing. After the sermon all were eager to
> find out the name of the student who had filled so
> acceptably the learned professor's place. That day was

9. Ibid., p. 389.

the first time I ever saw or heard the name, "John A. Broadus."[10]

Throughout his life Broadus retained his remarkable ability to capture an audience. He had what has been memorably called "the genius to be loved." That was undoubtedly one of Broadus's gifts, but it was not accidental. Among his prime bits of advice to the preacher is the admonition to "gain the sympathy of your audience." Broadus himself was a man of deep sympathy and understanding, and this concept finds ample expression in every sermon of his. Another contemporary of Broadus wrote of his preaching as a young man:

> Never can I forget how I would sit enwrapped in his eloquence which was scarcely surpassed afterwards, however much he may have grown. I think that later his sermons became more didactic and perhaps richer in the exposition of the Scripture; but oh, there was then a freshness and fervor and a flow of thought and language; and sentences from his lips are still in my memory as if heard yesterday.[11]

Although Broadus was an excellent thinker and scholar, his sermons are not particularly unique in thought. Their basic strength lies in their ability to describe with clarity and candor the basic issues in a passage of Scripture. Excellent use of imagination is a marked characteristic of the preaching of Broadus. He is at his best in historical description and biographical analysis. His sermons are not impressive for their embroidered elegance or for rhetorical tricks – they display more careful workmanship than flashing style. He was a warm, sympathetic, thoughtful preacher who always spoke with dignity and grace. He never sought to be impressive; nevertheless, men of intellect were impressed with the depth of his insight. Yet the common people, who made up the largest part of his audiences, heard him with appreciation. E. E. Folk wrote in *The Baptist and Reflector:*

> There is one thing about Dr. Broadus's preaching and speaking: Whenever you hear him you feel like you

10. Ibid., p. 71.
11. Ibid., p. 106.

want to be a better man, and that by God's help you are going to be a better man. At any rate this is always the way we feel after hearing him, and we presume that it is the same way with others. This is, we believe, the highest effect of preaching – to make people better.[12]

The many honors showered upon Broadus never affected his genteel modesty. After preaching at Madison Avenue Church in Philadelphia on February 24, 1876, and at Fifth Avenue Church in the evening of the same day, Broadus typically wrote: "Last night I preached here, Henson's dedication, and had the great satisfaction, with a magnificent congregation, of making one of my complete failures. The tamest broken-down sermons I made in Kentucky, when traveling with you, were better."[13] Apparently no one else was as disappointed as Broadus, but he was never afraid to admit to an inferior performance, at least by his own standards.

Broadus was a meticulous scholar and he left two large notebooks filled with the dates, places, and texts of all the sermons preached during his whole life. But he did not preach from a manuscript. He spoke extemporaneously, and many critics reported that the printed page was a poor substitute for the experience of actually hearing Broadus himself. W. C. Wilkinson, professor at the University of Chicago, reminded the readers of Broadus's sermons that his style was a spoken, not a written, style. Wilkinson took pains to illustrate the virtues of that style – naturalness, directness, familiarity, ease – as well as the faults of syntax which accompany oral style when printed. Actually, if Broadus had polished his sermons into the written style that was regarded as elegant in that day, his sermons would have been lacking greatly in the naturalness and directness that typified them.

Wilkinson pointed out that "wide reading and fine culture on his part are made evident enough," even though Broadus dealt sparingly in quotations from literature. He wrote:

> Charm is present everywhere in Doctor Broadus's discourse; but it is seldom a charm carried to the last, the consumate degree, by exquisite rhetorical form. You con-

12. Ibid., p. 422.
13. Ibid., p. 299.

stantly feel that the orator is too intent on what he will
say to be quite sufficiently solicitous as to how he will
say it—excepting always, or almost always, that he
will say it in a manner to have it instantly understood.[14]

In other words, Broadus was intent on *communicating* the
gospel—not indulging himself in rhetorical eloquence. This
slight criticism of Wilkinson—though he is generally complimentary to a high degree—only highlights the real strength in
the preaching of Broadus.

After quoting a particularly impressive section in one sermon, Wilkinson concluded his study with these words: "And if
the readers of this paper think the passage just shown them
beautiful in print, I can strongly say, 'You should have heard it
from the lips of its author!' There is a strand of pathos in tone
braided inseparably into the speech of Doctor Broadus. . . ."[15]

It is unfortunate, however, that the extemporaneous style
of Broadus did not leave us with more manuscripts. In May,
June, and July of 1877, he supplied the Calvary Baptist Church
in New York while Dr. MacArthur, the pastor, was absent.
Broadus had many of this series of eighteen sermons taken
down by a stenographer with a view of publishing a volume of
"Calvary Sermons." But he was disappointed at the results
and found it almost impossible to whip the stenographer's
report into decent shape. Apparently seeing his oral discourse in
written form was a bit too much for him, and Broadus gave up
on the idea. A few of these sermons appeared later in the volume of *Sermons and Addresses*. A. T. Robertson said, "He was
inimitable before an audience and unreportable, to the loss
of the reading public."

Broadus spoke mainly on the personal problems of individuals and preached a kerygmatic message with very little of
the prophetic overtone. He did not lay weighty emphasis upon
pressing social issues, even though in his personal life he
vigorously opposed secession and the activities of the Ku Klux
Klan, and worked diligently to reunite the North and the South.
Broadus was also well received by the Confederate soldiers and
frequently preached before thousands of troops and many of

---

14. Ibid., p. 370.
15. Ibid., p. 371.

the Confederate generals. J. William Jones, in the *Seminary Magazine* for April, 1895, wrote:

> I especially recall a sermon I heard him preach at Gen. Gordon's headquarters about sunset on the evening of the Confederate Fast Day (he preached four times that day). Gen. Gordon had sent around a special courier's notice that Doctor Broadus would preach, and there was an immense crowd—probably five thousand—in attendance. Generals Lee, A. P. Hill (an old schoolmate and special friend of Doctor Broadus), Ewell, Early, and a number of other generals were there, while all through the crowd the wreaths and stars and bars of rank mingled with the rude garb of the private soldier, and the vast sea of upturned, eager faces as the men sat on the bare ground, made the scene not easy forgotten. . . .
>
> The text was Proverbs 3:17, "Her ways are ways of pleasantness, and all her paths are peace." I have heard him preach from that text several times, but never with the pathos and power that he had that day. He caught the vast crowd with his first sentence, and held, and thrilled, and moved them to the close of the sermon. There were times when there was scarcely a dry eye among those gathered thousands, and all through the sermon "Something on the soldier's cheek washed off the stain of powder."
>
> It was touching to see the commander-in-chief and his great lieutenants and other officers, the very flower of our Confederate chivalry, mingling their tears with those of the "unknown heroes" of the rank and file. . . .
>
> At the close of the service they came by the hundreds to ask an interest in the prayers of God's people, or profess a new-found faith in the Lord Jesus Christ, and I doubt not that our beloved brother has greeted on the other shore not a few who heard him that day or at other points in the army.[16]

If Broadus was a faithful son of the South, he was also a courageous one and a mediating influence. One must remember that Broadus preached to a conquered nation. He preached to people whose homes had been destroyed, whose sons had been slain, whose fortunes had been lost. For them, the social issues

---

16. Ibid., pp. 208–9.

were finished. Their civilization was destroyed. They were disenfranchised, defeated, confused, bitter. It may be true that Broadus could have done more to expand their understanding of the seething times about them; but the words that he spoke against secession, lynching, rioting, and the Ku Klux Klan—as popular and powerful as all of these influences were in that day—took far more courage than some of the more outspoken expressions delivered in safer quarters.

Considering the almost unbelievable circumstances of tension, conflict, and privation under which he labored, the scholarly contributions of Broadus, as well as his superb preaching, are truly amazing.

It is a pleasure to present in this series of studies a selection of sermons previously unpublished in any collection of sermons by Broadus, taken from verbatim newspaper accounts of his day. They extend our knowledge and appreciation for the unusual pulpit ability of John A. Broadus.

Sermons

NOW A CERTAIN MAN WAS SICK

"Now a certain man was sick named Lazarus of Bethany, the town of Mary and her sister Martha" (John 11:1).

THIS BETHANY is distant from another town of the same name, beyond Jordan which had just before been alluded to by the Apostle as the residence of two Christians who had become well known, Mary and her sister Martha. And to make sure what persons they were, the evangelist adds, "It was that Mary which anointed the Lord with ointment, and wiped his feet with her hair." The Lord had declared that wherever this gospel was preached throughout the world that story should be told, and here a number of years later, Christians were presumed to be familiar with it. So the evangelist explains it was *that* Bethany, that Mary. This little town, an insignificant village in itself, has become so well known to all true lovers of the gospel that it would be well to begin the discourse this evening by some little account of the way it appeared a few years ago to the preacher.

You go out of Jerusalem on the East side through a gate they call St. Stephen's gate and immediately begin rapidly to descend a steep bank down into a ravine, down away down you go and across the valley of the Kedron – there is a stream of water there during the rainy season not at other times – perhaps a hundred yards you go and there you reach the foot of a long range of hill which we call the Mount of Olives. Just at the foot of it there is a little enclosure of less than an acre a high wall around it and some old olive trees 1000 years old and that is the place they call Gethsemane, we do certainly know that it was very near there, and you may try to imagine how you would feel if you should go to that spot. I remember one night about the time of Easter the Passover a party of us Americans got a permit and guard from the Turkish authorities to go there, and we knew as we knelt on the earth and prayed that we could not be far away from the spot where Jesus knelt, and fell, and writhed in his agony. If you wish to

A sermon by J. A. Broadus, delivered at Calvary Baptist Church, Sunday, June 17, 1877, at the evening service.

60

climb the Mount of Olives you will see that there are three paths. By the limestone ridges you can see that the paths are where they must have always been. They are long sloping depressions going down three ways. The paths must always have gone up those slight depressions and nowhere else. The northermost is the path King David went when he fled from Absalom. The southermost of these was the Roman paved road which to find a better grade passes some degrees to the south. There are pieces of pavement now on the road. There is one bit of pavement just alongside of the ridge of Olivet where Jesus came riding from Bethany in triumphant procession. You can find the very point and you can know that you are within five steps of the very place where Jesus was when he beheld the city and wept over it. There is a shorter path where our Lord and his disciples were wont to go, and if one finds that path he would be apt to seat himself on the rock there and look over the city just as Jesus did when he predicted the destruction of Jerusalem. When you reach the summit, you are one and a half miles from Bethany, or as we are told in the story fifteen furlongs. If you go beyond the ridge of Olivet you find an outlying rounded wall which is connected with the ridge of Olivet by a narrow neck of land having deep ravines on the north of it and the south of it, and as you go over that narrow neck of land you know that you cannot be away many paces from where his feet used to tread. Then you pass beyond the outlying wall towards the East and there is a town which has always been called Lazarus town. You can see the Dead Sea very plainly in the distance from the summit of the Mount of Olives. And just north of the little town there comes down a ridge or spine of land, and over that comes the same Roman road which has come winding around and then goes over that ridge towards Jericho and the Jordan. Over that little ridge came Jesus, even then, we fancy over that pavement. At one point of the road there is a limestone rock which may have been the spot where Jesus and his disciples sat down to rest when weary. It would be vain to try to describe the feelings with which you sit down here and take out your Bible and read the stories of what went on at Bethany.

I wish to speak this evening of the raising of Lazarus in particular, but first of all of the previous relations of Jesus to this family at Bethany. These relatives were singularly intimate and familiar. The first time we find the family mentioned is some months before this, the time he said, "One thing is needful." It is evident that he had often been there before. When Martha speaks it is with a certain kind of familiarity. They were persons of wealth it is evident, and so the large company of men could come as often as they pleased and would not be a burden to them. That they were persons of wealth appears partly from the fact that many Jews had gone out from the city to condole with them in their grief. It shows that they possessed what we call social consideration. Later than this we find that Mary had a valuable quantity of ointment which cost more than 300 Roman denares – that would be $400 or $500. It would have been out of question if this family had been poor, that this girl should have had such a valuable quantity of perfumery, and that explains Mary's course on the previous occasion. Now on this occasion what Martha did was probably not from a worldly spirit but probably from a desire natural with housekeeping women who in their desire to provide an elegant and elaborate entertainment carry it too far. And so in this case what Martha did was not from a worldly spirit but she went too far in expressing her love for the Prophet of Nazareth. This seems to have led also to a certain familiarity of friendship for we find them often speaking in a kind of fault finding way to Jesus. Martha comes in to tell the Lord that her sister has left her to do all the work alone, as if he ought to care. And so in our narrative before us we shall find them finding fault with the Master. Do you know I stop there and find myself touched by that. Jesus was not forbidding. Little children loved to come to him, and he loved to have them come, and his intimate friends would take liberties with him, and were surprised at his doing some things which they thought were strange.

In the next place consider our Lord's remarkable conduct when he received the news that Lazarus was sick. He was away beyond Jordan two or three days journey when the message was brought to him, and so far as we can see or judge he had no intimation of what would happen. Jesus stayed there two days still. And doubtless when the messenger returned, and Jesus came not, the beloved brother was dead already. They waited there the weary hours of a whole day and another slow moving day, and waiting they wondered that Jesus came not, just as you have wondered many a time, when you have been in trouble and did not need to send a messenger far away beyond a river, just as you have lifted up your heart in prayer to that same Savior now ascended and wondered that he seemed not to hear. You cried to him in your agony, and there came neither voice nor sound. There was no sign that he ever heard you at all, or ever would hearken to your cry of distress. But we know how it was with Martha and Mary. We know that he was preparing a richer, sweeter blessing for them than they had ever dared to dream of or hope for. Now when the disciples remonstrated with Jesus and said to him, "Master, of late the Jews have sought to stone thee, and goest thou thither again?" our Lord makes a reply which seems a little ambiguous but the general drift is plain. He says: "Are there not twelve hours in the day? If any man walk in the day, he stumbleth not, because he seeth the light of this world." The general thought is, that there is a time to do things, and when the time comes for doing a thing then you need not fear. It had been best that he should come away from Jerusalem to avoid collision with the authorities, but now there was a duty to be performed, and it was right that he should go back again. Ah, when a man can see his plain duty though it be perilous, what a comfort it is. To my mind, Christian friends, the sorest trials of life come when you cannot make up your mind what is your duty, when you see the time is coming that you will be compelled to decide and you don't know and can't determine what is your duty, but whenever a man can see plainly in his best judgment, and when the best counsel of others does seem the indication of God's providence and clear duty their duty is not much in this world after all. Ah duty will triumph over danger and the heart that is sure of duty can move forward without fear. When Lazarus was dying one of the disciples made a remark—Thomas called Didymus—"Let us also go that we may die with him." This was the man so often spoken of as the type of a skeptic or disbeliever. Thomas appears to be a low spirited man who took the worst view of things. He will die, he said, let us go and die with him.

In the third place notice our Lord's arrival at Bethany and what followed. Martha may have had somebody looking out for him, or else must have been very sharply looking out herself, for it was a little town. She met him before he entered the village. When Martha came where Jesus was she said, "Lord, if thou hadst been here"—the emphasis is not on the "thou." It is not "If *thou* hadst been here," but—"Lord, if thou hadst been *here*," or, anybody would have supposed that thou wouldst have been here, instead of beyond the Jordan, where so dear a friend was ill. "Lord, if thou hadst been here, my brother had not died." But she adds: "But I know that even now whatsoever thou shalt ask of God, God will give it thee." Do you see what she is thinking of? She is afraid to say it, afraid almost to think it, but the idea is in her mind that he may do something still. I suppose she had heard of like events before. I suppose that many a time when the disciples and the Master were at home, when Mary would have been sitting at Jesus' feet and listening to his profound discourse and they may have told her about the miracles and how when the little girl lay dead, Jesus had lifted her up alive and given her back to her parents, or how when walking along they happened to see a funeral procession and Jesus bade them set down the bier and touched the young man that lay dead and bade him arise, and he stood up and was restored to his mother. And so she has a thought in her mind which she does not dare distinctly to express. Now then Jesus said to her, "Thy brother shall rise again." Ah that is ambiguous. She says: "I know that he shall rise again in the last day." Jesus said: "I am the resurrection and the life; he that believeth in me, though he were dead, yet shall he live, and whosoever liveth and believeth in me shall never die." You see he passes as he often does from the idea of physical to spiritual life and death. Then came that woman Martha who is too often represented as contrasted with her sister as spiritual and she said: "Yea Lord; I believe that thou art the Christ, the Son of God which should come into the world." Did you ever talk with a Jew, a Jew of the present time to

to whom the question of all earth's questions was whether Jesus
Christ is the Messiah? Perhaps that would help you realize what was
meant when she said: "Lord, I believe that thou art the Messiah."
"And when she had so said she went her way and called her sister
secretly, saying, the Master is come and calleth for thee. As soon as
she heard that she arose quickly and came unto him." Many Jews had
come from Jerusalem, ladies and gentlemen to condole with the
family. They were seated in the house condoling after the Oriental
fashion. The Oriental fashion is to take a seat there and say nothing
scarcely ever speaking a word. Many a time when I was pastor I remembered to have observed, as physicians have observed how much
harm is done by words. Mary sat there with these friends and when
Mary was told that the master had come and called for her she got up
and went quickly out of the room. The friends supposed she had gone
to the grave to weep there. When Mary came to where Jesus was she
said the same thing that her sister had said, "Lord if thou hadst been
here my brother had not died," and then she said no more but fell to
weeping. With active and thoughtful Martha, Jesus reasoned; with
tender loving Mary, he wept. He always deals with his followers according to their disposition. Some will serve him in a cheerful way,
others in a half-desponding fashion. Some will serve him in contemplation more, some in activity. True love of Jesus Christ will show
itself as a different thing according to the temperament of the person
who exercises it. Let us not set up some standard and refuse to be
contented or grateful unless we can be just that, for, the standard
will often be just what we cannot attain to. Now as it is rendered,
Jesus groaned in spirit. That is not the meaning; the meaning is, "He
rebuked himself," he rebuked himself when he saw Mary weeping
and the friends around also weeping. He agitated himself; he tried to
keep from weeping. When a man feels like weeping, the first thought
is that he must restrain himself, when a woman feels like weeping she
will often allow herself to weep without effort. Jesus said, "Where
have ye laid him?" And then his feelings gave way, "Jesus wept."
My friend, O my friend, it is not any more important for you to realize
that he was more than man, than it is important for you to realize that
he was a man, a tender, loving man, a man with perfect, complete
humanity – only, blessed exception, that he was without sin. And so
they went on to the grave. It was a cave we are told. You will find a
number of old tombs around Jerusalem now, some only caves and
others artificial chambers, some opening into another in which bodies
wrapped in clothes were placed and clothes put over them. There is
just a little door at the side so that a huge stone rolled over it would
protect it from robbers and wild beasts. Jesus said as he came near,
"Take ye away the stone." Martha forgets what the Master had said in
the feeling that it would not do to take away the stone, and she in-
sinuates to the Lord that it would not do to take away the stone. Jesus

rebuked her, "Said I not unto thee, that, if thou wouldest believe, thou should see the glory of God?" Now my friends you know that story, you used to hear it told when you were a little child, and when you learned to read, that was one of the stories you loved to read. You know how Jesus stood there and said, "Father, I thank thee that thou hast heard me. And I know that—that—thou hearest me always; but because of the people that stand by I said it, that they may believe that thou hast sent me." In loving compassion for these Jews that were out there from Jerusalem, he wanted to say something which would make them believe for their own good. He spoke in a loud voice and said, "Lazarus come forth." I remember in Bethany one day I almost thought I heard come sounding down from the clouds above that loud voice with which the Redeemer called to the dead man in his tomb to come forth. And while they held their breath to listen, and their hearts stopped beating to hear, slowly, slowly, out of the tomb, moving with difficulty because wrapped in grave clothes—slowly, slowly came out of the tomb alive, the man, and with a cry of joy Martha rushed to their brother but Mary fell at the Redeemer's feet. My friends there are two or three of the many lessons which this marvelous, pathetic story teaches which I will indicate before we turn away. Cherish the miracles, cherish the miracles. We live in a day when many well meaning men puzzled with the idea of many physical forces, infatuated, will tell you they cannot believe in the possibility of miracles. "I believe there is a Creator, I believe there is a God, but I can't believe in miracles." If God made this universe, with all its physical forces, why can't he who made them control them? Ah if you believe in a Creator there cannot be any difficulty. When the material world seems closed in around us and men's minds are possessed with materialism so often in this day of ours, cherish the miracles, the Spirit of God who made the material world has in these miracles spoken to us bidding us understand that spirit is mightier than matter; that he is master of the world he has made and they are the sign-manual of the deity. Stamped upon the mission of his Son, and the teachings of his chosen one, cherish the miracles, and my brother, try to get near Jesus Christ and the Gospel. You may like to go to Palestine, to one who is prepared for it and will stay long enough to profit by it it is valuable. But it is not necessary to go to Palestine that you may come to Jesus. These stories carry about them in this world an atmosphere of their own, they carry Jesus with them, and if you will bend over these stories, you will find that you can come nearer Jesus. If you try to see him and try to hear him you will find that it becomes possible more and more as you grow older. Many cultivated people think the Gospel is for the Sunday School children, they possibly lose themselves in speculations about prophecy, or turn to precepts or devotions, but there is nothing we need more than to come to the Gospels and try to come there to the Savior, the personal Redeemer, who is the sum of all truth, the way, and the truth, and the life. Try to come near to Jesus in the Gospel, for after all, high or low, refined or rude, young or old, to get near to Jesus, to love him, and trust him, and follow him, and try to do what he wants us to do, to be exceedingly concerned to have others follow him too, that, that is to be a Christian. In all simplicity of soul, in loving trust and loving obedience try to get near to Jesus in the Gospel and then by the grace of his spirit to follow him through life.

BE CAREFUL FOR NOTHING

"Be careful for nothing, but in everything by prayer and supplication with thanksgiving let your requests be known unto God; and the peace of God, which passeth all understanding, shall guard your hearts and minds in Christ Jesus" (Philippians 4:6–7).

"BE CAREFUL FOR NOTHING." We are always telling the children and the servants to be careful of everything. But the word has changed its meaning; originally it meant full of care. In the revised edition of the Bible the word "anxious" is substituted, "in nothing be anxious"; that is the exact, full meaning.

How can we help it? How can any one help being anxious? Our possessions are held by an uncertain tenure. The possessions of the rich are a source of anxiety; and the anxieties of the poor are not proportioned to their possessions. Our very lives are uncertain; and the things that are dear to us awaken anxieties in our minds. We are anxious about those we love better than our lives. Your son stayed out late last night, and made an evasive answer when you questioned him about it. Could you fail to be anxious, as you stole a furtive look at him across the breakfast table? And your husband, you used to hope would become a Christian; but he hasn't, and he does not seem interested of late; he has not been to church in a good many Sundays. The little

---

A discourse preached in the Woodward Avenue Baptist Church, Detroit, August 11, 1889, by John A. Broadus, reprinted from *Christian Herald,* Detroit, Michigan, vol. 20, no. 33 (15 August 1889).

child in its second summer is sick; and you hear its pitiful wailing in the silence of the night. Can you keep from being anxious about it? Life, property, character, everything is uncertain. How is it possible to avoid being anxious? And yet the Apostle says it, secure in the promise of his Master, "In nothing be anxious."

Be not anxious for tomorrow. Be not anxious for what you shall eat and for what you shall wear; for One knows our needs and it is His purpose to supply all our needs through Christ Jesus our Lord. Worry is the friction of life.

We who live in this fag end of the 19th century find more causes for anxiety than those of any previous age. We want to go fast, walk fast, live fast, sing fast. The danger is that we will die too quickly.

See that man! He wants to catch a train. See how he strains every nerve and muscle until the beads of perspiration stand out upon his brow. Look at him, how fast he is walking! He is afraid he will not get there in time. He is a perfect type of the life of this great American nation.

Sir Arthur Helps, at one time private secretary to Queen Victoria, is the author of a work entitled *Friends in Council*. One of the essays, I remember reading to my wife. It was on the "Kingdom of Worry," and he says: "Worry reigns over more human beings than any other potentate." We wear our lives away with fatiguing, useless worry. Is there no remedy? Let us see:

"In nothing be anxious; but in everything by prayer and supplication let your requests be made known to God." Turn your troubles and anxieties into prayer by supplicating God. Now, the mere fact of telling one about our troubles is sometimes a partial relief. Don't you find it so? You have some dear friend—Oh, thank God for those friends! some dear friend whose sympathy you can count upon, and it is a comfort that you can tell that friend the cause of your anxiety. They may not have it in their power to aid you, but their sympathy is a great comfort to you. And so, "In everything let your requests be made known to God." It is a greater comfort to go to One with your troubles who understands you, and sympathizes with you, and who will not only listen, but will help you.

One hundred years ago there was a great deal of discussion in England, and in this country also, relative to the Bible. Some said praying to God is like a man in a boat who is given a rope that is fastened to some object on shore. By pulling at the rope he gradually pulls his boat to shore. He does not expect to pull the shore to him. And we can't expect to pull God to us, but we can pull ourselves toward God. But if that were all, the truth is we would never pray. The Bible does not allow us to so limit God's power. When we call upon Him, He will not only hear us; but he will heed and help us.

Will he always give us exactly what we ask for? Not he. He is too wise for that. "If ye who are evil know how to give good gifts to your children, how much more your Heavenly Father." If you who are evil make no mistakes in giving to your children, with how much more wisdom will an All Wise God deal with your requests. Suppose your child should ask for a serpent, thinking it a fish, would you not, instead of complying with the request, give it something else — something better? And so the child can come in its childlike limitations and ask the parent and the parent will know how to give good things to the child. Much more shall not your Father in Heaven know how to give good things to you, for he is not evil?

Suppose that you could have everything you asked, then just in proportion as your experience had been, you would be afraid to ask for those things you think you want. Many of us have lived long enough to see, that those things most longed for are not the things that are best for us to have; and we would be almost afraid to pray, if we were sure of getting just what, in our human judgment, seemed best. But our Heavenly Father knows our needs, and will give us just what is best for us to have.

"In nothing be anxious, but in everything by prayer and supplication, with thanksgiving, let your request be made known to God." "With thanksgiving." Did you notice that I had left that out? Don't ever leave that out. We are very apt to do so. We are so taken up with the affairs of the present that we don't have time to give thanks for the blessings of the past. And our prayers are not often those of thanksgiving. Why, my dear friends, in the greatest misfortunes of life we can still find occasion for thanksgiving.

"And the peace of God which passeth all understanding shall guard your hearts and minds in Christ Jesus."

"The peace of God!" O friends, have you ever been by the bedside of a dying Christian? Can you forget the anguish and suffering of that pale face, from which the life was ebbing? And then some words of comfort which touch the heart were spoken, and the anguished face would quiet down, and you would see it filled with peace, "the peace of God." No wonder the Apostle says the peace of God passeth all understanding. There are a great many things impossible for these human hearts of ours to believe, many things we can't understand. The peace of God passeth all understanding, but does not pass possibility of attainment.

But "can the peace of God enter my heart?" some person will ask. Can I, with these strange, passionate emotions ever know the peace of God? How can the peace of God rule my soul?

Mountains of waves are sweeping and raging o'er the sea of Galilee; a little boat with twelve occupants is struggling bravely against the storm; they can manage the boat no longer; it is filling with water. In the rear of the boat lies One sound asleep, while the waves roar around him unheeded. They can manage the boat no longer; and going to him, they say "Master, we are perishing." He arises from his slumber at their call, and noting the looks of fear depicted on their faces says, "Why are ye so fearful? O ye of little faith." And then he commands the waves, saying, "peace, be still." And in obedience to his commands the great waves subsided, the storm ceased, and all was calm. He who calmed the sea at the prayer of his beloved apostles, is he who can calm your storm-tossed soul into peace, if you only trust and ask him, O, ye of little faith! The peace of God, which passeth all understanding shall guard your minds and hearts in Christ Jesus. The fort may be old and weak as the one I saw in Mackinac last week, but if it has a strong garrison for its protection, that can "hold the fort"; and so the peace of God shall garrison your hearts and make them strong to battle with the world's worries and anxieties – there may be sad memories, and yet peace.

I remember seeing in Dresden the only picture of Mary Magdalene that I ever saw that seemed at all satisfactory. The ordinary conception is false to the idea. But this was a picture of a woman of middle age, once very beautiful, with deep furrows in her face, left there by terrible experiences. But the suffering is all past and a look of holy peace rests on the countenance. Peace purchased by sorrow and repentance, and yet, peace.

My friends, do you say that it is not possible that all this should be more than a dream? Do you say, "how can I be guarded and protected by something unseen?" I was writing an article on Solomon for the *Baptist Teacher* last week, and was reminded in connection with Solomon's early dreams, of a visit I made to Gibeon with a friend of mine. We were sitting on a housetop looking up some allusions to places of interest in that vicinity in our Bible, when a crowd of fifteen or more of the natives, attracted by strangers, came and formed a circle around us. I happened to take out my watch to see the time, while my friend was reading, and I noticed the eyes of the men gleam at sight of the gold. I said to my friend: "Just look at those fellows. Just see how they act," and I took out my watch again. Two of the younger ones started towards me, gazing on the gold with longing eyes; then they drew back. What were they afraid of? We were unarmed and without any means of defense and they could easily have overpowered us. Why were we so secure?

Our names were registered at Jerusalem in a large house over which floated the stars and stripes, and had we come to harm, search would have been made, and as the poor fellows were aware, the Turkish government would rather have destroyed hundreds of their people than offend the great Western Power. And thus, something those poor fellows never saw, and never will see, that unseen, far-away power made us safe.

It is a custom of modern medical men to guard against disease by using preventives, and in proportion as we are wise, we will guard against the disease of anxiety by the preventive of prayer.

Dear friends, the preacher is a stranger among you, and will soon go his way and be forgotten. The best wish he can make for you is, that you may know, living and dying, the meaning of this text: And the peace of God, which passeth all understanding, guard your hearts and minds through Christ Jesus.

THE CHRISTIAN RACE

"But I press on, if so be that I may lay hold on that for which also I was laid hold on by Christ Jesus. Brethren, I count not myself yet to have laid hold, but one thing I do, forgetting the things that are behind and stretching forward to the things that are before; I press on toward the goal, unto the prize of the high calling of God in Christ Jesus" (Philippians 3:12–14).

THIS PASSAGE is very familiar. What makes it so familiar? The fact that it is so rich in meaning. Paul is telling of his own actions, and his personal experience. We sometimes get troubled about these things and wish that his experience might be ours, and then we excuse ourselves and say: "That was the great apostle, and it is not to be expected that an ordinary mortal can act as he did. He was inspired, you know." Do you not see here that there was really no special inspiration? He speaks of his endeavor and personal experience as a Christian man. There is not one part of it but might come fully within the reach of our attainment.

The image as you all know is the image of a race. I love to think of those races of the olden times. The whole scene is grand. The great space allowed for the competitors, surrounded with stone seats, where crowds were gathered, as they gather with us now, to view our modern game. Yonder was a post, which was the goal; and when at the end of a course, some runner swifter than the rest reached forth and grasped the post, a great shout went up, that he had won the race. Let me say,

A discourse preached in the Woodward Avenue Baptist Church, Detroit, Sunday morning, August 25, 1889, by John A. Broadus, reprinted from *Christian Herald*, Detroit, Michigan, vol. 20, no. 35 (29 August 1889).

by the way, that I rejoice in every effort to promote athletic sports and in any innocent sport that keeps our young men apart from vice.

The image then is of a racer running a good race; and before him stands the goal, and the question is whether he will win the race and lay hold of the goal. The word "apprehended" is unfortunate in our old version. We speak of apprehending a thief; but in almost every other relation in which the word is now used, it conveys the idea of a mental grasp of an idea or subject. What is wanted here is just the plain term, "lay hold of." The thought is that Christ Jesus "laid hold of" him and set him to running this race. "I follow after that I may lay hold of the goal of life, that for which also I was laid hold of by Christ Jesus. Brethren, I count not myself to have laid hold. The goal of life is still before me, but one thing, forgetting the things that are behind and reaching forward to the things that are before, I press onward toward the goal, unto the prize of the high calling of God in Christ Jesus." You see then that the first thing we have to do in contemplating this image of the apostle and in appropriating it to ourselves is to realize that Christ Jesus laid hold of Paul, made him his own and put him to running this race. Paul, you remember, was in the pride and triumph of success, proud of his distinction as a Jew, fiercely persecuting the saints, when Christ Jesus laid hold of him and a voice out of the heavens almost made his heart stop beating. He stopped his persecutions and went in obedience to the commands of God to bear his name to the Gentiles. Well, that was peculiar. But as to the spirit of it, it was not peculiar. Christ Jesus laid hold of him and saved him, and made him his own no more truly than he lays hold of men today.

I once heard a forcible sermon of which I can give you the points: "First, I am not what I ought to be; second, I am not what I hope to be; third, I am not what I once was; fourth, by the grace of God, I am what I am." Does not every devout heart respond to that sentiment? "By the grace of God I am what I am." O men and women, let us humbly yield to this blessed power. Let us yield these human hearts to the divine grace and live by faith in the Son of God.

Our second thought is the Christian desire to complete the object for which Christ Jesus made us his own. "I follow after, if so be I may lay hold of that for which I also was laid hold of by Christ Jesus."

I have heard it said that baptism is the door of the church. If in any sense at all baptism is the door of the church, it is not the flowery door that leads to the castle of indolence. It is rather the door into the Lord's vineyard, where there is work for all.

At Alexandria in Egypt, in making port, the steamer stops at some distance out until the couriers from the hotels come on board. I remember noticing one Oriental in one of the boats. He gracefully fastened his little boat to the great ship, and then sat down in the bow, crossed his little legs, folded his arms and looked so contented and happy as the great steamer towed him into port. And I thought as I watched him: that is just the way some people think the church is going to save them. They have only to hitch on to be towed into the heavenly port.

There is nothing like Christianity to individualize men. If you turn to the fourteenth chapter of Romans you will find that it is there commanded that each man must do his own work. "Every one of us shall give account of himself to God."

And now we shall see that this passage is properly divided into two parts: that we may develop our own Christian character and that we may benefit our fellow men, and then through both together that we may glorify God. If Christ Jesus laid hold of you, he designed that you should yield to him and affiliate with the Christian family.

People are born again, but they are born babes in Christ. Minerva sprang from the brain of Jupiter, full grown in wisdom, according to ancient mythology, but we are born babes in Christ and have to grow afterward. There are cases, I suppose, where people just before death are completely transformed by divine grace. But the cases are rare and certainly it is against all analogies. We are born babes, and will have to grow according to the law of spiritual life – grow by nutriment and exercise combined. A healthy little babe is constantly exercising. Activity, with the nutriment it takes, is what makes it grow. You starve your soul for want of Christian food and you keep yourself idle and inactive, and then say you are a poor specimen of a Christian. I should think you would be.

Then the development of the Christian character and the benefit to our fellow men has to go on together. Neither will make much progress without the other. You say: "I would try to do more good if I only were a better Christian." And I say, when you cease to be ashamed of your own shortcomings, then you will be unfit to benefit anybody. If you think you are to go to people as some holy angel, you have got the wrong idea. Why were not angels sent to convert mankind? Because they are outside the range of human experience. If you think that you must keep away from all attempts at usefulness and turn your attention wholly to your own needs you make a great mistake. John Foster, who has written some of the finest things in our literature, was once solicited to give his aid to Christian missions. He wrote in reply: "I have not time to be occupying myself with the heathen. It is all I can do to look after my own religious life. I make such poor progress in my own work, I really haven't time for anything else." Did ever a great man say a more foolish thing? Andrew Fuller was the first secretary for foreign missions, and he had been in the habit of preaching very helpful and consoling sermons to the burdened members of his congregation. Most men and women go to church hoping to get consolation. He became identified with foreign missions which took up a great deal of his time and thought. After several years of the work it struck him that he must preach one of his comforting sermons to the disconsolate members of his congregation, but he did not find any in need of consolation. They had lost all need of it in trying to help others. O friends! we shall make small progress in the development of the Christian character unless we try to help others.

Some people will read a thrilling thing in a newspaper and after reading it will say: "O, if I could only do something of that sort!" "What can I do?" What can you do? If you will believe me you can do something that the tallest archangel that ever stood by the throne of God cannot do. You can do something that appeals to the very heart of the infinite God—you can win some souls to Christ. Oh friends! when life's opportunities are all past, will there be anything, can there by anything so sweet to look back upon, as to have been the means of saving a soul from death? You can do that. Somebody did that for you. Once somebody, by God's grace, won you to Jesus. And O, you can win somebody to Jesus! Go not alone into the palaces of God, Christian heart. You can't get there alone. We are so linked together that we must be trying to save others or we will not save ourselves.

And now, men, women, boys, girls, the preacher pleads with you to keep trying to become useful, trying to do good. What is life for but that you may do good? "My daughter," said a good man one day as he blessed the young bride, who was turning away with her young husband. "My daughter, you can get nothing out of life but usefulness." All the true joy of life has got to come as the unsought attendant upon usefulness. If you live to be happy, you will not be happy. If you live to be good and useful, happiness will come along of its own accord. Are you trying to be useful? Are you eagerly seizing on every opportunity to do good?

Do good on a large scale or on a small scale; but be sure to do good on any scale you can, and then maybe you will get more opportunities to do good on a large scale. Every one of you has a place to fill in the army of the Lord; and if you are not in your place there are weapons lying there that no one but you can wield. O do not leave them to rust. Nobody can fill another's place. You might as well think that another can be saved in your stead as that another can fill your place.

The third point is that the Christian here declares that he seeks continual progress. "Brethren, I count not myself to have laid hold, but one thing I do, forgetting the things which are behind and reaching out for the things which are before, I press onward toward the goal." "One thing." You don't like to meet a man with but one idea, always talking and thinking about the same thing. Such a man is called a crank, with his everlasting repetition of the one theme. But it is different if the idea is only great enough; if it takes in the limitless thought of Christian progress. Man has no right to be satisfied with merely doing well. "Forgetting the things that are behind I reach forward for the things that are before." You say: "I really would wish to do more for the Lord, but I am afraid that my experience, my doubts" – O get out of that and go to work! "But I am afraid that I was never really converted." Then "Let the dead past bury its dead" and turn your face to the future. If you never were really a Christian, then begin to be one now. Don't go hunting in the rubbish of the past but open your eyes on the future, and thank God for the life of the present. "Forgetting the things that are behind." We have no right to forget past mercies nor the blessings of past experiences, but be not satisfied with past attainments, and be not broken down with useless discouragement, but "reach out toward the goal," with your face toward the future.

Did you ever have occasion to watch a stream of water that flows calmly on for a while but by-and-by becomes stagnant and you notice that foul things creep on the bottom of the stream? That is an image of a life of inaction. On the other hand, do you see that stream hard by, bright and sparkling in the morning sun? How it widens and deepens gradually. This is the movement of life, a life of active usefulness. Is your life that stagnant pool? Can it be that sparkling stream?

And now I suppose you are disappointed. "I press onward toward the goal." I suppose you thought the preacher would try and say something about that; but the preacher can find nothing fit to be said about that place which from on high, he, our Lord, bends down to offer to us. What can I say? There is one thing more I must say. Oh, friends, Paul said in his last epistle to Timothy: "I have finished my course. I have fought the good fight and a crown of righteousness is laid up for me." Would you like to feel that was true of you, that you have nothing to do but wait for the crown, that you could repeat Paul's dying words of certainty and hope? Would you like to feel that you have finished the course your Lord and Savior set you to run? Then "forgetting those things which are behind press on toward the goal unto the prize of the high calling of God in Christ Jesus."

GOODNESS AS THE MORNING CLOUD

"O, Ephraim, what shall I do unto thee? O Judah, what shall
I do unto thee? For your goodness is as the morning cloud,
and as the early dew it goeth away" (Hosea 6:4).

IT IS TO BE FEARED that the prophecies of the opening chapters from
Hosea receive very little attention from the ordinary Bible reader.
The prophets seem so far away, and people have an idea that their
only business was to predict the future; and we try to read prophecy
and don't see exactly what it amounts to.

The prophets were inspired people, whose business it was to warn
people, to rebuke them, to exhort them, and to try to make people
live in the fear of God, as they ought to live; and they would tell them
of the history of God's dealings with them, and tell them of their present sins. And they would also, again and again, inspired of God, predict
future events by way of warning of the divine judgment that would
come, or of the coming of the divine presence. Prediction was not
their main business; they were inspired preachers to make people
turn from their sins and their folly. Prediction was just one of the
warnings they brought to bear, to make people live as they ought to.
Even in Hosea you will have any quantity of human nature appearing
in the state of things described. You will find that people were wicked
and worldly, and they are warning them of the consequences and
beseeching them to turn from their sins to God. So if you read between
the lines, and look down into it, you will find human nature there,
and learn of the efforts made to turn these people from their sins.

The prophets doubtless had a very hard time. They lived in a very
wicked period, in the northern country, and they came in contact
with all manner of wickedness. Hosea tried to rebuke and exhort, and
encourage as best he could. He had sore trials in his own life. His
wife proved unfaithful to him—the bitterest trial a man ever bears
in this life. And he was led by divine direction, as he thought, to
believe it to be his duty to condone the fault, to forgive her and keep
her still his wife, and to rear children that he knew were not his own
children. And out of this, he came to see a great and new thought
which he practiced, and which was adopted by many of the prophets
who came after him. This was the relation of human nature and
Jehovah; that He was like her husband, and nature was like his unfaithful wife that had wandered from him, and that Jehovah was calling unfaithful Israel to come back and he would forgive her. Among

A discourse preached in the Woodward Avenue Baptist Church, Detroit, August
10, 1890, by John A. Broadus, reprinted from *Christian Herald,* Detroit, Michigan, vol. 21, no. 33 (14 August 1890).

the great truths that the Bible abounds in, there is nothing more wonderful than God's compassion and forgiveness.

Now you read on in the book of this prophet, who had such trials,
and you think to yourself, "I wonder if he did any good, I wonder if
he made any one better. I cannot see that he did." So far as we judge
from this history, it is doubtful whether he made them any better,
but may be he did something to keep them from getting any worse.
In our home, in our church, and in our social relations, it is something if we can keep people from getting worse. It is one of the great
facts of life that the general propensities of people are downward.
It is something to keep people from getting worse, and certainly Hosea
did that, even among the difficulties that he had to encounter; among
the evils that afflicted his soul. As you look upon his people, both in
his own country and among the southern people of Judea, you will
see that much of their religion was superficial and transitory. They
made a great hubbub and ado of turning from their sins; they thought
it was the easiest thing to do; they abused divine mercy.

Do you not find anything, in all this, that suggests the doings of
today? People have a revival to get stirred up a great deal; and persons aroused by some personal affliction undertake to be more religious for a while, and when this is all gone, make light of it. We must
be terribly in earnest, if it is to be any use. Listen! Jehovah says:
"I will go and return to my place until they acknowledge their offence
and seek my face. In their affliction they will seek me early."

Now the people speak: "Let us return to the Lord, for he hath torn,
and he will heal us; he hath smitten, and he will bind us up." The
Lord is very forgiving; he will forgive us. After two days will he re-
vive us, and on the third day he will raise us up, and we shall live in
his sight.

"Again, O Ephraim, what shall I do unto thee? O Judah, what shall
I do unto thee? For thy goodness is as the morning cloud, and as the
early dew it goeth away." Transitory devotion. Superficial, transient
yearning. Have you been there?

Now, what I wish to say about it, is to see if I cannot point out some
things that will help us to just that mind to speak and think as he
did. Then we may exclaim, "Ah me, if the prophet were here, what
would he say for my life?" What can I say to keep undying that transient devotion? The first thing I would say is that we must enlist all
of our faculties in the struggle for true piety. There are a great many
people undertaking to be religious. But they put all their intelligence
into their worldly vocation.

Now, there are many people who put little intelligence into their
religion. Some of them, who have intelligence for the affairs of life,
feel that religion is an occasional feeling, an emotional matter, and so
on, and they do not presume that they are to be intelligent in their
religion; that they ought to think, that they ought to know religious

truth, that they ought to gain deep seated conviction of religion and of religious truth and duty. Why, truth is the life blood of piety. It is only in proportion as people have such circulation through their whole soul that they will have religious piety. So I say whatever proportion of it we can direct toward any object, let us direct our best-tried power toward religious truth and conviction, keeping ourselves freshly familiar with the great truths of Christianity. What exalted truths they are. What supreme ideas. If a man lay his naked soul upon the teachings of the Bible, what impressions he will get, and if he will constantly do this, the impression will be abiding. And I charge upon you, Oh my friends, that many of you have failed to bring your intelligence, as you ought to have done, to bear upon the truths of God, and thereby your religious life has greatly suffered.

Then again, there are men who neglect to enlist their sensibilities in the life of Christ; they have very critical convictions and ideas, and they can talk straight upon the subject, but their hearts are not in it. Their feelings are seldom moved by it, and some of them look down upon it. They say, "There are some people, you know, who are very emotional in their convictions, but I believe in a religion of intelligence." They will hide their religious character and blight their religious life, by trying to make it a mere matter of intelligence, not enlisting any emotions of their souls. We know that we do not accomplish anything in the affairs of life, that we do not amount to anything in the relations of home and society, till our heart is in the doing.

What satisfaction are you, husband, in your home, if you give your family only intelligence and support, and not your heart's affection. We must be interested in our religious life and we must bring our heart to bear upon it. We must bring this, our religious sensibility, and we are in no small danger of neglect in this respect.

We live in a time of characteristic activity, when everything in the world goes with a rush. I like to live in such an age, but we are in danger of neglecting the practice of religious affection and sensibility, and in special danger of criticising people who happen to show their feelings. It seems to some that it is not good to make mention of their emotions, hence their religious feelings decay and die out. Some person will say to himself, "Ah, me, it seems to be a sad thing, but I acknowledge I do not feel interested in religion. I hoped I would feel by this time as I used to feel. I wonder what is the matter." It is easy enough to see what is the matter.

The third element that must be enlisted in the life of piety is "will." Why, you know perfectly well that you will not accomplish very much without you use willpower upon it. A man will not expect to push business or make a successful struggle for money without "will."

I tell you, young people, you will do more with your situation if you make up your mind that you will. We talk a great deal about a helpless dependence upon a divine grace. This is very necessary, because there is a tendency in human nature to put too much confidence in itself, and fail to acknowledge dependence. You know with the matter of religion, one hopes that there will come some tide that will bear him along, and hopes that he will live to a time when it will be easier for him to be in earnest with religion, and hopes and prays that he will be better.

Do you mean to? Have you ever, in deep sincerity of soul, willed to be better? There is an old book of which John Wesley and Dr. Johnson speak, that they read when they were young, and which has been republished in our time, called *Law's Helps to a Holy Life.* I read it long ago, and remember one thought from it that I have retained and recalled a thousand times. I was startled by it at first, and afterwards wondered if it was strictly true: "A man is as holy as he ever really intended to be."

Not as holy as he may have sometimes wished to be; not as holy as he may have sometimes prayed to be, or vainly hoped that he would become, but he is as holy as he ever really intended to be. Think about it. And all men and women, young and old, who profess and call your-selves Christians, I solemnly caution you today, if you wish to be done with this superficiality and transient and ever decaying dullness of religious life, look up to God for help. Out of the reserve of your nature say, "God help me." Say it now, say it in your deep, earnest heart, "God help me. I will be a better Christian, I will, *I will, I will* be a better Christian!" Be in earnest about it. Enlist all the faculties; intelligence, sensibility, and will, in the Christian life.

The second thing is: We must have harmony between the inward and outward, in the life of piety. The two have to go together, and it is only when they work in harmony that the life of piety can be maintained. It is vain to try to have inward piety without outward. Some people attempt it; some very good people make this endeavor. I should not be surprised if you knew some among your acquaintances, who try with great sincerity to be pious altogether as an inner thing, and to an intimate friend to whom they are willing to talk, they would say, "Well, you know what I think, religion is a matter between the soul and God, and I don't quite see why there should be anything outward about it, and then I must confess (I do not mean to speak harshly) that I have seen Christians who were a reproach to their Christianity; I do not want to be one of that kind. I don't want them to talk that way about me. Religious life is inward, and I think that is the best. It will do for me."

There are some very beautiful characters who talk in that way of Christianity. O, my friend, take the right view of Him. He knew more about these things than you do. You may know more than all of us, but you do not know so well as he did. The Founder of Christianity laid it down definitely that people who undertook to be his must confess him publicly, and he knew a thing or two on the subject, did he not?

He laid it down definitely, that if you were to be his, you must confess him before men. There must be an outward as well as an inward life; we are soul, and also body. Our lives are inward, and also outward.

What would a mother think of her son if he were to tell her, now and then, that he loved her very much, and would not do anything for her, even when she asked him to. She would be glad to have him show his love for her by acts as well as words. That would be natural.

On the other hand, some persons attempt to meet the external life without the inner life. It is no light thing to retain outward forms without inner spiritual life. We must strive to maintain the life of piety and not sacrifice either to the other, nor neglect either for the other.

And now the third suggestion. If we want to do better in the life of piety, let us profit by our actual experience instead of dreaming about some other experience. You know how it is? A person will say: "I think I am unfavorably situated for being an earnest Christian. Circumstances are very unfavorable for religious life. My natural disposition is in some respects radically opposed to this. I think if I were otherwise constituted, or only situated differently, I could lead a religious life, and should be very glad, indeed."

O, how you dream. Profit by your actual experience. Now here is a person who is poor and labors for a livelihood and says, "If I were well off now, like some of these persons who go to church, dressed fine, you might talk to me about religion. When any one is poor, and hard pushed as I am, what is the use of talking to me." And little he knows that some of those who are rich are driven with cares, and are tempted in bitterness and agony of soul to say: "O, if I were but poor, may be I could be pious; but how can I be now?"

I say, we go dreaming as to how pious we could be, if things were only different with us, and all dreaming is idle, unless we profit by our actual experience. God Almighty has put us in this world, to try to make the best of things, for we can get good out of everything. It is one of the wonders of practical science in our age, how many things are turned to account now, and made profitable, which used to be thrown away in the process of manufacture. For instance, some of the most delicate perfumes, and some potent medicines are produced from the refuse of the factory, that used to go to waste. And so there are many things in our life (if we only had a more ingenious chemistry about us) out of which we could secure religious benefits, if we only had the heart to do so. Even poisons are now used by physicians as medicines. Poisons taken in proper quantities may prove a benefit. The worst trials of life may become means of religious good, and be useful, if we know how to make use of these things and benefit by them, and try to convert all our actual experiences as they are, into helps in the life of piety.

O, human heart, must we not do this; shall we not do this? And instead of just dreaming about how we could live, and what we could do, if things were otherwise, shall we not take things as they are, and by God's grace help make them to the forming of character, to the living of a life of true piety.

Now one more point:

The first was, we must enlist all our faculties in the life of piety. The second, we must make harmony between the inward and outward in the life of piety.

The third, we must employ our actual experiences as helps to the life of piety.

The last is, we must progress in the life of piety.

If we would stay where we are, we must always be going forward. There must be a going forward or we shall go backward. That is the law of nature. There is no use of arguing it; a man has daily proof of it. He cannot keep what he has, unless he is trying to get more. If a man has knowledge, he must constantly be endeavoring to widen and extend it. If you are rowing up stream, you must try to go farther, or you will be going down stream. All of the better endeavors of human life are in a sense a rowing up stream. Progress in the life of piety, is the only possible means of avoiding the otherwise inevitable result, floating backward and downward.

May God help us now, as we turn away from this morning's service, that we may try to live more as we ought; to make our religious life a thoroughly earnest one; to make it permanent, and deep, and lasting, and potent. God help us that it may never be true of us any more, that "our goodness is like the morning cloud, and as the early dew it goeth away."

ALL THINGS WORK TOGETHER FOR GOOD

"And we know that all things work together for good to them that love God, to them who are the called according to his purpose" (Romans 8:28).

THIS IS THE TRUE OPTIMISM. We hear the words optimist and pessimist often, and see them in the newspaper. The one believes this to be the

A discourse preached in the Woodward Avenue Baptist Church, Detroit, August 24, 1890, by John A. Broadus, reprinted from *Christian Herald,* Detroit, Michigan, vol. 21, no. 35 (28 August 1890).

best possible world and the other that it is the worst possible. There are those who do not accept God's word, and they look upon the disappointments and hardships about them and become pessimists. There are others who look upon the bright side, participate in the pleasures of life and see only its good side; they believe things are getting better and better—that it will all come out right, they are optimists. There have always been these two classes in society: the Greeks had their weeping and their laughing prophet.

The text is the basis of true optimism. "Whatever is, is right," is true only in a limited sense. It is not true that the thing is right in itself. The text, you observe, does not stop with the affirmation, "all things work together for good." Some people in quoting stop there; but the sentence is not complete without the words which follow "to them that love God." The individual thing may be harmful, and if it stood by itself would bring harm and harm only but the truth of the text is in the "all things" taken together.

If you had your way, you would have no wants ungratified; life would be all pleasure; no rude winds should blow, and no chilling blasts should touch the cheek of those you love. Life is very complex; all things, the pleasant, the sad, the helpful and the severe—all things are working together for good to those that love God.

Some say, do not deal with things so far away; give us thoughts that touch our everyday life. Don't these thoughts touch everyday life? The clouds some days look far away, but they come down to us in gentle showers, else all nature would become sere and brown, withered and dead. So these high, heavenly things must come down and influence our everyday lives.

The apostle says "we know that all things work together for good." How do we know? We understand scripture by taking it in its connection. Compare scripture with scripture. This text stands as the climax of that which went before. The apostle has been arguing concerning justification by the law, justification by faith, and sanctification, showing what the law can do towards making a man holy, and what is done under grace: "For, as many as are led by the Spirit of God, they are the sons of God" "if children then heirs, joint heirs with Christ, if so be that we suffer with Him, that we may be also glorified together." Observe the thought: "Joint heirs, joint sufferers, if so be we may be also glorified together." This, then, is a reason why God leaves his children here to suffer. Paul accounts for the fact that they are left to suffer until they be united with Christ in glory. You will never be successful in winning your child to the new life; you will never bring your Sunday school class to Jesus until you suffer; until you are deeply in earnest "for we know that the whole creation groaneth and travaileth in pain together" "and not only they, but ourselves also," "the Spirit itself maketh intercession for us with groanings which cannot be uttered." But says Paul "the sufferings of this present time are not worthy to be compared with the glory which shall be revealed in us."

The first point is consolation, in the assurance of future glory; the second point, we live in a suffering world, in earnest expectation, "waiting for the time when we shall be delivered from the bondage of corruption," and rejoice in the glorious liberty of the children of God. Mrs. Browning in the "Drama of Exile" takes Adam and Eve where Milton left them, exiles from Eden. Dimmer and dimmer sound the heavenly harmonies, and wailing and lament become more and more loud. Wild shriek the hawks, fierce howl the wolves.

> The heart of earth, once calm, is trembling like
> The ragged foam along the ocean waves:
> The restless earthquakes rock against each other.
> The elements move 'round me and I wail, I wail.

The golden age of the Greeks was in the past; the golden age of the Bible is in the future. This world is not a purgatory, neither is it a paradise. "All things," some pleasant, some sad, joy — sorrow, waiting for the redemption, which shall come.

The third point: we are saved by hope. Hope is something future, "if we hope for that we see not, then do we with patience wait for it."

Fourth: the Spirit helpeth our infirmities, helps us bear the ills and trials of life.

How does the Spirit help? Among the Greeks and Romans the advocate had a two-fold function. He not only appeared for the client, but he prepared the address which the client would deliver — prepared for him his plea. The Spirit not only maketh intercession for us, appears before the throne as our advocate, but teaches us what to say, gives right thoughts, works in us deep desire and strong purpose, indites our heart's petition, a prayer pleasing and acceptable to God: For "we know not what we should pray for as we ought." Now comes the text, as a climax: Why this suffering, why this intercession, why this hope? that we may know that all things work together for good: the suffering as important as the enjoyment.

How do we know these things? He tells in the words which follow: "All things work together for good, to them that love God, to them who are the called according to his purpose," for the reason, "Whom he did foreknow he also did predestinate." According to the eternal purpose of God, this constitutes a series of things sure to be; the last as important as the first link in the chain. These things are *sure* to those who love God.

So strange that we get hold of some passages of Scripture, and twist them and turn them to our own discomfort and hurt. We hear about that terrible doctrine of predestination. To the apostle this doctrine was the greatest consolation. It was the reason which assured him that all things shall work together for good. If the doctrine is a terrible one, it is because it is looked upon from a different point of view from that of the apostle. What is salvation worth if you save yourself? A salvation worth anything is that planned and perfected by Omnipotent, Almighty God. If one says "Well, if I'm predestinated to be saved I shall be. There is no use of my doing anything." If you say this, and thus, refuse to do, it is sure evidence that you are not a child of God. Jonathan Edwards said, "Perseverance to the end is the only infallible proof of being in a state of grace."

"The doctrine," says one, "is liable to perversion." Everything can be perverted. Salvation based upon God's eternal wish and purpose is not a doctrine to be afraid of — rather something for which to be profoundly grateful. If a man wants to love God, what is there to prevent it? If he doesn't wish to love God, why does he find fault about it? Everything will look kinky, and crooked, and wrong — from the standpoint of observation. Here is the foundation of our hope: "If God be for us who can be against us?" There are people and forces which may try to oppose and hinder, but "He that spared not his own Son, but delivered him up for us all, how shall he not with him also freely give us all things."

In the last days of the war, the good President spent much of his time hearing appeals of wives, mothers and sisters in behalf of husbands, sons and brothers. Military law was strict and severe, but the word of the President set it all aside. No matter for military law if the President signed a pardon. O, man, if God is for us, who can be against us? "He that spared not his own Son, but delivered him up for us all, how shall he not with him freely give us all things?" Such a priceless gift is assurance of every other gift.

"Who is he that condemneth? It is Christ that died, yea, rather, that is risen again, who is ever at the right hand of God, who maketh intercession for us," and so all things must, shall work together for good. "Who shall lay anything to the charge of God's elect? It is God that justifieth." "Who shall separate us from the love of Christ?" Not separate from *our* love to him, but from *Christ's* love to us? "Shall tribulation, or distress, or persecution, or famine, or peril, or sword?" These things seem 10,000 miles away from us at this day, but they were very near when Paul wrote these words. "Nay, in all these things we are more than conquerors. For I am persuaded that neither death, nor life, nor angels, nor principalities, nor powers, nor things present, nor things to come, nor height, nor depth, nor any other creature, shall be able to separate us from the love of God, which is in Christ Jesus, our Lord."

O, human heart, bowed down with grief and perplexity, trust in his love and submit with heart devotion, and bear in quiet, steady patience, all tribulation and trial, for we know that all these things "work together for good to them that love God."

We cannot fully understand now, but when we stand upon the

heights of glory, we shall look back with joy on the things we suffered, for we shall know then that our severest trials were a part of the "all things" which worked together for our eternal good.

AND ENOCH WALKED WITH GOD

Genesis 5:22–24

IT IS BUT LITTLE, certainly, we know of Enoch. "He walked with God, begat sons and daughters; and all the days of Enoch were three hundred and sixty five years and he was not for God took him." That is all we know of him, save the argument in Hebrews, based upon his faith.

The more we study men, the more we are impressed that humanity is the same in all ages in respect to essential vital principles. Get near these far away men and we see that they had the same temptations, the same conflicts, the same victories. Of course, there are questions impossible to answer. We do not know how it was that Enoch and his contemporaries lived so many hundreds of years. We cannot explain this and a great many other things. I cannot explain how in the ages ago glacier streams furrowed their paths through all this region and extended way down to Cincinnati. There are theories in respect to it, but I do not know if they be true; but I do know that one of the unwisest things in this world is to say of anything: "It can't be true, because we cannot explain it."

A few years ago a missionary wrote home that there was a snow-capped mountain right under the equator. Scientific men said that couldn't be; but said the missionary, "I have lived among the snow-capped Alps and think I ought to know a snow-capped mountain when I see it." Stanley now witnesses that the missionary was right, scientific negation notwithstanding.

When the Newtonian theory of gravitation was first published, no one believed, and later when they believed, they did not understand, and we cannot explain it. When it was first discovered that stones fell

A sermon preached in the Woodward Avenue Baptist Church, Detroit, August 31, 1890, by John A. Broadus, reprinted from *Christian Herald*, Detroit, Michigan, vol. 21, no. 36 (4 September 1890).

from the heavens, science said that cannot be. The Greeks and Romans believed that meteors fell out of the sky, but certain wise men in Europe reasoned: Stones could not fall from the sky unless they were first carried up by volcanic or other eruptive agency; and their reported descent is contrary to all laws of gravity, hence it cannot be. Nevertheless, we think we know, now, that contrary to all known laws of gravitation they do fall, and other phenomena are constantly taking place which we cannot reconcile with scientific law. We ought to be slow to say that we will not believe what we cannot explain: There are more things in heaven and earth than are dreamed of in our philosophy or in our science either. We ought to know better than to say we will believe only that which can be mathematically or scientifically demonstrated. Let no man speak lightly of science, we should think highly of anything which enables us to know concerning the works of God, and of anybody who teaches us things which we did not know.

While there will always be much which we cannot understand, there is much that is plain. Let us act upon what we know, and let go the mysteries which we cannot understand. There are new discoveries of truth and a great many things explained in the scriptures which were not known 40 years ago. But suppose they were not explained, what of it? The text says "Enoch was not for God took him." We cannot tell how he was taken, when he was taken, or where he was taken. You may ask a great many questions. We do not know! Nobody knows!

Enoch was a well known citizen among the people with whom he lived. He was well known to God. It ought to make an impression upon us. What was a mystery at that day is made clearer for you and me for our Lord rose from the dead "and if the spirit of him that raised up Jesus from the dead dwell in you, he that raised up Christ from the dead shall also quicken your mortal bodies."

There are several thoughts of practical importance:

I. Enoch Walked with God Amid Wicked Surroundings.

The progeny of Cain and their bad practices exemplify the law of heredity. The descendants of righteous Seth had been corrupted by association and intermarriage, "and God saw that the wickedness of man was great in the earth, and that every imagination of the thoughts of his heart was only evil continually." Amid all that, Enoch walked with God.

There never have been good times, *quite*, in the world. It is said that farmers are never satisfied. I once went into blue grass country in Kentucky and asked the farmers what about the crops. "O we never had such yield as this, but then the grass is so heavy and so high we can't get through it with the mower." Farmers are never satisfied. No, for if they were, they would be so entirely different from the rest of mankind. Did you ever know a missionary agent to visit the church on the opportune Sunday? The time for taking a collection is never just the right time. You never will find a time when everything is exactly right in this world. Enoch did not find it. It was not easy for him to be pious, it was not easy for David, it was not easy for Daniel; it was not easy in Christ's time—it is not easy now.

We read about the golden age of the past—golden nonsense! There never was a golden age. We just fool ourselves, if we think so. If we had lived then, it would have been just as hard to have been pious as it is now. We speak of the peaceful days of our fathers and think, well it was easier then. It was not! We speak of the millennium and think how favorable everything will be then; but if you cannot live a holy life *now* and *here* under the conditions which God has put around you, you never would and never will.

II. Enoch Walked with God in the Ordinary Walks of Life.

He was not a recluse. He did not withdraw himself from his kind, did not enter a retreat or go into a cave. He was a man among men. There are people who have given up all that is sweet in life, as the only condition of living a godly life. It was not so with Enoch, he was a husband and father. He was a good husband—not a perfect man by any means—but a man who believed in God and lived an upright, honest life. There is a story told of a man in Rhode Island who became pitiful for the sad lot of old worn-out horses and he made an asylum for them; and when he had gathered some 30 old horses and put them into a luxuriant pasture, it is said that his wife sued him for divorce, because he did not give her enough to eat. Now this may have been exaggerated, the man may have been consistent in his pitifulness, but a man is not truly pious who neglects the ordinary duties of life. It is not easy to be a good husband, to be unselfish, to be considerate, to be patient, to be prudent, to be wise, judicious and loving in control of the young. Ah, my friend let no glamour of civilization make you thoughtless of the little amenities of life. The best thing is to try to attend to these elementary, fundamental principles. Young man, determine to be a good husband and father. And you who are growing old, God pity you, if you have only bitter memories of austere and inconsiderate treatment of her whom you promised to cherish and love better than your own life. In these days there is a great deal said about the sphere of woman and her desire for broader usefulness, and realization of high aspiration and ambition—but God forbid that the time shall ever come when woman shall make the mistake of thinking that there is anything more honorable than to be a noble and true wife and mother.

III. Enoch Walked with God Amid Lowly Surroundings.

Civilization had but just commenced. The days were filled with humble tasks and the nights were spent in a lowly home.

How futile for people to think so much depends upon exterior surroundings. Some of the most pious men I have ever known were among the richest, and some of the most pious men I have ever known were among the poorest—lived in log cabins and could neither read nor write and so all the way between.

But didn't Jesus pronounce a special blessing upon the poor? Yes, when impressing upon the Jews a certain lesson; but in the parable of Lazarus and the rich man, Lazarus is represented as being carried to Abraham's bosom: To Abraham, a prince of the East and one of the richest of men.

Ah, well! if we are to be pious it depends a good deal more upon internal conditions than external surroundings.

I thank God that some of the most learned men in science are pious men. Some of the most noted statesmen are humble Christians, I thank God for the men of limited opportunity and attainment that know enough to be conscious of sin and the way to blessedness.

Let us consider the life of Enoch in some of its details, as the botanist analyzes the flower. He may spoil perfection of beauty in the flower, but he learns something. So, in studying men, we may mar the ideal picture of human perfection, but we shall learn something, and may profit thereby.

Enoch pleased God. The New Testament gives a more explicit statement of the ways in which Enoch pleased God. He was a man of faith. "Without faith it is impossible to please him: for he that cometh to God must believe that he is and that he is a rewarder of them that diligently seek him." Enoch believed God. Is that a small thing? I have met men who said they did not believe God. It is not a small thing to believe or to disbelieve. If you have doubts, they are nothing to be proud of, notwithstanding Tennyson says: "There lives more faith in honest doubt, Believe me, than in half the creeds."

I am not sure what Tennyson meant, and possibly he was not himself quite sure, but might it not be, that a man who believed an error had more faith than the man who professed faith in the truth in a formal, half-hearted way, and was ceremonially tied to a creed.

The honest doubt is thoughtful, considerate. It is not frivolous, it is not boastful, it is not proud, does not parade itself or make a display. It wishes to know the ground of belief. It investigates that it may believe. How is it in business? You wish to put money in this and that. There is doubt if the investment is a good one. But you do business; you invest, although you never can be really sure that any investment is good. Some good and true men are troubled by misgivings. Treat the honest doubter with consideration. He only questions to know. He is anxious and ready to receive the truth and learn.

If Enoch walked with God, he came to God and entered into relations of friendship with him. He did not say, "O, yes, I believe in God," and then didn't do anything. There are such; and they are the ones whom the professional doubters select when they say, "I live as well as your professing Christians, or mayhap, better." They always pick out some doubting Christian — always sure to pick out the worst specimen.

Enoch trusted God, believed in him. We don't know just how much he knew, for he lived in the twilight of religious knowledge. We know more, God be thanked! The eternal Son of God has come and we know him, and that in him God hath reconciled us to himself.

Enoch walked in the paths in which God walks. If we would walk with God, we must select the paths which please him. If you walk with a friend, you walk where your friend would prefer to go. You must not be heedless and unthoughtful. You must ask if it be a way in which God would go. If there be two ways, and one is doubtful, give to the right way the benefit of the doubt. You remember the story of the coachman. A man was testing applicants. Said he, "You count yourself skillful? How near the edge of a precipice would you dare drive and consider it safe?" "Within a foot," was the reply. The second, "Within six inches." The third, an Irishman, said, "Be shore, and I'd kape as far from the aidge as possible!" Pat wanted to be on the safe side, and take no risk. He got the position. So in questionable ways. Be sure and keep as far away from danger as possible. When you ask yourself, "Couldn't I do this?" "Couldn't I do that?" try to find the way which is plainly right. In God's word are described ways of pleasantness and paths of peace. Study the Bible; let it be a lamp to your feet, and when you find the right way, "walk ye in it."

If Enoch walked with God, he was in communion with him. If the preacher should ask you to come to the rostrum and relate your experience, you might hesitate and wish to be excused, but you would talk freely and without embarrassment with a friend. As friend talks with friend, they make themselves better known to each other; and do you not think it possible that those who try to walk with God know his thought and it makes its impress upon the heart?

Read the Bible also as a devotional aid, that thus you may learn the thought of God, and he will enter into your heart and life.

We come to the sanctuary, and we talk of these high things that pertain to the kingdom, and shall we turn away as if they were nothing to us, or shall we turn away, determined that we will walk with God?

FOR ADDITIONAL INFORMATION ABOUT JOHN A. BROADUS:

Ashby, Jerry Paxton. "John Albert Broadus: The Theory and Practice of His Preaching." Unpublished Th.D. dissertation, New Orleans Baptist Theological Seminary, New Orleans, La., 1968.

Broadus, John A. *Lectures on the History of Preaching.* New York: Sheldon & Co., 1876.

———. *On the Preparation and Delivery of Sermons.* Revised edition by Jesse Burton Weatherspoon. New York: Harper & Bros., 1944.

Jones, Edgar DeWitt. "John Albert Broadus." *The Royalty of the Pulpit.* New York: Harper & Bros., 1951.

Robertson, Archibald Thomas. *Life and Letters of John Albert Broadus.* Philadelphia: American Baptist Publication Society, 1901.

Taylor, George B. "John A. Broadus." *Virginia Baptist Ministers.* 4th series. Lynchburg, Va.: J. P. Bell Co., 1913.

Wilkinson, William Cleaver. "John Albert Broadus." *Modern Masters of Pulpit Discourse.* New York: Funk & Wagnalls Co., 1905.

FOR OTHER SERMONS BY JOHN A. BROADUS:

Favorite Sermons of John A. Broadus. Edited with an introduction by Vernon Latrelle Stanfield. New York: Harper & Bros., 1959.

Sermons and Addresses. New York: A. C. Armstrong & Son, 1891.

HENRY PARRY LIDDON

1829–1890

HENRY PARRY LIDDON, The Mansell Collection

HENRY PARRY LIDDON

1829   *Born August 10 at North Stoneham, Hampshire, England*
1847   *Entered Christ Church College, Oxford*
1850   *Took his degree from Oxford*
1852   *Ordained deacon in Church of England and assumed a curacy at Wantage*
1853   *Ordained priest in Church of England*
1854   *Served as vice-principal of Cuddesdon College until 1859*
1859   *Became vice-principal of St. Edmund Hall, Oxford*
1864   *Became prebendary of Salisbury cathedral*
1866   *Delivered the Bampton Lecture, "The Divinity of Our Lord and Saviour Jesus Christ"*
1870   *Became canon of St. Paul's, London, and Ireland Professor of Exegesis, Oxford*
1882   *Resigned his professorship*
1885   *Took a tour abroad*
1890   *Died; buried in the crypt chapel in St. Paul's Cathedral, London*

LOOKING TOWARD ST. PAUL'S CATHEDRAL, Bishop Blomfield of London remarked, "I wonder what that great building has ever done for the cause of Christ?" St. Paul's, designed by Sir Christopher Wren, is one of the famous churches of the world; its beauty has been praised by multitudes. But prior to the preaching of Henry Parry Liddon, crowds had seldom gathered in its cavernous halls to hear the Word of God proclaimed. Liddon changed that. Thousands crowded St. Paul's every Sunday to hear the brilliant preaching of Liddon.

LIFE AND TIMES

Born August 10, 1829, at North Stoneham, Hampshire, England, Liddon seemed destined almost from the beginning of his life to enter the Christian ministry. From his mother he learned an appreciation for literature, languages, and evangelical religion. His father, a captain in the British navy, provided him with an example of character and discipline. Liddon's high church tastes displeased his mother. Not long before her death she warned him, "You may be a good scholar, a good Churchman, yet not a good Christian."

During his high school days, Liddon was unusually intent upon studies and spiritual matters. He avoided games and athletics. Instead he gave himself to meditation, reading, and speaking to others about their spiritual responsibilities. In his higher education at Christ Church College, Oxford, he took small part in undergraduate life. He continued his bent toward theological scholarship.

During this time at Oxford, heated conflict erupted between the high church and the broad church members of the Church of England. John Henry Newman, the famous high church Anglican who became a Roman Catholic, wielded a deep influence upon the young men of Oxford. Liddon faced a choice. He could go, as many were doing, into the Church of Rome. He could participate in the popular broad church movement which tended to de-emphasize ecclesiastical issues. Or he could join with the high church group—often noted more for their cold, calculating devotion to dogma than for their genuine concern for persons. Liddon chose what in many ways was the most difficult option: he aligned himself with the high church party within the Church of England.

Rome had an appeal for him as it did for most other high church Anglicans. He seriously considered entering the Church of Rome but could not accept some of its basic doctrines, particularly that of papal infallibility. He visited Rome, talked with Roman scholars, and even had an audience with the pope. Describing his visit to the pope, Liddon wrote: "At length I reached the apartment in which the Pope was sitting. He was at a desk, writing, surrounded with books and papers. I knelt first on entering the room, and a second time to kiss his feet. He was anxious to talk, and spoke for some minutes. He spoke in French; said that he hoped that I had enjoyed Rome—of course I had—and then went on to express his hope that I should pursue my studies with constant recourse to prayer to God, without Whose aid nothing would be obtained, and Who would ultimately lead me into the Truth."[1] In spite of the concern and interest shown by the Catholic hierarchy, Liddon refused to align himself with Rome.

After his ordination as deacon in the Church of England, he assumed a curacy in Wantage. His health—never robust—was not able to endure the strain of the parish ministry. After a brief time he was forced to resign and return to Oxford. After ordination to the priesthood he became vice-principal of Cuddesdon College. There he worked with young men to develop their spiritual life and to kindle their enthusiasm for Christian ministry. His gifts suited him to the task. But his views were out of step with the prevailing sentiment of the school and the church most closely associated with it. He was considered soft on Catholicism. After five years he was forced to resign his position. Of this experience he wrote in his diary, "I do not see any future whatever. My first great attempt at work in life has failed. This is, no doubt, good for my character!"[2]

Liddon became vice-principal of St. Edmund Hall, Oxford. His duties were not in keeping with his great intellectual and personal gifts. But he did not complain. He displayed compassion for all and sought at every opportunity to guide the lives of those around him to God. During this time his preaching became widely acclaimed. He preached at Oxford, and the students flocked to hear him. Many were deeply impressed with the Christian faith as he presented it. His preaching was not limited to Oxford, however; he also preached throughout England. In 1863 he delivered his first sermon at St. Paul's Cathedral on April 19. In his diary on April 18 he wrote: "Feel very unequal to preaching at St. Paul's to-morrow, both spiritually and physically. O Lord Jesus, help me—a poor sinner." After the sermon he wrote: "Did as well as I could; but feel that the sermon was a mess. The Dean told me that it was 1 hour 10 minutes, and that I exerted myself too much to be heard."[3]

Meanwhile his theological abilities were being recognized

---

1. John Octavius Johnston, *Life and Letters of Henry Parry Liddon* (London: Longmans, Green, & Co., 1904), p. 24.
2. Ibid., p. 47.
3. Ibid., p. 55.

also. In 1866 he delivered the Bampton Lecture. His subject was "The Divinity of Our Lord and Saviour Jesus Christ." This series of lectures has been rated by many scholars as an example of the finest discourse on the subject in the English language. The lectures revealed his conservative bent, his defense of the faith against German rationalism, and his unapologetic devotion to the fundamentals of the Christian faith as historically understood. Notes in his diary during preparation of the lectures reveal his humility: "They will be a very feeble production." "I am wretched about them. They will be poor and thin beyond all words." "In very low spirits about my lectures. I cannot make way with them or arrange them satisfactorily. O Lord, help me, though most unworthy."[4]

In 1870 he became canon of St. Paul's Cathedral in London. In the same year he was named Ireland professor of exegesis at Oxford. The dual role of preacher and professor suited him. He was a gifted preacher and yet seemed ill-equipped to handle a regular church assignment. Liddon delighted in academic pursuit, but he was more of a popularizer than a technical theologian. His two positions, therefore, allowed him to blend the best qualities of his life into a harmonious whole.

Preaching in St. Paul's was no easy task. Liddon was never a man of great physical strength, and preaching to the vast multitudes gathered in the huge cathedral took immense physical effort. After a preaching assignment in St. Paul's Liddon often would be ill for days. To compound the difficulty he preached long sermons—frequently over an hour. His assignment therefore amounted to standing before a great multitude and shouting at the top of his voice for a solid hour. The architecture of the building was such that the walls often swallowed his words before they reached his hearers. Added to the physical difficulty was the emotional frustration of seeing puzzled looks on people's faces and realizing that they were not hearing what was being said.

Liddon was analytical in his preaching, yet popular. He preached a positive message of hope. He dealt with the main themes of the Christian faith. Though committed to high church principles, he was not without appreciation for what others of different persuasions accomplished. For example,

---

4. Ibid., p. 83.

in a sermon at Oxford he praised Moody and Sankey and their work in Great Britain:

> Last year two American preachers visited this country to whom God had given, together with earnest belief in some portions of the Gospel, a corresponding spirit of fearless enterprise. Certainly they had no such credentials of an Apostolic ministry as well-instructed and believing Churchmen would require, . . . and yet, according to the light which God had given them, they threw themselves on our great cities with the ardor of apostles; spoke of a higher world to thousands who pass the greater part of life in dreaming only of this, and made many of us feel that we owe them at least the debt of an example which He who breatheth where He listeth must surely have inspired them to give us.[5]

Not only did he appreciate men with the evangelistic zeal of Moody and Sankey, he also appreciated the saintly scholarship of men such as John Henry Newman who had left the Church of England for the Church of Rome. Less than a month before his own death, Liddon had heard of the death of John Henry Newman and wrote in his diary, "Found it impossible to think of anything else throughout the day." He deeply felt the tragic loss of a man of Newman's greatness.

Liddon died September 9, 1890. He was buried in St. Paul's after a stately but simple funeral ceremony. England mourned his passing. But at the funeral there were none of the usual trappings of mourning—even the altar was covered in white. Liddon's life was too full of the positive expression of faith to allow grief to crowd out triumphant hope.

PREACHING AND SERMONS

Robertson Nicoll characterized Liddon as "the debtor to the wise." By that expression Nicoll intended to suggest that Liddon was specially called to minister to the "wise." His congregations were composed of many intellectuals and he had unique success in preaching to university audiences. No

---

5. Harry C. Howard, *Princes of the Christian Pulpit and Pastorate,* 2d series (Nashville: Cokesbury Press, 1928), p. 247.

doubt Liddon himself was an intellectual and attracted the intellectual classes in an unusual way, but another description of his work suggests that his appeal was broadly popular:

> The audience listening to Liddon was scarcely less remarkable than was the preacher. All sorts and conditions of men gathered there, and they came from all parts of the London suburbs into the great silent city. . . .
> The tinge of sacerdotalism, the unconscious assumption of being in the apostolical succession, the priestly air of one who had little sympathy with the Protestant Reformation, and gloried in calling himself an ecclesiastic, the dogmatic insistence of a schoolman . . . , all of these were minor matters, which might be blemishes or might not. What was certain was that here was a preacher who drew about him a vast crowd, thoroughly cosmopolitan and made up of "many nations and of all varieties of creed."[6]

Liddon might have been a great favorite among the educated, but the average people also flocked to hear him. His popular appeal was proved by the throngs at his afternoon services in a great London cathedral. In few other instances has a preacher of academic tastes and intellectual culture been so effective in preaching to the common man. Liddon was not only intellectual and scholarly, but he was also gifted with a vivid imagination which he used to explain the profound truths of the Christian faith so that everyone—intellectual or not—might understand.

His high church views were firmly proclaimed in his sermons. He believed in dogmatic preaching and sometimes he carried his dogmatism too far. He could be rigid and uncompromising in his approach; he seemed to preach with one eye on his opposition. Liddon's preaching also was decidedly apologetic in tone. It was more concerned with the defense of the Christian position than most. He had a profound distrust of the modern world, and particularly modern higher criticism. He felt himself called to be an apologist for the Christian faith. Nevertheless, his method of refuting his enemies was earnest and sincere. Many of his critics disagreed violently with his

6. Ibid., pp. 272-73.

conclusions, but they never disagreed with his spirit. Liddon was never petty nor tedious in his arguing; he concerned himself with the larger issues of the faith.

In spite of his dogmatic tendencies, Liddon preached relevant sermons to his own time. He was an avid newspaper reader and became deeply involved with many practical concerns. Elegant critics in his day suggested that his preoccupation with the newspapers "doubtless injuriously affected his style." If he had not read the newspapers, Liddon could never have spoken as plainly nor with such relevance as he did.

When Liddon first began preaching at St. Paul's, the preaching services were conducted in the choir loft. The building was famous for its architecture (it was designed by Sir Christopher Wren) but not for its preaching. After Liddon came, the crowds came: Sunday afternoon services, which were customarily taken by the canon in residence, soon reached three thousand to four thousand people per week. The archbishop of Canterbury described his preaching:

> He unites many charms. His beautiful look and penetrating voice are powerful over one, and then his reasoning is very persuasive. . . . All his physical and intellectual structure is quite swallowed up in spiritual earnestness. . . . One feels that his preaching in itself is a self-sacrifice to him—not a vanity nor a gain. . . . He does not look as if he were in pain, yet you cannot help thinking of it.[7]

Liddon may *well* have been in pain—the acoustics of the place were so miserable that he almost literally preached himself to death. Friends constantly urged him not to expend so much energy in his preaching; yet Liddon found it necessary to exert all his physical energy in order to be heard—and even then he was not successful.

John A. Broadus, who delivered one of the Yale lectures and authored the widely distributed text on preaching, *On the Preparation and Delivery of Sermons*, heard Liddon on September 26, 1870, immediately after having heard Spurgeon in the morning. His comparison of the two is interesting as are his comments on Liddon's voice.

---

7. Ibid., p. 260.

We went straight toward St. Paul's, where Liddon has been preaching every Sunday afternoon in September, and there would be difficulty in getting a good seat. We lunched at the Cathedral Hotel, hard by, and then stood three quarters of an hour at the door of St. Paul's, waiting for it to open. Meantime a good crowd had collected behind us, and there was a tremendous rush when the door opened, to get chairs near the preaching stand. The crowd looked immense in the vast cathedral, and yet there were not half as many as were quietly seated in Spurgeon's Tabernacle.

There everybody could hear, and here, in this grand and beautiful show place, Mr. Liddon was tearing his voice in a vain attempt to be heard by all.[8]

Yet the people heard enough to make them want more, and thousands came to hear him preach.

Many writers refer to the "melancholy" manner of Liddon. There was a kind of mystical attraction about him, not as pronounced as in Newman, but real nevertheless. He became totally immersed in his sermons. Even though he read from a meticulously worded manuscript, his audiences never seemed to grow weary. One writer remarked that he had heard him many times and still could not understand the secret of his attention-getting abilities, particularly because of his constant reading from a manuscript.

Contemporaries repeatedly described his preaching with one word: loftiness. Yet they emphasized that though his themes, his tone, his style, and his feeling might be lofty, he himself was never aloof or haughty. He demonstrated personal affection for those who were entirely opposed to his thinking. He humbly asked the great nonconformist, R. W. Dale, for his prayers. He cordially recognized the Christian character of free church ministers and had good fellowship with them—though he doubted the validity of their ordination.

Liddon was a master of sermon construction. At times his arguments were too intricate, but he never suffered from weak structure in his preaching. His ideas proceed logically, and he shows skillful transitions between points of development. He had a superb grasp of his subjects, even when they involved

---

8. A. T. Robertson, *Life and Letters of John Albert Broadus* (Philadelphia: American Baptist Publication Society, 1901), pp. 243-44.

intricacies of both theology and philosophy, and he had a gift for explaining abstractions in a concrete and understandable way. His style does not suit the modern picture-conscious mind, but in his day Liddon was regarded as a model of homiletical excellence.

His delivery was not perfect. Liddon spoke rapidly, so rapidly and energetically that his articulation suffered. His voice, however, was rich and flexible, characterized with all the passion of Phillips Brooks or Thomas Chalmers. When he was not speaking so rapidly, as in addressing smaller groups, his articulation was described as "exquisite, almost over-refined, the very note of culture." His gestures were free and natural. A listener in 1868 described him: "His eyes glow and flash, every line of his face quivers with emotion, his gestures are so free, so expressive, so illustrative, that you might almost say his body thought. He leans far out from the pulpit, spreading himself, as if it were, over the congregation, in an act of benediction."

There was a time, although a brief time, when Liddon preached without a manuscript. On the advice of Dr. Pusey he applied himself to the extemporaneous method with great success, and he was described as possessing "a splendid gift of extemporaneous oratory." Nevertheless in the long run he made no extensive use of it, largely because of his belief in carefully worded, closely reasoned, dogmatic preaching. He gained the reputation "as a preacher of very long, very eloquent, and very impassioned sermons." This pilgrimage in methods of preparation — from manuscript to extemporaneous preaching to manuscript — has been described as follows:

The sermons preached in St. Edmund Hall Chapel were mostly written out, like his earlier Cuddesdon addresses. But for most of his other sermons he made a few notes on an ordinary sheet of notepaper, and delivered them without any external aids to his memory. In 1861 he began the habit of writing out, at the earliest opportunity after delivery, a minute analysis of each sermon that he preached. There are two or three notebooks of these analyses, written out in his clear handwriting, without any erasures.

The elaborateness of the arrangement of these sermons, the fulness of the thought, the wealth and range of his illustrations, the simple and ungrudged outpouring of his learning, the deep knowledge of the Bible and the clear grip of its inner meaning, and the fervour of his exhortations, strike the mind even more readily in looking over these analyses than in reading his printed sermons.[9]

It is fascinating to speculate on what success indeed Liddon might have had if his preaching had been less dogmatic and more pictorial and spontaneous in its method.

When Canon Liddon died in 1890, the vast area of the cathedral was crowded for his funeral as for one of his Easter sermons. On the following Sunday morning Canon Scott Holland preached from the same pulpit which the gifted preaching of Liddon had raised to such honor. His words serve as an effective evaluation of the preaching of Henry Parry Liddon:

> Can there be a better test of the spiritual sincerity of a man than this – that we feel no shock when he speaks to us the Bible language? And was it not this which was the entire secret of Liddon's power over us when he preached? As we listened, that inner world that lies before the spiritual eye was once more felt to be laid bare. . . . Our world . . . ; that world of shifting resolution, and bewildered doubts, and miserable timidities, and haunting hesitations; that world of ours was parted asunder! It was pierced through and through by that vibrating voice. . . . As I speak of him . . . it is I who should be dumb. It is this silent pulpit which speaks to you![10]

---

9. Johnston, p. 53.
10. Ibid., p. 389.

Sermons

INFLUENCES OF THE HOLY SPIRIT

"The wind bloweth where it listeth, and thou hearest the sound thereof, but canst not tell whence it cometh, and whither it goeth" (John 3:8).

WHO HAS NOT FELT the contrast, the almost tragic contrast, between the high station of the Jewish doctor, member of the Sanhedrin, master in Israel, and the ignorance of elementary religious truth, as we Christians must deem it, which he displayed in this interview with our blest Lord? At first sight it seems difficult to understand how our Lord could have used the simile in the text when conversing with an educated and thoughtful man, well conversed in the history and literature of God's ancient people; and, indeed, a negative criticism has availed itself of this and of some other features in the narrative, in the interest of the theory that Nicodemus was only a fictitious type of the higher classes in Jewish society, as they were pictured to itself by the imagination of the fourth Evangelist.

Such a supposition, opposed to external facts and to all internal probabilities, would hardly have been entertained, if the critical ingenuity of its author had been seconded by any spiritual experience. Nicodemus is very far from being a caricature; and our Lord's method here, as elsewhere, is to lead on from familiar phrases and the well-remembered letter to the spirit and realities of religion. The Jewish schools were acquainted with the expression "a new creature"; but it had long since become a mere shred of official rhetoric. As applied to a Jewish proselyte, it scarcely meant more than a change in the outward relations of religious life. Our Lord told Nicodemus that every man who would see the kingdom of God which He was founding must undergo a second birth; and Nicodemus, who had been accustomed to the phrase all his life, could not understand it if it was to be supposed to mean anything real. "How," he asks, "can a man be born when he is old? Can he enter a second time into his mother's womb, and be born?"

Reprinted from *The World's Great Sermons*, comp. Grenville Kleiser, vol. 7 (New York: Funk & Wagnalls Co., 1909), pp. 123–41.

Our Lord does not extricate him from this blundering literalism; He repeats His own original assertion, but in terms which more fully express His meaning: "Verily, verily, I say unto thee, Except a man be born of water and of the Spirit, he can not enter into the kingdom of God. That which is born of the flesh is flesh; and that which is born of the Spirit is spirit. Marvel not that I said unto thee, Ye must be born again." Our Lord's reference to water would not have been unintelligible to Nicodemus; every one in Judaea knew that the Baptist had insisted on immersion in water as a symbol of the purification of the soul of man. Certainly, in connecting "water" with the Spirit and the new birth, our Lord's language, glancing at that of the prophet, went very far beyond this. He could only be fully understood at a later time, when the sacrament of baptism had been instituted, just as the true sense of His early allusions to His death could not have been apprehended until after the crucifixion. But Nicodemus, it is plain, had not yet advanced beyond his original difficulty; he could not conceive how any second birth was possible, without altogether violating the course of nature. And our Lord penetrates His thoughts and answers them. He answers them by pointing to that invisible agent who could achieve, in the sphere of spiritual and mental life, what the Jewish doctor deemed so impossible a feat as a second birth. Nature, indeed, contained no force that could compass such a result; but nature in this, as in other matters, was a shadow of something beyond itself.

It was late at night when our Lord had this interview with the Jewish teacher. At the pauses in conversation, we may conjecture, they heard the wind without as it moaned along the narrow streets of Jerusalem; and our Lord, as was His wont, took His creature into His service – the service of spiritual truth. The wind was a figure of the Spirit. Our Lord would not have used the same word for both. The wind might teach Nicodemus something of the action of Him who is the real Author of the new birth of man. And it would do this in two ways more especially.

On a first survey of nature, the wind arrests man's attention, as an unseen agent which seems to be moving with entire freedom. "The wind bloweth where it listeth." It is fettered by none of those conditions which confine the swiftest bodies that traverse the surface of the earth; it sweeps on as if independent of law, rushing hither and thither, as though obeying its own wayward and momentary impulse. Thus it is an apt figure of a self-determining invisible force; and of a force which is at times of overmastering power. Sometimes, indeed, its breath is so gentle, that only a single leaf or blade of grass will at distant intervals seem to give the faintest token of its action; yet, even thus, it "bloweth where it listeth." Sometimes it bursts upon the earth with destructive violence; nothing can resist its onslaught; the most solid buildings give way; the stoutest trees bend before it; whatever is frail and delicate can only escape by the completeness of its submission. Thus, too, it "bloweth where it listeth." Beyond anything else that strikes upon the senses of man, it is suggestive of free super-sensuous power; it is an appropriate symbol of an irruption of the invisible into the world of sense, of the action, so tender or so impe-rious, of the divine and eternal Spirit upon the human soul.

But the wind is also an agent about whose proceedings we really know almost nothing. "Thou hearest the sound thereof"; such is our Lord's concession to man's claim to knowledge. "Thou canst not tell whence it cometh, and whither it goeth"; such is the reserve which He makes in respect of human ignorance. Certainly we do more than hear the sound of the wind; its presence is obvious to three of the senses. We feel the chill or the fury of the blast; and, as it sweeps across the ocean, or the forest, or the field of corn, we see how the blades rise and fall in graceful curves, and the trees bend, and the waters sink and swell into waves which are the measure of its strength. But our Lord says, "Thou hearest the sound thereof." He would have us test it by the most spiritual of the senses. It whispers, or it moans, or it roars as it passes us; it has a pathos all its own.

Yet what do we really know about it? "Thou canst not tell whence it cometh, and whither it goeth." Does the wind then obey no rule; is it a mere symbol of unfettered caprice? Surely not. If, as the psalmist sings, "God bringeth the winds out of his treasuries," He acts, we may be sure, here as always, whether in nature or in grace, by some law, which His own perfections impose upon His action. He may have given to us of these later times to see a very little deeper beneath the surface of the natural world than was the case with our fathers. Perchance we explain the immediate antecedents of the phenomenon; but can we explain our own explanation? The frontier of our ignorance is removed one stage farther back; but "the way of the wind" is as fitting an ex-pression for the mysteries now as it was in the days of Solomon. We know that there is no cave of Aeolus. We know that the wind is the creature of that great Master who works everywhere and incessantly by rule. But, as the wind still sweeps by us who call ourselves the chil-dren of an age of knowledge, and we endeavor to give our fullest an-swer to the question, "Whence it cometh, and whither it goeth?" we discover that, as the symbol of a spiritual force, of whose presence we are conscious, while we are unable to determine, with moderate con-fidence, either the secret principle or the range of its action, the wind is as full of meaning still as in the days of Nicodemus.

When our Lord has thus pointed to the freedom and the mysterious-ness of the wind, He adds, "So is every one that is born of the Spirit." The simile itself would have led us to expect — "So is the Spirit of God." The man born of the Spirit would answer not to the wind itself, but to the sensible effect of the wind. There is a break of correspondence be-tween the simile and its application. The simile directs attention to the divine Author of the new birth in man. The words which follow direct attention to the human subject upon whom the divine agent works. Something similar is observable when our Lord compares the kingdom of heaven to a merchantman seeking goodly pearls; the kingdom really corresponds not to the merchantman, but to the pearl of great price which the merchantman buys. In such cases, we may be sure, the natural correspondence between a simile and its application is not disturbed without a motive. And the reason for this disturbance is presumably that the simile is not adequate to the full purpose of the speaker, who is anxious to teach some larger truth than its obvious application would suggest.

In the case before us, we may be allowed to suppose, that by His reference to the wind our Lord desired to convey something more than the real but mysterious agency of the Holy Spirit in the new birth of man. His language seems designed, not merely to correct the materialistic narrowness of the Jewish doctor, not merely to answer by anticipation the doubts of later days as to the spiritual efficacy of His own sacrament of regeneration, but to picture, in words which should be read to the end of time, the general work of that divine person whose mission of mercy to our race was at once the consequence and the completion of His own.

It may be useful to trace the import of our Lord's simile in three fields of the action of the holy and eternal Spirit; His creation of a sacred literature, His guidance of a divine society, and His work upon individual souls.

I. As, then, we turn over the pages of the Bible, must we not say, "The wind of heaven bloweth where it listeth"? If we might reverently imagine ourselves scheming beforehand what kind of a book the Book of God ought to be, how different would it be from the actual Bible. There would be as many bibles as there are souls, and they would differ as widely. But in one thing, amid all their differences, they would probably agree; they would lack the variety, both in form and substance, of the holy Book which the Church of God places in the hands of her children. The self-assertion, the scepticism, and the fastidiousness of our day would meet like the men of the second Roman triumvirate on that island in the Reno, and would draw up their lists of proscription. One would condemn the poetry of Scripture as too inexact; another its history as too largely secular; another its metaphysics as too transcendental, or as hostile to some fanciful ideal of "simplicity," or as likely to quench a purely moral enthusiasm. The archaic history of the Pentateuch, or the sterner side of the ethics of the psalter, or the supernaturalism of the histories of Elijah or of Daniel, or the so-called pessimism of Ecclesiastes, or the alleged secularism of Esther, or the literal import of the Song of Solomon, would be in turn condemned.

Nor could the apostles hope to escape: St John would be too mystical in this estimate; St. James too legal in that; St. Paul too dialectical, or too metaphysical, or too easily capable of an antinomian interpretation; St. Peter too undecided, as if balancing between St. Paul and St. James. Our new Bible would probably be uniform, narrow, symmetrical; it would be entirely made up of poetry, or of history, or of formal propositions, or of philosophical speculation, or of lists of moral maxims; it would be modeled after the type of some current writer on English history, or some popular poet or metaphysician, or some sentimentalist who abjures history and philosophy alike on principle, or some composer of well-intentioned religious tracts for general circulation. The inspirations of heaven would be taken in hand, and instead of a wind blowing where it listeth, we should have a wind, no doubt, of some kind, rustling earnestly enough along some very narrow crevices or channels, in obedience to the directions of some one form of human prejudice, or passion, or fear, or hope.

The Bible is like nature in its immense, its exhaustless variety; like nature, it reflects all the higher moods of the human soul, because it does much more; because it brings us face to face with the infinity of the divine life. In the Bible the wind of heaven pays scant heed to our anticipations or our prejudices; it "bloweth where it listeth." It breathes not only in the divine charities of the gospels, not only in the lyrical sallies of the epistles, not only in the great announcements scattered here and there in Holy Scripture of the magnificence, or the compassion, or the benevolence of God; but also in the stern language of the prophets, in the warnings and lessons of the historical books, in the revelations of divine justice and of human responsibility which abound in either Testament.

"Where it listeth." Not only where our sense of literary beauty is stimulated, as in St. Paul's picture of charity, by lines which have taken captive the imagination of the world, not only where feeling and conscience echo the verdict of authority and the promptings of reverence, but also where this is not the case; where neither precept nor example stimulates us, and we are left face to face with historical or ethical material, which appears to us to inspire no spiritual enthusiasm, or which is highly suggestive of critical difficulty. Let us be patient; we shall understand, if we will only wait, how these features of the Bible too are integral parts of a living whole; here, as elsewhere, the Spirit breathes; in the genealogies of the Chronicles as in the last discourse in St. John, though with an admitted difference of manner and degree. He "bloweth where He listeth." The apostle's words respecting the Old Testament are true of the New: "All Scripture is given by inspiration of God, and is profitable for doctrine, for reproof, for correction, for instruction in righteousness." And, "Whatsoever things were written aforetime were written for our learning, that we through patience and comfort of the Scriptures might have hope."

"But thou hearest the sound thereof, and canst not tell whence it cometh, and whither it goeth." The majesty of Scripture is recognized by man, wherever there is, I will not say a spiritual faculty, but a natural sense of beauty. The "sound" of the wind is perceived by the trained ear, by the literary taste, by the refinement, by the humanity of every generation of educated men. But what beyond? What of its spiritual source, its spiritual drift and purpose, its half-concealed but profound unities, its subtle but imperious relations to conscience? Of these things, so precious to Christians, a purely literary appreciation of Scripture is generally ignorant; the sacred Book, like the prophet of the Chebar, is only "as a very lovely song of one that hath a pleasant voice, and can play well on an instrument." Or again, the "sound thereof" is heard in the admitted empire of the Bible over millions of hearts and consciences; an empire the evidences of which strike upon the ear in countless ways, and which is far too wide and too secure to be affected by the criticisms that might occasionally seem to threaten it. What is the secret of this influence of Scripture?

Not simply that it is the Book of Revelation; since it contains a great deal of matter which lay fairly within the reach of man's natural faculties. The Word or eternal Reason of God is the Revealer; but Scripture, whether it is a record of divine revelations or of naturally observed facts, is, in the belief of the Christian Church, throughout "inspired" by the Spirit. Inspiration is the word which describes the presence and action of the Holy Spirit everywhere in Scripture. We know not how our own spirits, hour by hour, are acted upon by the eternal Spirit, though we do not question the fact; we content ourselves with recognizing what we can not explain. If we believe that Scripture is inspired, we know that it is instinct with the presence of Him whose voice we might hear in every utterance, but of whom we cannot tell whence He cometh or whither He goeth.

II. The history of the Church of Christ from the days of the apostles has been a history of spiritual movements. Doubtless it has been a history of much else; the Church has been the scene of human passions, human speculations, human errors. But traversing these, He by whom the whole body of the Church is governed and sanctified, has made His presence felt, not only in the perpetual proclamation and elucidation of truth, not only in the silent, never-ceasing sanctification of souls, but also in great upheavals of spiritual life, by which the conscience of Christians has been quickened, or their hold upon the truths of redemption and grace made more intelligent and serious, or their lives and practise restored to something like the ideal of the Gospels. Even in the apostolic age it was necessary to warn Christians that it was high time to awake out of sleep; that the night of life was far spent, and the day of eternity was at hand. And ever since, from generation to generation, there has been a succession of efforts within the Church to realize more worthily the truth of the Christian creed, or the ideal of the Christian life. These revivals have been inspired or led by devoted men who have represented the highest conscience of Christendom in their day. They may be traced along the line of Christian history; the Spirit living in the Church has by them attested His presence and His will; and has recalled lukewarm generations, paralyzed by indifference or degraded by indulgence, to the true spirit and level of Christian faith and life.

In such movements there is often what seems, at first sight, an element of caprice. They appear to contemporaries to be onesided, exaggerated, narrow, fanatical. They are often denounced with a passionate fervor which is so out of proportion to the reality as to border on the grotesque. They are said to exact too much of us, or to concede too much. They are too contemplative in their tendency to be sufficiently practical, or too energetically practical to do justice to religious thought. They are too exclusively literary and academical, as being the work of men of books; or they are too popular and insensible to philosophical considerations, as being the work of men of the people.

Or, again, they are so occupied with controversy as to forget the claims of devotion, or so engaged in leading souls to a devout life as to forget the unwelcome but real necessities of controversy. They are intent on particular moral improvements so exclusively as to forget what is due to reverence and order; or they are so bent upon rescuing the Church from chronic slovenliness and indecency in public worship as to do less than justice to the paramount interests of moral truth. Sometimes these movements are all feeling; sometimes they are all thought; sometimes they are, as it seems, all outward energy. In one age they produce a literature like that of the fourth and fifth centuries; in another they found orders of men devoted to preaching or to works of mercy, as in the twelfth; in another they enter the lists, as in the thirteenth century, with a hostile philosophy; in another they attempt a much-needed reformation of the Church; in another they pour upon the heathen world a flood of light and warmth from the heart of Christendom. It is easy, as we survey them, to say that something else was needed; or that what was done could have been done better or more completely; or that, had we been there, we should not have been guilty of this onesidedness, or of that exaggeration.

We forget, perhaps, who really was there, and whose work it is, though often overlaid and thwarted by human weakness and human passion, that we are really criticizing. If it was seemingly onesided, excessive or defective, impulsive or sluggish, speculative or practical, esthetic or experimental, may not this have been so because in His judgment, who breatheth where He listeth, this particular characteristic was needed for the Church of that day? All that contemporaries know of such movements is "the sound thereof"; the names with which they are associated, the controversies which they precipitate, the hostilities which they rouse or allay, as the case may be. Such knowledge is superficial enough; of the profound spiritual causes which really engender them, of the direction in which they are really moving, of the influence which they are destined permanently to exert upon souls, men know little or nothing. The accidental symptom is mistaken for the essential characteristic; the momentary expression of feeling for the inalienable conviction of certain truth. The day may come, perhaps, when more will be known; when practise and motive, accident and substance, the lasting and the transient, will be seen in their true relative proportions; but for the time this can hardly be. He is passing by, whose way is in the sea, and His paths in the deep waters, and His footsteps unknown. The Eternal Spirit is passing; and men can only say, "He bloweth where He listeth."

III. Our Lord's words apply especially to Christian character. There are some effects of the living power of the Holy Spirit which are invariable. When He dwells with a Christian soul, He continually speaks in the voice of conscience; He speaks in the voice of prayer. He produces with the ease of a natural process, without effort, without the taint of self-consciousness, "love, joy, peace, longsuffering, gentleness, goodness, faith, meekness, temperance." Some of these graces must be found where He makes His home. There is no mistaking the atmosphere of His presence: in its main features it is the same now as in the days of the apostles. Just as in natural morality the main elements of "goodness" do not change; so in religious life, spirituality is, amid great varieties of detail, yet, in its leading constituent features, the same thing from one generation to another.

But in the life of the individual Christian, or in that of the Church, there is legitimate room for irregular and exceptional forms of activity or excellence. Natural society is not strengthened by the stern repression of all that is peculiar in individual thought or practise; and this is not less true of spiritual or religious society. From the first, high forms of Christian excellence have often been associated with unconscious eccentricity. The eccentricity must be unconscious, because consciousness of eccentricity at once reduces it to a form of vanity which is entirely inconsistent with Christian excellence. How many excellent Christians have been eccentric, deviating more or less from the conventional type of goodness which has been recognized by contemporary religious opinion. They pass away, and when they are gone men do justice to their characters; but while they are still with us how hard do many of us find it to remember that there may be a higher reason for their peculiarities than we think. We know not the full purpose of each saintly life in the designs of Providence; we know not much of the depths and heights whence it draws its inspirations; we can not tell whence it cometh or whither it goeth. Only we know that He whose workmanship it is bloweth where He listeth; and this naturally leads us to remark the practical interpretation which the Holy Spirit often puts upon our Lord's words by selecting as His chosen workmen those who seem to be least fitted by nature for such high service.

The apostle has told us how in the first age He set Himself to defeat human anticipations. "Not many wise men after the flesh, not many mighty, not many noble, are called"; learned academies, powerful connections, gentle blood did little enough for the gospel in the days when it won its first and greatest victories. The Holy Spirit, as Nicodemus knew, passed by the varied learning and high station of the Sanhedrin, and breathed where He listed on the peasants of Galiee; He breathed on them a power which would shake the world. And thus has it been again and again in the generations which have followed.

When the great Aquinas was a student of philosophy under Albertus Magnus at Cologne, he was known among his contemporaries as "the dumb Ox"; so little did they divine what was to be his place in the theology of Western Christendom. And to those of us who can look back upon the memories of this University for a quarter of a century or more, few things appear more remarkable than the surprises which the later lives of men constantly afford; sometimes it is a failure of early natural promise, but more often a rich development of intellectual and practical capacity where there had seemed to be no promise at all. We can remember, perhaps, some dull quiet man who seemed to be without a ray of genius, or, stranger still, without anything interesting or marked in character, but who now exerts, and most legitimately, the widest influence for good, and whose name is repeated by thousands with grateful respect. Or we can call to mind another whose whole mind was given to what was frivolous, or even degrading, and who now is a leader in everything that elevates and improves his fellows. The secret of these transfigurations is ever the same. In those days these men did not yet see their way; they were like travelers through the woods at night, when the sky is hidden and all things seem to be other than they are.

Since then the sun has risen and all has changed. The creed of the Church of Christ, in its beauty and its power, has been flashed by the Divine Spirit upon their hearts and understandings; and they are other men. They have seen that there is something worth living for in earnest; that God, the soul, the future, are immense realities, compared with which all else is tame and insignificant. They have learned something of that personal love of our crucified Lord, which is itself a moral and religious force of the highest order, and which has carried them forwards without their knowing it. And what has been will assuredly repeat itself.

A DOOR OF HOPE

"I will give the valley of Achor for a door of hope" (Hosea
2:15).

No ISRAELITE, we may be sure, could have heard this language from
the lips of Hosea without being deeply moved, for it would have carried him back to the early history of his race, when, under the Divine
guidance, his forefathers were taking possession of the promised land.
It would have reminded him of a great failure, and, as the word
"Achor" means, of a great trouble – nay, of a new tragedy. It implied
to him that history was repeating itself, that old sins were to be followed by old punishments, and that beyond those punishments, as
of old, there was hope. Israel, in Hosea's days, was largely apostate
and idolatrous. It was again morally and spiritually, although not literally, in Egypt, encompassed by and yielding to the attractive fascinations of a widespread idolatry; and the old sins were to be followed by
the old discipline.

"I will allure Israel and bring her into the wilderness, and speak
comfortably unto her. And I will give her vineyards from thence, and
the valley of Achor for a door of hope." Here, as so often in the prophets, Israel is addressed as the bride, too often as the unfaithful bride,
of the Lord Jehovah; and the wilderness from which vineyards were
again to be given her, and the valley of Achor which was to be once
more a door of hope, would have suggested that while the generations
and the centuries pass, God remains unchanged in His purposes of
mercy and of judgment – the same everlastingly. The valley of Achor
– it recalls those early days, of which we have lately been reading
in the daily Lessons, when, under the captaincy of Joshua, Israel was
taking possession of the land of promise. The memory of a deed of
heroism or a deed of blood seems in the minds of men to hang somehow about a narrow valley, as though the human imagination read
in the rocks which close in on this side and on that the eager witness
of inanimate nature, pressing forward to express its mute sympathy
with the champions of right or with the victims of cruelty.

Had Glencoe been in the lowlands of Scotland its associations with
one of the darkest crimes in the history of Great Britain, would,
ere now perchance, have been at least enfeebled, but a framework of
natural beauty surrounds the scene of the tragedy and condemns its
authors to at least an earthly immortality of shame. The valley of
Achor lay along the line of Israel's advance from Jericho to Ai. When
Jericho had fallen, the invading host of Israel moved on towards Ai,

Reprinted from H. P. Liddon, *Forty-Two Sermons on Various Subjects,*
4th series (London: Charles Higham, 1886), pp. 97–104.

and 3,000 men were sent forward to conquer it. As the entire population of Ai was only 12,000 it would have seemed that 3,000 fighting men were advancing to an easy victory, and yet the 3,000 fled before the men of Ai, and this so suddenly, and with so little effort of resistance, that only thirty-six of them were slaughtered. The demoralisation of the Israelites was complete. The hearts of the people melted and became as water.

It was a critical moment, and Joshua, as was his way, lost no time in asking for guidance and for help. He rent his clothes and fell to the earth upon his face before the ark of the Lord until the evening, he and the elders of Israel, and put dust upon their heads. He asked God, with reverent boldness, why so much had been done for Israel, only that help might be withdrawn when it was needed most, and what would be said among the heathen of Him, the Lord of Israel, if, after covenanting to give the people the land of Canaan, He should now permit Israel to be destroyed. Joshua was told that it was a time for action rather than for prayer. If Israel had been smitten before the heathen, it was because Isreal went into the battle in a moral condition answering to that of a man with heart disease, and only to be paralysed by the weakness which came with secret sin.

We shall understand this if we remember that Israel was not only a nation, but Israel was a Church, and its wars, when they were in accordance with the will of God, were carried on for moral and religious objects, just as the wars of the surrounding heathen were carried on for purposes connected with their material interests. In conquering Canaan and destroying its inhabitants, Israel was carrying out the sentence of condemnation that had been passed upon a race quite exceptional in its corruption; and as Jericho was the first city of Canaan that was taken, it was devoted, as our authorised version less happily renders it, "accursed" to the Lord, in order to show that the conquest of the land was God's gift to Israel. In other cases the cattle and the property became the booty of the victors, but Jericho was devoted as the first fruits to God. With the exception of Rahab, every living thing was put to death, and the spoils, silver and gold, were to be brought into the treasury of Israel. Such was the order, but Joshua was warned that it had been disobeyed. Some of the devoted treasures had been stolen, and the theft had been covered by deceit.

If Israel had been merely a secular heathen people, the moral character of its soldiery might have mattered little. As it was, sacrilege and lying meant for Israel physical weakness, and if the career of victory which had been begun was to continue, the Israelites' first duty was to discover and punish the offender. "For thus saith the Lord God of Israel, there is an accursed thing in the midst of thee, O Israel: thou canst not stand before thine enemies, until ye take away the accursed thing from among you," and then took place that solemn enquiry which we all remember as children as among the most stirring incidents even of the book of Joshua. In the early morning the host was marshalled tribe by tribe, in its social and military array, and the lots were drawn; they were drawn as they were afterwards, in the cases of Jonathan and Jonah, to discover the guilty. It was felt that on this occasion, an occasion of such moment to the welfare of Israel, a higher power would preside, and that when the lot was cast into the lap the disposing thereof would be from the Lord, and so, as the inquest proceeded from tribe to family, and from family to household, and from the collective household to its several members, the meshes closed more and more closely round the sinner who had brought on Israel this ruin and this shame.

The tribe of Judah, the family of the Zarhites, the household of Zabdi – those were the steps by which discovery advanced towards Achan. Achan was Zabdi's grandson and a person himself, it would seem, of substance and consideration, and Joshua pressed Achan to glorify God by telling the truth, and Achan confessed that he had taken and hidden away the rich robe of Syrian manufacture and two hundred shekels of silver and a solid wedge of gold. They were found, as Achan had said they would be found, hidden in the earth beneath his tent, and the proof of guilt was complete; and then what follows can only be told in the language of the Bible, "And Joshua, and all Israel with him, took Achan the son of Zerah, and the silver, and the garment, and the wedge of gold, and his sons, and his daughters, and his oxen, and his asses, and his sheep, and his tent, and all that he had: and they brought them unto the valley of Achor. And Joshua said, Why hast thou troubled us? the Lord shall trouble thee this day. And all Israel stoned him with stones, and burned them with fire after they had stoned them with stones. And they raised over him a great heap of stones unto this day."

Achor, as you will have observed, is the Hebrew word for "trouble," and Joshua gave the valley this name from the likeness of this word Achor to Achan. It was in truth a terrific act of penal retribution by which Achan and his family met their deaths, and it requires an effort to ask ourselves how the spot which witnessed this scene of torture and of shame could be a door of hope. It was then first of all a door of hope for Israel, because Achan's sin, while undiscovered, had about it this terrible distinction, that in an eminent degree it brought with it weakness and ruin to the public cause of Israel. Israel was not fully pure-hearted while the Assyrian robe, which ought to have been burnt, and the gold and silver which ought to have been placed in the treasury of the Lord, were sacrilegiously hidden away in the earth beneath Achan's tent; and a serious effort, like the attack on Ai, revealed the presence of moral unsoundness somewhere which, so long as it festered at the heart of Israel, made further progress impossible. When Achan had been discovered and punished, Israel's weakness at once disappeared. The Lord turned from the fierceness of His anger, and Ai fell easily before the first assult.

Achan's sin was not, let us observe, an open scandal which brought dishonour on the cause of God by its publicity. It was not in this respect like the sins of the sons of Eli who made the Lord's people to transgress, nor like the sin of Jeroboam who made Israel to sin. It was akin to that of Ananias and Sapphira, not in its precise form, since Achan took what never had been his, and Ananias kept back part of that which he had vowed to give God; but certainly in its motive, which was covetousness, and in the deceit which was employed to shield him, and in the fact that what was taken in the one case and kept back in the other belonged to God; so that the offence had the aggravated character of sacrilege. Such secret sins are more common than public ones. They satisfy the sinful instinct more economically, and those who commit them are tempted to persuade themselves that because they do not corrupt others by the taint of bad example they are really much more venial. Such, no doubt, would have been Achan's view of his case – at least he kept his wrong-doing to himself – at least he had not persuaded others to join in this sacrilege and in concealing it he was all alone – at least he had not had fellowship with the deceitful. Ah, we often wonder why great causes fail or flag, why so little comes of schemes for doing good into which much heart has been thrown, and for which great sacrifices have been made; why the results are so poor or disappointing of enterprises or societies for propagating the faith, or for setting on foot works of charity, or for maintaining the Christian character of education, or for improving public conduct in this respect or that, or for carrying morality into legislation, or into the relations which exist between nations professedly Christian. We count up, we measure, we lay stress on the difficulties of the undertaking itself, and we satisfy ourselves that these difficulties furnish the real reason of the failure. "Ai," we say, "is too strong to be taken, its soldiers are more than a match for the men of Israel."

May it not be that all the while the true cause of failure lies nearer home, that something is hidden away in the tent of the soul, hidden beneath the earth, which one conscience at least that is concerned in the enterprise cannot forget, and that this fatal memory makes the heart sick and unnerves the hand when the time for decisive action comes? And moral weakness, mark you, is contagious; it radiates from soul to soul just as does moral force. We feel its presence by a sure though inexplicable instinct, when we cannot give an account of it to ourselves or to others; but in any case those invisible beings who are the witnesses of all human efforts, and above all, He Who is their Lord and ours, see well and clearly what is really the case, and the enterprise is blessed or rejected accordingly. Depend on it, dear brethren, that as the strength of the Church of Christ lies not in her external circumstances, not in the support or the countenance which she may receive from the great or the powerful, but in the secret prayers and deeds of souls whose names are unknown, it may be, on earth, but already registered in heaven, so the weakness of the Church lies not in the number or fierceness of her enemies, which God may and does turn to His praise, but in the secret unbelief and sins of her children.

Achan, Judas, Diotrephes, these had a fearful power of traversing God's purpose of mercy; and perhaps if we knew more, as one day we may hope to know, what are the secrets of the moral government of the world, we should see how God acts at times even now by His Providence as He acted of old by Joshua; how men are removed with swift decisions from this earthly scene because they bring to the cause of truth and goodness that moral paralysis and collapse which comes with cherished wrong-doing, and how their removal restores the public vigour and hope which their sin had forfeited. We dare not, of course, think of individuals, but the general laws of God's government do not vary from age to age, and the subject is surely full of warning for each of us. None of us are too high, none too low to promote or to weaken the cause of Christ in the world, and *salus populi suprema lex* – the well-being of God's Israel from age to age is the law of God's constant government, and the valley of trouble for the individual wrong-doer is the door of hope for the Church, for the nation, for the race.

But the valley of Achor might have been a door of hope for others than those survivors who passed on to the conquest of Ai. The fate of the sons and daughters of Achan was one of the stock objections to this part of the Bible narrative which was urged by the Deists in the last century; and I suppose that to a child reading the Bible for the first time, and with the interest which the narratives of this part of Scripture always possess for children, it does seem hard sometimes that the sons and daughters of Achan were made to share in the dreadful punishment of their father. And here it is by no means sufficient to say with a recent writer, who means at least to be religious, that the history before us only illustrates the sanguinary severity of oriental nations, which has in all ages involved the children in the punishment of their father, for we cannot but remember that the Jews had received a law which has specially insisted on the sacredness of human life, and it is difficult to see how the slaughter in question was other than a high crime against the Sixth Commandment, unless it could appeal to some independent principle, which justified and explained it. It is, indeed, more than probable that Achan's family were, to a certain extent, accomplices in his sin. They must have been privy to the concealment of the stolen spoil in the tent, and they knew what was involved in stealing and in concealing it. But, besides this, we cannot doubt that Achan and his family are here regarded as forming, in some sense, a moral whole, and not simply as a set of individuals, each of whom was on his or her trial.

Scripture does take these two views of human beings. Sometimes it treats us as each one entirely separate from all besides, both in probation and in judgment; and sometimes it merges the individual in a wider association of which he forms a part; and whether it be the family, or the race, or the church, or humanity, it merges him in it so completely as to treat him as though he were merely a limb of the great whole to which he belongs, and both of these views of men are true to, and they are based on the nature of things, since man is by the terms of his creation at once a personal being complete in himself, and yet a part of a larger organism—the human family. On the first of these aspects the Gospel, no doubt, specially insists, but it does not by any means ignore or dispense with the second. When the Apostle tells us that in Adam all die, and that by one man sin came into the world, and death by sin, he treats every descendant of Adam as part of a family which is united in its natural head, and which is fatally compromised by the acts of that head. This principle of the reality of a common human nature which we all share explains our loss of righteousness in Adam; but it tells to our advantage even more decisively, for it explains our recovery of righteousness in Christ. "In Christ shall all be made alive," "As by the disobedience of one many were made sinners, so by the obedience of one shall many be made righteous."

How can this be unless Christ, too, is the head of a family which He endows with His saving righteousness, just as Adam endowed his descendants with a legacy of sin and death, a family which is united to Christ by the gift of His new nature through the spirit and the sacraments just as truly as the old and wider family is connected with Adam by the tie of natural life transmitted in the way of human generation. This principle of the solidarity—if I may be allowed the word—of human beings, tells for good as it tells for evil; and just as Levi, though in the loins of his father Abraham paid tithes in Abraham to Melchisedek, and so determined the character of his priesthood, so Achan's act compromised his family in the real sense which cannot possibly be ignored without rebelling against the facts of nature as well as against the teaching of Scripture; for, putting revelation altogether aside for the moment, do we not see the operation of this law in the physical and social life of man written in characters too plain to be mistaken? What means that inheritance of impoverished and diseased life which a parent, whose frame has been shattered by excess and debauchery, bequeaths to children or grandchildren who are yet unborn? What means the transmission, with the gift of life, of a moral character and predispositions—a transmission so certain as to have suggested the error that the personal soul itself is transmitted instead of only being impressed by the transmitted organ which encases it? How can we deny that good or bad circumstances of an earlier generation, that the splendour of the great name or the forfeiture of all self-respect, are, whether we will or no, a fatal entail from parents to their children? There is no mistaking these facts of human nature, and when Christianity tells us of an original sin descending from Adam and of a gift of righteousness descending from Christ, it grafts those high doctrines on facts which are already matters of experience and which no true philosophy of human nature can possibly ignore.

Achan's children were involved in their father's guilt on a somewhat like principle. As they had shared his credit and standing in the ranks of Israel, so they shared the shame and the pain of his fall, and yet when this and much more that might be said has been said, a higher justice still asks whether the destruction of all the members of Achan's family is fully accounted for. Do not your hearts, my brethren, echo this repressed murmur, do they not whisper, "Your theology may be right, but there is something in our moral sense which is still unsatisfied"? The truth is that we see here a deeper sense in which the valley of Achor was a door of hope. In order to explain the tragedy which it witnessed we must resort to that larger conception of the destiny of man which was affirmed with varying degrees of distinctness by the Jewish revelation. If all ended with this life it would be difficult if not impossible to explain occurrences of this sort of consistency with the belief that the world is governed by an absolute and unerring justice. It would seem as if there was no room in this visible world for such a justice to take adequate measures – I will not say for self-vindication but for self-satisfaction, and so all is quite purposely left incomplete with the deliberate intention of making belief in a future life inevitable for all who believe in a moral government of the world.

Certainly those who do not believe in a future after death are perfectly right in taking as they do the very gloomiest view of our present existence; while on the other hand faith in such a future enables us to understand how the tragedies of human life and history are strictly consistent with the moral attributes of God. If any members of Achan's family were punished beyond the measure of their personal deserts in respect of Achan's crime, the valley of Achor was for them a door of hope. It opened into, it suggested a future life in which all would be more than redressed by a just and holy God. No doubt in later ages than Joshua's the separate relation of each individual soul with God was more distinctly marked by revelation. When Ezekiel's contemporaries complained that the fathers had eaten sour grapes and the children's teeth were set on edge, Ezekiel proclaimed that "the soul that sinneth it shall die" and that "When the wicked man turneth away from his wickedness and doeth that which is lawful and right he shall save his soul alive"; and Christ our Lord, if I may say so, yet further extricated the individual soul from the mass of human nature and placed it face to face in an awful and a blessed solitude with the mercy and with the justice of God.

Each Christian is redeemed as though redemption had been wrought for him alone; each is to pass through death to judgment as though the judge of all the world had only to do with a single soul, and yet the law which makes us part of a vast family is not thereby cancelled. Since death, which awaits us all, is a legacy of our first natural parent, life is full of blessings and of sorrows which come from those who have preceded us. The fate of Achan's family was as much a prophecy of a coming adjustment of deserts and awards as the fall of the Tower of Siloam, or the Tay Bridge disaster. It left accounts to be settled in a vast hereafter, and it was thereby a door of hope. Nay, is it not at least possible that to Achan himself the valley of Achor may have been a door of hope? We dare not dogmatise, but his confession at the instance of Joshua is not without traces of a true repentance. He was no Judas, hurrying by his own act into the presence of the Judge, and God may have spoken to his soul in those last moments of agony and shame, and he, on his part, may have used the last efforts of will that were at his disposal to accept his punishment as deserved, and as coming from God; and if this was the case, Achan's lot was, in reality, happier than that of others who have sinned as he did, but who, in this life, have escaped punishment.

"Some men's sins," says the Apostle, "are open beforehand, going before to judgment, and some men they follow after"; and surely of these the last are in the worst case, when everything which conscience threatens, and which justice renders inevitable, is reserved for the future. Achan was punished here; his trouble may have been even to him a door of hope; and the general truth, which is independent of the cases of Israel and of Achan, that the punishment which God sends may open the way to life's choicest blessings, or to blessings which lie far away beyond it, is too plainly written in Scripture to be mistaken. It was true for the Israel of Joshua's day, it was true for the Israel to which Hosea addressed these warnings so full of sternness and of love, it is true for every one of us now, true for individuals and for great bodies of men, true for parties, for nations, for churches. We cannot use our Psalter with any approach to intelligence or sincerity without confessing it. "Before I was troubled I went wrong, but now have I kept Thy word." "It is good for me that I have been in trouble, that I may learn Thy statutes." "I know, O Lord, that Thy judgments are right, and that Thou of very faithfulness hast caused me to be troubled." "Heaviness may endure for a night, but joy cometh in the morning." "Blessed is the man whom Thou chastenest, O Lord, and keepest him in Thy law."

Surely at this season of the year the truth receives its highest consecration at the sepulchre of our risen Lord. He, indeed, was in Himself, holy, harmless, undefiled, separate from sinners, but in His love and condescension He took upon Him the whole weight of human sin. He became in Gethsemane the representative penitent. "He was made sin for us Who knew no sin, that we might be made the righteousness of God in Him." "To Him also the valley of trouble was a door of hope. The passion was the herald of the resurrection." "Being found in fashion as a man, He humbled Himself, and became obedient unto death, even the death of the cross. Wherefore, God also hath highly exalted Him, and given Him a name which is above every name"; and it was for the hope that was set before Him that He endured the cross and despised the shame. What is of most importance is that when trouble comes to each one of us it should be recognised as coming from God, and accepted as His will, as due certainly to our sins, and therefore as the best thing possibly that could happen.

Many a reverse in life is relatively worse for a man than Israel's defeat before Ai. Many men die in their beds in more painful tortures than did Achan in the valley of Achor. Nothing sweetens family anxieties, failures in business, mental anguish, the loss of friends, the inroads of illness, the felt approach of death, so effectively as this conviction that the trial is from God, and that there is, therefore, if we only will, a hope beyond it. Of this hope Easter is the warrant and the consecration, and the more simply and truly we hold communion with our risen Lord, the better shall we be persuaded of the reality of that hope within the veil, sure and steadfast, which makes all trouble not merely tolerable, but, to God's true servants, welcome.

THE POWER OF THE RESURRECTION

"That I may know Him, and the power of His Resurrection" (Philippians 3:10).

THE POWER of Christ's Resurrection! Here is one of those phrases which we only understand when we remember that it is in tacit contrast to another phrase which suggests it. "Power" seems here to be contrasted with "fact." In every occurrence, whether great or unimportant, there are to be considered, first, the fact, or, that which actually occurred, and secondly, its consequences, actual or possible,

Reprinted from H. P. Liddon, *Easter in St. Paul's: Sermons Bearing Chiefly on the Resurrection of Our Lord,* 2 vols. (London: Rivingtons, 1885), 1:163–79.

or, what St. Paul calls its power. We know the fact of an occurrence when we have handled the proofs which show that it really took place; when we know how it has been described, what were its several aspects, near or distant, seen from without or from within. We know the fact when we have mastered its scene, its mechanism, its dimensions. But we know the power of an occurrence when we can trace what its effects have been, or what, but for disturbing or interrupting causes, they might have been, or might be, whether in the world at large, or upon individuals, whether upon others or upon ourselves. It is easier to apprehend a fact than to take the measure of its consequences, its practical meaning, its power. If I throw a stone as far as I can, I can ascertain without much difficulty the weight of the stone, the moment at which it leaves my hand, the distance of the spot at which it touches the ground from the spot on which I am standing. So much for the fact. But what is hard to ascertain is the effect of the stone's passage through the air; the thousands or millions of insects instantaneously disabled or destroyed by it; the radiation of disturbance caused by the displacement of the atomsphere, and extending, it may be, into regions which defy or escape calculation.

All of us understand, more or less, at least, the general outline and succession of recent events in Egypt, but what will be, in the course of years, their import and influence upon the condition and history of our own country and of the world who shall say? This is a matter much less easy to determine: it needs the lapse of time, observation, reflection, very varied experience, in order to do so with any approach to accuracy. So on Good Friday morning we were all of us startled by hearing that a great lawyer and statesman had passed away: and it is not necessary to subscribe to all of Lord Cairns's opinions in order to do justice to the great ability and to the fearless conscientiousness which have throughout marked his career. But what will be the effect, or as St. Paul would say the "power," of the withdrawal of so prominent a figure from the public life of our country, and at such a time as the present? This question also can only be answered some months, perhaps some years, hence; and even then, the influence of a single mind upon those with whom he acts, or upon men in general, is not easy to measure with anything like exactness. You see, my hearers, to apprehend a fact is one thing; it is quite another to understand its power.

When then St. Paul utters his earnest prayer that he may know the power of Christ's Resurrection, he implies that he already has knowledge of the fact. He had indeed no sort of doubt about it. Here perhaps some of you may recall ground over which, at this sacred season, we have travelled together in former years; I mean the nature and vigour of the witness which St. Paul in particular bears to the fact of the Resurrection, and by which accordingly he unveils before our eyes the basis of his own conviction. St. Paul wrote his first Epistle to the Corinthians before any of the Gospels had been written; and that

Epistle is one of the only four books in the New Testament against the genuineness and authenticity of which unbelieving criticism has found absolutely nothing to allege. There is, in fact, in a purely sceptical judgment, no more reason for doubting that St. Paul wrote that Epistle than for doubting that Sir Walter Scott wrote *Waverley*.

And what does St. Paul tell the Corinthians about our Lord's Resurrection? He tells them that, while he was writing, there were more than two hundred and fifty persons still living who had seen our Saviour on one occasion after His rising from the dead. "He was seen of five hundred brethren at once; of whom the greater part remain unto this present" (1 Cor. 15:6). Now here was an assertion which the Corinthians might, if they would, verify for themselves. There was intercourse enough between Greece and the coast of Syria; and any Corinthian who thought that St. Paul was too impetuous, or too credulous, or anything else of the kind, had only to investigate the accuracy of his statement by paying a visit to some of the two hundred and fifty survivors, and cross-questioning them for himself. St. Paul's statement was itself a challenge to do so . And if, so far as we know, the challenge was not accepted, this would only have been because men felt that unless the Apostle had been quite sure of his ground, the statement would never have been made. Even those who do not, with the Church, venerate in St. Paul a glorious Saint and Apostle, enthroned, now that his life of toil and suffering is over, not far from the very Throne of Christ in heaven — even they must, and do, gather from his writings that he was a remarkably clever man, and a man of shrewd common sense. And as such, putting for the moment his inspiration out of sight, he never, we may be sure, would have made an assertion like that before us had he believed it to be liable to be disputed upon examination; had he been less than certain of its literal and severe accuracy. St. Paul was convinced that Christ had risen, for other reasons, as we know, but also because more than two hundred and fifty people were still living who, if questioned, would say that they had seen Him.

And St. Paul, being thus sure of the fact of the Resurrection, was not embarrassed by any *a priori* doctrine bidding him ignore it; he was not like those schoolmen whom Lord Bacon condemned, and who, instead of learning what to think about nature from the facts of nature, endeavoured to persuade themselves that the facts of nature corresponded to what they already thought about it. If a man says that miracle is impossible or incredible, no amount of proof that the Resurrection actually occurred is likely to satisfy him. When some early navigators, of whom Herodotus tells us, coasted round Africa, and returned with the story that they had reached a region at which their shadows at noonday pointed toward the south, their report was treated as ludicrous by the inhabitants of the Mediterranean seaboard, and among them, by the great historian himself; since the constant experience of their own neighbourhood furnished them, as they thought, with ample reason for thinking that nothing of the kind was possible. When asserting the fact of the Resurrection, St. Paul planted his foot upon the rock of experience; he was proof against the seductions of the idols whether of the den or of the cave. He had no need to pray, as have many in our time, that he might be assured of the fact of Christ's Resurrection. What he did pray for was that he might increasingly know its power.

Now, we may be sure we can trace only very partially the range of power which attaches to such an event as the Resurrection of our Lord. But let us do what we may within such narrow spheres as are the thought and life of man.

I

The power of Christ's Resurrection, then, may be observed, first of all, and generally, in the way in which a true belief in it enables us to realise habitually the moral government of the world by God.

Our age has many characteristics which honourably distinguish it from earlier times, and which will be pointed to hereafter by historians. But it is not an age in which men believe, as they believed in the past, that, whatever happens or is permitted, all is overruled by a Being Who is perfectly Good and perfectly Wise.

When people are not deliberately and consciously sceptical about this, they often believe it only in a languid, hesitating way. They feel the doubt which floats in the intellectual air around them, and which enervates their mental grasp of the truth. We may perhaps flatter ourselves that this weakened hold on elementary truths is the result of a wider mental culture than was enjoyed by our fathers; of greater readiness to welcome new impressions; of a more judicial and balanced habit of mind. In this manner disbelief in an overruling Providence may assume in our eyes the colours of a distinction, if not of a virtue. And it is only when we find ourselves at one of the sterner crises in life, and the heavens seem as brass above our heads, and we cry, and there is, we think, none to answer, that we understand the extent and the misery of our loss.

And when some man,[2] not a clergyman, appears on the scene of our public life, to whom the Divine government of the world is as certain and as obvious as the action and language of his friends, or of the members of his family; a man to whom prayer is the most natural form of conversation, and the Bible and the imitation of Christ the rule of conduct; we experience almost a new sensation, as at the presence of a striking and original apparition. Yet if we knew more of the

---

2. The late General Gordon, killed at Khartoum, January 1885.

days that have preceded us, we should know that the type which for the moment so fascinates and astonishes us, has been heretofore even the prevailing type among the sincere worshippers of Jesus Christ.

There are circumstances, no doubt, in the modern world which make belief in the Divine government harder for us than it was for our ancestors. One such circumstance is our wider outlook. Thanks to the press, the railway, the telegraph, we know a great deal more of what is going on all over the world, at the same time, than has any previous generation of men. And one consequence is that human life presents itself to many minds as a much more tangled and inexplicable thing than it ever did before. The picture which is brought before us is so complex, so blurred; the details are so much more importunate than any obviously presiding and ruling principle; the disappointments in store for the conscience which is searching for clear traces of a law of right vigorously asserting itself are so frequent and so great, that men lose heart where heart and purpose are especially needful. They lazily acquiesce in some indistinct conception of the world which treats it as an unexplored and inexplicable moral chaos, amid the confusions of which it is vain to look for any clear note of a Reign of Righteousness maintained behind the veil.

Now here the certainty that Jesus Christ rose from the dead asserts what St. Paul calls its power. For when Jesus Christ was crucified, it might have seemed, it did seem, that the sun of God's justice had gone down behind thick clouds; and that a moral darkness, of which that in the sky was but a shadow, had settled on the earth. It might have seemed that while all the vices were being crowned and feasted in Rome, all the virtues could be crucified, and crucified with impunity, in Jerusalem. It might have seemed that we lived in a world where nothing was more surely at a discount than moral beauty, and nothing more certain of the future than physical and brute force.

And when He burst forth from the grave in which they laid Him under seal and stone, He proclaimed to men's senses, as well as to their consciences, that the real law which rules the world is moral, not material law; and that if the sun of God's righteousness is at times overclouded in human history, it is sure to reappear. To know that Jesus Christ rose from the dead is to know that, whatever may be the perplexities of the moment or of the age, the world is really swayed by God's most holy and overruling Providence.

II

Next, the power of the Resurrection of Christ is seen in the firm persuasion which it should create, in our own days as in those of the Apostles, that the Christian Creed is true; true as a whole, and in its several parts. Thus the Resurrection of Christ has a twofold aspect.

It is at once a proof that the Christian Creed is true, and a truth of the Christian Creed.

There are many truths of Christianity which do not contribute anything to prove its general truth, although they could not be lost sight of or denied without fatally impairing its integrity. Take for an example the truth of our Lord's perpetual intercession in heaven. Nothing tells more powerfully upon the life and conscience of a believing Christian than the knowledge that our living but unseen Saviour is ever engaged in one ceaseless act of self-oblation on high on behalf of His members and servants here on earth; on behalf of all and of each of them. "He ever liveth to make intercession for us." But this truth does not attest the truth of any other part of our Creed; although it is, if we may reverently say so, their inevitable complement. We believe in our Lord's intercession because His Apostles have so taught us. We do not believe in the Creed as a whole because we believe in His intercession.

It is otherwise with the Resurrection, which, as I have said, is not only an article of the Christian faith, but a proof that the Christian faith is true as a whole. It is this because it is the certificate of our Lord's mission from heaven, to which He Himself pointed as the warrant of His claims. He laid this stress on His coming Resurrection on two occasions especially: in His saying about the destruction and re-building of the temple, and in His saying about the sign of the Prophet Jonah. His words came in effect to this: "You Jews doubt whether I have any right to teach you, and to proclaim Myself as I do. Very well; wait a short while, and an event will take place which will prove that your misgivings or doubts are unwarranted. I shall be put to death, and then I shall rise from the dead on the third day. This will be a counter-sign of My mission from heaven: if it does not take place, reject; if it does, believe Me."

It is a mistake to say that our Lord referred to His Resurrection only on rare occasions, and that it had no such place in His mind as in the teaching of His Apostles. For it is plain from the Gospels that He was constantly dwelling on it. Thus He alluded to it, at least by implication, in the synagogue of Capernaum, when He spoke of the Son of Man ascending up where He was before. He foretold both His Death and Resurrection explicitly after the confession of His Divinity by Simon Peter at Caesarea Philippi. While coming down from the Mount of the Transfiguration, He bade the disciples who had been with Him tell no man what they had seen until the Son of Man was risen from the dead. After healing the demoniac, He is crossing Galilee, and He explains to His disciples that He will be delivered into the hands of men, and that they will kill Him, and the third day He will rise. Still more striking is the saying that in dying He does not submit to the irresistible; that no man takes His life from Him; that He has power to lay it down, and has power to take it again. In going up to Jerusalem He repeats the prediction about dying and rising with great detail and precision; and in the Upper Chamber the gracious promise, "A little while and ye shall see Me," certainly points to the Resurrection. Even on the road to Gethsemane, when the little company had left the Upper Chamber, and had sung a hymn, He assures them, "After I am risen again, I will go before you into Galilee."

The Resurrection was thus constantly before His mind, because it was to be the warrant of His mission. And when He did rise, He redeemed the pledge which He had given to His disciples and to the world. The first preachers of Christianity understood this. The Resurrection was the proof to which they constantly pointed that our Lord was really what He claimed to be. "Jesus and the Resurrection" was the popular name at Athens for the Gospel as taught by St. Paul. "This Jesus, Whom ye have crucified, hath God raised up," had been the keynote to the early teaching of St. Peter. The Resurrection was the truth which filled the early Church with its first converts. The Resurrection was the decisive proof that Christianity was from God.

Let us ask, more precisely, What is the true value of the fact that our Lord rose from the dead among the credentials of Christianity? what is the measure of its evidential power?

Here, it would seem, there are two opposite mistakes to be avoided.

There is the mistake which was made nearly a century ago by a writer of genius, who was, however, unduly influenced by the wish to simplify questions which are not always really simple—I mean, Archdeacon Paley. Paley wanted to put the evidence of the truth of Christianity, as the phrase goes, in a nut-shell; and, in his well-known *Evidences,* he makes the whole case of Christianity rest upon the fact that the Resurrection was so certain to its first preachers that they willingly gave their lives to attest it. Paley's mistake lay, not in insisting upon this fact, which is indeed of the first importance as an evidence of Christianity, but in insisting on it, as if it stood alone, and would, of itself and unsupported, prove to all minds the truth of the Christian Creed. The consequence has been that, in many minds of our own and two preceding generations, Paley's book has failed to create or to reinforce the convictions which its author was anxious to serve; men have felt that more stress has been laid on a single line of evidence than it will properly bear. The truth is, that the evidences of Christianity are not one and simple, but many and complex. Their strength lies in their convergence; and the conviction of the truth of the Resurrection which was held by the Apostles is only one of several lines of argument which point towards a single and central truth, although of these it is the most important. And when this is overlooked, there is always risk of a catastrophe: the fabric which its Divine Architect meant to rest upon a group of pillars cannot be safely rested by us on one.

The other mistake is of later date, and much more serious. From saying that the Resurrection alone proves Christianity to be true, men have, in some instances, come of late to say that it is of no value whatever as an evidence of Christianity. Christianity is said to be recommended solely by the moral character of Christ. The supernatural incidents of His earthly life, and notably His Resurrection, are treated as an embarrassing addition to what else would be a simple and convincing exhibition of moral excellence. We believe the Resurrection, men have said, if we do believe it, for the sake of the religion which seems to warrant it; we do not believe in Christianity for the sake of the Resurrection.

Enough has already been said to show that this estimate of the evidential value of the Resurrection is altogether opposed to the mind of our Lord and His Apostles. They did not mean the Resurrection to stand alone, but they assigned to it a high, nay the highest place, among the facts which go to show that Christianity is true. The real value of the Resurrection, as an evidence of Christianity, would seem to be that it is a countersign in the world of nature to the teaching of our Lord in the court of conscience. The outward miracle assures us, through the senses, that the Being Who is the Author of nature is the same Being as He Who speaks to conscience in the Moral Law, in the Beatitudes, in the Sermon on the Mount, in the Last Discourse, in the whole character and teaching of Jesus Christ. If we heard the inward verdict of conscience alone, we might doubt whether there was anything external to ourselves which really warranted it. If we witnessed the outward miracle alone, we might see in it a mere wonder, with no moral significance, with no ascertainable relation to the inward and the spiritual.

But when the Teacher Whose voice pierces, rouses, quickens conscience, is accredited by an interference with, or a suspension of, the observed course of nature, the combined evidence is reasonably overwhelming: deep answers to deep, sphere to sphere, the moral and the material are in felt harmony, and the combination is more than sufficient to warrant that assent of the mind and heart which we call faith. And in this way a persuasion of the literal certainty of the Resurrection is at the present day, as of old, a power which has weight with the most well-informed and thoughtful minds, as decisively attesting the claims of Christianity.

III

And thirdly, the power of the Resurrection should be traced and felt in the spiritual and moral life of Christians.

Let us remind ourselves that our Lord Jesus Christ is not merely our one authoritative Teacher, not merely our Redeemer from sin and death, but also, and especially, through real union with us, the Author of a new life in us. He gives us a new nature, which is indeed His Own. St. Paul teaches us this truth again and again, and by a great variety of expressions. Sometimes he speaks of our Lord as though He were a sphere of being within which the Christian lives: "If any man be in Christ, he is a new creation: old things are passed away; behold, all things are become new." Sometimes he speaks of Him as of an inhabitant of the Christian soul. "Christ in you," he says to the Colossians, "the Hope of Glory."

This union is not in St. Paul's mouth the language of metaphor; it is to him just as real a thing as eating or walking, or reading or preaching, or going to Athens or to Jerusalem. It is an actual experience of which he is certain. It began with him when he was baptized by Ananias; for "as many as have been baptized into Christ have put on Christ." It was deepened and strengthened in many ways, but especially by the reception of that other Holy Sacrament, in which, unlike the careless Corinthians, he really "discerned the Lord's Body," and knew that he was admitted to the closest contact with the Source of his highest life.

Let none think that, in insisting on the presence of Christ in the bodies and souls of Christians, we are forgetting the office of the Holy Spirit, or confounding the work of the Spirit and the Son. The office of the Spirit is to convey Christ's nature and to interpret His teaching to Christians. This is one of the reasons for His being so constantly termed in the New Testament the Spirit of Christ. "He shall take of Mine, and shall show it unto you," was our Lord's description of His office. And thus He is the Agent Who makes the Christian Sacraments effectual in conveying Christ's Human Nature to Christians. The baptized puts on Christ, but he is born of water and of the Spirit; the communicant eats the Body and drinks the Blood of Christ, but it is the Spirit that quickeneth the dead elements, and makes them veils and vehicles of the unseen Gift. Our Lord then dwells in Christians; their bodies and souls are temples of His Presence, His Incarnation is perpetuated in His living Church. And, as a consequence, the New Testament teaches us that the mysteries of His earthly life are reproduced, after a measure, in the Christian soul.

If Christ is born supernaturally of a Virgin Mother, the Christian is made God's child by adoption and grace, and Apostles are in travail until Christ be formed in their converts. If Christ is crucified on Mount Calvary, the Christian, too, has a Calvary within, where he is crucified with Christ, where he crucifies the flesh with the affections and lusts. If Christ, while His disciples behold, is taken up into heaven, and sits at the Right Hand of God, the Christian in heart and mind with Him ascends, and with Him continually dwells; nay, he is, as St. Paul says, made to sit together with Him in heavenly places. And in like manner, if Christ rose from the dead the third day, according to the Scriptures, the Christian also has experience of an inward resurrection. As at a primitive baptism the adult neophyte was plunged beneath the waters, and then lifted up amid prayers and benedictions, so in this Sacrament Christians are still buried with Christ, and raised to newness of life. And if the baptismal gift be impaired or forfeited, a second putting forth of the Resurrection power becomes necessary. A resurrection in penitence is a new effort of the power of recovery from sin and death, issuing from contact with the Risen Redeemer.

All this seems to be the language of metaphor, or the language of mysticism, until it has been discovered to be the record of an experience. St. Paul knew that it meant, or might mean, a solemn reality. It was this inward power of Christ's Resurrection, in its ever-increasing fulness, that he chiefly desired to know. Of this power of Christ's Resurrection lodged in the recesses of the Christian soul, of this moral and spiritual resurrection which issues from, and corresponds with, the literal Resurrection of Jesus Christ from His grave, there are three leading characteristics.

1. Our Lord rose really. It was not a phantom that haunted the Upper Chamber, or the road to Emmaus, or the shores of the Sea of Galilee; the Apostles had but to handle Him, and see, for a phantom had no such flesh and bones as they might see He had. And an Easter resurrection from sin should be no less real, will be no less real, if it is His power by which we are rising. The flesh and bones, the actual substance of recovered life, true prayers, true confessions, true resolutions, truth in thought and word and act, are indispensable. To have a name that we live again, and yet to be dead, is only too easy: it is scarcely less easy to impose upon ourselves than upon others with false appearances of life. Little indeed will a phantom-resurrection avail us here or hereafter; let us pray for that first mark of Christ's Resurrection power — reality.

2. Our Lord really rose, but He rose to lead, for the most part, a hidden life. On the day of His Resurrection He appeared five times, but rarely afterwards during the forty days that preceded the Ascension. So it is with the risen life of the soul. It is not constantly flaunted before the eyes of men; it seeks retirement, solitude, and the sincerities which these insure. They whose religious life is perpetually displayed to the public eye may have risen really. But at least they are very unlike our Risen Lord. "If ye then be risen with Christ, seek those things that are above, where Christ sitteth at the right hand of God. . . . For . . . your life is hid with Christ in God. When Christ, Who is your life, shall appear, then shall ye also appear with Him in glory."

Reserve in speaking about ourselves may make heavy demands upon buoyant and impetuous natures. Frequent retirement for communion with God is not natural to flesh and blood: it fails to satisfy the demands for excitement and human sympathy, which enter so largely into much of our modern religion. But let us be sure that it is a true note of the presence of Christ's Resurrection power, that we should be thankful to be often alone with God.

3. And thirdly, our Lord "being raised from the dead dieth no more; death hath no more dominion over Him. For in that He died, He died unto sin once: but in that He liveth, He liveth unto God." His Resurrection power does not lend itself to the perpetual alternations of relapse and recovery, which mark the lives of so many Christians: "Christ, being raised from the dead, dieth no more." It is sad work when Easter is only reached to forfeit by relaxation what little may have been gained in Lent and Passion-tide. We may sink into the grave of sin once too often. Surely we should pray with the Ancient Church —

> O Jesus, from the death of sin
> Keep us, we pray; so shalt Thou be
> The everlasting Paschal joy
> Of all the souls new-born to Thee.

God grant to all of us that St. Paul's desire may be fulfilled, alike in our convictions and in our lives; and that we may know something of what the power of Christ's Resurrection really is. As the years go by, our natural forces become sensibly weaker; they will fail altogether at the approach of death. But here is a Power which death cannot extinguish or arrest, since it is itself the conquest and repudiation of death; a Power which may enable the weakest of us to feel that, while his bodily strength decays, he is enriched with a new energy that comes from heaven.

GEHAZI'S LIE

"But he went in, and stood before his master, and Elisha said unto him, Whence comest thou, Gehazi? And he said, Thy servant went no whither" (2 Kings 5:25).

Reprinted from H. P. Liddon, *Forty-Two Sermons on Various Subjects*, 4th series (London: Charles Higham, 1886), pp. 217–24.

THE PAGES of the Bible describe a great many lies, but no one lie more complete and deliberate than this which Gehazi told Elisha. Let us endeavour to consider it in as practical a spirit as may be this afternoon, since, human nature being what it is, the subject is never without present and immediate interest.

And first of all we will remind ourselves of the preceding and surrounding circumstances as they are recorded in the First Lesson for this morning.

Naaman, the Syrian general, had risen at the court of Damascus to a position of the very first importance. He had, in all probability, distinguished himself in the war of independence against Assyria, which, as we know from recently-discovered inscriptions, had been carried on by the Syrians of Damascus some few years before, and had been brought to a successful issue. Naaman, however, though a great soldier, was a leper. His leprosy seems to have been of that lighter sort which did not disable a man for the discharge of many public duties. Still, any man in his position would have been thankful to be cured of a painful and humiliating disease; and in Naaman's household there was a slave girl who was both able and willing to help him.

She was by birth an Israelite. She had been carried away from her home by the wild Syrian cavalry in one of the raids which were then made at intervals, as it seems, into the territory of Israel, and she was now in the service of Naaman's wife. She one day expressed to her mistress a wish that her lord could meet Elisha, the great prophet, working and teaching in Samaria. The leprosy, she thought, would soon be cured if this only could be arranged. Her words were repeated to the Syrian king, who sent Naaman himself with a letter of introduction to the reigning king of Israel, Jehoram, and, as was usual in the East, a present, consisting, in this instance, of a large sum of money and ten complete suits of dress. Jehoram was asked to effect somehow Naaman's cure, the Syrian king probably meaning that Jehoram was to bid the prophet, as his subject, to work the necessary miracle. But Jehoram had no serious belief in the mission and power of Elisha. He looked at Elisha as men of the world often regard a powerful religious influence – with quaint alternations of cynicism and uneasiness, but without any such trust, any such sympathy, as would enable him to apply to Elisha for counsel and assistance.

In point of fact, Jehoram saw in the Syrian king's letter only an attempt to create a pretext for a new war by preferring a request which he could not possibly grant. In his alarm and agitation Jehoram rent his clothes, an act which, in the East, when it did not express mourning for the dead, implied the greatest distress and perplexity of mind; and Elisha, on hearing of this occurrence, reproached the king of Israel by a messenger for forgetting that God had a prophet in Israel, and desired that Naaman might be sent on to himself. The great Syrian came; he came as he was bid. His splendid equipages drew up before the humble cottage in which the prophet lived. Elisha deemed it well to teach him of how little account this world's magnificence may be in the eyes of a spiritual man. Elisha did not even go out to the door to see his illustrious visitor. He merely sent a message to the effect that Naaman was to wash seven times in the sacred waters of the Jordan, and then he would be healed.

Naaman was offended both with the substance of the message and with the way in which he had been treated. Naaman had pictured to himself Elisha working a miracle then and there for his benefit in an imposing way. "I thought," he cried, "I thought he will surely come out to me, and stand and call on the name of the Lord his God, and strike his hand over the place and recover the leper." As to going to wash in the foreign, the Jewish river, the notion was intolerable. Why would not the Syrian streams do just as well – the Abana and the Pharpar which watered the fields and the gardens of Damascus? The prophet's conduct and his message combined were simply insulting. Naaman was very angry.

But the leprosy was as bad as ever. Time passes, and as time passes passion cools. Naaman's trusted slaves pointed out to him that, after all, he was not asked to do very much. If he had been enjoined to attempt some great duty, they said, he would have at once obeyed. Why should he hesitate when obedience was so simple, so easy? And Naaman did obey. The sevenfold washing in the waters of the Jordan did its work. Naaman's flesh came again as the flesh of a little child, and he was clean. And then it was that, in his gratitude and in his joy, Naaman paid his second visit to the prophet Elisha. He came, not merely to thank the prophet for the counsel which had proved to be so wise, but also to announce his own conversion from paganism to Israel's faith in the one true God. "I know," he said, "that there is no God in all the earth but in Israel." He begged Elisha to receive a valuable present of dress and money; but Elisha steadily declined. And then, after a few words as to the conduct he might rightly pursue when waiting on his royal master in his heathen home, Naaman took his leave of the great prophet, rejoicing in his recovered health of body, but rejoicing more, we may believe, in his knowledge of Him Who is the source of all blessings whether of body or soul.

Naaman was gone, but one person, at least, who had witnessed the scene, was not well pleased. As Elisha's servant, Gehazi, no doubt, was well satisfied that Naaman should be cured of his disease, and that he should be converted to the faith of Israel; but then was it not reasonable that he should pay for these advantages? In Gehazi's opinion a great opportunity had been recklessly lost. It was not, however, too late to repair the mistake, at least to some extent, by relieving Naaman of part of his treasure; and Gehazi accordingly set out in pursuit of him.

Naaman showed the high honour in which he held Elisha by alighting down from his chariot to receive even Elisha's servant and the message which, presumably, that servant bore. Gehazi explained that two young students from one of the two schools of the prophets in Ephraim had arrived suddenly on a visit to Elisha, that these young men wanted money and clothes, and that Elisha now would be glad to accept a talent of silver and two suits of clothing. This was, indeed, much less than Naaman had originally offered to give, but Gehazi could not have asked for more without exciting Naaman's suspicion that something was wrong. Naaman begged Gehazi by all means to take two talents instead of one; and so Gehazi returned with his ill-gotten spoils. He took the precaution, we are told, of stopping beyond a hill close to Elisha's house, which, it seems, shut off the view of the Damascus road. He then dismissed Naaman's servants who had carried his packages, lest they should attract his master's eye, and so, after stowing his treasures away in some room or cupboard of the prophet's dwelling, he went and, as is the wont of Eastern servants, stood before Elisha, looking as if nothing in particular had happened since Naaman's departure.

If Gehazi thought that he could escape detection he was soon undeceived. The old man looked up at him and asked him where he had been, and Gehazi ventured to say that he had been nowhere; and then the prophet delayed no longer. He had marked Gehazi's act; he knew Gehazi's motives. Gehazi had thought himself alone, but Elisha had accompanied him in the prophetic spirit at that critical moment when Naaman alighted from his chariot on the Damascus road. Gehazi thought that, at the least, his intentions were his own secret; but Elisha, by his reference to olive-yards, and vineyards, and sheep, and oxen, and men-servants, and maid-servants, showed that he had read in the servant's heart the projects of social splendour which, as Gehazi fondly hoped, might be realised by the aid of Naaman's wealth. There was a stern justice, at the least, in the penalty that followed. Naaman's leprosy should go along with his wealth. In grasping at the one, Gehazi had succeeded in inheriting the other. Already the foul disease was full upon him, and he went out from Elisha's presence a leper as white as snow.

Gehazi's punishment is startling, but its justice will be more apparent if we proceed to consider what it was in Gehazi's conduct which led up to his lie, and which, from his point of view, made it at the moment necessary for him to tell the lie.

Gehazi's conduct, then, involved, first of all, a violation of the trust which his master had reposed in him. Confidence, my brethren, is to society what cement is to a building—it holds all together. From the necessity of the case, we all of us place confidence in some persons, whether our elders or our children; whether our superiors or our servants; whether those from whom we learn or those whom we trust not to abuse the information with which we furnish them. And from the necessity of the case, no less, we all of us, until we have by some great crime forfeited our relations to society altogether, are the objects or recipients of confidence on the part of others, often of a great deal more confidence than we at all suspect, or than we deserve to have reposed in us. Confidence—it is the venture which every human being has to make in dealing with other human beings around him. Confidence—it is the honour, the high and ennobling honour, which in some degree every human being receives at the hand of his fellows, and which associates him, so far, with that highest power and goodness to which, in the last resort, we all of us commit our destinies and our lives. All our occupations in life, all our relations with one another, depend for their well-being upon the maintenance of confidence; and to justify confidence on the one hand, and to learn to place confidence largely in other men on the other, are essential conditions of any department of a man's public daily work.

Nowhere, I apprehend, is this better understood than here in London, the mistress and the centre of the commerce of the world. The conditions upon which trade is conducted are so largely, as we speak, artificial, that a shock to confidence is felt to be nothing less than a disorder of grave importance, and a violation of confidence a crime which can be with difficulty, if at all, atoned for by the offender. And this, mark you, is by no means a matter of arbitrary or merely human arrangement, it belongs to the very structure of society. It is the way in which one part of the law of God makes itself felt to be essential, even here and now, to the well-being of man. Confidence, I say, as vital to the well-being of society, is just as much God's appointment and work as the due action of the heart. As vital to the well-being of the human body is God's appointment and work. And society is guided by a true instinct when resenting and punishing a violation of confidence even with a severity which may, at first sight, appear to be violent or excessive.

Gehazi, then, was an offender against the obligations of confidence; for he was not merely Elisha's servant; he was also, to a great extent, a trusted companion; I might dare to say, in a sense, his partner. Consider the part assigned to Gehazi in Elisha's dealing with the good Shunammite. On two occasions Elisha sends Gehazi with delicate messages to this distinguished lady. It is Gehazi who makes the suggestion that she is childless, and so leads the prophet to promise her a son. It is Gehazi who is sent on before the prophet and the sorrowing mother to lay Elisha's staff upon the face of the dead child. It is Gehazi who, in after years, when the Shunammite was claiming her property at the hands of the king of Israel, describes in glowing terms the deeds of the master from whose presence he was now banished for the remainder of his days. Yes, when it was all too late, Gehazi could feel what had been the honour of this association with the great teacher, with the lofty and saintly character, with the man who, in his simple and austere life, had such power with God that pagans, as well as Israelite kings and statesmen, as well as many of the people, trembled and bowed before him.

It was association with such a man—it was this alone—which gave Gehazi what we call "a position." To be Elisha's servant was of itself a privileged post of commanding influence. We have already seen how the Syrian general acknowledged it. To be associated with Elisha in his work, to share his sympathies, and to a certain extent his counsels, to know what never could have been known but for this high companionship, would have been felt by a man with even the natural sense of honour to impose great and lasting obligations. And, accordingly, when Gehazi had once so far yielded to his covetous desires as to go after Naaman and negotiate for the treasure, his conscience told him—told him at once—that he had done that which his sense of honour itself condemned. To use the great position which his relation to Elisha had secured to him for a purpose which he knew Elisha would have disallowed—to employ the knowledge, the experience, the influence with other men, which such an intimacy conferred, in order to compass an end which he dared not acknowledge to the master whose generous confidence had made him what he was—this was to do an act which the pagans of Damascus, in their better moments, would have shrunk from doing.

And Gehazi could hardly stop here. We have heard, perhaps, of some clerk in a public office, or in a great mercantile house, who has sold information to which his position gave him access, with the result of enriching himself, but to the embarrassment, or to the serious loss, of his employers. No man having committed an act like that can say that he can go no farther. He may well have no choice. The man who has acted against his sense of right is on the brink of lying against his sense of truth. Gehazi had to choose between a lie and humiliation; and when he had brought himself to prefer two talents of silver and two changes of raiment to the love and the trust of his great friend and patron, there is not much doubt what his choice would be.

And why was Gehazi's act so wrong in the eyes of Elisha? Because it involved a serious injury to the cause of true religion. What is said of our Lord and Saviour by the aged Simeon in the *nunc dimittis* was in a measure true of the religion of the prophets of Israel also. That religion had a double aspect. It was "prepared before the face of all people to be a light to lighten the Gentiles, and to be the glory of God's people." When St. Paul wishes to mark the degradation of the Jews of his time he quotes a warning which, in slightly different terms, had been given by Nathan to David, by Isaiah and Ezekiel, respectively, to the men of their day, "The name of God is blasphemed among the Gentiles through you." Israel had duties to the heathen; not, indeed, the great duty which is laid upon the Church of Jesus Christ, of bringing them all, as quickly and as surely as may be, into the true fold, but the duty of letting them at least see that there was a lamp of truth burning in the hearts of the one chosen people, by the light of which, if they would, they might read God's best lessons about themselves and about Him in nature and in history.

In Elisha's eyes the main interest of Naaman's visit was not that it was calculated to establish friendly political relations between Israel and Syria so long estranged, or yet that it had resulted in a bodily cure which, from the eminence of the patient, could not but be famous throughout the neighbouring countries of the East, but that it had, and was likely to have, important results on the progress of true religion. Naaman, as we have seen, was, in effect, converted to faith in the one true God, and, therefore, everything that was likely to strengthen or weaken him in the religion of his choice was, in Elisha's eyes, of great importance – an importance altogether distinct in kind from that of any political or social event whatever; and here it was that conduct like Gehazi's was likely to act so very disastrously. Elisha – he had been careful to refuse all and any of the splendid presents which Naaman offered. If Naaman was to carry back with him a sound body, and, what was better, a soul illuminated by Divine truth, Elisha was determined that these great blessings should not be associated in his mind with the petty details of a commercial transaction. God's great gifts in grace should surely resemble His gifts in nature in being bestowed with an open-handed generosity. The heathen were to come, in the language of prophecy, to the waters of salvation and to the waters of healing, without money and without price.

But Gehazi's act, as it must have presented itself to Naaman, had all the appearance of an after-thought on the prophet's part, which would be fatal to his first and high idea of the prophet's disinterestedness. It may well have seemed to Naaman as if Elisha had repented at the last moment of his first large-heartedness, as if he had originally declined the presents from an impulsive enthusiasm which, after reasoning, would not last; as if the prophet of the true God was, after all, just like the rest of mankind in looking upon the high gifts of heaven as having a marketable value, just like any of the wares that were exposed for sale in the bazaars of Damascus. Elisha foresaw this result as too likely to follow upon his servant's act; he foresaw the cynical recoil; perhaps, the ruin or the apostasy of the recent, probably still hesitating, convert; and hence his searching, agonising question to Gehazi, "Is this a time to receive money, and to receive garments, and oliveyards, and vineyards, and sheep, and oxen, and men-servants and maid-servants?"

We may be sure, brethren, that Gehazi's conscience was sufficiently enlightened by association with Elisha to have anticipated and endorsed Elisha's feeling on the subject; and this would have been with him a second and more powerful reason for concealment, so long as he thought it possible, at any cost – for Gehazi would hardly have tried to persuade himself that, after all, he was not a prophet, and that a high view of duty, which would have been becoming in his master, was not necessary in him.

It is, I take it, the modern conscience which indulges in these refinements upon the broad responsibilities of a position in life. Those who are associated with God's work in some capacity, less than the most responsible, are yet, in their degree, answerable for the success of that work—are bound, at the least, to do nothing that can hinder or can injure it. Not ordained clergymen only, but those who are connected with them by family ties, as wives or daughters, and those who, without being ordained, take part in the service of the Church whether in choirs or schools, or works of charity, are answerable, every one of them, for the effect of their conduct and bearing on men who are without any religion, but who, perhaps, are seeking one. Inconsistencies or works on the part of those who are associated with the work of Christ in the world, if not actually consecrated to promoting it—inconsistencies of which little is thought by those who are guilty of them —may, oh! believe it—be only too easily taken by others to be the measure of the practical worth of the Christian creed, and may have the effect of driving an enquirer back into the desert, when he is already almost within sight of the towers of Jerusalem. It is not the clergy alone—they have, indeed, to remember it, but it is not the clergy alone —who have to remember that there are things better worth living and working for than the two talents of silver and two changes of raiment which may possibly be filched from the world.

It was, then, Gehazi's sense of the character of his act in following after Naaman which led him into his great and deliberate sin against the law of truth. He had, indeed, found it necessary to deceive as soon as he began to do wrong. There is a nexus between one sin and another, just as there is a connection between one virtue and another. A man cannot stop his boat at will in the strong currents that run just above Niagara, though he might have avoided those currents at one time altogether. Gehazi's fiction about the needs of the two imaginary students from the schools of the prophets, his dismissal of Naaman's servants while under the cover of the hill which hid the proceeding from Elisha's eye—these were the preliminary stages of a falsehood by which Gehazi's connection was fatally and surely hardened up to the decisive point of declaring before his master that he had not been in pursuit of Naaman at all.

And here, as almost always, we remark the blindness of sin— blindness in the midst of so much ingenuity, so much contrivance. No one can know better than Gehazi that Elisha knew a great deal that was going on beyond the range of his eyesight. Why? As we have heard in this afternoon's Lesson, the slaves of the king of Syria said to their master that Elisha repeated to the king of Israel the words that the Syrian king uttered in his bed-chamber. Gehazi had had large opportunities of taking the measure of Elisha's power, and yet he set to work as if Elisha could know nothing that he did not witness with his bodily eyes. And this was the point of the other reproachful question, "Went not my heart with thee when the man turned again from his chariot to meet thee?" It was folly, but it was folly of which almost every criminal trial in our courts affords a fresh example. Sin blinds men to the real circumstances with which they have to deal. Above all, it destroys their power of apprehending the presence and the omniscience of God. What Gehazi thought of Elisha, all sinners, with infinitely less reason, think about Almighty God. "Tush, the Lord shall not see; neither shall the God of Jacob regard it." The wasted ingenuities of a diseased or a violated conscience, culminating first in outrageous falsehood, and then in conspicuous disgrace, are, as the moral world goes, quite in order.

Gehazi's punishment seemed severe, but it marks a fact which we do well to remember – the fact that the injury which a deliberate falsehood inflicts on the moral nature is, in this life, irreparable. I do not say that a lie cannot be forgiven. God forbid! That would be to limit His mercy in Jesus Christ; nor do I say that a habit of substantial truthfulness may not be restored. God forbid! That would be to limit the efficacy of His grace in Jesus Christ. But when the lie has been pardoned and the habit of truth re-established, the effect of the lie still remains. The shock which it has inflicted on the more delicate fibres of the moral nature issues in a permanent weakness which shows itself when any demand or strain is put upon high principle. A man who has once told a very deliberate lie – mark, I do not speak of any form or degree of involuntary falsehood – the man, who, looking truth right in the face, has deliberately contradicted it knowing it to be truth – is like a man who has lost a lung. He may get on pretty well so long as over-exposure and over-exertion do not tax his resources. He is of the nature of a moral invalid, and there is no saying when or how his constitution may not give way.

And Gehazi's leprosy expressed this. It was a visible symbol of the moral and inward fact – the fact that Gehazi's moral nature was permanently damaged. Gehazi could not be again as he was. He must carry with him to his grave the brand of humiliation and of weakness. He could not, either as a liar or as a leper, live with Elisha. The matter was forbidden by the terms of the Jewish law. The former was inconsistent with the rule of every good Israelite's household. "There shall no deceitful person dwell in my house. He that telleth lies shall not tarry in my sight." And so Gehazi went forth, to mourn for a lifetime the folly and the wickedness which had led him to throw away the companionship and the confidence of so good and great a friend.

And Gehazi's fall teaches us three practical lessons. One is to keep our desires in order if we mean to keep out of grave sin. As St. James says, "Lust" – or desire – "when it hath conceived, bringeth forth sin, and sin, when it is finished bringeth forth death." That is the order of growth in evil, and the practical rule is, therefore, *obsta principiis*, put a stop to the process, if you can, in the very beginning. If Gehazi had not cast those longing eyes upon the Syrian wealth, he would never have entered upon the series of acts which culminated in his great lie, and in his life-long leprosy. If Christ our Lord is to reign over our hearts and tongues, He must be enthroned, first of all, by His Spirit, in those hearts out of which, in His absence, evil desires are flowing.

And a second lesson is the danger of thinking that great religious advantages of themselves protect a man against grievous sins. The illusion is common. Experience in all ages quite contradicts it. What religious advantages in that day could be greater than those of Gehazi? Naaman, while still a pagan, could have told Gehazi that a lie is moral degradation; and the high aspirations for a new religious life in the court and the people of Israel, which Gehazi would have often heard from his master's lips, should have led him to think that he, too, lived in a moral atmosphere in which attention to the simplest and primary rules of good living might be taken for granted. A lofty ideal, like the Sermon on the Mount, or like the discourse in the upper room, does not oblige those who have it before their eyes to be true even to those virtues which the heathen honoured; the grace of the Holy Spirit, and of the Christian sacraments, does not put force upon reluctant wills, or compel us to practise even natural goodness if we are not so minded. What can be more distressing than the spectacle of men whose education and friendships and work at times, it may be, pointed to all the higher standards of the Gospel, and who yet, in the presence of temptation, have fallen below what is required of men of the world? "Let him that thinketh he standeth take heed lest he fall."

And the last lesson is the priceless value of truthfulness in the soul's life. No advantage whatever of mind, or body, or estate, can counterbalance the misery of indifference to truth. No faults, however grave, are irreparable when the soul still clings to a love of truth. Truth is the basis of all other natural virtues in the human soul. It is the basis of all true religion, courage, justice, temperance. What are these but products of the sense of truth, dictating the forms of virtuous effort which are required by different circumstances? It is the sense of truth, as well as the voice of the Apostle, which tells us that if we say that we have no sin, we deceive ourselves, and the truth is not in us; but that if we confess our sins, God is faithful and just to forgive us our sins. It is the sense of truth which bids us pray for God's pardoning mercy in Jesus Christ, because we know what we are as sinners. It is the sense of truth which leads us to seek God's grace from His Holy Spirit and in His sacraments, for we know our weakness when we are left to ourselves. Truth — it is the one condition of all moral and religious progress. It were, indeed, better, in the phrase of the old Greeks, even to perish in the light than to miss truth altogether; but, as matters stand, we Christians know that "if we walk in the light as God is in the light, we have fellowship one with another," and that, for the rest, "The blood of Jesus Christ His Son cleanseth us from all sin."

FOR ADDITIONAL INFORMATION ABOUT HENRY PARRY LIDDON:

Howard, Harry C. "Henry Parry Liddon." *Princes of the Christian Pulpit and Pastorate.* 2d series. Nashville: Cokesbury Press, 1928.
Johnston, John Octavius. *Life and Letters of Henry Parry Liddon.* London: Longmans, Green & Co., 1904.
Nicoll, W. Robertson. "Dr. Liddon." *Princes of the Church.* London: Hodder & Stoughton, 1921.
Russell, George William Erskine. *Dr. Liddon.* London: A. R. Mowbray & Co., 1905.
Wilkinson, William Cleaver. "Henry Parry Liddon." *Modern Masters of Pulpit Discourse.* New York: Funk & Wagnalls Co., 1905.

FOR OTHER SERMONS BY HENRY PARRY LIDDON:

Sermons Preached Before the University of Oxford. 8 vols., 2d series. Oxford: Oxford University Press, 1868–1879.
Some Words for God. 8 vols., 1st series. Oxford: Oxford University Press, 1865.
Also: *Thoughts on Present Church Troubles* (1881), *Christmastide in St. Paul's* (1889), *Sermons on Some Words of Christ* (1892), *Sermons on Some Words of St. Paul* (1898).

ROBERT WILLIAM DALE

1829-1895

ROBERT WILLIAM DALE, The Mansell Collection

ROBERT WILLIAM DALE

1829	*Born December 1 in London*
1843	*Experienced religious conversion*
1846	*Entered Spring Hill College, Birmingham, England*
1853	*Graduated from college and became copastor of Carr's Lane Congregational Church in Birmingham*
1858	*Lectured at Spring Hill College*
1859	*Became pastor of Carr's Lane Congregational Church*
1866	*Published sermons,* Discourses on Special Occasions
1869	*Elected to chairmanship of Congregational Union*
1877	*Delivered the Yale Lectures on Preaching*
1887	*Visited Australia*
1895	*Died on March 15*

BY THE TIME he was seventeen years old he had preached his first sermon and published his first book. For the rest of his life his main interest would center in preaching and writing. Robert William Dale was no child prodigy, but early in life he knew his goal and set out to attain it. He became one of England's most effective – and controversial – preachers.

LIFE AND TIMES

Dale was born in a modest home in London. Except for a younger brother born when Dale was a teenager, he was the only surviving child of several brothers and sisters. His mother exerted a strong religious influence over her son, and more than any other one person was probably responsible for his decision to become a preacher.

During his early years of school Dale did not distinguish himself as a scholar. At fourteen he left home and became an assistant schoolmaster at Andover. But he found that the teaching profession was not suited to him; after eighteen months in the position, he was ready to quit. From outward appearances these months were a total failure. Yet during that time he experienced a crisis in his religious experience which was to alter the direction of his life. In these months as an assistant schoolmaster he seriously pondered his relation to God. A sermon Dale heard when he was thirteen had awakened his religious interests. He initiated a search to try to discover peace in the midst of the religious storm raging within him. Finally he came to a sense of assurance about his salvation. About this experience he said, "How I cannot tell, all came clear; I ceased thinking of myself and of my faith, and thought only of Christ; and then I wondered that I should have been perplexed for even a single hour."

When he was fourteen years old, Dale was received as a member of the Congregational Church at Andover. About a year later he began to do some preaching. Realizing that he needed special training he searched for the financial support necessary to attend college, but he was unsuccessful and returned to teaching. When he was seventeen, the school in which he was teaching was closed because of financial difficulty. Friends guaranteed the money he needed to enter college, and Dale began his studies at Spring Hill College in Birmingham. Birmingham was to be his home for the rest of his life.

Dale preached from time to time in the churches near the college, including Carr's Lane Congregational Church, where he relieved the pastor, Dr. J. A. James, who was ill at the time. He made such an impression upon the people that he was asked to return. Finally he became the associate pastor of the church. His preaching excited not only interest but controversy. Dale was no man to back away from controversy. He continued to preach sermons in which his doctrinal emphasis severely troubled a number of the members of the congregation. Unknown to Dale, the pastor, Dr. James, intervened and urged the people to be patient with the young minister.

When James died, Dale became the pastor of the church. This was to be his only church; he was thirty when he became its pastor and served for thirty-six years. Dale was a successful minister. Noted more for his civic interests than for his pastoral ability, he nonetheless provided a balanced ministry for the church.

His activities carried him beyond the realm of the local church in Birmingham. He was also an author and a theologian. He was editor of *The Congregationalist*, a paper published by the Congregationalists in England. More important, he was the author of numerous books, pamphlets, articles, and sermons. In his biography, the list of Dale's writings takes eight pages; a total of 128 items are listed. Many of these publications were on theological themes. He was regarded by many of his contemporaries as a perceptive and creative theologian.

Civic activities also consumed much of his time. He believed that a minister had a responsibility to be active in citizenship affairs. He was a member of the Liberal party in England. Among his close friends were Gladstone and Chamberlain. He was so influential in Birmingham that the city's representatives in Parliament were often referred to as "Dale's men." It was generally conceded that a politician who was opposed by Dale had little chance of winning any election in Birmingham.

His civic duties also led him into the field of education. He worked hard at improving education not only in his own city but throughout England. Dale served as a member of the Birmingham school board and a member of the Royal Commission on Elementary Education. He was instrumental in moving Spring College from Birmingham and establishing it as Mansfield College at Oxford.

Dale displayed rare balance in his ministry. He was a strong advocate of missions, a believer in evangelism, and a proponent of ethical preaching. He displayed the rare quality of weaving all of these interests together in a complementary rather than a conflicting way. He frequently made appeals for mission causes. He was exceptionally persuasive in this concern and led many to become active in mission associations in England. In evangelism, he not only stressed evangelism within his own church but also cooperated in broader evangelistic efforts. When Dwight L. Moody came to Birmingham, Dale cooperated with him and supported him. The after-meetings and follow-up efforts particularly excited Dale. He welcomed into his church over a hundred persons who were the fruit of the Moody revival.

Others, however, emphasized missions and evangelism in his era, but none were his superior when it came to preaching on ethical themes; some of his greatest sermons were on these subjects. Sermons such as "Christ and the State," "Christ and the Controversies of Christendom," and "Christian Worldliness" are not only among his best sermons, but also rank among the best expressions ever of the Christian faith as it is applied to life.

Dale emphasized many ethical subjects. Birmingham was an industrial city under the strains of the Industrial Revolution. Much of his emphasis was directed toward the privileges and problems of family life in an industrial and urban society, the relation between employer and employee, wealth and property as stewardship, and the municipal duties of Christians. He also spoke to specific local and national issues as they arose.

He stressed the virtues of socialism but was also aware of its weaknesses. He realized that a radical transformation of human nature would be necessary if socialism were to succeed. A popular description of socialism states: "Socialism says, 'What is thine, is mine'; Christianity says, 'What is mine is thine'; the difference is infinite." Dale added his own emphasis: "Christianity really teaches us to say, 'What seems thine is not thine; what seems mine is not mine; whatever thou hast belongs to God; and whatever I have belongs to God; you and I must use what we have according to God's will.' "[1]

The most striking aspect of his ethical teaching concerned civic duties. He dismissed as flagrant hypocrisy the idea that political duty was inconsistent with spirituality. He was convinced that it narrowed the message of Christ to limit it to individual souls and not to extend that message to the social order. Dale insisted that a man might have as clear a divine call to become a member of Parliament or a municipal councilor as to go as a missionary to a foreign land. He called for Christians to run for public office; it was not enough merely to vote; a citizen should serve in positions of responsibility. To do otherwise, he stressed, was to open the doors to a downhill plunge into the pit of social chaos. According to Dale, the will of God must be done not only in the church but also in the

---

1. R. W. Dale, *Laws of Christ for Common Life* (London: Hodder & Stoughton, 1911), p. 35.

family, on the farm, in the counting-house, in the courts of the kings, in the college, in the school, in all of life.

A key to the thought of Dale on the Christian's responsibility in the world is his concept of the relation of secular and sacred. He declared that as the doctrines and the ethics of the Christian revelation are inseparable, so also are the secular and sacred orders inseparable. This statement reaches the heart of his thought: "God himself has done and is always doing a great deal of work that we must call secular." He further states: "It is as secular a work to create the sun to give light in the daytime, as to make a lamp, or to build gas works, or to manufacture gas to give light at night." In consequence he said, "A secular work is just of the same kind as a great part of God's work."[2]

Dale added a divine luster to daily work. He called upon all men engaged in worthy vocations to look upon themselves as laboring for God's cause. He insisted that vocations are complementary comrades fighting side by side in a great army under the command of God against want, ignorance, disorder, and sin.

No man can be as deeply involved in the issues of his day as Dale without being controversial. And Dale was most certainly controversial. Nevertheless, he had a quality about him which seemed to spare him from much personal enmity. He created hostility by the stands he took on many issues, both theological and social. Dale tackled most of the tough and explosive topics of his time and tried to deal with them from the perspective of the Christian faith. Controversial issues in theology were rampant at that time; the struggles between liberalism and orthodoxy swept many into verbal combat. The conflict between Calvinism and Arminianism often disrupted the fellowship of church groups. Dale dealt with the themes of Calvinism, of Christian doctrine, and of the Christian faith as it related to modern thought.

The most explosive theological controversy of his career centered on the established Church of England. Dale insisted that financial support of the Church of England by the government as the only established church was wrong. He believed that establishment was bad both for the church and for the state. He argued persuasively and frequently against the exclusive establishment of the Church of England. This stand

2. Ibid., p. 5.

won many enemies for him among the ranks of the established clergy. Yet the best-known preacher of the Church of England, Henry Parry Liddon, corresponded cordially with Dale and even requested his prayers.

He was also frequently entangled in social controversies. Many felt that he should remain silent on political issues; he believed that to do so would be treasonous not only to his nation but also to his faith. Therefore he took an active role in politics and stood clearly in the ranks of the Liberal party.

Conflicts between the poor and the rich, between labor and management, between the aristocracy and the common man engaged Dale's attention. His sympathies were clearly on the side of the common poor. He called for reform in the economic system; he insisted that every man should have the opportunity to work and to earn a decent wage. Dale not only talked about such issues, but he was willing to become involved in the political machinery necessary to bring about reform.

Issues within his own denomination also received his careful attention. He served in responsible positions within his denomination: in 1869 he was elected to the chairmanship of the Congregational Union, and in 1887 he visited Australia at the request of Australian Congregationalists who invited him to come in an effort to revitalize the churches.

The personality of Robert Dale was molded by his home, his education, and his times. His health also played a large role in his life; he suffered from ill health throughout his life. This weakness resulted in several breakdowns and may have accounted for some of his tendency to withdraw and to remain aloof from people. He was so absorbed in his work that he quite often forgot to relate personally to those around him. Toward the end of his life he became even more distant and lonely. He withdrew from most of the organizations in which he had played such a significant role.

From time to time some zealous Christians have contended that evangelism and ethics cannot be mixed, and that a preacher should remain aloof from public affairs. Robert William Dale is evidence that such sentiments are false. He was a man who blended evangelism and ethics, preaching and public service in an effective ministry. "Dale of Birmingham," as he was affectionately called, was known as "an unworldly man of the world." This is as he would have liked it.

When he died on Wednesday evening, March 13, 1895, he left behind not only a significant body of writings and a great reputation, but also a virile, active, dynamic church. His successor was to be another famous preacher, J. H. Jowett.

PREACHING AND SERMONS

In 1877 Dale delivered the seventh in the series of Yale Lectures on Preaching. He was the first Englishman invited to participate in this historic lectureship. His work was among the best ever done in the series, and the excellent quality of these lectures was largely responsible for establishing a high standard of performance for the subsequent lectures. Canon Liddon, an objective and qualified critic, was enthusiastic in his praise of Dale's lectures.

Whatever Dale's power in the pulpit – and he has been called "probably the most impressive pulpit personage of the Free Churches in the nineteenth century"[3] – it was certainly not due to his appearance. His face was so swarthy that an old lady who had previously refused to contribute to missions began to give after hearing him preach; she said that after having seen what God could do "with that poor Hindoo," she could refuse no longer. Others describe him less strikingly as "dignified" and "a personable gentleman."

The Yale Lectures provide the primary source for understanding the preaching methods of Dale; without them a major conflict of opinion about Dale's preaching would be left unresolved. This conflict concerns Dale's effectiveness in sermon delivery. John Brown, in his *Puritan Preaching in England*, described Dale's delivery as monotonous and lacking in emotion. He attributed this fault to his "close, compact, and weighty style of writing."[4] Brown asserted that only one thing could be learned from Dale's delivery: ". . . that *stateliness* of style, elaborate literary finish, even in the hands of a master, is *not* the most effective style for the pulpit. That which may make a man's work good as literature may mar it for spoken discourse."[5]

---

3. Horton Davies, *Worship and Theology in England, 1850–1900* (Princeton: Princeton University Press, 1962), p. 322.
4. John Brown, *Puritan Preaching in England* (New York: Charles Scribner's Sons, 1900), p. 252.
5. Ibid., pp. 257–58.

Dale himself admitted in his diary that his primary preaching quality as described by others — whether spoken as a criticism or a complaint — was "stateliness." He said: "I have a dread of aiming at the 'popular' method of treatment, arising from a dread of aiming at 'popularity.'" Later he described his tendency to sacrifice communication for intellectual weightiness as "a fatal defect."

There must be some truth to these criticisms of his delivery. Once when his church was conducting a study of means for improving their worship, a layman delivered a paper on the place of the pulpit in the church. As a criticism he stated that Dale's preaching "moved at a height — intellectual and spiritual — far above that of the congregation generally." This criticism pained Dale greatly and kept him awake for many nights. And yet on reflection, he came to feel that the criticism was just. Garvie said of this incident, "His delivery of the sermons was, as a hearer testified, adversely affected by this mode of composition. It tended to monotony, and lack of pathos; the intellectual predominated over the emotional." All of these comments reflect a heavy, pedantic pulpit style marked by weighty argument and serious thought but lacking in natural, extemporaneous expression.

On the other hand, Edgar DeWitt Jones, in *The Royalty of the Pulpit,* said that Dale ". . . was an impassioned orator when the occasion so demanded and always he was a lucid, fluent speaker. . . ."[6] Nicoll, writing at the time of Dale's death, attributed to him "one of the most perfect styles in the whole range of ancient literature," and spoke of Dale as "eloquent." Dale himself said that he believed in an extemporaneous style; he advocated a careful and exact preparation which provides a man with "what he is going to say," but not with the exact words with which he will clothe his thoughts — all of which is entirely in conflict with the other reports on his preaching.

Without Dale's lectures on preaching the matter would remain in utter confusion. In his sixth lecture, however, "Extemporaneous Preaching and Style," Dale quickly clears up the confusion:

> About the comparative advantages of preaching from a manuscript and preaching extemporaneously, I have

6. Edgar DeWitt Jones, *The Royalty of the Pulpit* (New York: Harper & Bros., 1951), p. 27.

some difficulty in speaking. It seems to me that the over-whelming weight of the argument is on the side of extemporaneous preaching; but I have very rarely the courage to go into the pulpit without carrying with me the notes of my sermon, and occasionally I read every sentence from the first to the last.

The contrast between my theory of preaching and my practice is in this respect very glaring. . . . Some of the worst faults . . . which I have entreated you to avoid, are the faults and the mistakes which I have found it most difficult to avoid myself; and the bitterness with which I may have spoken of these vices has come from the soreness of heart with which I remember the extent to which they have impaired the power of my own preaching, and from the resentment I feel against them as my own persistent enemies — resentment which has been intensified by prolonged and not very successful struggles to escape from their power. The methods of work which I recommend to you are not mere the-oretical suggestions. I have tested their value; but some of them I began to try too late.[7]

This statement explains the reason that many of Dale's listeners objected to his preaching style, while other critics could speak of him as "eloquent." Apparently Dale believed in extemporaneous preaching and could do it effectively when he chose, but his nerve usually failed him and he carried a manu-script — or at least full notes — with him into the pulpit. This statement in the Yale Lectures suggests that he attempted to change his method toward the end of his life, but that he also doubted his success in doing so.

Other facts about Dale's preaching ability are not so hard to determine. He was predominantly a doctrinal preacher and an evangelical one. He did not believe in theological speculation: "Let me recommend to you, therefore, to build up your theology in private, and not to perplex your congregations with specula-tions which are only half finished, with theories which are in process of formation. Let the walls of the building be dry before you ask people to come in and live in it."[8] He followed his own advice; as a preacher he was thorough in his thought and care-ful in his interpretation. He believed that it was his first and

7. R. W. Dale, *Nine Lectures on Preaching* (New York: George H. Doran Co., n.d.), pp. 151–52.
8. Ibid., p. 15.

foremost duty to instruct his people in the great truths of the Christian faith.

No doubt part of the criticism of his preaching resulted from his thorough treatment of doctrinal matters. That criticism must not become overbalancing, for there is abundant evidence that his preaching was thoroughly appreciated by his congregation, even if occasionally it was a bit too much for them. When someone heard that Dale was preaching doctrinal sermons at Carr's Lane, he said to him, "I hear that you are preaching doctrinal sermons to the congregation at Carr's Lane; they will not stand it." Dale's immediate reply was, "They will have to stand it." His congregation did stand it, and more than that, they developed an intense pride in the quality of their pulpit.

Dale succeeded as a doctrinal preacher because of his practical approach to the subject:

> Christian doctrine was not to him merely an intellectual system. . . . He preached doctrine, not as an intellectual system, but as a means of conveying God's saving truth and grace to men through Christ. Doctrine in this sense was inseparable from man's salvation; . . . Doctrinal preaching, then, in his hands was not remote or abstract, but personal and experimental. Doctrine was verified in Christian experience.[9]

He believed in using plain language. He challenged the preacher to develop to the highest his ability to use the English language: "You have no more right to injure the national language than to chip a statue or to run a penknife through a picture in the national museum."

Although Dale was deeply involved in social action and has been remembered for his vigorous involvement in civic affairs, he was zealously concerned about the personal conversion of individuals to the Christian faith. J. Guinness Rogers, speaking on March 17, 1895, at the Sunday morning memorial service for Dale which preceded his funeral on Monday, said:

> His work was pre-eminently that of the preacher. It is true that he never confined his activities to the pulpit, and that he was a great citizen as well as a great preacher.

9. Harry C. Howard, *Princes of the Christian Pulpit and Pastorate,* 2d series (Nashville: Cokesbury Press, 1928), pp. 298–99.

... But the master-passion of his life was the conversion of souls, and for this he toiled and watched, he
wept and prayed.[10]

In the evening service, Dr. Fairbairn agreed: "He was indeed a
genuine son of the Evangelical Revival. He had its love for
souls, its passion for saving men, its belief in the Gospel as the
Power of God unto salvation." Fairbairn said that even his
doctrinal preaching had a personal note: "He believed that
theology lived in living men, and that apart from the true medium of the renewed spirit it could not live at all."[11]

Dale's sermons are characterized by their balanced blending
of ethical concern, Christian doctrine, and personal appeal.

---

10. *Memorial Sermons Preached in Carr's Lane Chapel on Death of Dr.
R. W. Dale*, unpublished pamphlet, funeral bulletin from Carr's Lane Chapel,
1895, p. 11.
11. Ibid., p. 13.

Sermons

THE WORK OF THE HOLY SPIRIT IN THE CONVERSION OF MEN

"Ye men of Israel, why marvel ye at this? or why look ye so earnestly on us, as though by our own power of holiness we had made this man to walk?" (Acts 3:12).

IT WAS VERY NATURAL that the people who saw the lame beggar, whom they knew so well, walking and leaping and praising God, should crowd round Peter and John, who had healed him, and should look at them with wonder and awe. I think that we should have done the same. They had seen the man carried morning after morning to the gate of the temple; they had seen him lying there every hour in the day; they probably knew that he had been born lame; many of them, no doubt, had often thrown him a few copper coins as they passed through the magnificent gate; and now they saw him not only walking, but, as was natural in a man who had just got the use of his feet, leaping and praising God. The man would not let the apostles go, but kept fast hold of their long Eastern robes. The people came thronging into the cloisters, called Solomon's porch, on the eastern side of the temple, and stood looking at Peter and John, greatly wondering.

Peter, seeing the temper of the crowd, addresses them. He tells them that the miracle had been wrought by the power of Jesus of Nazareth, whom they had killed, but whom God had raised from the dead. They thought that His claims were crushed when He was crucified on Calvary; but God had glorified Him, and He, through the faith which the apostles had in Him, had made the man strong whom they saw and knew.

The disposition of the crowd to make heroes of the apostles when they should have recognised in the miracle the power of God is an illustration of a common instinct. The instinct is not altogether mischievous. When through foreign invasion or internal revolution the

Reprinted from R. W. Dale, *The Evangelical Revival and Other Sermons* (London: Hodder & Stoughton, 1880), pp. 171–92.

154

institutions of society are broken up, the blind submission which a whole nation sometimes yields to a popular chief, whose words or achievements have touched its imagination, or to the heir of an illustrious name associated with the past glories of the State, sometimes renders it possible to restore law and order. The intellectual supremacy of great men, a supremacy which has been acknowledged in some rare cases for a long succession of centuries, has also its uses; it preserves something like order in our intellectual life. Aristotle and the great poets of Greece have not only received the homage of the commonalty of mankind, they have ruled and directed the men of genius of later ages, and have prevented a great waste of intellectual power. It is the same with that conspicuous moral excellence which wins more reverential homage than that which we offer to genius in even its loftiest forms. The lives of philanthropists, patriots, and saints have stimulated obscure and unknown men to live nobly, and have raised the common standard of morality; their example has been a law to successive generations.

But have you ever observed that there is nothing that can be called hero-worship either in the Old Testament or the New? The Jews had their daring fighting men, their poets, their orators, their statesmen, their saints; but you find no disposition in the Old Testament Scriptures to attribute to any of them the kind of authority attributed to great men by other races; you find no disposition to surround them with the same kind of glory. The heroism of Wallace is commemorated in the national songs of Scotland, and the Swiss have transmitted from generation to generation the story of the heroism of William Tell; but there is no Psalm to celebrate the heroism of David. The women of Israel came out to meet him after one of his victories, and welcomed him with songs of triumph; but then, as far as we can see, the personal celebration was over. Nor does Jewish history exalt Moses as the history of Europe exalts Charlemagne, as the history of England exalts Alfred or Elizabeth. The genius of Isaiah does not receive the same kind of homage that we concede to the genius of Dante or of Shakespeare. There is the same absence of hero-worship in the New Testament. Christ stands apart. He is God manifest in the flesh. To have seen Him is to have seen the Father. But the apostles assume no personal greatness; no personal greatness is claimed for them. Their authority was the authority of their Master. Luke never analyses their power nor dwells upon their personal qualities. He tells the story of their work with what might appear a complete absence of admiration for the men themselves. That they were in any way remarkable and eminent is never intentionally suggested. The saints of the Old Testament and the saints of the New are transparent; God shines through them. Their own personal importance is not merely suppressed; neither they nor their historians ever had to suppress it; it is never thought of. The history of the very greatest of them is a striking commentary on the words of our Lord: "Let your light . . . shine before men that they may glorify your Father who is in heaven."

That is the Christian law; and, indeed, as I have said, it is the law which had been illustrated in the Jewish Scriptures long before Christ appeared. Are men steadfast in righteousness, fervent in charity, temperate, fearless? Do not glorify *them;* glorify God who made them so good. Are they wise? Glorify God who is the Giver of wisdom. Have they genius? Glorify God who kindled its fires. Have they wrought great deliverances for mankind? Why look ye on *them* as though by their own power or holiness they had wrought these deliverances? Joshua fought well; but when the men of later days look back upon his victories, they say—

"We have heard with our ears, O God, our fathers have told us, what work Thou didst in their days, in the times of old. How Thou didst drive out the heathen with Thy hand, and plantedst them. For they got not the land in possession by their own sword, neither did their own arm save them: but Thy right hand, and Thine arm, and the light of Thy countenance, because Thou hadst a favour unto them."

This was the temper of the nation in its noblest times.

And when we come to the New Testament we find the greatest of the apostles saying, "I planted, Apollos watered, and God gave the increase." This address of St. Peter's about the miracle is a vivid illustration of the spirit of both Testaments. Good works are God's works; it is His strength which makes us strong, His wisdom which makes us wise. We are His servants, and the honour of all our success is His and not ours.

In recent times we have failed to maintain the traditional spirit of Judaism and of Christianity. We dwell on the personal goodness, the temperament, and the intellectual power of Peter, Paul, and John; we treat them as ordinary historians treat sovereigns like Elizabeth and Cromwell, statesmen like Burghley and Walpole and Chatham. We inquire what there was in the men that accounted for the success of their work—what power, what holiness, explains their achievements. No doubt their personal character and their intellectual force had a direct relation to their work. Peter's vehemence and warmth of nature, his natural audacity and his vigorous sense; Paul's keen, logical subtlety, his passion, his restless enterprise and his affectionate heart; the quiet depths in the soul of St. John, lying far beneath the stormy energy of his passion, as the calm depths of the Atlantic lie beneath the winds and tempests which sometimes disturb its surface—all these had a part in determining the kind of service to which each of them was appointed. They received supernatural gifts varying according to their native capacity, and according to the type of character which had been formed by their personal history. But the gifts were from God; their power was His. Their work was God's work, not their own. In the spiritual, as in the natural life, when the blind receive sight, Christ gives it; when the lame walk, it is Christ who makes them strong; when the dead rise, they rise at Christ's voice: "His name through faith in His name, hath made this man strong" is the explanation of all wonders.

Wycliffe, Luther, Calvin, Baxter, Wesley, and Whitefield, what were they all but ministers, servants of God by whom England or Europe came to know and believe a truer Gospel than it knew or believed before? They should be transparent to us as the Jewish prophets and heroes were transparent to the ancient saints, and as the Christian apostles were transparent to the early Chruch. Their noble qualities, their eloquence, their learning, their courage, their zeal, may be recognised, and may be honoured as God's gifts; but still it was not their power or their holiness that first loosened and then broke the fetters by which the spiritual life of nations was bound – drove the darkness away and brought in the true light that now shineth – called men from the graves into the upper air and the sunlight of heaven; it was *God* who did it all.

This holds true of all effective spiritual work in our own time, and it is a truth which we may well consider this evening. We are meeting in connection with the ordination of the Pastor of many persons who are in this congregation. He will conduct your worship; he will teach those of you who know something of the infinite love and righteousness of God how to do God's will. I want you to remember that it will not be by the "power" or the "holiness" of your minister that your worship will be made devout or that your knowledge of God will be enriched. Apart from the light and power of the Spirit of Christ the work of my friend will be a failure.

I understand that the congregation has been formed very recently, and that a great part of my friend's work will be directed to those who have not yet taken sides with Christ. Perhaps, therefore, it is especially necessary that I should insist on the truth that when men are prevailed upon to submit to Christ's authority, to break with sin and to begin to live a Christian life, their great decision is not to be attributed to the impassioned eloquence, the vigorous argument, the pathetic entreaty of the preacher, nor to his personal sanctity, nor to his fervent zeal; it is not to be attributed, I say, either to the preacher's "power" or to the preacher's "holiness," but to the direct appeal of the Spirit of God to the conscience and to the heart. This is the truth on which I intend to speak to-night.

You remember that Christ promised that when the Spirit came He would do a wonderful work in the world as well as in the Church. During His earthly life Christ Himself had been the great preacher, and when He was about to die the apostles must have been in despair, not only about themselves, but about the fortunes of the Gospel. What lips had a charm like His? Who could speak with the pathos, the tenderness, the authority with which He had spoken? What faultless beauty as well as perfect simplicity there was in His parables! What power in His appeals to the consciences of men! How wonderfully He could excite their hopes, fire their imagination, melt their hearts! What terror there was in His threatenings! How was the Gospel to be preached to any purpose when He was no longer in the world to preach it? But if it was expedient for His friends that He should go away, it was also expedient for the world; for when the Spirit came He would convince the world concerning sin and righteousness and judgment. The Spirit was to comfort, strengthen, and teach those who loved Christ already; the Spirit was also to bring the enemies of Christ to Christ's feet.

The leaders of the Evangelical Revival believed this with all their heart; they relied upon the presence and power of the Spirit of God for the conversion of men. I wonder whether we have the same faith.

Everything short of the actual conversion of men to God we can accomplish without God's help. Canvass the town for children and you can fill your Sunday schools. Make the teaching interesting and attractive, let the rooms be bright and warm and pleasant, have cheerful singing, let the teacher be kindly, genial, and earnest, and you can keep the children when you have them; and not only keep them, but enable them to pass excellent examinations in Old Testament history and New Testament doctrine; and, more than that, you can soften their manners and refine their tastes and elevate their morals. All this you can do without God; if you are satisfied with this there is no need to pray to God. But if you want the children to love and serve Christ, the Spirit of God must be with you, and must work directly on the inner thought and life of your scholars.

Build an attractive church, get a good organ and choir, let there be an educated and earnest and eloquent man in the pulpit—fearless, thoughtful, and kindly—and you can get a crowd of people to hear him. He may produce a profound impression by his preaching. The great topics of the Christian preacher—life, death, and eternity, the righteousness of God and the sin of man, the Divine pity and human sorrow, human temptations and human duties, the fair hopes of childhood, the hot passions of youth, the cares of maturer years, the lassitude and weariness of old age, the struggles of the Church in other centuries and in our own days, its reverses and its triumphs, its doctrinal controversies, its conflicts with doubt and with sin—all these are topics which have an incomparable and unrivalled charm for all sorts of men. Let the preacher have learning, intellectual vigour and freshness, wit, imagination, ardour, and sympathy, he can use them all, and men will throng to listen to him. They will listen with admiration and sometimes with deep emotion; they will be agitated and excited; yes, and they will become ashamed of many of their sins and will begin to discharge many neglected duties; religious sentiment will be created; they will sing devout hymns with profound feeling; will listen to prayers with reverence and awe. All this may be done without God; but if men are to be moved to real penitence, and are to be inspired with real faith, the light and power of the Holy Spirit must reach individual hearts.

Many of us know what this means. For years we were familiar with truths which ought to have exerted irresistible control over us; we believed them; sometimes we felt their power. But we can remember when these very truths came to us as though we had never known them before. Perhaps there was excitement when they came, perhaps they came to us in our most quiet moods. However they came, it seemed hardly possible to resist them. The Divine love in its tenderness, the Divine authority in its majesty, the infinite mercy of Christ, the guilt of unbelief, the beauty, the righteousness, and the immortal hopes of the Christian life, these, or some of these, were presented to us in a way which carried our whole nature with them. Perhaps we were listening to a sermon; but we had listened to sermons before, and to sermons not less clear, not less impressive, not less earnest, and had listened unmoved; others heard the same sermon and it did not touch them. Perhaps we were reading a book; but we had read the book before, and it had never taught us what we now learnt, and others have read the same book and learnt nothing from it. What made the difference was a silent voice to which then, for the first time, we consented to listen. The Spirit of God came to us, and we suffered Him to lead us into the truth.

This work of His is not, as some theologians have described it, a work of irresistible grace; it is the direct appeal of the Infinite Spirit to the human spirit, fruitful if yielded to in immortal blessings; but, like other appeals, it may be resisted.

Our perverse reluctance to think of God aright, and to believe with all our heart that all life and light come from Him, is inexplicable. We have to learn the same lesson over and over again in many forms —our life seems spent in learning it; and we look back upon wasted years, years of unvictorious struggle, of unprofitable labour, of hope only partially fulfilled or perhaps altogether baffled, and mourn that we had not learnt the open secret earlier which would have made all those years bright with noble and glorious success.

The lesson has to be learnt at the beginning of the religious life, and some of us learn it very slowly. We want the pardon of sin and that change in the very centre and root of our religious life which will render it possible for us to do the will of God. And we try—perhaps for months, perhaps for years—to make our penitence for sin more agonising and our hunger and thirst for righteousness more keen, hoping that at last we shall have rest of heart, the assurance that sin has been forgiven, and strength to keep God's commandments. It is all in vain; and then we discover what we knew from the first — that we can trust God to forgive us our sins, and to forgive us our impenitence too, and to inspire us with the life and power of the Holy Ghost: we trust Him and we pass into a new world.

But the lesson has to be learnt over again. We are now liberated from distress about our past guilt, and we know that we are the sons of God and the heirs of His glory; but we find that we are unequal to many duties, and are overcome by many temptations. We subject ourselves to discipline; perhaps we fast; we certainly pray; we think upon the transcendent motives to righteousness — the judgment to come, the infinite mercy which died for us, the beauty of holiness, the glory, honour, and immortality which are to crown patient continuance in well-doing. It is all in vain; we make no way; we are perpetually thwarted, hindered, defeated. And then, again, we discover what a child might have taught us, what we always knew, that evil passions are to be burnt down to their very roots by the fire of God; that we are to be strong for holy living in the strength of God: we trust in Him once more, and as long as we trust we are kept in perfect peace, and our life is free and bright and triumphant.

But we have not learnt the lesson even now. We engage in Christian work, and are hot and eager to rescue men from sin and eternal death. We do our best — teachers, preachers, or visitors, whatever else we may be — yes, our very best, and hardly anything comes of it. We put all our strength into our work — God has a right to ask for it; we spare no time, no energetic effort of thought; we ask how other men have succeeded, and try to learn from them how we may succeed ourselves; we are in deadly earnest and struggle as if for our own salvation, and still we accomplish nothing. Then once more we discover what we always knew; God and only God can bring right home to man the truth which is on our lips: we trust in Him, and then our work begins to prosper.

I was never more deeply convinced than I am now that for the work of the Christian ministry it is necessary to secure men of conspicuous intellectual power, and men who have received the most thorough and stimulating and invigorating intellectual training. For the most ordinary duties of the ministry some fair measure of learning is necessary; and if a man is to speak on religion to any purpose, he must have the kind of power and discipline and knowledge which would enable him to speak to some purpose on other subjects. We have had enough, and more than enough, of ignorance, shallowness, and imbecility in the Christian pulpit. There is an Antinomianism in relation to Christian work not less fatal and far more subtle than the Antinomianism of the Christian life.

Men have argued that since they can do nothing for their own salvation without God, they will attempt nothing, and will leave all to Him. They might as well say that they can get no harvest without the rain of heaven and the heat and light of the sun, and that therefore they will not plough nor sow. And men have argued, that since Christian work can never achieve its highest results apart from the direct appeal of the Spirit of God to the souls of men, the intellectual power and cultivation of the teacher and preacher are worthless, that learning is worthless, and eloquence worthless, and that we should leave everything to God. What folly, what insanity there is in this! It is, I repeat, the very spirit, showing itself in Christian work, which when it shows itself in the personal Christian life we call Antinomianism.

But among ourselves there are not many who are likely to be infected with this heresy. Our peril—your peril and mine—lies in the opposite direction. We are in danger of forgetting that when we have done our utmost, everything will be in vain apart from the power of God.

We look back upon the great evangelists of past generations and think that if we could only have them with us again the most glorious days in the history of the Church would return. If St. Bernard were here, with his fiery passion, a passion which kindled his intellectual life as well as his heart; if Luther were here, with his frankness, his audacity and his immense moral force; if Whitefield were here, with his affectionate spirit and his charming eloquence; if Wesley were here, with his calm and resolute strength and his keen sagacity—then we might hope to see a great religious reformation in England. But what can *we* do—we whose ardour is so easily chilled, whose faith is so easily shaken, and to whom the spells by which genius can touch and subdue the hearts of men are quite unknown. This self-distrust is only the specious cover of a want of faith in God. The illustrious preachers of former days are with us no longer and seem to have left no successors; but the great Preacher of all is with us still—the only Preacher whose voice can raise the dead, the Preacher whose power achieved all the triumphs which we connect with the famous and sacred names in the history of Christendom. It is not for us to despair because Bernard, Luther, Whitefield, Wesley, have passed away. The despair would be the sign that we had ascribed their success to their own "power and holiness," instead of to the Spirit of God. Could these great saints come back again, it would not be to take the work from our hands because we are unequal to it, but to tell us that the same Spirit that was with them can still reach the hearts and consciences of men.

Even when we pray we sometimes forget that our trust should be in the Spirit of God. We ask that for the success of our work we ourselves may have a larger knowledge of the thought of God, a more fervent passion for the honour of Christ, a profounder solicitude for the rescue of men from their sorrows and their sins—wise and necessary prayers, but incomplete, fatally incomplete. For the prayers imply that if we ourselves had greater "power," the power which would come to us from a deeper knowledge of God and a firmer loyalty to Christ and a more ardent love for mankind; if we had greater "holiness" — the holiness which would be the result of a more complete consecration of all our strength to God's service — we should be certain to be successful. This was not what the apostles thought — "Paul planted, Apollos watered, God gave the increase."

Let us cease to trust in men and trust only in God. Yes, in *God*; not in men; and not in ecclesiastical systems. For what is true of men is also true of ecclesiastical systems. It is not the perfection of its organisation that enables a Church to redeem men from their sins and to lead them in the paths of righteousness. There have been preachers in the Church of Rome, spite of its monstrous polity, who have done infinitely more for mankind and for God than whole crowds of preachers, eloquent, learned, and orthodox, in the purest of Protestant Churches. There is no "power," no "holiness" in Presbyterianism, in Methodism, in Congregationalism, in Episcopacy, to work the spiritual miracles by which the lives of individuals and of communities are transformed. The chief merit of an ecclesiastical system lies in the measure in which it is transparent and lets the glory of Christ shine through. We are in the right, as I think, in our ecclesiastical polity; we refuse to cover the windows of our church organisation with the purple and golden glories of a stately hierarchy; but if there is no sun shining in the heavens the simplest windows will let in no more light than those which are thickly covered with sacred legends. For it is not the windows that give the light, they only let it come into building. And even when the sun is shining — to keep up the illustration — it sometimes happens that the simplest windows are so covered with dust and dirt as to prevent the glory from breaking through, while windows of another sort, kept bright and clean, may permit the whole building to be filled with splendour. It is not a good ecclesiastical system, I repeat, that saves mankind, but Christ; the best system is that which lets nothing come between Christ and the Church.

The same test is to be applied to all theologies and to all methods of spiritual discipline. It is an incidental measure of their wisdom and their truth. Do they make us forget ourselves and remember only Christ? Do they break down everything that comes between the soul and Him who is the fountain of mercy and of power? The question of the *truth* of theologies is the first question to be settled, but this is an incidental test of their truth.

Tell me that my good works are necessary before Christ will forgive my sins, and you put months, and perhaps years, of painful moral struggle between me and Christ; tell me that He will forgive me at once, as soon as I come to Him, and that then He will stand by me in all my endeavours to keep His commandments, and Christ is already at my side at the very beginning of my new life. The doctrine of justification by works seems less likely to be true than the doctrine of justification by faith.

Tell me that to make sure of the Divine forgiveness I must confess my sins to a priest, and there is danger lest the priest should come between me and Christ. Tell me that I can confess to Christ Himself, and that the priest is unnecessary, then, again, Christ is near to me while I am in the agony of my repentance and while the dark shadow of evil years still lies heavily on my heart. The doctrine which affirms that the priest has power to absolve seems less likely to be true than the doctrine which denies it.

Tell me that the priest must consecrate the bread and the wine before the Church can have the Real Presence of Christ at the Lord's Supper, and then the Church must wait till the priest has pronounced the words of mystery and power. Tell me that wherever two or three are gathered together at the table of Christ, Christ is among them, and then there is no delay, either in His access to us, or our access to Him. Those who maintain the theory of Sacramentalism seem less likely to be in the right than those who reject it.

But here, too, we must remember that the truest and simplest doctrine may be made a fetich, an idol, and may come between the soul and Christ. If you think that any doctrine is so true and so simple that by its own "power" or "holiness" it will regenerate and save men, you will be separated from Christ as completely by the soundest belief as other men are by the most corrupt.

The truths which we have been considering should teach us all to be of good heart about the work which we call ours, but which is Christ's rather than ours. I appeal to ministers who are in the congregation to-night, and especially to you, my friend, whose ordination has brought us together. We are conscious — all of us — that we have little strength to do any noble service for God and for mankind. The consciousness deepens as we grow older. In our youth, perhaps, we had unmeasured hopes; we had not learnt the narrow limits of our powers; but the discovery has come to us with increasing years. We still think that we know something of God; but how dim our knowledge is! We love Him, and we love Him better than when our work began; but our love is very fitful, and even when most fervent it seems very cold. We try to speak for Him, but we speak with stammering lips. Ours is not the secret which some preachers have mastered, and by which they seem to have been able to charm great crowds of grown men and little children to live righteously and to rejoice in the love of God. We have neither the "power" nor the "holiness" to work any deliverance for our race.

It may be so; but at least we may have faith in Christ; and we may

be driven to a simpler faith in Him by the discovery that there is absolutely no reason for having faith in ourselves. If we thought we had
"power" we might trust in it; if we thought we had "holiness" we
might trust in it; but if we have learnt that we have neither, what can
we do but appeal to the mercy of Christ, who died for men, and to the
power of Christ, who is able to give to men the very life of God?

Neither our weakness nor our unworthiness is a reason for de-
spondency. If we had to measure our own strength and earnestness
against the difficulties of our work we might despair; but our confidence is in the strength and in the grace of the Lord Jesus Christ.
The results of our labour will transcend all that could be anticipated
from the labour itself. This kindles our enthusiasm, and is a motive
for strenuous exertion. If we are only loyal to Christ, perfectly loyal,
even *we* may do very much for the rescue of men from their sorrow
and their sin, and for the triumph of the love and righteousness of God.

The true minister of Christ does not stand alone; he is in alliance
with Christ Himself; this is the secret of the minister's power. Yes;
but he is also in alliance with his Church; and this may be the source
either of power or of weakness. I turn from my friend, who has been
ordained to-day, to you the members of his congregation, and ask you,
for your own sake, and for the sake of your minister, whom you are
welcoming with such cordiality of affection and such generous hope,
to remember that the success of his ministry depends as much upon
your fidelity to Christ as on his own. You and he are henceforth
confederate in one great work. Your prayers in solitary places will
inspire his words to crowded congregations with Divine power; cease
to pray, and the power will be absent. Your silent but hearty concurrence in his appeals to men to forsake sin and to do the will of God
will secure that mightier appeal of the Holy Spirit to the conscience
and the heart, in response to which alone men submit to the authority
of Christ, and trust in His infinite love; if you listen without deep
spiritual sympathy, without a keen solicitude for the conversion of
men, the energy of the Divine Spirit will be withdrawn. Your personal
integrity in the common duties of life, your kindliness and charity,
your earnestness in all good works, will be the most effective support
of the ethical and spiritual teaching of your minister and the supreme
proof of its power; your personal inconsistencies will defeat all his
exhortations to righteousness.

You remember the famous description of an orator. It was not his
voice alone that spoke; his eyes, his face, his hands, his feet—they
were all eloquent. And a Church is a living body. The minister is its
voice; but, if he is to speak to any purpose, the voice must not come
from a body struck with death, with fixed features, glassy eyes, and
rigid limbs; there would be something ghastly in *that*. Eyes, hands,
face, feet, must all have life and passion in them, and must all speak;
they must share the sorrow and alarm with which the minister tells

men of the infinite evil of sin, and the rapture with which he triumphs in the infinite love of God. Share his work and you will share his joy and his final reward. In every man rescued by his ministry from an irreligious life; in every man who through his words finds in God strength for the exhausting, monotonous struggle with temptation, and consolation in the troubles by which our earthly condition is perplexed and saddened; in every man who through his instruction, entreaty, and encouragement continues patiently in well-doing, and wins glory, honour, and immortality, you will see the answer to your own intercessions, and the triumph of your own earnestness and zeal.

CHRIST AND THE STATE

"Jesus therefore perceiving that they were about to come and take Him by force, to make Him king, withdrew again into the mountain Himself alone" (John 6:15).

WERE NOT THE PEOPLE wholly in the right? Did not our Lord miss a great chance when He refused the position which they offered Him? If a nation has the good fortune to discover such a man as our Lord was — a man so upright, so fearless, with such pity for suffering, such hatred of injustice, and with resources so immense — what can it do better than place in his hands supreme political power, all legislative, judicial, and administrative authority? For a king, according to Jewish ideas and traditions, was not a constitutional sovereign, limited by a Parliament, but a real king, governing as well as reigning. The people might have said — to use our modern language — "If we make this man king, He will give us an ideal economic and social order, just judges, an equitable system of taxation, institutions which will relieve and diminish existing poverty and will gradually make poverty impossible; He will bring prosperity to the whole nation." According to Plato, the

Reprinted from R. W. Dale, *Fellowship with Christ*, The Expositor's Library (London, New York: Hodder & Stoughton, 1891), pp. 192–215. The Annual Sermon preached on behalf of the Home Missions of the Baptist Union in Westbourne Park Chapel (Rev. Dr. Clifford's), on Friday evening, April 24th, 1891.

world will never be happy till its kings are philosophers, or its philosophers kings; and here was One whose wisdom transcended all the
wisdom of mortal men. A great opportunity had come to the Jewish
nation—an opportunity such as never came to any nation before, and
could never come to any nation again. They tried to take Jesus by force
and make Him king. Were they not wholly in the right?

And I ask again, Did not Jesus miss a great chance? Had He accepted the supreme authority, might He not have introduced into the
Jewish State economic reforms, which would have lessened the
hardships of large numbers of the people, changed the conditions
which made it difficult for them to live an upright and devout life,
brought home to them in the most effective way the power and the
beauty of His teaching concerning God and God's relations to mankind, and the relations of men to each other? Might He not have made
the Jewish State the illustration of an ideal political and social righteousness? Would not the visible realization of the principles and spirit
of His teaching in the actual order and life of a nation, have invested
His Gospel with an irresistible charm and been a decisive demonstration of its Divine origin? And our Lord Jesus Christ really claimed
sovereignty over men; He was the king of ancient Jewish prophecy
and hope—Why did He not consent to reign?

I

Yes, He claimed to be King, but not a king of the kind that these
people desired—a political Ruler, a Prince mightier indeed than other
earthly princes, but belonging to the same order, surrounded with
similar splendour, the leader of armies, imposing laws to punish
crime and to regulate agriculture and commerce, levying tribute on
subject races. This was their conception of a king; it was not His.

Suppose that He had consented to reign. Imagine that He has driven
out the Romans, that His armies are holding the roads into Palestine
from the North the South and the East, that He has powerful fleets at
Tyre and Sidon and riding off Joppa, so that the country is absolutely
safe from invasion. Imagine Him in Jerusalem, accepted there, as
well as in Galilee, as King of the Jewish nation. Now, what is He to do?
He has to provide for the administration of justice all over the country;
is it certain that He will be able to find just, sagacious, and courageous
magistrates? Even among the men who had lived with Him during a
great part of His earthly ministry there were conflicts for personal
supremacy; and one of them robbed the common purse. After re-
moving Caiaphas and the rest of the unscrupulous men who exercised
under the Romans supreme authority in Jerusalem, where is He to
look for men whom He can perfectly trust to fill their places?

What kind of laws can He establish? What social and economic order
can he set up? Ideal laws and an ideal order are only for an ideal people.

In constructing institutions it is necessary to take account of the capacity and the virtue of the people who have to work them. The best social and economic order for any particular nation is an order largely determined by its actual, material, intellectual, and moral condition. For example, representative institutions are admirable for a people on whom you can rely for public spirit, a willingness to undertake laborious and difficult duties in the public service, and a capacity for forming sound judgments on large questions of public policy. It may take time even for such a people to learn how to govern themselves wisely. They may make serious blunders, and may bring upon themselves great misfortunes; but the discipline of intelligence and of character which is secured by the discharge of grave public responsibilities will more than compensate for the transient sufferings which follow their political errors. If, however, those great qualities, which are necessary for the effective working of representative institutions, do not exist, if the germs of them do not exist, there will be such confusion and corruption in the conduct of public affairs, that by an imperious necessity these institutions will soon give place to another kind of government. Had Christ become King, He could not have organized the national life of the Jewish people on a noble model, for their national life itself was not noble.

Or take the department of criminal jurisprudence. Laws which are not supported by the moral convictions of the great mass of the people are always ineffective; they may do something, no doubt, to educate the national conscience, but they fail to do even that if they are far in advance of it. It would be useless for a Government to enact laws against theft, if the national conscience did not condemn theft; useless for a Government to enact laws protecting the sanctity of contracts, if the national conscience did not regard contracts as sacred. Take an illustration: the law of divorce which was given to the Jews was given to them, Christ says, because of the hardness of their hearts. In a social condition which allowed men to dismiss their wives at their own pleasure, it would have been useless to insist on the sacredness and permanence of the institution of marriage. Some check was imposed on this brutal licence when a man who divorced his wife was required to set down in writing the reasons why he divorced her. That was a very slight advance towards a better regulation of marriage, but it was an advance, and apparently it was all the advance that was possible. Your jurisprudence, I say, must take account of the actual moral condition of the people. Laws which punish as crimes acts which the national conscience allows, are powerless; if maintained at all, they must be maintained by a constant exertion of force. It may be necessary, in order to hold society together, and to lay the foundations of a better and nobler organization of the national life, for a Government to fight hard against practices which the moral sense of large masses of the people does not condemn; but while this struggle lasts the foundations of national order are shaken; there is civil war, though there may be no armies in the field.

If Christ Himself had become the King of the Jewish people, His legislation would necessarily have been lowered towards the level of the national morality. He would have had to tolerate many grave evils and to leave many grave offences unpunished. His laws could not have been the ideal laws of an ideal State.

There were other reasons which might well have prevented Him from accepting the power which the people wished to force upon Him. It was the miracle of the loaves and the fishes, of which you heard earlier in this service, that provoked the popular enthusiasm. No doubt the people thought that if He were their King all their material wants would be certain to receive satisfaction. Ah! but it is not Christ's first object to secure for men in this life outward conditions favourable to universal ease and comfort. That was clearly not His object in the creation of the material universe which He has built for our home. Men have to live by the sweat of their brow, and in most parts of the world they have to work hard in order to live. There are fogs and floods; harvests are blighted; there is intolerable heat; there is intolerable cold; men are disciplined to endurance by physical discomfort; their intellectual life is provoked to strenuous activity by the hardships and difficulties of their condition. The proverbial garden of the sluggard is not a reproach to Providence but to the sluggard. It was God's will that he should have not only a garden bright with flowers but that he should have the physical vigour, the industry, the intelligence that would come from cultivating it. God cares more for the man than for the garden. Nor is it Christ's first object to give us a social and political order that shall certainly secure for men universal physical happiness. Government is a Divine institution, but it is through human virtue, human self-sacrifice, human patience, human sagacity, that the material blessings which are possible through the social condition are to be actually won. And it is not God's will that we should have the material blessings apart from the virtues and intellectual labours which are necessary for the maintenance of a just social order. It was impossible that Christ should accept power on the terms upon which He knew that it was offered Him.

II

The relations of Christ to the political, economic, and social order have exercised the thoughts of men ever since He returned to His glory. He declared before His ascension that all authority had been given to Him in heaven and on earth; the great words of the Psalmist had been fulfilled; not the elect race only, but all nations, had been given to Him as His inheritance, and the uttermost parts of the earth as His possession. During His earthly ministry He and His apostles had declared that the kingdom of heaven was at hand; after His resurrection that proclamation ceased; the kingdom was no longer at hand, it had actually come, for the King had come; and through the redemption which He had achieved the whole race stood in a new relation to God. He was King of kings and Lord of lords, King by Divine right, Lord by Divine appointment. There were no longer any aliens from the Divine commonwealth; every man was a subject of Christ by birth. Revolt was still possible, but revolt is a crime of which only subjects can be guilty. Men are the subjects of Christ by the Divine will, though it lies with their own will to determine whether they will be obedient to His laws and loyal to His throne.

His authority extends over every province of human life; over the business of men and their pleasures; over science, literature, art; over the family; over the State as well as over the Church. This is acknowledged, but the question, How is that authority to be asserted in relation to the State, and to the economic and social organization of the State? has received many answers. I am not clear that the final answer has yet been given. Perhaps the final answer can never be given. During the last thirty or forty years the question has been discussed with great seriousness and earnestness; it is being discussed now on all sides with vehemence and passion. The subject is so intimately related to the great work which has drawn us together this evening – the evangelization of England – by which I mean the realizing in our own country of the Christian ideal of personal, social, and national life – that I may be permitted, perhaps, to say something about it.

III

I suppose that we should all agree that during the present generation there has been a gradual change among Evangelical Nonconformists in their conception of the State and of the functions of the State. Half a century ago there was a very general acceptance among us of the theory that the whole business of the secular Government is to repress force and fraud. The State was even regarded by many of us as founded on a kind of mutual contract for the purpose of protecting life and property – a Limited Liability Company, with its objects and powers strictly defined in the articles of association. To restrict its action within the narrowest possible area was supposed to be the first duty of a wise and liberal politician. Many of us, I suppose, owed our emancipation from that theory, partly to Mr. John Stuart Mill, whose authority was at its zenith in 1850; partly to Edmund Burke, who taught us that the State is a great historical growth, not an artificial creation, and that instead of having any analogy to a voluntary association with limited liability, it is a "partnership in all science, in all art, in every virtue, in all perfection."

To Mr. Frederick Denison Maurice, probably more than to any other man, many of us owe the original impulse which started us on another line of thought. I think that I am not in error when I say that many Evangelical Nonconformists had come to have a vague impression – it was not inherited from their greatest ecclesiastical ancestors – but they had come to have a vague impression that political activity lies beyond the true province of the Christian life. When I was a young man I believe that that impression was a very general one. Mr. Edward Miall had already done something to dissipate it, but it had not disappeared. The State, with all its affairs, was regarded by large numbers of Christian people as belonging in an evil sense to this world, and to be political was to be worldly. They went to the polling booth, many of them, no doubt; but they went, as many Christian people now go to the theatre, feeling that they were hardly in their right place. Mr. Maurice insisted that the State is a Divine institution – like the Family, like the Church; many of us, I say, probably owe to him more than to any other man the original impulse which started our thought in that direction. But as soon as we began to look seriously into the New Testament we found it there, and we were astonished that we had not found it before.

Paul had taught that the powers that be are ordained of God – "therefore he that resisteth the power withstandeth the ordinance of God: and they that withstand shall receive to themselves judgment." He was writing to the Romans when Nero was Emperor of Rome and master of the world – Nero, whose murders, whose brutal lusts, whose tyranny, whose insane follies have covered him with eternal infamy. Even then, according to Paul, rulers were "not a terror to the good work, but to the evil." Government, though administered by bad men, and administered badly, was still a Divine institution; as long as it held society together it was better than no government at all. And men were to "be in subjection" – they were to acknowledge the Divine sanction of the authority even when the authority was wickedly used. They were to "be in subjection, not only because of the wrath," through fear of the penalties of disregarding the law, but also "for conscience' sake" – their obedience was to be as unto the Lord, not unto men. At what point a nation may determine that the Government has become so bad that it is justifiable and necessary to resist it by force, and to transfer the authority which is exercised in the name of God to worthier hands, is a question which there was no occasion for Paul to discuss. When it emerges it is a question of appalling difficulty. That a nation may be driven to this awful extremity is, however, our assured belief.

But Paul's principle – and it is that about which I am speaking – is clear. The State is a Divine institution, the political ruler is the minister of God. Having learned this, most of us have been teaching for many years past, that in a country like our own, where the ultimate choice of those who are to administer both local and national government, lies with the great mass of the people, it is the duty of Christian men to use the franchise and to use their political influence so as to secure that rulers, who are the ministers of God, shall discharge their trust according to the will of God. In the State, as in the Church and in the family, the will of God is supreme.

Yes, in the State as in the Church and in the family, the will of God is supreme. But the State, the family, the Church, are different institutions, existing for different ends, and securing their ends by different methods. In each there is Authority, but in each the Authority is of a different kind, possesses different powers, and asserts those powers by different instruments. We want the will of God to be done in the State; we want the laws of the State and the policy of the State to be in harmony with the will of God; but what is the will of God in relation to the State?

It is our belief that the Church and the State, though both of them are Divine institutions, are Divine institutions of such a different description, and with such different immediate objects, that any organic alliance between them is certain in the long run to be injurious to both. The State is primarily the visible representative and defender of the Divine justice in the temporal order; the Church is primarily the visible representative of the Divine mercy and the Divine redemption in the eternal order. The State has other functions; the Church has other functions; but there is that deep distinction between them. When listening to Christ in the Church, and learning His conception of what our life should be, we hear Him say, "Resist not him that is evil, but whosoever smiteth thee on thy right cheek turn to him the other also; and if any man would go to law with thee and take away thy coat, let him have thy cloak also." But when we want to learn the Christian conception of the function of the civil ruler, we discover that if any man does evil he is not to expect the ruler to treat him after that manner; and that it is not the will of God that the ruler should treat him after that manner. "If thou do that which is evil be afraid, for he beareth not the sword in vain; for he is a minister of God, an avenger for wrath to him that doeth evil."

That is the ruler's function — to assert in the visible order the principles of eternal justice. The ultimate ground of punishment is, that the criminal deserves to suffer. Apart from that, punishment is unjust and intolerable. You have no right to subject a man to suffering for the sake of doing him good, for the sake of reforming him, unless he deserves to suffer. You have no right to subject a man to suffering merely for the sake of giving a wholesome lesson to the community; unless he deserves to suffer, the man becomes a martyr for the public benefit, instead of a criminal.

What theologians call retributive justice is as real an element in the Divine life as compassion and grace, and the ruler is the minister of the retributive justice of God in the temporal order. This austere task is imposed upon him, and he cannot decline it without unfaithfulness to his trust. We on whom this heavy burden is not directly laid, are graciously called to kindlier duties. But in one memorable precept we are reminded that, if *we* are destined to be compassionate and merciful, it is not because the punishment of wrong-doing is contrary to the Divine will, but because God has provided for it without our aid: "Avenge not yourselves, beloved, but give place unto the wrath"– leave room for the anger of God against wrong-doing to its own stern work, "for it is written, 'Vengeance belongeth unto Me; I will recompense, saith the Lord.'" Within limits, this work is to be done by the civil ruler–"He is a minister of God, an avenger for wrath to him that doeth evil."

IV

The State, the Church, both are Divine institutions; the State, the Church, in both the will of God is to be supreme; but the characteristic function of the State is to assert the authority of law; of the Church to reveal the infinite wealth of grace. The State is to secure to all men their due in the temporal order as far as its powers extend; to protect the peaceful, upright, industrious citizen in his person, property, and reputation; to punish the disorderly and the violent. The Church, on the other hand, by its very constitution and the ends for which it was founded, is not to deal with men after their sins, nor to reward them according to their iniquities. It is to declare to all men the remission of their sins in Christ. It is to shelter men from evils which they have deserved; to rescue them from miseries into which they have fallen by their own follies and crimes. This sharp contrast between the characteristic functions of the Church and the characteristic functions of the State cannot, as I believe, be obliterated without peril. When ecclesiastical authorities have become princes they have weakened the foundations of the political order, and they have paralysed the redemptive powers of the Church.

And yet the growth of the Church, by which I mean the gradual conquest of the people of any country by the spirit and truth of Christ, must have and ought to have a great and increasing effect on national laws and national policy. This will happen even under an absolute government; it will be illustrated on a greater and more impressive scale in a country which has achieved political freedom. The State is a Divine institution, and some of its ends are definitely determined by its very nature; if these are not secured it will be broken up, and will have to be re-organized. But it is not a Divine institution of the same kind as the solar system, which is fast bound in the iron chains of necessity. It has to be realized by the concurrence of free agents, and its actual form and activity will vary with their sagacity and their folly, their public spirit, their courage, their unselfishness, their purity, their intellectual vigour and cultivation, their baseness, their cowardice, their covetousness, their sensuality, their intellectual feebleness and sluggishness. Change the people by the power of the Christian gospel, and you will change their laws. The State is still the representative of justice; but as a nation becomes increasingly penetrated with the spirit of Christ, its ideal of justice in that temporal order which is under the control of the civil ruler will be gradually elevated. The austere severities of government will not be weakly relaxed, but there will be eager questionings as to the possibility of effecting changes in the political and economic order which, without making justice less awful, shall contribute to the relief of misery, give to the unfortunate a chance of comfort and ease, and add to the brightness of the life of the whole community.

The material prosperity and physical happiness of the community can never be the exclusive or even the chief aim of those who desire to carry into the State the spirit they have received in the Church for in the Church they have learned that these do not constitute the supreme good either of individuals or of nations. Personal righteousness, the discipline of both the robust and the gracious virtues, so far as they can be disciplined by political and economic institutions, will take precedence of mere physical ease and enjoyment; and yet the compassionate works of Christ will be always remembered, who, after charging His disciples to seek first His kingdom and His righteousness, and not to be anxious about what they should eat or drink or wear, added, "Your Heavenly Father knoweth that ye have need of all these things."

In our own country during the present century the power of religious faith over the nation has been shown in great public acts of compassion. It was the new energy of the religious life created by the Evangelical revival which gave intensity and passion to the great movement against the slave trade, and which, at last, by a splendid act of generosity, abolished slavery throughout the possessions of the Crown. The justice of that achievement was as conspicuous as its mercy. It was not the triumph of a cheap philanthropy, which was willing to confer a great good if it could be conferred without great cost. Hateful, intolerable, iniquitous as was the system which gave to the master a property in his slave, the property had been sanctioned by national opinion and protected by national law, and the nation gave £20,000,000 in order to cancel the master's rights. Legislation of other kinds, and affecting our own population, has had its origin in that pity for the poor, that reverence for all men, which the Church has caught from Christ, and which the world has caught from the Church. Act after Act has been passed limiting the hours of labour of women and children employed in factories and workshops, and preventing them from working at all in mines. Acts have been passed for protecting the life and limbs of persons exposed to accidents from machinery. Attempts have been made, not I trust wholly unsuccessful, to prevent men from being sent to sea in ships that are unseaworthy. Local authorities have acquired new powers for compelling owners of houses to keep them in a sanitary condition. Here and there a great municipality has begun to build healthy homes for the less fortunate classes of the community. One great town after another has provided public baths, public gardens, public parks, free libraries, and art galleries. The Education Acts of 1870, 1876, and 1880 have secured a public elementary school for every child in the kingdom that needs it, and have provided that every child shall be sent to school and kept there until it has received a moderate measure of education. These are but examples of the social legislation of the present century, and they have come, not from a fierce and violent struggle of the poor for a larger share in the public wealth, but mainly from the sincere and earnest desire of the more prosperous classes in the State to secure for all classes of the people an easier and a happier life. We are but at the beginning of the tasks which must be undertaken if the miseries which still remain are to be lessened, and if a life of honourable industry, of comfort and dignity, is to be made possible to all our countrymen.

The precise forms of the social troubles which now perplex and confound us are new. They are largely the result of the breaking-up of the ancient order which in France was violently destroyed by the great Revolution, and which in this country has perished more peacefully as the result of the immense development of our manufacturing industry in the last half of the last century and the first half of this. To discover the solution of the new problems which have thus been forced upon us is not easy. Patience is necessary as well as zeal, or attempts at reform may issue only in worse confusion and worse suffering. A genuine love for man, and an intense desire that God's thought concerning our national life should be fulfilled—let these inspire and guide our policy, and then, though we may commit some great errors, we may be certain that, as time goes on, the real strength and happiness of the nation will be constantly augmented.

V

But in the work which has drawn us together tonight we are sure to be wholly in the right. If the social order is to be just, men must be just; if the social order is to be kindly, men must be kindly. We can only hope for great and enduring changes for the better in the social order, as the result of great and enduring changes for the better in the spirit and character of the whole people. The ethical quality of the organization of a State, political, economic, social, must, I suppose, be always more or less inferior to the general ethical life of the nation. Reforms which are far in advance of that life may be carried, as the result of transient enthusiasm, but they will not be effective, and they will not endure.

We ought to take our full share, we Christian people, in every movement for the practical amelioration of the condition of our fellow-
countrymen. But speaking as one who for many years took an active
part among the obscurer members of a great political party, I think
that we must often be doubtful whether political and social schemes
which are full of promise may not, from causes which human sagacity
is unable to anticipate, turn out mischievous. In endeavouring to
draw individual men to Christ — in disciplining to Christian intelligence, to righteousness and sanctity, those who already acknowledge
His authority — we cannot go wrong. Every man that has received the
Spirit of Christ, and is eager to do the will of Christ, is a new power for
bringing in more just and more gracious conditions of economic and
social life. John Wesley and George Whitefield did more for the social
redemption of England than all the politicians of this century and the
last, whose names are associated with great reforms; under God,
they created those moral and spiritual forces which have rendered all
reforms possible.

In this work, I say again, we cannot go wrong. We trust that future
generations of men, inheriting our name, speaking our tongue, living
on English soil, will achieve an organization of life so just and so
beautiful, that the poverty, the crime, the ignorance, the social strife
of our own days shall seem to them an evil dream. But the great harvests of the world ripen slowly. We rejoice that while they are ripen-
ing it is possible, through God's grace, for God's lost children to be
found and brought home to their Father. Their life in this world is
brief at the longest. They are destined by the thought and purpose of
God to an endless life of righteousness and wisdom, of joy and glory.
That thought and purpose are not to be defeated by the inequalities
and confusions of their earthly condition. The Apostles did not wait
till slavery was abolished before they preached the Christian Gospel
to slaves; slaves received the Gospel, and, remaining slaves, became
children of the Eternal and heirs of the glory of God. Nor need *we*
wait till the social miseries of many of our own countrymen disappear
before we endeavour to make clear to them that they are born to an
inheritance in the infinite love of God, and in the redemption which
has been achieved for the human race by Christ. To those who are
suffering from these miseries in their intenser form we should carry
material relief, which, thank God, the Church has always been eager
to give to the wretched. But with the material relief we should also
carry the animating and glorious hope of a larger, freer, and nobler
life when their earthly troubles are over. But the immense majority
of our people are not worn with anxiety, wasted with hunger, crushed
by despair; and among these there are millions who know nothing of
the power and blessedness of the Christian Redemption. To these we
have free access; there is nothing in their circumstances and condi-

tion to prevent them from receiving the Gospel of Christ, and from living according to His will. Let *them* learn to acknowledge Him as the true King of men, and within a generation the whole life of the country would be changed. Have courage, have faith. In the power of Christ, and in the power of the truth of Christ, we may confidently hope to recover our country both from its sorrows and its sins.

And in this great work you are asked to take some part to-night. There are many in this congregation who could speak with a larger knowledge than I can of the work which is being carried on all over England by the Baptist Home Missionary Society, on behalf of which I have now to plead. But of this I am sure — you cannot tell what light, what consolation, what hope, what strength for righteousness, what endurance for suffering, are carried to lonely cottages by the colporteurs and evangelists associated with this society; you cannot tell how much of the best life of England in obscure places is sustained by the Churches and the pastors that you are asked to stand by to-night. Ah! Dr. Clifford, it is pleasant enough for you and me to preach the Gospel; but what courage is necessary, what faith, what zeal, by multitudes of our brethren in the country districts of England! You are asked to show by your contributions to-night that you have some sympathy with them in their heroic struggle.

You know, many of you, what they are doing, and you know it to their cost; for young men and women who in these country districts have been trained to faith in Christ and loyalty to the great ends for which the Free Evangelical Churches exist, come in crowds to the great towns and cities of England; and among our most effective workers in the Churches in the great towns and cities are those who have been disciplined and trained by the men and the Churches for whom I plead to-night. You need not go to your secretaries to learn what they are doing; look round your Sunday schools, look into your diaconate, look at those who are taking part in all the mission work connected with your own Churches, and you will learn the kind of work which — shall I say? — these men and these Churches turn out, and you may judge with what fidelity and earnestness they are discharging the trust which they have received from God.

I wonder when the imagination of our Churches will be touched by this Home Mission work as it has been touched from time to time by the great work of evangelizing the heathen. Do not misunderstand me. I have never found that the men who are most disposed to criticize the work that we are carrying on in remote countries are the men who either consecrate personal service or give large contributions to sustain evangelistic work at home. Let them earn the right to criticize our missions to the heathen by doing more for our missions to our own countrymen; if they distrust our foreign work, there is ample room for all they can give and all they can do in connection with our evangelistic work at home. But, I repeat, I wonder when our imagination will be touched, and when our passion will be stirred, by this work of evangelizing England, as they have sometimes been touched and stirred when a new nation has been thrown open to the Gospel of Christ. How is it that splendid gifts are not consecrated to this work, as splendid gifts are sometimes consecrated to the other? How is it that this work is not regarded as being just as heroic under many conditions as that? England for Christ is surely as lofty an aim as China for Christ, or India for Christ. I trust that there will be a change in the scale of contributions to our home missionary work among the Free Evangelical Churches of this country. And I ask you to begin that change to-night.

FAITH AND PHYSICAL SCIENCE

"No one knoweth the Son, save the Father; neither doth any know the Father, save the Son, and he to whomsoever the Son willeth to reveal Him" (Matthew 11:27).

"NEITHER doth any know the Father, save the Son, and he to whomsoever the Son willeth to reveal Him"—that is an august and unique claim; the Lord Jesus Christ declares that only through Himself can any man come to know God. The august and unique claim has been followed by an august and unique history.

I

During the eighteen hundred years which have passed since the earthly life of our Lord ended in the crucifixion, it is apparent that His influence on the thought of the human race has been immense. It has guided and governed the highest forms of intellectual energy. For more than a thousand years after the meeting of the Council of Nicaea, early in the fourth century, it is hardly possible to mention the name of a single man of great speculative power in Europe, in Northern Africa, in Western Asia, who was not a Christian theologian;

Reprinted from R. W. Dale, *Fellowship with Christ*, The Expositor's Library (London, New York: Hodder & Stoughton, 1891), pp. 171–91.

the only striking exceptions are to be found among the scholars who illustrated the brief but brilliant period of Saracenic civilization. The great poets, the great painters, the great orators, the great architects also did homage to the supremacy of Christ. It was confessed that He stood alone and apart, and that in Him man had found God.

And even since the great revolution in European thought which originated, partly in the recovery of the splendid creations of the genius of ancient Greece, partly in the early triumphs of modern physical science, a long succession of men of the keenest, most vigorous, and most courageous intellect have found a more intense and more stimulating speculative interest in the Christian revelation than in any of those new fields of inquiry which have yielded to the patience and genius of recent times such dazzling and exciting results.

The influence which Christ has exerted on the thought of the commonalty of those nations which have accepted the Christian faith is not less remarkable. He has made the loftiest and sublimest conceptions of God, of the Universe, of the dignity and destiny of mankind, the common possession, through age after age, of uncounted millions of men who knew nothing of the learning of the schools and were familiar with only the rudest forms of secular literature — peasants whose strength was worn by their labour in the fields in the summer's heat and the winter's storm, shepherds who kept their flocks on lonely hills, workmen at the bench and at the forge.

But the influence of the Lord Jesus Christ has extended far beyond the limits of the intellectual life of man. The central elements of the Christian faith have vital relations to conduct. They imply and form a specific type of character. They contain a law of perfection. All the mysteries of the Christian revelation — the Trinity, the Incarnation, the Death of Christ for the redemption of the human race, the remission of sins, the gift of eternal life, the discovery of that city of God of which all Christian men are citizens, Judgment to come, the glory, honour, and immortality to which God has destined us in Christ — all these are directly related to the Christian virtues which are commanded in the Sermon on the Mount. In the teaching of Christ doctrine and duty, promise and precept, go together. Christian mysteries which transcend the most adventurous speculation affect the humblest and obscurest forms of Christian practice. The fires of the sun in the distant heavens are not more necessary to ripen the wheat or to perfect the grace of the wild-flower than are the great revelations of Christ concerning God to create and sustain the characteristic Christian virtues. The religion of Christ regulates, inspires, and sustains the morals of Christ. The morals are a part of the religion.

II

But it may be contended — it has been contended — that Art is also a religion, and that delight in beauty, and the study of beauty, may also create gracious and noble forms of morality; that Science – the patient, laborious investigation of the structure and laws of the physical universe – may render the same service. Dismissing the first of these contentions – the contention for the religious and ethical functions of Art – I propose, before considering more closely the great claim of Christ in the text, to say something about the contention for the religious and ethical functions of Science.

It is maintained that Science may answer some of the great ends which have hitherto been answered by Religion – may, in fact, have many of the attributes of Religion, may contribute similar, if not the same, elements to human life – may exert a similar, if not the same, influence on human character.

The discussion of this question may, perhaps, recall to some of you a book of great interest, published a few years ago by a very eminent living author; and it is necessary, therefore, that I should say that I am not attributing to the writer of that book the claims on behalf of the religion of Science which I propose to examine, although he has stated these claims with a clearness and force which I cannot find elsewhere. The argument of his book was missed by some of his readers; it was no part of his intention to maintain that what he described as Natural Religion could, without grave loss to mankind, take the place of the Christian faith.

But it is contended, I say, that Science – the investigation of the physical universe – is a kind of religion; and that the scientific man, though he rejects the Christian Gospel, and rejects every form of belief commonly described as Theistic, still retains what may be properly called a religious faith.

(1) For – "That man believes in a God who feels himself in the presence of a Power which is not himself, and is immeasurably above himself, a Power in the contemplation of which he is absorbed, in the knowledge of which he finds safety and happiness. And such now is Nature to the scientific man."

"Immeasurably above himself" – there, perhaps, lies one of the chief perils of a deep devotion to the study of the physical universe. We are in danger of being mastered by its immensity, by the awful energy of its forces, by the contrast between our own brief and uncertain years and the ages of its vast duration – ages stretching back beyond the reach of the most daring thought – lost in clouds which imagination cannot pierce. But this is to surrender our regal claims, and to consent to the suppression and paralysis of those very powers of our nature to which religion appeals. The universe – the universe which lies within the range of the physical sciences – "immeasurably above" ourselves! I refuse its title to supremacy. I decline to confess inferior rank. The universe above me! – it is not my equal; much less is it great enough to be in any sense my God.

Do the planets know the laws which constrain them to keep their orbits? The man who can calculate their path is greater than the planets. Is the sun conscious of the fierce heats of its secular fires? The man who, at the distance of nearly a hundred millions of miles, can tell us about the fuel which feeds them is greater than the sun. The painter, or the poet, whose imagination kindles at the vision of mountain and river, cloud and sky, and who reveals on canvas or in song a diviner beauty than was caught by the outward sense, is greater than the physical earth and the physical heavens, which are unconscious of their own loveliness and to which no dream of a greater glory has ever come.

Let us stand erect, and scorn ourselves for the baseness which would acknowledge the supremacy of the unintelligent and unconscious forces of physical nature. Reason, memory, speculation — these raise us to a nobler rank.

It is no answer to this protest on behalf of the greatness of humanity, that our intellectual activities, wonderful as they are, may be only functions of our physical organization, and that our physical organization is the felicitous growth and creation of those unconscious powers whose last secret will in future centuries be wrested from them by physical science; if the case is so, the dignity of the race still remains, and we can but say that these mysterious powers have achieved something that transcends themselves. In the presence of mere physical phenomena, however glorious, and of mere physical forces, however immense, the superior rank of the intellectual life asserts itself. Its titles are not imperilled by any impeachment of its origin and ancestry. It needs no other vindication of its supremacy than its own intrinsic and apparent greatness.

(2) It is said that in the presence of the physical universe the man who has a large knowledge of the revelations of modern science may be filled with a wonder and awe that are too rarely present in popular religion. This may be true. Our sense of the infinite greatness of God has been impaired. Religious thought in recent times has deserted those mountain solitudes in which devout hearts learnt to fear and to reverence the Eternal as well as to trust and to love Him. And a sense of the awful majesty of God is necessary not only for reverential worship and for some of the deeper experiences of the spiritual life, but for many moral virtues. It is the discipline of humility; it is the inspiration of fortitude; it contributes to the vigilant self-command which is one of the guarantees of fidelity to the highest law. The very virtues of a man who is not conscious of living under the control of a power immeasurably above himself will miss a certain refinement and a gracious dignity which are necessary to perfection. But we must take care that the power which we reverence is really above us. The servility of slaves who are held down by a stern and irresistible force is something different in quality from the loyal courtesy and the manly reverence with which a free people regard an august

throne. Science may render a service to the religious life of our times by its illustration of the immensity and grandeur of God's works; for if the universe is great, God is infinitely greater. But our religious awe must be reserved for God Himself.

(3) It is said further that—"the true theist should recognise his Deity as giving him the law to which his life ought to be conformed," and that to the scientific man his science is a religion because he believes that all happiness depends upon the careful adaptation of human life to the laws of nature.

There is no doubt an admirable ethical temper encouraged by devotion to scientific pursuits; and the patience and accuracy which they demand are the discipline of certain excellent ethical habits; but when the claim is preferred that scientific discovery discloses the laws to which human life ought to be conformed, the claim must be challenged.

For in what province of physical investigation has the scientific man any occasion to use the word "ought" in announcing his discoveries? Where does he find the idea for which the word stands? It belongs to a region of inquiry in which his instruments and methods are altogether valueless. He is conversant with facts and with facts which are not of the highest order; with the idea of duty he has nothing to do. He has to tell us what is, what has been, what will be, in certain limited regions of observation and experience; he passes into another and a higher world when he begins to speak of what ought to be.

What are called the laws of Nature are in no proper sense laws of conduct. They give us no assistance in determining what are the true aims and obligations of human life; they can only inform us when the aims have been already determined, how some of them may be reached; when the obligations have been already accepted, how some of them may be discharged; they perform even this humbler service imperfectly at the best, and sometimes they fail us altogether. In relation to "the law to which human life ought to be conformed," the function of science is secondary and ministerial, not authoritative and supreme. We must derive the law from religion and ethics; science can only assist us to discover the methods by which in some cases the law is to be fulfilled.

Take one of the most obvious illustrations. The physician, with his scientific resources, may tell me the methods by which I may be able to maintain my health, or to check the growth of a disease by which my life is endangered. But are the directions of the physician final in relation to conduct? Clearly not. They are submitted to another and higher tribunal. Some of them are approved, some dismissed, on the authority of laws which lie beyond the reach of physical science. The physician tells me to drink claret instead of sherry, and to eat less meat. I obey, for I can do it without violating any ethical or religious duty. But he tells me that I must live near the moors or the sea; that I must leave my books and my desk; must spend five or six hours every day in the open air; must ride, or drive, or fish, or shoot; that if I go on working I shall break down in a very few years, and, a year or two later, shall die. That may be all true, but it contains no law which I am under any obligation to obey. Even supposing that I have the resources necessary to carry out his directions, it may be perfectly clear that I am bound to disregard them. My work may be of a kind which I have no more right to desert for fear of breaking down in health and shortening my life than a soldier has to desert his post for fear of being shot. It is the clear duty of the soldier to run the risk of being shot — that is his vocation; and no scientific demonstration of the mischievous effects of a gunshot wound in the chest can in any way affect his duty; it may be just as clearly my duty to keep to my work at the risk of ruining my health and of dying before my time; and no scientific demonstration of the mischievous effects of those habits of life which are incident to my work can relieve me from guilt and dishonour if I leave the work undone. Is it a man's first duty to preserve his health and to live as long as he can? Does this take precedence of the duty of a statesman and a soldier to defend the safety and honour and prosperity of their country? Does it take precedence of the duty of a poet, of an artist, to enrich mankind with the most perfect creations which can be achieved by their genius? Does it take precedence of the duty of a man who has received a great faculty for scientific discovery to extend the boundaries of human knowledge? To these questions physical science can give no answer; the answer must come from higher sources.

But this is only an example and illustration of the inability of science to give us a law to which human life should be conformed, and of the invalidity of the claim that man is to find his happiness in obeying the laws of Nature. The laws of Nature are not to be obeyed; the knowledge of them is to be used in obedience to the laws of another and diviner authority.

And where — in all the discoveries of physical science — can you learn the obligations of truthfulness, of justice, of pity, of showing mercy to those who have erred and gone astray from the paths of righteousness, of self-sacrifice, or devotion to the public good? The man who recognises Nature as his Deity, and who receives from her "the law to which his life should be conformed," will find in the sacred books which contain the revelations of her will, neither the Sermon on the Mount nor even the Ten Commandments.

(4) But further, it is alleged that the scientific man finds in the contemplation of the universe endless delight. Nature is not only a power immeasurably above us; she is infinitely interesting and infinitely beautiful, interesting and beautiful not only in those aspects which are open to the common eye, but in the regularity of her methods; in the fascinations of mysteries partially revealed; in the broken

clouds which half disclose and half conceal the wide regions which have as yet been only imperfectly traversed and imperfectly surveyed by scientific thought. It is suggested that the delight of the scientific man in the vision and admiration of Nature has a certain analogy to the delight of the Theist and the Christian in the vision and worship of God.

But as the greatness of our intellectual life requires us to assert our superior rank in the presence of the unconscious forces which are revealed in the phenomena of the physical universe, so the still higher greatness of our moral life requires us to demand a diviner object of admiration and diviner fountains of delight than can be discovered in the infinite beauty and infinite interest of Nature and her laws.

Our deepest reverence and joy should be reserved for that which is really greatest; and if we are arrested by any subordinate and secondary glories, our own life must suffer harm. The order of Nature is majestic; but to the majesty of Eternal Righteousness is due a more devout and reverential homage. We may be fascinated by the beauty of Nature; but the mercy of the living personal God —

> Mercy carried infinite degrees
> Beyond the tenderness of human hearts,

should inspire a far more passionate affection and a far intenser delight.

The moral virtues — justice, courage, generosity, truthfulness, kindness, pity, self-sacrifice — belong to a nobler order than the fairest and most brilliant discoveries that in recent times have filled the world with wonder; and whatever indications of the moral perfections of God may be found in Nature by the man who has discovered them elsewhere — these lie beyond the limits of the physical sciences, and what the scientific man admires in Nature by virtue of his science can have no moral element in it. It does not belong to him to inquire whether the laws which he investigates are just, or whether Nature is kind and pitiful: these are terms which belong to men of other pursuits; he has learnt their meaning from other teachers than those who have achieved their authority and fame in those provinces of discovery which he can claim as his own, and which are sometimes spoken of as if they included all human knowledge.

Nature as revealed to science is not great enough for us to worship. The courage and fidelity of martyrs are greater than anything that science has discovered in the heavens above or on the earth beneath. The purity of saints is greater. The pity of kindly hearts for human suffering is greater. The dear affections of home and kindred, the loyalty of friends, the cheerful patience of old age, the innocence of childhood, are greater. Nature, as revealed by science, has no love; and —

> The loving worm within its clod
> Were diviner than a loveless God
> Amid His worlds.

A famous Frenchman said, that in the great moments of life he was "stifled by the universe"; and if you ask me to worship Nature, I answer—I have seen visions of something infinitely fairer and more wonderful; and in the worship of Nature my highest powers and my strongest affections are suppressed, pent in: they struggle for the freedom which they can find only in the presence of the Living and Personal God.

It would, indeed, be ungrateful for a Christian preacher not to remember, that in addition to the knowledge — precious for its own sake — with which physical discoveries have enriched the human race, and in addition to the new and wonderful command which they have given us over the power and resources of the material universe, they have rendered services of many kinds to the Christian faith. Of these services, one of the greatest may some day be attributed to that lofty scientific idea which, within our own memory, has secured such a rapid ascendency in every field of scientific inquiry. We have come to think of the work of creation as unfinished, and of ourselves as spectators of the mystery. The ages are as yet in the remote future in which the universe will reach that consummate perfection to which it was destined by the forces which have determined its development and history. Perhaps that perfection may never be actually achieved, but the mighty movement which in the past has struggled forward through storm and conflict and suffering, may some day pass into a peaceful progress towards an ideal glory, a progress to be prolonged through eternity.

This new scientific conception of the order of Nature will compel Christendom to revise some of its theological conceptions of the life of God — conceptions which have been largely derived neither from the Jewish nor the Christian scriptures, but from a cold metaphysical philosophy. For some theological definitions of God which pass as Christian have come from deism rather than from Jewish prophets and psalmists, or Christian evangelists and apostles. We have been taught to think of Him as a necessary hypothesis to account for the origin of all things; but that ever since He created all things His power has been inactive except in miracle. That was not the faith of Jewish saints. They believed that God not only "laid the foundations of the earth, that it should not be moved for ever," but that through age after age, before their own eyes, He continued to work: "He causeth

the grass to grow for the cattle, and herb for the service of man."
To all His creatures He gave their meat in due season: "Thou openest
Thine hand: they are satisfied with good." It was He who in the spring-
time renewed the face of the ground; and in the winter fire and hail,
snow and vapour fulfilled His word. "My Father," said Christ, "worketh hitherto" – worketh on holy days, set apart for the rest of man, as
well as on days which man spends in common toil – "My Father worketh hitherto, and I work." It will be something if science enables us to
recover a firmer hold of the ancient faith, and enables us to see for
ourselves the present activity of God.

We have been taught to think of creation as if by a few successive
exertions of the Divine power, God achieved and completed an ideal
universe. That was not what Paul believed. Knowing nothing, suspect-
ing nothing, of the tragic story of long millenniums of conflict and
pain which preceded the appearance of man on the earth, the great
Apostle, grasping the true conception of the manner in which the
thoughts of God are fulfilled, used language which might have been
taken as the motto and text of many a recent scientific treatise, and
told the Christians at Rome that "the whole creation groaneth and
travaileth in pain together until now," and that its blessedness and
glory are still to come. God, too, has His unrealized ideals; He, too, is
in pursuit of an unachieved perfection; He is thwarted, hindered,
baffled by we know not what hostile powers; but "He fainteth not,
neither is He weary"; and though age after age may pass, the golden
years will come when the eternal purposes of His righteousness and
His love will be fulfilled. In this perpetual effort of God to reach a perfection that still lies far before Him, we may find new grounds for
faith in His sympathy with ourselves in the pursuit of an ideal righteousness.

Yes, Physical Science may render service to Religious Faith; but
first of all Religious Faith must render a greater service to Science by
teaching her that Nature is not God, and that although the Heavens
declare His glory, and the earth is full of His goodness, in Nature God
is not seen at His highest and best.

"Neither doth any know the Father save the Son, and he to whomsoever the Son willeth to reveal Him." I say again, as I said at starting,
that this is an august and unique claim. The Lord Jesus Christ declares
that it lies with Himself, depends upon His personal volition, whether
any man shall have a true knowledge of God. In no age, in no country,
in no Church, can any man discover God for himself, or learn from
priest or theologian what is revealed concerning God by Christ. It is
not enough to have the tradition of Christ's own teaching, or even the
authoritative record of the discourses and parables in which He
assured the men and women of His own time that they were the children of the Eternal. He deals with us one by one – not in crowds.

"Neither doth any know the Father save the Son, and he to whomsoever the Son willeth to reveal Him."

Think what it means. He tells us of the ardours of love for the human race that glow in the Divine heart; He tells us that we are God's children; but that we cannot know our Father except He – Christ – wills to make the Father known to us. The claim is more daring – or more sublime – than if He had said that God's rain fell on no man's meadow, God's sun ripened no man's wheat, except by His will – that He determined whose grass should be parched by drought and whose grass should receive the kindly showers; whose fields should be green at harvest time, and whose should be rich with the golden wheat.

If He had said simply that only through His teaching could the men of His own time and country come to know the Father, and that in other lands and in later generations only those who were reached by the traditions or written record of His teaching could come to know the Father, this would have been wonderful. But He said infinitely more than this. In the crowds that heard the Sermon on the Mount and the Parable of the Prodigal Son, He determined whether this man or that should receive the revelation of God. Among the millions that have heard or read the sermon or the parable in after centuries He has determined whether to this man or that He would reveal the Father. Just as it was by His will, exerted in individual cases, that blind men received sight and dumb men recovered speech, so it is by His will, exerted in individual cases, that men reach the knowledge of God.

We must take Christ's teaching as it stands, and this unique claim is not separable from the rest of it. It affirms that you cannot learn what Christ reveals of God by reading any treatise of Christian theology as you learn Newton's theory by reading the *Principia;* that you cannot learn what Christ reveals of God by reading even the four gospels as you learn the thought of Socrates by reading Xenophon or Plato. It is as if you needed Newton himself to enable you to master the *Principia,* Socrates himself to enable you to understand the *Memorabilia* or the *Republic.* Do you care to know God – to know God, in your measure, as Christ knew Him – as Christ knows Him? You need Christ. You must appeal to the living Teacher, must be taught by Him who is the Eternal Word – the Eternal Revelation of God.

How He may answer that appeal He only knows. Not, perhaps, by sudden illumination, but after long and painful discipline may the knowledge come. He may see that to you, however it may be with others, a protracted search is necessary to make you capable of the final discovery. Who knows? It is not for us to make terms with the Giver of that supreme knowledge which is eternal life, or to be impatient if His methods perplex and trouble us. Of this, however, you may be sure, that He who descended from the heights of eternal blessedness and glory to reveal God will not withhold the revelation from any man that desires to receive it, and will grant it as soon as the power to receive it is present.

The new light may begin to shine, the dawn may break, at unexpected points of the horizon. Christ may prepare you for the revelation of God by teaching you first to love and to care for men. He may remind you of forgotten duties. He may trouble your heart by reproving follies and sins which your conscience has ceased to rebuke. Whatever word of His comes to you, however simple, however elementary it may be, receive it with reverence, with devout fear; listen and obey; the path of righteousness is the path to God. It may be that for a long time whole regions of the truth He taught may be covered with dense clouds; but if as you read the gospels – remembering that He is at your side – a sentence here, a sentence there – not those perhaps which you desired to master – begins to brighten under a divine light, let your thought and heart dwell on what He is revealing, and wait patiently till in His own good time, and as you are able to bear it, the clouds break and reveal the rest.

And then life, throughout the whole range of its duties, its pleasures, its sorrows, will be drawn into close relations with the Eternal, and you will discover that you have passed into that fair city which is the home of the saints. The visible creation will be the symbol of a diviner order, and the common paths of thought will all end in God. You will become conscious of your kinship with the Creator; and the universe, with all its infinitely varied phenomena of glory and of terror, instead of being a power above you, will lie beneath your feet. You will not be humiliated by the awful procession of ages which moves before your imagination when you look back upon the history of Creation; you will look up to the Creator and say, "Before the mountains were brought forth or ever Thou hadst formed the earth or the world, from everlasting to everlasting thou art God; and as for me, I am more than Thy creature; I am Thy child; in Christ Thou hadst made Thine eternal life my own." You will find God; God will find you: and in the blessedness of that meeting life will reach its consummate perfection and power.

THE GOSPEL OF SUFFERING

"Count it all joy, my brethren, when ye fall into manifold temptations; knowing that the proof of your faith worketh patience. And let patience have its perfect work, that ye may be perfect and entire, lacking in nothing. But if any of you lacketh wisdom, let him ask of God, who giveth to all liberally and upbraideth not; and it shall be given him. But let him ask in faith, nothing doubting: for he that doubteth is like the surge of the sea driven by the wind and tossed. For let not that man think that he shall receive anything of the Lord; a double-minded man, unstable in all his ways. But let the brother of low degree glory in his high estate: and the rich, in that he is made low: because as the flower of the grass he shall pass away. For the sun ariseth with the scorching wind, and withereth the grass; and the flower thereof falleth, and the grace of the fashion of it perisheth: so also shall the rich man fade away in his goings" (James 1:2–11).

THE EPISTLE opens in an heroic strain. "Count it all joy," James says, "when ye fall into manifold temptations, knowing that the proof of your faith"—that which tests its strength—"worketh patience." This is a stern doctrine. These trials bring misery, he says, but you Christian men and women are to look beyond them, and to find the light even in the misery. Why? Because the trials discipline you to patience; and he adds, "Let patience have its perfect work." Do not give way after you have borne suffering well for a time, else all will be lost. Be faithful, as our Lord says to the Church at Smyrna—"be faithful unto death." Endure not merely bitter persecution, loss of property, loss of liberty, but carry your faithfulness through to the last extremity. "Be faithful unto death, and I will give thee the crown of life." Or, as James puts it, "Let patience have its perfect work, that ye may be perfect and entire, lacking in nothing."

This, I say, is stern doctrine. To count it all joy when suffering comes upon us, and suffering that tests our faith, how is this possible? It is only possible when we come to think of righteousness as being infinitely more precious than comfort, happiness, or peace; when we come to see that the great thing for us in this life is not to enjoy ease and prosperity, to get rich, to rise in the world, but to become better men. For this we require wisdom—a true estimate of the nature and ends of human life.

"If any of you lacketh wisdom let him ask of God." *Wisdom* was a

Reprinted from R. W. Dale, *The Epistle of James and Other Discourses* (London: Hodder & Stoughton, 1895), pp. 9–21.

great word among the Jews, especially during the centuries immediately before Christ. There was a distinct class of Jewish literature
called The Wisdom literature, represented by the Book of Proverbs,
and the Book of Ecclesiastes, and the Book of Job. "The wise men,"
says Professor Driver, "took for granted the main postulates of Israel's
creed, and applied themselves rather to the observation of human
character as such, seeking to analyse conduct, studying action in its
consequences, and establishing morality, upon the basis of principles
common to humanity at large. . . . They have been termed . . . the
Humanists of Israel. Their teaching had a practical aim." It related to
conduct and to education. And further, "the observation of human
nature . . . naturally leads on to reflection on the problems which it
presents." The inequalities among men, the prosperity of bad men, the
sufferings of good men, the apparent vanity of human pursuits—
these problems are discussed in Job and Ecclesiastes. And so when
James speaks of wisdom, he means a true understanding of human
life, and of the moral order of the world—the power and habit of forming a just judgment on wealth and poverty, joy and sorrow, ease and
pain, public honour and public dishonour, and all the incidents of human experience—a clear vision of the laws which should regulate
conduct, of the principles which should form character. It is, as some
one has said, a living insight into Christian duty; it is the art of Christian
conduct. "If any man lack this wisdom let him ask of God."

We all greatly need it, for there are large numbers of Christian men
and women who not only mean well, but who at times set their hearts
very earnestly on doing well; yet they make nothing of it. There is no
dignity or force or consistency in their life. You can see the traces and
outlines of a noble plan, but the plan has never been carried out. They
discover their mistakes too late to mend them—mistakes in their
personal habits, mistakes in the ordering of their homes, mistakes in
the choice of their friends, mistakes in the objects for which they have
spent time and money and strength. "Experience," as Coleridge says,
"is too often like the stern-lights of a ship; it illuminates only the path
over which we have travelled, and it gives no enlightenment of guidance for conduct in the future." We want this divine gift of wisdom,
the power to judge things according to their true worth, and in their
relation to our own plan of life. It shows us what life really is, and how
we are to make the best of it.

James implies that if we had it we should count it all joy when we
fall into trouble. What a difference that would make to many of us!
And even if we came short of rejoicing, and were only able to subdue
our discontent and impatience, and to rise above the transient troubles
to the eternal treasure which it cannot lessen, the eternal glory which
it cannot dim, how great a thing it would be! This wisdom, if we had it,
would transfigure life. You have an unreasonable employer; wisdom
would teach you to regard his unreasonableness as a divinely ap-

pointed discipline to train you to good temper. A man has greatly wronged you; wisdom would teach you to regard the wrong as giving you the opportunity of fulfilling our Lord's precept: "Bless them that curse you, pray for them that despitefully use you." Your occupation is dreary, monotonous, badly paid; wisdom will teach you to do your work as unto the Lord and not unto men, and this will bring down into your work-room light from heaven. You lose money that you have worked hard for; wisdom will teach you that this loss will help you not to put your trust in uncertain riches. And so when a man once comes to see that human life is surrounded by infinite horizons, all things will be changed; conduct will have a new law, the heart will find new peace.

The objects for which a man will spend his time and strength and money will be changed. With regard to many things to which he has attached great importance, he will cease to care for them, and will feel that they do not concern him. When Napoleon was in the East it was suggested to him that he should visit Jerusalem. "No," he answered, "Jerusalem does not come within the field of my operations." That was the kind of answer that such a man was likely to make; it suggests one of the great secrets of his greatness; he saw what would count for the success of his campaign, and he cared for nothing else. And wisdom will enable us to discern what are the true ends of life, and how we are to secure them. As for what would not contribute to these, we shall say they do not come into the field of our operations; they count for nothing: I will spend no time on them, no thought, no money. There are higher aims and loftier purposes than those – achieving righteousness, winning God's favour, securing eternal glory. These are the objects towards which we press. These are the supreme motives for those whose eyes wisdom has opened to see things as they are – to whom wisdom has revealed the inner law of life.

And if we "lack wisdom," we are to "ask of God, who giveth to all liberally" – freely, unconditionally, making no bargain – "and upbraideth not." If we discover that we are wanting wisdom, are troubled by the want of it, and ask for it, He will not rebuke us for our folly. But, says James, "let him ask in faith, nothing doubting; for he that doubteth is like the surge of the sea driven by the wind and tossed. For let not that man think that he shall receive anything of the Lord; a double-minded man, unstable in all his ways."

These last words suggest a long train of reflection, which we cannot now pursue. The man who has some confidence in God and yet doubts, who asks for wisdom, hopes that God will give it, and yet is uncertain – he is "a double-minded man." He will not only be hesitating in his prayers, he will be "unstable in all his ways." That is the trouble with many of us – high thoughts to-day, to-morrow they have all disappeared.

Now look at the words which follow: "Let the brother of low degree glory in his high estate: and the rich, in that he is made low; because as the flower of the grass he shall pass away. For the sun ariseth with the scorching wind, and withereth the grass; and the flower thereof falleth, and the grace of the fashion of it perisheth: so also shall the rich man fade away in his goings."

"Let the brother of low degree" — the poor man, the obscure man — "glory in his high estate"; he is a child of God through Christ, heir of eternal blessedness; instead of resenting his poverty and being discontented with his obscurity, let him remember that he is a prince, and glory in it. He is a prince on his way to his kingdom, travelling by rough roads, enduring many hardships, suffering from hunger, cold, and weariness, and the people among whom he is travelling do not know anything about his greatness; but *he* knows; "let him glory in his high estate."

It is a hard thing for a Christian man to maintain this high and cheerful temper while he is enduring hardships. The hardships are so near, so real, so distressing, that they fill all his thoughts. How is it possible for him not to be depressed? It is only possible when he really comes to see how brief are his earthly sufferings when compared with eternal joy, how light they are when compared with eternal glory. Let him look at things as they are; let him have true wisdom, wisdom to form right judgments about this world and the next, about earthly sorrows and divine blessings, and then the brother of low degree will "glory in his high estate."

On the other hand, the rich brother is to glory "in that he is made low." That is harder still. He is to glory in whatever reminds him that his wealth is transient, that he will cease to be a rich man when he dies, and may cease to be a rich man long before he dies. So far as he is merely a rich man and nothing more, "as the flower of the grass he shall pass away. For the sun ariseth with the scorching wind, and withereth the grass, and the flower thereof falleth, and the grace of the fashion of it perisheth: so also shall the rich man fade away in his goings." The rich man is very likely to forget all this. He is likely to pride himself on his wealth, as though it were an enduring possession, to find his satisfaction in the pleasant things of life, to forget how brief these satisfactions are, and to disregard the awful, the glorious life which lies beyond death. He is likely to think too highly of himself because his wealth purchases him the consideration of others. He is likely to become self-confident, to be masterful and arrogant, to suppose that because he is better off than his Christian brother he is therefore a better man.

Let us translate James's meaning into modern language. If a bank breaks and he loses a large sum of money, the rich man must rejoice, because it compels him to see that he may lose everything, and that he is just as dependent on God as the poorest of his brethren. If he invests half his fortune in a rotten company, and is obliged to live in a smaller house and to part with his horses and carriages, he is to rejoice, because it forces him to think of the treasure which moth doth not corrupt and which thieves cannot steal. That is very hard. If he finds that with all his riches he cannot get into the kind of society which he likes, that poorer men win more affection and more respect – if in any way he is humbled, he is to rejoice; for it makes him see the difference between what he has and what he is. What he has will soon disappear, and the great question for him to consider is what he is. And he may discover that his money represents all that he is worth, and that apart from his money he is worthless. He is to "glory in that he is made low" – in whatever makes clearer the real truth about himself and his wealth he is to rejoice; it is always best to know how we really stand, though the knowledge may be very painful to us. That a rich man should glory in whatever brings him down from his imagined security of eminence is, I repeat, a hard lesson to learn, and a rich man needs a great deal of the grace of God to learn it.

However, there are very few, if any, of us who are subjected to this severe test. Compared with the rich and the great, we are all, I suppose, "brothers of low degree" – not wealthy, not distinguished by high birth or high position. Our perils are of another kind; we are in danger of being discontented and envious. The workman with thirty shillings a week sometimes envies the foreman with three pounds. The foreman sometimes envies the master; the draper's assistant sometimes envies the head of the firm; the merchant's clerk sometimes envies the merchant. The small manufacturer and the small shopkeeper sometimes envy the great people in their own way of business. The doctor with a poor practice sometimes envies the doctor who attends wealthy people and gets large fees; the lawyer who can hardly afford to keep a clerk sometimes envies the prosperous solicitor and famous barrister. Thank God it is not always so. Indeed, I believe that envy of this kind is far less common than we often imagine. I have long ceased to bring sweeping charges against whole classes of men, if it was ever my foolish habit to bring such charges. It is the people who are proud of their prosperity, and who despise men that are less fortunate than themselves, who think that the less fortunate envy them, just as people who envy the greater prosperity of other men think that the prosperous despise them.

We have seen how sternly James deals with the rich; there is sternness in his dealings with the brother of low degree. He was a compassionate man for real distress, as appears later in the Epistle, but here there is no softness. He does not tell the brother of low degree that he is badly used, that society is hard upon him, that many a poor man deserves to be rich, many an obscure man to be distinguished and famous. Here he expresses no sympathy with the man who is not so prosperous as other men, whose place is among the undistinguished millions of ordinary people. Sympathy? No! That is not his present mood.

"Let the brother of low degree glory in his high estate." There is something manly, something really Christian in that. Do not complain of your want of riches, of your hard work, of your want of distinction. Glory in the greatness of your wealth, and in the greatness of your position as sons of God and heirs of eternal blessedness. Think what you are. The eternal God loves you with as warm a love as that which He has for the richest and most eminent of your Christian brethren. You are as dear to Him as if you had the estates of a duke. You are as dear to Him as if you had in your veins the blood of a long line of noble ancestors. You are as dear to Him as if you were a famous minister, or a great orator, or a great poet. You who are His child, "glory in your high estate." You are poor, but you are not at home. You are on a journey, on your way to the home that God has prepared for you. Even princes do not wear their robes and their crowns while they are travelling, nor do rich men carry their wealth with them. You, too, my poor brother, are rich enough at home. And you are on your way there. Glory in your high estate.

There is a famous passage in Macaulay's *Essay on Milton,* in which, with all the brilliance of his rhetoric, though not without its characteristic defects, he describes the Puritans. "If their steps were not accompanied by a splendid train of menials, legions of ministering angels had charge over them. Their palaces were houses not made with hands; their diadems crowns of glory which should never fade away. On the rich and the eloquent, on nobles and priests, they looked down with contempt; for they deemed themselves rich in a more precious treasure and eloquent in a more sublime language; nobles by the right of an earlier creation, and priests by the imposition of a mightier hand."

That is a great passage, with all its imperfections, and if we make one correction it describes the true temper of a Christian man. Contempt, whether for nobles or for priests, whether for the rich or the poor, should never have a place in a Christian heart. The Christian man should "glory in his high estate," but should never despise others. For them, too, though they may not know it, Christ died. They, too, even when unconscious, are encircled by divine love. They, too, are the heirs of an eternal glory. They, too, are among those whom Christ came to seek and to save.

What a different life Christian men and women would live throughout the week if they kept in their thoughts the palaces which are to be their homes, the crowns which they are to wear, the dignity which belongs to them already, and the greater dignity which they may win by the gentle speech, by the courteous manners, the gracious temper, the truthfulness, the uprightness, the industry, the purity which should distinguish them as the sons and daughters of God – if they would think of all the wealth and glory that are theirs, however humble may be their earthly condition.

I was returning yesterday from Church Stretton, where I had been for a few days' rest. It was a brilliant afternoon, and as we came through Shropshire and North Staffordshire the country seemed perfectly beautiful. When we reached Wolverhampton there was a great contrast. You know the country – huge masses of cinders and black waste upon the mounds; dreary workshops, rows of mean houses, foul with dirt and smoke; the very grass, where it would grow at all, unlovely and dingy. I said, "What a change!" but then I lifted my eyes, and above all that dreary waste there was a divine glory. In the west the sun was sinking in a sea of flame. The heavy clouds were of rich purple, fringed with fire; lighter clouds, touched with the sun, were of a brilliant orange. It was a vision of transcendent splendour.

And that may be a true type of your life. Your earthly condition may be poor, mean, ignoble. But over you too God's heaven is hanging. It is always there – the sun in its splendour by day, the shining hosts of stars by night; these are the heritage of the brother of low degree, as well as of the rich and the great. Every promise of divine love, every gift of the divine grace, every dignity that belongs to the children of the Most High, every immortal hope – they are all yours. Live like men whom God has so greatly blessed. "Glory in your high estate."

FOR ADDITIONAL INFORMATION ABOUT ROBERT DALE:

Brown, John. "R. W. Dale." *Puritan Preaching in England.* New York: Charles Scribner's Sons, 1900.

Dale, A. W. W. *The Life of R. W. Dale.* London: Hodder & Stoughton, 1898.

Dale, R. W. *Nine Lectures on Preaching.* New York: George H. Doran Co., n.d.

Edwards, John. "Dr. R. W. Dale of Birmingham." *Nineteenth Century Preachers and Their Methods.* London: Charles A. Kelly, 1902.

Howard, Harry C. "Robert William Dale." *Princes of the Christian Pulpit and Pastorate.* 2d series. Nashville: Cokesbury Press, 1928.

Nicoll, W. Robertson. "Dr. R. W. Dale." *Princes of the Church.* London: Hodder & Stoughton, 1921.

FOR OTHER SERMONS BY ROBERT DALE:

The Evangelical Revival and Other Sermons. London: Hodder & Stoughton, 1880.
The Ten Commandments. London: Hodder & Stoughton, 1885.
Also: *Fellowship with Christ* (1891), *Week-Day Sermons* (1867).

WILLIAM BOOTH

1829-1912

WILLIAM BOOTH, photograph, courtesy of the Salvation Army, London.

WILLIAM BOOTH

1829	*Born April 10 in Nottingham, England*
1842	*Apprenticed to pawnbroker; father died*
1844	*Converted*
1849	*Went to London*
1852	*Entered Methodist ministry*
1854	*Left Wesleyan Church and united with Methodist New Connexion*
1855	*Married Catherine Mumford*
1861	*Became independent of any religious denomination and entered evangelistic work in London*
1865	*Began mission work in East London*
1878	*Constituted the Salvation Army*
1887	*Began expansion of social services*
1890	*Catherine Booth died on October 4;* In Darkest England and the Way Out *published*
1912	*Died on August 20*

REARED IN POVERTY, he became the leader of an army of two million dedicated to fighting poverty. As a child he lived in a home which was at best cold to religion, but as a man he preached a "hot" religion that led hundreds of thousands into deep religious experience. As a young preacher he was jeered and stoned by riotous thugs, but as the aged leader of the Salvation Army he was cheered and honored not only by the masses but also by kings, queens, and presidents. William Booth was a preacher without parallel in the Christian movement.

LIFE AND TIMES

On April 10, 1829, William Booth was born in Nottingham, England. Although his father, Samuel Booth, was not a devout man he did want his children to be in the church. Two days after William was born he was baptized in the Church of England at Nottingham. His parents seldom attended worship services, but William was not completely deprived of religious influence. Relatives and friends spoke to him from time to time about spiritual matters and he occasionally attended Sunday school.

His family was not only lacking in religion but also in economic stability. His father experienced financial setback again and again until finally the family was reduced to poverty. Shortly before his death, when William was only thirteen years of age, Samuel Booth apprenticed his son to a pawnbroker. Realizing that his death was near, the father wanted to provide in some way for his son and family, and this seemed to be the only way out. For six years William Booth served in the pawnshop. He had practically no income as an apprentice and watched helplessly as his mother and sisters suffered the hardships of poverty.

Two years after his father's death William Booth was converted. He described this experience as follows:

> When as a giddy youth of fifteen I was led to attend the Wesley Chapel, Nottingham, I cannot recollect that any individual pressed me in the direction of personal surrender to God. I was wrought upon quite independently of human effort by the Holy Ghost, who created within me a great thirst for a new life.
>
> I felt that I wanted, in place of the life of self-indulgence to which I was yielding myself, a happy, conscious sense that I was pleasing God, living right, and spending all of my powers to get others into such a life. I saw that all this ought to be, and I decided that it should be. It is wonderful that I should have reached this decision in view of the influence then surrounding me. . . .
>
> Yet I had that instinctive belief in God which, in common with my fellow-creatures, I had brought into the world with me. I had no disposition to deny my instincts, which told me that if there was a God His laws ought to have my obedience and His interests my service.
>
> I felt it was better to live right than to live wrong, and as to caring for the interests of others instead of my own, the condition of the suffering people around me, people with whom I had been so long familiar, and

whose agony seemed to reach its climax about this time, undoubtedly affected me very deeply.[1]

William Booth had an overwhelming desire to share the good news of Jesus Christ with others. Immediately after his conversion he began to tell about his experience. From the very beginning he decided to tell the poor, the sick, and the outcasts about Jesus Christ. His early witnessing and preaching added strength to his Christian conviction. He needed all of the strength he could get—he received no encouragement from his family or even from his church.

After completing his apprenticeship in the pawnshop, Booth left Nottingham and traveled to London. He wanted very much to leave the pawnbroking business, but in London he could find no other employment. For three years he worked for a pawnbroker during the day and preached at night on the streets of London. On Sunday he preached in some Methodist chapels and on the streets. He came to feel that he should devote all of his time to preaching; about this conviction he wrote:

> How can anybody with spiritual eyesight talk of having no call, when there are such multitudes around him who never hear a word about God, and never intend to; who can never hear, indeed, without the sort of preacher who will force himself upon them? Can a man keep right in his own soul who can see all this, and yet stand waiting for a "call" to preach? Would they wait so for a "call" to help some one to escape from a burning building, or to snatch a sinking child from a watery grave . . . ?
>
> And are there not persons who know that they possess special gifts, such as robust health, natural eloquence or power of voice which specially makes them responsible for doing something for souls?
>
> And yet I do not at all forget that above and beyond all these things there does come to some a special and direct call, which is peculiarly fatal to disregard, and peculiarly strengthening to enjoy and act upon.
>
> I believe that there have been many eminent, holy, and useful men who never had such a call; but that does not at all prevent any one from asking God for it,

1. Quoted in William Hamilton Nelson, *Blood and Fire: General William Booth* (New York: Century Co., 1929), pp. 29–30. Used by permission of Meredith Press, New York.

or blessing Him for His special kindness when He gives it.[2]

In 1852 Booth began to give full time to preaching. In this same year he met Catherine Mumford. Soon Catherine stopped addressing William as "my dear friend" and began addressing him as "my dearest love." Her letters were signed, "your own loving Kate." In a short time they were engaged. She brought to their relationship a superior mind, a cultured background, and a deep devotion to Christ. She too was a Methodist. She sensed William's strong ambition and urged him to control it. She recognized his bent toward overwork and pled with him to pace himself. She was also responsible for turning him from alcohol to a position of total abstinence. In 1855 they were married—only William's lack of financial resources delayed the wedding for so long.

Booth continued to preach within the Methodist fold, but increasingly he was irritated by the religious bickering which divided Methodism. In 1854 he had left the Wesleyan church to unite with the Methodist New Connexion. Within this fellowship he served as pastor and revivalist. By 1861 he was convinced that he should sever ties with any religious denomination and enter independent evangelistic work in London.

In his move to religious independence, as in all other important decisions of his life, his wife played a significant role. Catherine Booth was not only a devoted wife but also an effective preacher and author. Her first preaching took place when she was thirty-one years old and while Booth was still in the pastorate. Booth was confined to his house by the doctor, and Catherine took his place in the pulpit. Women preachers were a novelty in that day, and news of her preaching spread quickly over England. During Booth's illness she not only preached for him but also wrote a pamphlet and carried on many other activities of the church. This activity is all the more amazing in light of her physical condition: she was a semi-invalid, much of the time confined to her bed with painful spine trouble; she had a weak throat and was often in the grips of a cold; she had borne four children in five years, had nursed them, made their clothes, and cared for them through numerous childhood illnesses.

Booth's entrance into evangelistic work was an act of faith.

2. Ibid., pp. 52–53.

He had no assurance of financial support. He and his family lived on the brink of poverty. Soon the effective preaching of William and Catherine Booth attracted attention. Financial backers established them in a home in London.

After a series of evangelistic campaigns Booth returned to London and began a revival meeting in Whitechapel, East London. It was here that he began the work which was ultimately to extend around the world. Walking through this poverty-stricken section of London, Booth was certain that this was the place where he was to plant his life. He told his wife: "O Kate, I have found my destiny! These are the people for whose salvation I have been longing all these years. As I passed by the doors of the flaming gin-palaces tonight, I seemed to hear a voice sounding in my ear, 'Where can you go and find such heathen as these, and where is there so great a need for your labors?' And there and then in my soul I offered myself and you and the children up to this great work. These people shall be our people, and they shall have our God for their God."[3]

Booth began his mission work in East London in 1865. At first the work was disappointingly fruitless. Opposition was strong, many were indifferent, and the people were suspicious of religion in general. The tent in which he began his mission was destroyed by a gang of toughs. He moved into a dance hall where people danced on Saturday nights and continued until early Sunday morning; then Booth and his followers cleaned out the hall, set up benches, and had preaching services. Soon people began to come in great crowds and the hall was crowded to capacity—about six hundred people—every Sunday. In addition to the Sunday meetings, Booth preached in the open air, led processions, and held night meetings during the week in an old wool warehouse.

Persecution was great from the beginning. Hoodlum boys and drunken loafers threw fireworks through the windows of the warehouse; sometimes they would pour gunpowder in the room and create a blinding flash by setting fire to it. Gangs frequently hurled mud and stones through the windows at the preacher and the crowd. The liquor dealers worked hard to have Booth kicked out of East London. The police were no help; in fact, they often broke up outdoor meetings and accused Booth's followers of being the cause of all the trouble.

---

3. Ibid., pp. 131–32.

By 1878 the Christian Mission became the Salvation Army. William Booth assumed the title of "General." A thorough organization was created and publications such as the *War Cry* were instituted. But persecution continued to plague Booth and his army. One Salvation Army officer came into a meeting loaded down with dead cats and rats; he explained these had been thrown at him, and that he caught and held the dead animals because if he dropped them the crowd would merely pick them up to throw again. Pots of human urine were often dumped on the street preachers. Beatings were not uncommon: in 1889, at least 669 Salvation Army members were assaulted— some were killed and many were maimed. Even children were not immune; ruffians threw lime in the eyes of a child of a Salvation Army member. The newspapers ridiculed Booth. *Punch* referred to him as "Field Marshal von Booth."

Soon a band of thugs and ruffians organized themselves into the "Skeleton Army" and devoted themselves to disrupting the meetings of the Salvation Army. They often attacked Salvation Army members as they paraded through the streets or held open-air meetings. They frequently stormed Salvation Army meeting halls by the hundreds, broke out the window panes, and wrecked the inside of the buildings. At first the police did little to stop the "Skeleton Army." Instead of helping they frequently harassed Booth and his followers.

The beginning of change in public attitude came with the expansion of the Salvation Army's social service activities. Booth had always been dedicated to evangelism and he never wavered in this dedication. But the horrible conditions of the poor made him realize that as a Christian he had to do something to alleviate their suffering. In spite of all of the arguments to the contrary, he commanded his army to move to meet the needs of the poor.

Booth had always been sympathetic with the poor—he had known poverty as a youth and had never really escaped it. But in his earlier days he believed that conversion in itself was fully adequate to place a man on the road to Christian growth. With maturity he realized that a person needed more than a religious experience if he were to climb above the horrors of poverty in urban London.

Booth noted that in the winter men and women often slept in the open with nothing but paper to protect them from the icy air. He saw thousands of children sold into prostitution before they were fourteen years of age. He gazed upon multitudes of people gripped by alcoholism. He deplored the widespread unemployment and the inability of many who wanted to work to find a job. He smelled the stench from the tenements where whole families were packed into one room without adequate ventilation or sanitation. He sickened at the sight of armies of rats and bugs feeding on the flesh of the poor. His sensitive spirit suffered as he saw the wealthy grow even wealthier on the suffering and hopelessness of the poor.

In response to such needs, Booth moved with zeal to establish numerous services and institutions. A list of all his programs would fill several pages. He set up programs for the starving, for the drunkards, for the poor, for the unemployed, for the homeless, for the criminals, for the prostitutes, for the sick, for missing persons, for the emotionally disturbed, and for the uneducated. He established factories, farms, training schools for emigrants, and loan services. He did not claim that his efforts would eliminate poverty, but he hoped that they would alleviate the suffering caused by an economic system which plunged millions into poverty.

His book *In Darkest England and the Way Out* set forth his plans for social action. Many ridiculed his schemes. Others saw them as dangerously socialistic. Booth shrugged off the criticism and plunged ahead. About his efforts he said, "We saw the need. We saw the people starving, we saw people going about half-naked, people doing sweated labour; and we set about bringing a remedy for these things. We were obliged — there was a compulsion. How could you do anything else?"[4]

Gradually the poor began to realize that Booth cared for *them*, not just for their souls. And in spite of their objections to some of his methods, even the leaders of church and state began to recognize the sincerity of Booth's motives and the effectiveness of some of his methods. Men with such diverse temperaments and backgrounds as Winston Churchill, Charles Haddon Spurgeon, and Cardinal Manning praised Booth. During his last years William Booth became an honored guest in the courts of kings and in the residences of national leaders throughout the world.

---

4. Richard Collier, *The General Next to God*, p. 175. Copyright © 1965 by Richard Collier. Published by E. P. Dutton & Co., Inc. and reprinted with their permission and the permission of Collins Publishers.

After a vigorous discussion of prison reforms with Winston Churchill, an old friend, Churchill cracked: "Well General, am I converted now?" Booth shot back, "Oh no, I wouldn't say you're converted, but I think you're *convicted*." His humor sometimes appeared in his sermons, too, as when he told his favorite story of the man who confessed between sobs, "I'm a convert, all right, General, but when I came into this place I'm damned if I had any idea of getting saved."[5]

Even before King Edward VII, his lively humor was evident. On June 24, 1904, at Buckingham Palace, the king asked what the churches then thought of his work. Booth replied, "Sir, they imitate me." The king laughed and then begged Booth to write in his autograph book. The old man summed his life work:

> Your Majesty,
> Some men's ambition is art,
> Some men's ambition is fame,
> Some men's ambition is gold,
> My ambition is the souls of men.[6]

Nevertheless, many found him dictatorial and hard to work with — members of his own family even denounced him as their leader and formed separate organizations. His methods were often dramatic and showy. Yet none could deny his compassion.

When he died in 1912 on August 20, the world mourned. As his funeral procession moved through the streets of downtown London, all traffic was stopped for two hours. England had reason to pause: one of her most famous generals was dead.

Vachel Lindsay captures the spirit of Booth best in his historic poem, "General William Booth Enters into Heaven."[7]

General William Booth Enters into Heaven

(To be sung to the tune of 'The Blood of the Lamb'
with indicated instrument)

I

(Bass drum beaten loudly.)
Booth led boldly with his big bass drum —
(Are you washed in the blood of the Lamb?)

---

5. Ibid., p. 241.
6. Ibid., p. 215.
7. Reprinted with permission of The Macmillan Company from *Collected Poems* by Vachel Lindsay. Copyright 1913 by The Macmillan Company.

The Saints smiled gravely and they said: 'He's come.'
(Are you washed in the blood of the Lamb?)
Walking lepers followed, rank on rank,
Lurching bravos from the ditches dank,
Drabs from the alleyways and drug fiends pale —
Minds still passion-ridden, soul-powers frail: —
Vermin-eaten saints with moldy breath,
Unwashed legions with the ways of Death —
(Are you washed in the blood of the Lamb?)

. . . .

II

(*Bass drum slower and softer.*)
Booth died blind and still by faith he trod,
Eyes still dazzled by the ways of God.
Booth led boldly, and he looked the chief
Eagle countenance in sharp relief,
Beard a-flying, air of high command
Unabated in that holy land.

(*Sweet flute music.*)
Jesus came from out the court-house door,
Stretched his hands above the passing poor.
Booth saw not, but led his queer ones there
Round and round the mighty court-house square.
Then, in an instant all that blear review
Marched on spotless, clad in raiment new.
The lame were straightened, withered limbs uncurled
And blind eyes opened on a new, sweet world.

. . . .

(*Reverently sung, no instruments.*)
And when Booth halted by the curb for prayer
He saw his Master thro' the flag-filled air.
Christ came gently with a robe and crown
For Booth the soldier, while the throng knelt down.
He saw King Jesus. They were face to face,
And he knelt a-weeping in that holy place.
Are you washed in the blood of the Lamb?

PREACHING AND SERMONS

There is an incredible variety among the men who have achieved distinction as preachers of the Christian gospel, but

General William Booth is unique among them all. No one who ever saw him could forget his appearance on the platform, aggressive and dominating, on fire with a passion for souls. He once said that he liked his tea as he liked his religion — H-O-T! — and he always preached a hot religion.

He never intended to found a great movement, nor did he intend to become involved with social action. He was an evangelist first and foremost, and it was his concern for souls that led him into his concern for the physical needs of men. He told his followers, "Go for souls, and go for the worst." He began as an evangelist and through all his life he remained a flaming evangelist. He believed that all men were infected with sin and condemned to a fiery hell. His enthusiastic, intense preaching blazed with a passion to rescue men from that fate.

One description of him late in life is particularly pointed:

> Tall and attenuated, with slightly stooping shoulders, the frail body of the man would have seemed almost feeble but for the vigor and distinction of the strong head. His hair, which was snow-white, grew long, and was brushed carelessly standing up from the brow and falling backwards to the neck and ears. His face was almost bloodless in its pallor. The rather small eyes, under dark and restless eyebrows, had the brightness of beads. The lower part of his face was covered by a mustache and beard as white as his hair. It seemed as if he were a figure carved out of chalk. In repose, he was like a tired man who observes and reflects between spells of nodding sleep, but in action, with his thin arms raised above his head, his eyes blazing, and his powerful voice hurtling out his thoughts, he was like a prophet.[8]

Booth was a complex man: vehement, moody, impulsive, stern and disciplined, consumed with the interests of his "army." By the end of his life he had succeeded in alienating most of his family. In their younger days, Booth's children enjoyed many frolics with their father, who, for all of his dedication, enjoyed romping with his family. But he was imperious and demanding as he grew older and many people found it virtually impossible to work with him. His stomach

---

8. Alexander Gammie, *Preachers I Have Heard* (London: Pickering & Inglis, n.d.), pp. 54–55.

was a source of constant pain to him and he neither ate nor slept regularly. Occasionally Booth grew irritable with his aides, even harsh tempered; some men admitted that he made them "almost bleed at the pores with nervousness." Nevertheless he was also a man of great compassion, and whatever his personal failings in his dealings with others, he had infinite compassion for tired and broken humanity.

His sermon style was as vigorous and startling as his life. When he preached in the United States in 1886 during a whirlwind eleven-week campaign from New York to Kansas City, he spoke for almost 200 hours and was heard by 180,000 Americans. Town after town listened spellbound as Booth thundered at the crowds, his long body swaying back and forth on the platform, his hair and flowing beard rumpled, his arms clasped behind his back, right hand over left wrist, his eyes like fiery coals.[9]

As he neared the conclusion of one sermon during that tour, he said:

> *Sin is a real thing,* a damnable thing. I don't care what the scientists call it, or what some of the pulpits are calling it. I know what it is. Sin is devilish. It is sin and sin only which prevents the world being happy. Sin! Go into the slums of the great cities, pick up little girls six years of age, sold into infamy by their own parents. Look at the drunken mother murdering her own child. Look at the father, strapping his crippled boy. Sin! That's what I call sin . . . something beastly and filthy and devilish![10]

Booth had a gift for vivid allegories that drove home his message until his audiences were spellbound:

> Look at that man going down the river, going down in a boat with Niagara beyond. He is got out into the stream . . . the rapids have got hold of the boat . . . he is going . . . my God! He has gone over—and he never pulled in an oar! That is the way people are damned; they go on; they have no time; they don't *think;* they neglect Salvation—and they are lost.[11]

---

9. Collier, p. 166.
10. Ibid.
11. Gammie, p. 55.

Sometimes he was even more dramatically sensational, as when he pictured Lot going out to warn his sons-in-law on the last night in Sodom. Booth would turn up his coat collar, seize somebody's hat and jam it on his head, and go stalking across the stage, while the whole audience vividly imagined the dark streets of Sodom, the coming disaster, and the mocking laughter of the young men. His son, Bramwell Booth, said that he had seen thousands of people transfixed as the general spoke of the various classes of sinners suffering in hell, and among them one counting, always counting – "one – two – three – four – five – then ten – eleven – twelve – thirteen" – until you could have heard a pin drop as he came to "twenty-eight – twenty-nine – thirty. Why it is Judas!"[12]

He urged the outcasts, "Come drunk or sober." New converts, released from a life of debauchery, would shout in the midst of his services, "I *do* believe – He *does* save me!" When one who was overcome with excitement cried out, "I must jump!" the evangelist urged him, "Then jump!" Some fell into near trances and were carried to rooms close by. Booth often kept doctors standing nearby, but none ever found that the converts had suffered physical harm.[13]

Once while preaching in his home country in the Midlands following the execution of wife-murderer John H. Starkey, Booth was urged by an aide to preach a funeral-service sermon on Starkey that same night. An ugly crowd packed the hall, jeering and ridiculing, stamping their feet upon the floor, until Booth's voice cracked like doom: "John H. Starkey never had a praying mother." In the startled silence that followed, every man there felt his hold on life grow uneasy.[14]

It would be easy enough to dismiss such tactics as sheer, raw sensationalism. But it must be remembered that Booth's converts were not the ordinary, middle-class individuals who normally occupied churchly pews. They were men from the hardest and crudest kinds of life, without education or inclination toward religion. They knew nothing of churches and even less of God. William Booth was an evangelist who spoke their language, one who understood their sins and needs. He believed in publicity – "Anything that gets us into the papers,

12. Ibid.
13. Collier, p. 60.
14. Ibid., p. 79.

is good" — but he was canny and shrewd in his use of publicity, and his immediate as well as ultimate end was always to bring men unto Christ, never to elevate himself.

At times Booth could use the sharpest kind of personal application in his sermons. Standing in Red Lion Square, hemmed in by a gang of loafers, he flayed them unmercifully; the world was in chaos because of sins like theirs. His voice knifed straight through to them in that early sermon:

> I want to put a few straight questions to your souls. Have any of *you* got a child at home without shoes to its feet? Are *your* wives sitting now in dark houses waiting for you to return without money? Are you going away from here . . . *to spend on drink money that your wives need for food?*[15]

Booth learned his preaching style from fiery evangelists. After his conversion, he frequently attended the tall Wesleyan Chapel on Broad Street in Nottingham. During the "Hungry Forties," many revivalists enthralled crowds at the chapel. Booth learned something from them all. He learned the value of a subdued opening that warmed steadily to a white heat from the Reverend James Cauthey, an angular, black-cloaked Irish-American preacher from Burlington, Vermont. He learned his style of simple parables from the preaching of Isaac Marsden, of Doncaster, Yorkshire. And from them all he caught the spirit of enthusiasm that never left him. But Booth was more enthusiastic than them all, much to the scandal of his Methodist brethren.

From the beginning of his ministry Booth preached, like Wesley, in the open air. Never dismayed, he preached in alley-ways, perched on chairs or barrels, to crowds of three at the most, exhorting them to join a forthcoming meeting in a nearby cottage. In Nottingham Booth preached one of his first sermons in such a cottage. An inverted box flanked by flickering candles served as his pulpit; his audience was largely composed of poor women who carried their own chairs to the parlor. Those who heard it never forgot Booth's strangely gentle parable of a mother watching her child's first efforts to walk. Would she rebuke it for its failures, or sit unmoved if it fell and hurt itself? It was just as hard, Booth said, for a man to follow Christ.

---

15. Ibid., p. 30.

Harsh words were no help to a falling man; the answer must be an effort by everyone to help him learn to walk.[16]

But Booth took to street preaching in earnest when he discovered that people would not come into the comfortable, though meager, New Connexion churches that he pastored. At the age of thirty-six Booth came to the stunning realization that the aching needs of East London would never be met by inviting people to come into churches.

In a memorable walk he pushed his way through the ragged, brutalized, shrieking crowds of match-sellers and Irish flower girls, hawking laborers and starving children digging through heaps of rotten plums outside of the fruit-seller's shop. He saw five-year-old children blind drunk, alcoholics before the age of six. It was a shocking world. He was determined to reach these people, and he knew that to do so he must preach in the streets where they were. Outside a pub he stopped and cried, "There is a Heaven in East London for *everyone,* for everyone who will stop and think and look to Christ as a personal saviour." Only jeers and oaths came from inside the pub, but some were listening in spite of themselves. Then from the rear a rotten egg came whizzing to find its mark; and with the yolk trickling down his face, Booth bowed and prayed, and then walked on through the streets.[17]

Many times in his life Booth would be stoned, battered, shoved, cursed, and almost killed along with many of his followers. But he never gave up his belief in street preaching, even when he was dismissed from the New Connexion churches because of it. In his later days Booth may have been the only evangelist in the world to have a private bodyguard — Peter Monk, an Irish prize fighter converted by Booth, who became famous as "the General's boxer." At times when thugs threatened to silence Booth, Monk would stalk ominously up and down the aisles while Booth continued his sermon.

Booth was a perfectionist in his preaching as in his life. When he preached inside, he insisted on preaching only in well-ventilated halls with adequate lighting. He sent one of his associates to the back of the auditorium as he began his sermon; then, if his voice could be heard, his assistant would have a white handkerchief indicating that every word could be

---

16. Ibid.
17. Ibid., pp. 21-22.

clearly distinguished. Booth never had a good voice, but toward the end of his life it became even more harsh and cracked. Gammie said:

> By the time I heard him, the General was already an old man. His voice had suffered from constant use, particularly in the open air. It was as rasping as a saw; someone described it as "a queer, worn, torn, corncrake voice." But the passion vibrating in every tone made it powerful and impressive.[18]

From his early days as an independent street preacher Booth learned enthusiasm and directness. As a young man enrolled as a student under William Cooke, Booth studied Greek and Latin as a painful discipline, but his preaching he took to with enthusiasm. On the day of his enrollment in Cooke's classes in South London, Booth preached at the local Brunswick Chapel and made fifteen converts. He pictured the world's sinners as shipwrecked men whom only Christ could save, and he jumped upon the pulpit chair, wildly waving his pocket handkerchief as a distress signal.

Booth's ability as an evangelist was quickly recognized by the New Connexion churches and he was allowed to pursue his enthusiastic preaching in a series of revival efforts. His wife, Catherine, was a great source of help to him. He once wrote to her: "I want a sermon on the Flood, one on Jonah, and one on the Judgment. Send me some bare thoughts; some clear startling outlines. Nothing moves the people like the terrific. . . ."[19]

He gained great success in his early revivals. During a short revival at Hyle, Cornwall, which eventually was extended to a mammoth eighteen-month campaign, fishermen rowed ten miles across turbulent seas and villagers walked for miles over the hills to hear him. "Business is no longer carried out," a local citizen wrote. "The shopkeepers and their customers are all busily engaged in the Booth meetings. . . ." Booth claimed 7,000 Cornishmen became Christians.

Strangely enough, however, in his early days of preaching to the poor, Booth was not at all successful. His naturally impet-

---

18. Gammie, p. 54.
19. Collier, p. 37.

uous style had tamed considerably during his days as a Methodist minister; he not only wore a black frock coat but he had a black-frock-coat manner. One night the answer to his frustration came to him suddenly. While addressing an audience of 1200 at Whitechapel, Booth was perplexed and frustrated by his indifferent audience. Then he called upon an old gypsy hawker, who had been converted a few weeks earlier, to give his testimony. As the old man spoke, a strange quiet and fascination swept across the meeting. Now Booth learned the sober truth: ordinary men giving their testimony could command such attention as he could not. He told his son, Bramwell: "I shall have to burn all those sermons of mine and go into the gypsy's."

Booth had been forced to withdraw from the formal, sedate sermons of the age in order to reach the poor he wanted to win. He told his followers later, "Just don't start preaching, I've got quite enough broken down parsons on my hands without that." No doubt he was thinking of his own days spent in frustration as he attempted to reach the poor with ordinary, conventional, sedate sermons. But there was no lasting danger of that: Booth was by nature a firebrand, and he forced his rugged style upon his followers. He urged them never to become settled nor to remain in one place. He refused to allow his followers to become static communities of the pious, sitting under a favorite preacher. He urged them to become "Godly go-ahead daredevils." He told one volunteer, "Make your will, pack your box, kiss your girl, be ready in a week." He told another, "You must be like the Irishman's gun — go off, loaded or not!"[20]

Booth followed his own advice: during the years of his sensational ministry, he became a legend in his own time by traveling five million miles in his sixty years of ministry and preaching sixty thousand sermons.

But no matter how much his fame grew, Booth always retained the simple language with which he had begun preaching in the streets of Nottingham and East London. His appeal was always to the heart, and his vocabulary was that of a common man — simple, direct, earthy. He liked to say: "Use words that Mary Ann will understand, and you will be sure to make yourself clear to her mistress; whereas if you speak only to her mis-

20. Ibid., p. 56.

tress, you will very likely miss her, and Mary Ann as well."[21]

He made no attempt to instruct or edify in his preaching. Even though his filing cabinet held three hundred classified sermons,[22] his one message all over the world was that of Jesus Christ and his salvation. He instituted the "Penitent-form," an early altar call that summoned men to come forward and kneel, confessing their sins and accepting Christ as their Savior. He was a vigorous, direct messenger of the almighty God, calling men to the altar for repentance. In his lifetime Booth succeeded in bringing hundreds of thousands of men to a new life.

Whatever his faults, he shook the teeth of conventional Christianity. In a real way, Booth inaugurated a new day in Christian preaching.

---

21. Gammie, p. 56.
22. Officials of the Salvation Army in London report, however, that they cannot locate any sermon manuscripts by Booth at this time. This loss may be due to the fact that many of their records were destroyed in the bombing of London during World War II.

Sermons

THE ATONEMENT OF JESUS CHRIST

Titus 2:11; Hebrews 2:9

WHAT DO WE MEAN by the Atonement? The word itself simply means *at-one-ment*, the uniting of two beings who had been separate or apart. In everyday language the word is used to signify something done by the wrongdoer to make amends for injuries he has inflicted on others. In religion the word Atonement is used to signify the sacrifice which Jesus Christ offered for our sins, by His death on the Cross, by which offering the reconciliation of God and man was made possible.

Some mistaken notions are entertained with respect to the benefits flowing out of the Atonement. The controversies with respect to the character and measure of the benefits resulting from Christ's sacrifice have been many and bitter, although the intensity of feeling aroused by these differences has been greatly modified in recent years.

While the controversies of the present day refer to aspects of the subject different from those of former times, the opinions of those days are still advocated with some degree of earnestness. In some parts of the world this is more markedly the case than in others. It is, therefore, of importance that officers should have correct ideas as to what those different opinions are. To several views of this doctrine, entertained by some churches, we take strong exception.

Salvationists object to the view that Christ by His sacrifice made salvation possible or certain to a chosen portion only of the human race, leaving the remainder outside the possibility of that salvation. This doctrine is generally described by the terms "election" and "reprobation," and is more commonly known as Calvinism. It sets forth the belief that one portion of mankind is elected by God to Everlasting Life, and the remaining portion reprobated to everlasting

Reprinted from *The Founder Speaks Again: A Selection of the Writings of William Booth*, [comp.] Cyril J. Barnes (London: Salvationist Publishing & Supplies, 1960), pp. 3–15, by permission of Salvation Army, London.

death. This doctrine is condemned by Salvationists on various grounds:

It is in opposition to the emphatic declarations of the Bible that Christ died for all men. "For the grace of God that bringeth salvation hath appeared to all men" (Titus 2:11). And again: "That He by the grace of God should taste death for every man" (Heb. 2:9).

It is in opposition to what we know of the nature of God, as set forth in the Scriptures. He is described in the Bible as a just and benevolent Being, which this doctrine seems most emphatically to deny.

It is in opposition to our natural sense of justice. That multitudes of human beings should be appointed to suffer everlasting death, independently of any choice or action of their own, is revolting to our conceptions of right and wrong, to say nothing about our natural sympathies with suffering.

Neither do we mean by the Atonement, as is maintained by some theologians, that Jesus Christ, by His sacrifice, met and satisfied the claims of the law man had broken, so as to render any further obedience to that law, by the entire human race, unnecessary. This view of the Atonement implies that every man you meet — whether you find him drunk in a public-house, or wallowing in the filth of a brothel, or expiating his murderous offences on the gallows — is on his way to Heaven, the punishment of his sins having been endured by Jesus Christ on the Cross. Such an idea is emphatically contradicted by the plainest declarations of the Bible. For the Bible has no meaning at all if it does not reveal a difference in the final destiny of the good and the bad — of the "saved" and the "unsaved."

Whatever may be the character of the punishment of the wicked, the Bible repeatedly, explicitly and emphatically states that it will be everlasting in its duration. It says that the wicked are to "go away into everlasting punishment: but the righteous into life eternal."

A third view of the Atonement from which the Army dissents maintains the theory that Jesus Christ paid our debt; by which is meant that He satisfied the claims of the broken law for every human being and secured the salvation of all men — on the simple condition of their believing the glad tidings. This is known as "the payment of debt theory" or "only believe and you shall be saved."

This view of the Atonement will, I think, be seen to be an impossible one. If it were true, it would secure the entrance of every human being into Heaven; because if Christ has satisfied all the claims which the law has upon those who transgressed it, He must have satisfied also the claim involved in the unbelief entertained down to the last moment of life. Consequently, "if the debt is paid, the obligation is discharged, and the debtor is free." It would follow inevitably that, whether I believe the good tidings or not, my unbelief cannot affect the fact; and whatever wickedness may be involved in my refusing to believe, that wickedness itself is also paid for if all my debt is discharged—I am free. As the hymn sung by the believers in this doctrine says:

> The payment of my debt cannot be twice required—
> First at my Surety's hand, and then at mine.

Another mistaken view of the benefits flowing out of the sacrifice of Christ, although it does not directly refer to the Saviour's death, is closely connected with it; this is known as the doctrine of "imputed righteousness." Jesus Christ, this notion says, by voluntarily placing Himself under the law to which man was subject, rendering a perfect obedience to that law, and sealing that obedience with His own Blood, thereby not only did purchase the forgiveness of sin for those whom He redeemed, but merited for us through His obedience a perfect righteousness; clothed in this His people will appear at the Judgment Bar, and it will constitute not only a preparation for Heaven but a right of entrance there.

This doctrine declares that the righteousness of Christ is imputed to those who believe on His name, not only to make up for their own unrighteousness, but to create a righteousness which should be regarded as their own. Though they have not obeyed the law, Christ has obeyed it for them, and therefore they are entitled to just the same blessings as though they had obeyed it themselves.This, I need hardly say, is a mistaken notion, seeing that one being cannot, in this sense, obey the law for another. Every creature in Heaven and on earth is placed under that law of Benevolence which claims all the love and service he is able to render, according to the capacity of his nature— whether it be that of an angel, of a man, or of a little child.

In becoming a man Jesus Christ voluntarily placed Himself on the same level, in this respect, as Peter and John; that is to say, the Law required from Him, as truly and really as it did from them, all the love and service which His powers enabled Him to render. The extent of the Saviour's capacity determined the extent of His obligation. Having an infinite capacity He was under obligation to love and serve in an infinite degree.

But if concerning the Atonement we do not entertain these notions, we do believe that Jesus Christ, by His death, offered a sacrifice for the sins of men which was of sufficient value to make amends for the damage done to the honour of the Law by man's transgression. This made it possible for God to forgive the sins of all who truly repent and believe on His Son and determine to live lives of faith and obedience. And we believe that, in virtue of this sacrifice, full forgiveness can be granted to the transgressor, without in any way diminishing, in the estimation of mankind, the honour of God whom he has offended, the majesty of the law he has broken, or the evil of the sin he has committed. By this divine scheme God can be just, and yet be the Justifier of him that believeth in Jesus.

I want now to mention some of the reasons which are given for refusing to accept the doctrine of the Atonement in any form.

The first of these affirms that this doctrine is a reflection upon the justice and benevolence of God. Those who bring forward this objection say that while the Bible and our natural instincts represent God as a loving and beneficent Father, this doctrine describes Him as a fierce and angry Being, who cannot forgive a poor sinner without His Son coming from Heaven to suffer the shame and agony of the Cross.

But this is a false representation of the subject; it is not the doctrine of the Bible, nor the doctrine of The Salvation Army. The true doctrine is just the opposite. The Atonement was not necessary to create compassion in the bosom of God for sin-stricken man; it was the compassion of God that generated the Atonement. The sacrifice on the cross was not offered to appease the angry wrath of the Father; it was in the compassionate bosom of the Father that the sacrifice of the Cross was born.

Christ's sacrifice was devised to maintain the dignity of the Law man had broken, and at the same time to rescue man from the penalty he had incurred. So far, therefore, from the Atonement being a reflection on the justice and benevolence of God, it is perhaps the greatest evidence we possess both of His unswerving justice and of His boundless love.

In the second place, the Atonement is declared by these objectors to have been unnecessary. This objection is taken on three grounds:

The objectors deny that in man's conduct any serious offence has been committed. They affirm that nothing has been done that could correctly be described as sin—meaning by sin the transgression of the divine Law. They say that the offences which the Bible describes as sins are not really sins at all, but merely irregularities resulting from errors of judgment; or, that they are involuntary, the working out of man's unbalanced nature; or, that they are the inevitable outcome of some hereditary inclination or disposition for which the individual cannot justly be held responsible.

Let us look carefully at this statement that no real sin has been committed, assuming several simple truths, to which I do not think these objectors would demur. God is, as we all believe, a benevolent Being, and the Author of our existence. Having arranged for our coming into the world, God must be desirous of our well-being. Knowing that our well-being must be largely dependent on our conduct, and knowing the kind of conduct which is likely most surely to lead to the happiest and most useful existence, it is certain that God would prefer that we should adopt that course of conduct. These preferences and judgments with respect to the conduct of our lives God has caused to be written in the books of providence, conscience and Scripture; and they constitute the rules, that is the laws, by which He seeks to control that conduct.

The transgression of these laws constitutes sin – which is, therefore, an offence not only against ourselves and our neighbours, but against God. In the everlasting death that is announced in the Bible you have the penalty God has connected with the transgression of His law. In the gift of Jesus Christ you have the expression of God's compassionate desire to save men from the penalty which is the consequence of their wrongdoing. And in the suffering and death of Jesus Christ you have the Atonement, by which act He displayed His high regard for the Law man had broken, His deep hatred of sin, and His boundless compassion for the transgressor. The Atonement enables Him at the same time consistently to rescue all who comply with the conditions attached to it, from the doom to which they have exposed themselves.

The second argument in support of the objection that the Atonement was unnecessary is as follows: "If God *is* the God of mercy that He is represented to be, and if man *has* sinned against Him, as he is said to have done, and if God *did* compassionate man, as the Bible says He did – why could He not forgive him, and remit the penalties attached to his wrongdoing without all the humiliation and suffering which is implied in the doctrine of the Atonement?"

To this I reply: There is a real difference between what is right and what is wrong, and this difference constitutes a gulf of infinite width and infinite depth – a gulf so wide and so deep that neither men, nor angels, nor even God himself can disregard it. For God, omnipotent and wise as He is, cannot make right wrong or wrong right. Upon this essential difference between what is right and what is wrong the whole fabric of the moral law of the universe is based. Thus God must be under the strongest obligation to do all that lies within His power to maintain, before all the creatures under His care, the manifest rightness of what is right and the manifest wrongness of what is wrong. This object God seeks to accomplish by the institution of the Law – the declaration of what is right and what is wrong in human conduct, and the demand for obedience upon all to whom the Law applies.

The needed respect for Law, and the importance of obedience to it, are guarded by the infliction of a penalty bearing some proportion to the magnitude of the transgression. And when Law is broken the infliction of penalty must inevitably follow. In the case of man's sin the penalty included: everlasting condemnation as wrongdoers, and everlasting separation from God. Quite possibly, indeed probably, the same or a similar penalty applies to every transgressor of divine Law in every part of the universe, seeing that divine Law is an expression of the divine nature and will. It is evident that, great as God is, it was morally impossible for Him to remit the penalty due to sin without some sacrifice being found which would have the effect of making the Law appear as honourable, and the offence appear as awful, as would have been the case had the penalty been inflicted.

Now, God's heart yearned over man in his transgression, prompting Him to desire man's deliverance from the consequences of that transgression. How was this deliverance to be effected? Something must be done which would make a similar impression upon the mind of man as to the importance of keeping the Law and the evil of breaking it as the infliction of the penalty due would have done; and which would at the same time awaken in him a sense of the shame and guilt of his transgression, and a desire to cease from his disobedience. This was done by the life and death of Jesus Christ, so that now every sinner who will, on God's terms, accept the deliverance provided for him, may go free.

A third objection to the necessity of the Atonement declares: "If the offence of man was the serious evil that you assert, and if God could not forgive that offence without some remarkable intervention on the part of some great Being who should become a wonderful example of freedom from sin, and yet of suffering for it – then are we not justified in believing that the holy life of Jesus Christ and the death He endured were sufficient to impress humanity with the required sense of the value of the Law, and the evil of the offence that had been committed against it, without our being called upon to regard Him as a *divine* Being? That is – could He not have made the needed sacrifice without being more than man?"

No! We do not think He could. If He had been nothing more than man He must Himself have been a transgressor of the Law, seeing that "all have sinned, and come short of the glory of God" (Rom. 3:23), and in that case He would have required a sacrifice for His own sins. Even if that difficulty were surmounted, but Jesus Christ had been only a human being, it would have been impossible for Him to furnish sufficient merit to meet the needs of a world of sinners. Again, in whatever meritorious work Jesus Christ performed, or whatever sufferings He endured, if He had been merely human, instead of being *the* Saviour of the world, as He is presented to be, He would have been only one of the saviours of the world.

If He were not more than man, the Christian world has been deceived for two thousand years as to the value of the Blood He shed, the intercession He has made and the worship that has been rendered Him. If His work for me were nothing more than human wisdom devised, and human passion compelled, and human nature endured, then I can accept it or reject it as I think fit, without condemnation from anyone. If Jesus Christ were not a divine Person there would be nothing more to make me condemn myself for not accepting Him as my Saviour, than in my refusing to believe in some other human benefactor. Finally, if He was not more than man, and if His life and death have no more bearing upon my destiny than those of any human philanthropist, then His claims are without foundation, and the hopes they have raised in my soul are a delusion: He must have been either the prince of impostors or, what He really was, the Lord of lords, the King of kings, the Saviour of mankind.

The objectors of whom we are speaking argue further that such a transaction as the Atonement was improbable. "How," they ask, "could God weep and be depressed, and feel Himself forsaken, and die, as the Bible represents Him to have done?" These objectors find it difficult to credit that these events occurred, and consequently they find it difficult to trust their souls upon them.

If, however, we were to go so far as to admit that the story of the Atonement has the appearance of *improbability,* that would be no positive *disproof* of its truthfulness. Many things are constantly occurring under our very eyes, which we should think were most unlikely and should refuse to believe, if we had not had some personal acquaintance with the actual occurrence.

It is argued further that it is an unjust arrangement for one being to be sacrificed in the interests of another, as in the case of the Atonement.

It seems to me to be most curious that such an objection should be raised in a world that is so full of sacrifice at every turn you take in it. When we look round us it seems as though in this life sacrifice were a law of existence. It appears as though we could have joy only as a result of the sorrows of others, as if we could have life only by their death.

The *material* world is full of sacrifice. Matter is sacrificed to propagate and support every sort of vegetable, as well as animal life. Coal has to be burned in order to create warmth, prepare food and supply the means of motion. The vegetable world is sacrificed to sustain animal life. And the animal world is sacrificed, with a vengeance, for the maintenance of human life.

Husbands sacrifice themselves for their wives, or ought to do so. Wives are sacrificed for their husbands. Parents are sacrificed for their children. Patriots are sacrificed for their country. And in some Eastern lands one human being is accepted as a sacrifice for another.

On the one hand the highest admiration of men of all stations is given to those who sacrifice their interests or even themselves for the good of others. On the other hand selfishness — taking care of yourself, and allowing other people to suffer or perish, sometimes through your unwillingness to suffer on their account — is everywhere despised; although, alas! alas! largely practised by those who hold it in such contempt.

And when we come to the *religious* world we find sacrifice everywhere taught. No religion has a powerful hold upon the people that has not sacrifice as a principle of its action, if not a main reason for its existence. Without sacrifice religion would not be religion at all.

Why then should it be counted an unreasonable or unjust arrangement for the Son of God to inhabit a human body for a season, in order that He might be a Man of sorrows and die a suffering death, to make a sacrifice for our sins and leave behind Him an example for us to imitate?

Another objection to the doctrine of the Atonement affirms that the benefits flowing out of the sacrifice are not equivalent to the amount of humiliation and suffering that Jesus Christ endured.

In answer to this objection let us consider some of the blessings flowing out of the Atonement, and show that they constitute incontrovertible reasons why we Salvationists should hold to the doctrine with all our might.

We must hold on to the doctrine of the Atonement because of the marvellous revelation it affords of the love of God to man.

You have the revelation of that love in the *Creation*, the provision made for man's health and happiness.

You have a revelation of that love in *Providence*. All things work together for our good. That we do not understand why things that appear opposed to our welfare come to us does not disprove the fact.

You have a revelation of that love in the *Bible*. Who would ever have dreamed of many of the things we know about God if they had not been there revealed?

You have a revelation of that love in *Grace*. Grace is the sign of the infinite compassion, love and beauty of God in the conversion, sanctification, preservation and utilization of His people, and in their final triumph over death and hell.

But in Christ—in His hanging, dying on the Cross—we have a manifestation of the heart of love which made all this possible, and which, in importance, far transcends it all.

We must hold on to the doctrine of the Atonement because it forms a strong incentive to us to love God in return.

As I kneel before His bleeding form, and remember who He was, and why He came there, I can do no other than say, from the depths of my being:

> Were the whole realm of nature mine,
>   That were a present far too small;
> Love so amazing, so divine,
>   Demands my soul, my life, my all.

We must hold on to the doctrine of the Atonement because of the picture it presents of the majesty of the divine Law, and the importance of its maintenance.

As I look upon the suffering Christ, not only am I compelled to think of the high estimate God sets upon the law that keeps the universe in order, but my heart bounds to render obedience to that Law.

We must hold on to the doctrine of the Atonement because of the revelation it makes of the evil of sin.

If I were permitted to witness the agonizing miseries that sin brings upon men in this life; if I could wander over the battle-fields and through the slums and prisons and hospitals and other habitations of human vice and crime and woe — I should, without doubt, get some faint idea of what an evil and bitter thing it is to sin against God. If I were permitted to go down into Hell itself, and witness the terrible sufferings and listen to the agonizing regrets of the lost, I should gain some further idea of the dreadful consequences that follow the transgression of the holy law of God. But, altogether, I should not find such a telling expression of the awful nature of sin as I see when I behold the suffering form of my Saviour — the eternal Son of God — on the bloody Tree, and know that it was sin that nailed Him there.

We must hold on to the doctrine of the Atonement because of the door of mercy which it flings widely and gloriously open for all mankind.

Millions have entered the gates that lead to the Celestial City with the sentiment in their hearts which we Salvationists express by our song, "His Blood can make the foulest clean." Millions upon millions more will reach the Golden Pavement who have never heard His precious name before they gained the Heavenly Shores. There can be no question that sincere souls who, by living up to the light they possess, prove that if they had had the opportunity they would have laid themselves at the Saviour's feet, will not have to suffer banishment on account of their ignorance. You will remember Paul says, "In every nation he that feareth Him, and worketh righteousness, is accepted with Him" (Acts 10:35). This shows that God is going to deal with people according to their sincerity. If they are obedient to what they hear, there will be salvation for them; and if they have never heard but would have been obedient if they had heard, they will not be rejected.

We must hold on to the doctrine of the Atonement because it justifies us in believing in the transference to the Heavenly Shores of multitudes of young children who have never heard His name below.

More than half the human race die in infancy and, in view of the holy examples set before them by the Heavenly host, grow into celestial maturity in the Heavenly Canaan.

We must hold on to the doctrine of the Atonement because of the example the Saviour Himself furnishes for imitation.

Nowhere in the history of the human race, from Adam down to the present hour, have we any being, until we come to Jesus Christ, to whom we can point with confidence, and say, "Take not only the precepts of His mouth as your guide, but the example of His life and death." The value of such an example is greater, I need not say, than anything human or angelic can calculate.

We must hold on to the doctrine of the Atonement because of the material, mental, moral and spiritual blessings which stream from it out into our dark and desolate world.

We must hold on to the doctrine of the Atonement because of the fire of compassion and love for the sinning, suffering bodies and souls of men, which it kindles in the hearts of those who yield themselves to its influence.

We must hold on to the doctrine of the Atonement because of the fulness of the Holy Spirit's influence which it makes possible to men.

"I will pray the Father, and He shall give you another Comforter, that He may abide with you for ever; even the Spirit of truth" (John 14:16–17).

We must hold on to the doctrine of the Atonement because of the preparation for Heaven it makes certain for those who accept it.

Think of the multitude which no man can number, already assembling on the Heavenly Plains, who have washed their robes and made them white in the Blood of the Lamb, and the multitudes more who have availed themselves of the same preparation and are coming on.

We must hold on to the doctrine of the Atonement because of the verification it affords of the prophecies, promises and general statements of the Bible.

To take the Atonement out of the Bible would not only rob the sacred volume of its chief, if not its entire interest, but largely destroy its power to bless the souls of its readers. In fact, without the Atonement the Bible would cease to be one of the lights of the world, and would speedily vanish from the earth in the gloom that would surround it.

We must hold on to the doctrine of the Atonement because its loss would rob multitudes of the holiest men and women of the most powerful motive to purity of heart and life.

We must hold on to the doctrine of the Atonement because it constitutes our most powerful weapon in the fight with the godless crowds.

Whether in the churches, the market-places, the theatres, the music halls, the public-houses, the brothels, their own homes or elsewhere, the death of Jesus Christ is our battle cry of victory. Christ weeping, suffering, dying for them, and waiting to wash away their sins in His Blood, constitutes the most powerful motive to submit themselves immediately to God, accept His mercy and commence a new life calculated to please Him, promote their own happiness and ultimately lead them to Heaven. Without this inducement our talking would lose its influence on the conscience of men, and the Penitent-form would be banished from the world for ever.

We must hold on to the doctrine of the Atonement because the loss of it would spoil every song we sing.

If there were no Atonement, we should soon abandon singing altogether. Take away the Cross, and the river of our peace would cease to flow; the joy of our religion would come to an end.

We must hold on to the doctrine of the Atonement because it is the greatest, most influential and most soul-stirring truth in the universe. Where should we be without the Cross? Comrades, let us avail ourselves to the uttermost of the salvation and the conquering power that the Atonement of our Lord Jesus Christ makes possible to us in our inward experience; and let us resolve that, with renewed energy and increased enthusiasm, we will proclaim the redeeming virtues of the Cross to the whole world.

WHO CARES?

DURING ONE OF MY RECENT JOURNEYS I was led out into a train of thought respecting the conditions of the multitudes around me living regardless of all that concerned their eternal welfare, and in the most open and shameless rebellion against God. I looked out upon the millions of people around me given up to their drink and their pleasure, their dancing and their music, their business and their anxieties, their politics and their troubles, and thousands of other things; ignorant – wilfully ignorant, in many cases – in other instances knowing all about it; but all of them sweeping on and up, in their blasphemies and devilries, to the Throne of God. While thus musing I had a vision.

I saw a dark and stormy ocean. Over it the black clouds hung heavily; through them every now and then vivid lightnings flashed and loud thunders rolled, while the winds moaned, and the waves rose and foamed and fretted and broke and rose to foam and fret and break again.

In that ocean I thought I saw myriads of poor human beings plunging and floating, shouting and shrieking, cursing and struggling and

Reprinted from *The Founder Speaks Again: A Selection of the Writings of William Booth,* [comp.] Cyril J. Barnes (London: Salvationist Publishing & Supplies, 1960), pp. 61–67, by permission of Salvation Army, London.

drowning; and as they cursed and shrieked, they rose and shrieked again, and then sank to rise no more.

And out of this dark angry ocean I saw a mighty rock that rose up with its summit towering high above the black clouds that overhung the stormy sea; and all round the base of this rock I saw a vast platform; and on to this platform I saw with delight a number of the poor, struggling, drowning wretches continually climbing out of the angry ocean; and I saw that a number of those who were already safe on the platform were helping the poor creatures still in the angry waters to reach the same place of safety.

On looking more closely I found a number of those who had been rescued scheming and contriving by ladders and ropes and boats and other expedients more effectually to deliver the poor strugglers out of this sea. Here and there were some who actually jumped into the water, regardless of all consequences, in their eagerness to "rescue the perishing"; and I hardly know which gladdened me most – the sight of the poor people climbing on to the rocks, and so reaching the place of safety, or the devotion and self-sacrifice of those whose whole being was wrapped up in efforts for their deliverance.

And as I looked I saw that the occupants of that platform were quite a mixed company. That is, they were divided into different "sets" or castes and occupied themselves with different pleasures and employments; but only a very few of them seemed to make it their business to get the people out of the sea.

But what puzzled me most was the fact that though all had been rescued at one time or another from the ocean, nearly everyone seemed to have forgotten all about it. Anyway, the memory of its darkness and danger no longer troubled them. Then what was equally strange and perplexing to me was that these people did not seem to have any care – that is, any agonizing care – about the poor perishing ones who were struggling and drowning before their eyes, many of whom were their own husbands and wives, mothers and sisters and children.

And this unconcern could not have been the result of ignorance, because they lived right in sight of it all and talked about it sometimes, and regularly went to hear lectures in which the awful state of the poor drowning creatures was described.

I have already said that the occupants of this platform were engaged in different pursuits. Some of them were absorbed night and day in trading, in order to make gain, storing up their savings in boxes, strong rooms and the like.

Many spent time in amusing themselves with growing flowers on the side of the rock; others in painting pieces of cloth, or in playing music, or in dressing themselves up in different styles and walking about to be admired.

Some occupied themselves chiefly in eating and drinking, others were greatly taken up with arguing about the poor drowning creatures in the sea and as to what would become of them in the future, while many contented themselves that they did their duty to the perishing creatures by the performance of curious religious ceremonies.

On looking more closely I found that some of the crowd who had reached the place of safety had discovered a passage up the rock leading to a higher platform still, which was fairly above the black clouds that overhung the ocean, and from which they had a good view of the mainland not very far away, and to which they expected to be taken off at some distant day. Here they passed their time in pleasant thoughts, congratulating themselves and one another on their good fortune in being rescued from the stormy deep, and singing songs about the happiness that would be theirs when they should be taken to the mainland, which they imagined they could plainly distinguish just "over there."

And all this time the struggling, shrieking multitudes were floating about in the dark sea, quite near by — so near that they could easily have been rescued. Instead of which there they were, perishing in full view, not only one by one, but sinking down in shoals, every day, in the angry water.

And as I looked, I found that the handful of people on the platform whom I had observed before were still struggling with their rescue work. O God, how I wished there had been a multitude of them! Indeed, these toilers seemed to do little else but fret and weep, and toil and scheme for the perishing people. They gave themselves no rest, and sadly bothered everyone they could get at around them by persistently entreating them to come to their assistance. In fact, they came to be voted a real nuisance by many quite benevolent and kind-hearted people, and by some who were very religious too. But still they went on, spending all they had and all they could get on boats and rafts, drags and ropes, and every other imaginable device they could invent for saving the poor, wretched, drowning people.

A few others did much the same thing at times, working hard in their way; but the people who chiefly attracted my attention were at the business all the year round; indeed, they made such a terrible to-do about it and went at it with such fierceness and fury, that many even of those who were doing the same kind of work, only in a milder way, were quite angry with them and called them mad.

And then I saw something more wonderful still. The miseries and agonies, perils and blasphemies of these poor struggling people in this dark sea moved the pity of the great God in Heaven; moved it so much that He sent a Great Being to deliver them. And I thought that this Great Being whom Jehovah sent came straight from His palace, right through the black clouds, and leaped right into the raging sea among the drowning, sinking people; and there I saw Him toiling to rescue them, with tears and cries, until the sweat of His great anguish ran down in blood. And as He toiled and embraced the poor wretches, and tried to lift them on to the rock, He was continually crying to those already rescued—to those whom He had helped up with His own bleeding hands—to come and help Him in the painful and laborious task of saving their fellows.

And what seemed to me most passing strange was that those on the platform to whom He called, who heard His voice and felt they ought to obey it—at least, they said they did—those who loved Him much and were in full sympathy with Him in the task He had undertaken—who worshipped Him, or who professed to do so—were so taken up with their trades and professions, and money-saving and pleasures, and families and circles, and religions and arguments about it, and preparations for going to the mainland, that they did not attend to the cry that came to them from this wonderful Being who had Himself gone down into the sea. Anyway, if they heard it they did not heed it; they did not care; and so the multitude went on struggling and shrieking and drowning in the darkness.

And then I saw something that seemed to me stranger than anything that had gone before in this strange vision. I saw that some of these people on the platform, whom this wonderful Being wanted to come and help Him in His difficult task, were always praying and crying to Him to come to them.

Some wanted Him to come and stay with them, and spend His time and strength in making them happier.

Others wanted Him to come and take away various doubts and misgivings they had respecting the truth of some letters which He had written them.

Some wanted Him to come and make them feel more secure on the rock—so secure that they would be quite sure they should never slip off again. Numbers of others wanted Him to make them feel quite certain that they would really get on to the mainland some day; because, as a matter of fact, it was well known that some had walked so carelessly as to miss their footing, and had fallen back again into the stormy waters.

So these people used to meet and get as high up the rock as they could; and, looking toward the mainland, where they thought the Great Being was, they would cry out, "Come to us! Come, and help us!" And all this time He was down among the poor struggling, drowning creatures in the angry deep, with His arms around them, trying to drag them out, and looking up—oh! so longingly, but all in vain—to those on the rock, crying to them, with His voice all hoarse with calling, "Come to Me! *Come, and help me!*"

And then I understood it all. It was plain enough. That sea was the ocean of life—the sea of real, actual, human existence. That lightning was the gleaming of piercing truth coming from Jehovah's Throne. That thunder was the distant echoing of the wrath of God. Those multitudes of people shrieking, struggling, agonizing in the stormy sea, were the thousands and thousands of poor harlots and harlot-makers, of drunkards and drunkard-makers, of thieves, liars, blasphemers and ungodly people of every kindred, tongue and nation.

Oh, what a black sea it was! and, oh, what multitudes of rich and poor, ignorant and educated were there, and all so unlike in their outward circumstances and conditions, yet all alike in one thing – all sinners before God; all held by, and holding on to, some iniquity, fascinated by some idol, the slaves of some devilish lust, and ruled by some foul fiend from the bottomless pit!

"All alike in one thing?" Nay, in two things – not only the same in their wickedness but, unless rescued, alike in their sinking, sinking, sinking, down, down, down to the same terrible doom.

That great sheltering rock represented Calvary; and the people on it were those who had been rescued; and the way they employed their energies and gifts and time represented the occupations and amusements of those who profess to be rescued from sin and Hell and to be the followers of Jesus Christ. The handful of fierce, determined saviours were salvation soldiers, together with a few others who shared the same spirit. That mighty Being was the Son of God, "the same yesterday, and today, and for ever," who is still struggling to save the dying multitudes about us from this terrible doom of damnation, and whose voice can be heard, above the music, machinery and hue-and-cry of life, calling on the rescued to come and help Him to save the world.

My comrades, you are rescued from the waters; you are on the rock. He is in the dark sea, calling on you to come to Him and help Him. Will you go?

Look for yourselves. The surging sea of life crowded with perishing souls rolls up to the very spot on which you stand. Leaving the vision, I now come to speak of the fact – fact that is as real as the Bible, as real as the Christ who hung upon the Cross, as real as the Judgment Day will be, and as real as the Heaven and Hell that will follow it.

Look! Don't be deluded by appearances – men and things are not what they seem. *All who are not on the rock are in the sea.* Look at them from the standpoint of the Great White Throne, and what a sight you have! Jesus Christ, the Son of God, is in the midst of this dying multitude, struggling to save them. And He is calling on *you* to jump into the sea – to go right away to His side and help Him in the holy strife.

Will you jump? That is, will you go to His feet and place yourself absolutely at His disposal?

A soldier came to me once, saying that for some time she had been giving her Lord her profession and prayers and money, and now she wanted to give Him her body. She wanted to go right into the fight. In other words, she wanted to go to His assistance in the sea. As when a man from the bank, seeing another struggling in the water, lays aside those outer garments that would hinder his efforts and leaps to the rescue, so will you who still linger on the bank, thinking and singing and praying about the poor perishing souls, lay aside your shame, your pride, your care about other people's opinions, your love of ease and all the selfish loves that have hindered you so long, and rush to the rescue of this multitude of dying men.

Does the surging sea look dark and dangerous? Unquestionably it is so. There is no doubt that the leap for you, as for everyone who takes it, means difficulty and scorn and suffering. For you it may mean more than this. It may mean death. He who calls to you from the sea, however, knows what it will mean; and knowing, He still beckons you and bids you come.

You must do it. You cannot hold back. You have enjoyed yourself in religion long enough. You have had pleasant feelings, pleasant songs, pleasant meetings, pleasant prospects. There has been much of human happiness, much clapping of hands and firing of volleys – very much of Heaven on earth.

Now, then, go to God and tell Him you are prepared as far as necessary to turn your back upon it all, and that you are willing to spend the rest of your days grappling with these perishing multitudes, cost you what it may.

You *must* do it. With the light that has now broken in upon your mind, and the call that is now sounding in your ears, and the beckoning finger that is now before your eyes, you have no alternative. To go down among the perishing crowds is your duty. Your happiness henceforth will consist in sharing their misery, your ease in sharing their pain, your crown in bearing their cross, and your heaven in going to the very jaws of hell to rescue them. *What will you do?*

"DARKEST ENGLAND" SCHEME

THE CAB-HORSE CHARTER

I SORROWFULLY ADMIT that it would be utopian in our present social arrangements to dream of attaining for every honest Englishman a

Reprinted from *The Founder Speaks Again: A Selection of the Writings of William Booth*, [comp.] Cyril J. Barnes (London: Salvationist Publishing & Supplies, 1960), pp. 151–56, by permission of Salvation Army, London.

jail standard of all the necessaries of life. Some time, perhaps, we may venture to hope that every honest worker on English soil will always be as warmly clad, as healthily housed, and as regularly fed as our criminal convicts – but that is not yet.

Neither is it possible to hope for many years to come that human beings generally will be as well cared for as horses. Mr. Carlyle long ago remarked that the four-footed worker has already got all that this two-handed one is clamouring for: "There are not many horses in England, able and willing to work, which have not due food and lodging and go about sleek coated, satisfied in heart." You say it is impossible; but, said Carlyle, "The human brain, looking at these sleek English horses, refuses to believe in such impossibility for English men." Nevertheless, forty years have passed since Carlyle said that, and we seem to be no nearer the attainment of the four-footed standard for the two-handed worker. "Perhaps it might be nearer realization," growls the cynic, "if we could produce men only according to demand, as we do horses, and promptly send them to the slaughter-house when past their prime" – which, of course, is not to be thought of.

What, then, is the standard toward which we may venture to aim with some prospect of realization in our time? It is a very humble one, but if realized it would solve the worst problems of modern society.

It is the standard of the London cab horse.

When in the streets of London a cab horse, weary or careless or stupid, trips and falls and lies stretched out in the midst of the traffic, there is no question of debating how he came to stumble before we try to get him on his legs again. The cab horse is a very real illustration of poor, broken-down humanity; he usually falls down because of overwork and underfeeding. If you put him on his feet without altering his conditions, it would only be to give him another dose of agony; but first of all you'll have to pick him up again. It may have been through overwork or underfeeding, or it may have been all his own fault that he has broken his knees and smashed the shafts, but that does not matter. If not for his own sake, then merely in order to prevent an obstruction of the traffic, all attention is concentrated upon the question of how we are to get him on his legs again. The load is taken off, the harness is unbuckled or, if need be, cut, and everything is done to help him up. Then he is put in the shafts again and once more restored to his regular round of work. That is the first point. The second is that every cab horse in London has three things: a shelter for the night, food for its stomach, and work allotted to it by which it can earn its corn.

These are the two points of the Cab-horse Charter. When he is down he is helped up, and while he lives he has food, shelter and work. That, although a humble standard, is at present absolutely unattainable by millions – literally by millions – of our fellow men and women in this country. Can the Cab-horse Charter be gained for human beings? I answer, yes. The cab-horse standard can be attained on the cab-horse terms. If you get your fallen fellow on his feet again, docility and discipline will enable you to reach the cab-horse ideal, otherwise it will remain unattainable. But docility seldom fails where discipline is intelligently maintained. Intelligence is more frequently lacking to direct, than obedience to follow direction. At any rate it is not for those who possess the intelligence to despair of obedience, until they have done their part. Some, no doubt, like the bucking horse that will never be broken in, will always refuse to submit to any guidance but their own lawless will.

The first question, then which confronts us is, what are the dimensions of the evil? How many of our fellow men dwell in this Darkest England . . . below the cab-horse standard to which it is our aim to elevate the most wretched of our countrymen? . . . Three millions or, to put it roughly one-tenth of the population. . . .

Darkest England, then, may be said to have a population about equal to that of Scotland. Three million men, women and children, a vast despairing multitude in a condition nominally free, but really enslaved. These it is whom we have to save. . . . Can anything be done for them? Or is this million-headed mass to be regarded as offering a problem as insoluble as that of the London sewage, which, feculent and festering, swings heavily up and down the basin of the Thames with the ebb and flow of the tide?

This Submerged Tenth—is it, then, beyond the reach of the nine-tenths in the midst of whom they live, and around whose homes they rot and die? No doubt, in every large mass of human beings there will be some incurably diseased in morals and in body, some for whom nothing can be done, some of whom even optimist must despair, and for whom he can prescribe nothing but the beneficently stern restraints of an asylum or a gaol.

But is not one in ten a proportion scandalously high? The Israelites of old set apart one tribe in twelve to minister to the Lord in the service of the temple; but must we doom one in ten of "God's Englishmen" to the service of the great twin devils—Destitution and Despair?

The Essentials to Success

The first essential that must be borne in mind as governing every scheme that may be put forward is that it must change the man when it is his character and conduct which constitute the reasons for his failure in the battle of life. If he is a drunkard, he must be made sober; if idle, he must be made industrious; if criminal, he must be made honest; if impure, he must be made clean; and if he be so deep down in vice, and has been there so long that he has lost all heart and hope, and power to help himself, and absolutely refuses to move, he must be inspired with hope and have created within him the ambition to rise; otherwise he will never get out of the horrible pit.

Secondly: *The remedy, to be effectual, must change the circumstances of the individual when they are the cause of his wretched condition, and lie beyond his control.* Among those who have arrived at their present evil plight through faults of self-indulgence or some defect in their moral character, how many are there who would have been very differently placed today had their surroundings been otherwise?

Thirdly: *Any remedy worthy of consideration must be on a scale commensurate with the evil with which it proposes to deal.* There must be no more philanthropic tinkering, as if this vast sea of human misery were contained in the limits of a garden pond.

Fourthly: *Not only must the scheme be large enough, but it must be permanent,* to go on dealing with the misery of tomorrow and the day after, so long as there is misery left in the world with which to grapple.

Fifthly: *But while it must be permanent,* it must also be *immediately practicable.*

Sixthly: *The indirect features of the scheme must not be such as to produce injury to the persons whom we seek to benefit.* Mere charity, for instance, while relieving the pinch of hunger, demoralizes the recipient.

Seventhly: *While assisting one class of the community, it must not seriously interfere with the interests of another.* In raising one section of the fallen, we must not thereby endanger the safety of those who with difficulty are keeping on their feet.

TEMPORAL SALVATION

I have nothing to say against those who are endeavouring to open up a way of escape without any consciousness of God's help. For them I feel only sympathy and compassion. In so far as they are endeavouring to give bread to the hungry, clothing to the naked and, above all, work to the workless, they are to that extent endeavouring to do the will of our Father which is in Heaven; and woe be unto all those who say them nay! But to be orphaned of all sense of the Fatherhood of God is surely not a secret source of strength. It is in most cases — it would be in my own — the secret of paralysis. If I did not feel my Father's hand in the darkness, and hear His voice in the silence of the night watches bidding me put my hand to this thing, I would shrink back dismayed; but as it is I dare not.

How many are there who have made similar attempts and have failed, and we have heard of them no more! Yet none of them proposed to deal with more than the mere fringe of the evil which, God helping me, I will try to face in all its immensity. Most schemes that are

put forward for the improvement of the circumstances of the people
are either avowedly or actually limited to those whose condition least
needs amelioration. The utopians, the economists, and most of the
philanthropists propound remedies, which, if adopted tomorrow,
would only affect the aristocracy of the miserable. It is the thrifty,
the industrious, the sober, the thoughtful who can take advantage
of these plans. But the thrifty, the industrious, the sober and the
thoughtful are already very well able for the most part to take care of
themselves. No one will ever make even a visible dint on the morass
of squalor who does not deal with the improvident, the lazy, the vi-
cious and the criminal. The scheme of social salvation is not worth
discussion which is not as wide as the scheme of eternal salvation
set forth in the gospel. The glad tidings must be to every creature,
not merely to an elect few who are to be saved while the mass of their
fellows are predestined to a temporal damnation. We have had this
doctrine of an inhuman cast-iron pseudo-political economy too long
enthroned amongst us. It is now time to fling down the false idol and
proclaim a temporal salvation as full, free and universal, and with no
other limitations than the "Whosoever will" of the gospel.

To attempt to save the lost, we must accept no limitations to human
brotherhood. If the scheme which I set forth in these and the following pages is not applicable to the thief, the harlot, the drunkard and the
sluggard, it may as well be dismissed without ceremony. As Christ
came to call not the saints but sinners to repentance, so the new message of temporal salvation, of salvation from pinching poverty, from
rags and misery, must be offered to all. They may reject it, of course.
But we who call ourselves by the name of Christ are not worthy to
profess to be His disciples until we have set an open door before the
least and worst of these who are now apparently imprisoned for life
in a horrible dungeon of misery and despair. . . .

To get a man soundly saved it is not enough to put on him a pair of
new breeches, to give him regular work, or even to give him a university education. These things are all outside a man, and if the inside remains unchanged you have wasted your labour. . . . What is the
use of preaching the gospel to men whose whole attention is concentrated upon a mad, desperate struggle to keep themselves alive?
You might as well give a tract to a shipwrecked sailor who is battling
with the surf which has drowned his comrades and threatens to drown
him. He will not listen to you. Nay, he cannot hear you any more than
a man whose head is under water can listen to a sermon. The first
thing to do is to get him at least a footing on firm ground, and to give
him room to live. Then you may have a chance. At present you have
none. And you will have all the better opportunity to find a way to
his heart, if he comes to know that it was you who pulled him out
of the horrible pit and the miry clay in which he was sinking to perdition. . . .

No compulsion will for a moment be allowed with respect to religion. The man who professes to love and serve God will be helped because of such profession, and the man who does not will be helped in the hope that he will, sooner or later, in gratitude to God, do the same; but there will be no melancholy misery-making for any. There is no sanctimonious long face in the Army. We talk freely about salvation, because it is to us the very light and joy of our existence. We are happy, and we wish others to share our joy. We know by our own experience that life is a very different thing when we have found the peace of God, and are working together with Him for the salvation of the world, instead of toiling for the realization of worldly ambition or the amassing of earthly gain.

FOR ADDITIONAL INFORMATION ABOUT WILLIAM BOOTH:

Booth, Bramwell. *Echoes and Memories.* New York: George H. Doran Co., 1925.

Booth, William. *How to Reach the Masses with the Gospel.* London: Marshall, Morgan, Chase & Scott, 1872.

_____. *The Founder Speaks Again.* Compiled by Cyril J. Barnes. London: Salvationist Publishing and Supplies, 1960.

Collier, Richard. *The General Next to God.* New York: E. P. Dutton & Co., 1965.

Mead, Frank S. "William Booth." *Rebels with a Cause.* New York: Abingdon Press, 1964.

Nelson, William Hamilton. *Blood and Fire: General William Booth.* New York: Century Co., 1929.

Railton, G. S. *The Authoritative Life of General William Booth, Founder of the Salvation Army.* New York: George H. Doran Co., 1912.

Sandall, Robert. *History of the Salvation Army.* 3 vols. London: Thomas Nelson, 1947.

FOR OTHER SERMONS BY WILLIAM BOOTH:

The sermons of General Booth were preached to the millions on the streets of the world, but according to the officials of the Salvation Army he left no sermon compilations for posterity.

JOSEPH   PARKER

1830-1902

JOSEPH PARKER, photograph by Ernest H. Mills, London, from Alexander Gammie, *Preachers I Have Heard* (London: Pickering & Inglis, n.d.), p. 40.

JOSEPH PARKER

1830	*Born April 9 in Hexham-on-Tyne, Northumberland, England*
1851	*Married Ann Nesbitt*
1852	*Became assistant to John Campbell, pastor of Whitefield Tabernacle, London*
1853	*Became student at University College, London, and pastor of the Banbury Congregational Church in Oxfordshire*
1858	*Moved to Cavendish Street Congregational Church, Manchester*
1862	*Received D.D. degree from University of Chicago*
1869	*Called as pastor of Poultry Church, London*
1874	*Led in building of City Temple, London*
1902	*Died November 28*

THE ARCHITECT employed to design the projected City Temple of London asked Joseph Parker what style of architecture he wanted. Parker replied: "Any style! But build me such a church that when Queen Victoria drives into the City she will say, 'Why, what place is that?' – and she will be told, 'That is where Joseph Parker preaches!'"

A thoroughgoing individualist, Parker has often been accused of being a gross egotist – a charge probably not without foundation. Once when he was invited to become pastor of a much smaller church than City Temple, he replied, "An eagle does not roost in a sparrow's nest!"

Blessed with a unique personality, Joseph Parker enjoyed a successful ministry in London. He became so well known that his church was included as a stopping point for tourists; and if the tour were on Sunday, its itinerary would certainly include a sermon at City Temple by Joseph Parker.

His fame is even more remarkable when other preachers

of his era are named: Charles Spurgeon, Alexander Maclaren, F. B. Meyer, Robert Dale, Henry Liddon, John Newman, and Henry Ward Beecher. Among such great preachers a lesser light would never have been noticed, but Joseph Parker never lacked for attention.

LIFE AND TIMES

Joseph Parker, born in Hexham-on-Tyne, Northumberland, England, April 9, 1830, grew up in a family which gave him religious training and a rugged character, but little formal education. Joseph's father was a stone mason "with deepest love of prayer," according to his son's own testimony. His mother, a devout woman, gave Joseph his early thirst for religious knowledge. Both parents were dedicated Christians and Congregationalists. During a church dispute his parents attended a Methodist congregation for a while, but Joseph's main tie remained with the Congregationalists.

The influence of family and church resulted early in profound religious experiences. Later in his life Parker wrote about the night he first professed Christ:

> I remember the Sunday night, when walking with my father and a most intelligent Sunday-school teacher, I declared my love to Christ and asked Him to take my child-heart into His own gracious keeping. The whole scene is ever before me. The two men, father and teacher, explained to me what they knew of the power and grace of Christ, and by many loving words they tempted my tongue into its first audible expression of thought and feeling.
>
> It was a summer evening, according to the reckoning of the calendar, but according to a higher calendar it was in very deed a Sunday morning, through whose white light and emblematic dew and stir of awakening life I saw the gates of the Kingdom and the face of the King.[1]

His "first audible expression" of the Christian faith soon gave way to a flow of words. He began to teach a Sunday school class, and this experience was soon followed by public speaking in

---

1. William Adamson, *The Life of Joseph Parker* (New York: Fleming H. Revell Co., 1902), pp. 12–13.

behalf of the Christian faith. When he was eighteen, he preached his first sermon. He stood on the crossbeams of a sawpit in the open air and, with characteristic Parker conviction, boomed forth the gospel.

Because of the poverty of his family there was no opportunity for him to go to college. But he was not without education. Arising at six o'clock in the morning, he studied Greek and read theology. He preached everywhere he had opportunity and learned from each experience. He journeyed to London and became assistant to John Campbell of Whitefield Tabernacle; Campbell constructively criticized Parker's sermons and helped immensely in his Christian development.

His first pastorate at the Banbury Congregational Church in Oxfordshire challenged him. The church was run down and offered little prospect for growth. Under Parker's vigorous ministry the church sprang to new life. A new chapel had to be built because the crowds were too large for the old building. Soon the new building became inadequate for the throngs which crowded to hear Parker preach. Not content to be merely a pulpiteer, the young pastor was busy writing, studying, and developing administrative skills.

Many churches urged him to become their pastor, but he refused them all until a call came from Cavendish Street Congregational Church in Manchester. He moved to Manchester and immediately became an influence in the city. While there, the University of Chicago recognized his ability and conferred on him the D.D. degree. Although he had not received college training, the doctor's degree was not inappropriate for his learning; he loved writing and many volumes poured from his pen.

In Manchester too he tasted of deep sorrow. His wife died in 1863. This experience sobered his personality; until then, he had not really tasted of defeat or real sorrow. Yet his spirits were by no means broken.

His greatest ministry came in London. In 1869 he was asked to come as pastor of the Poultry Church in London. He accepted the invitation on the condition that a new building would replace the old as soon as possible. As a result of his planning and labors, the renowned City Temple was soon built near Holborn Viaduct.

City Temple rapidly expanded under Parker's dynamic leadership. A church with a many-faceted program developed. He gave little time to visiting, but he administered the church in a masterful way. In the midst of his responsibilities as leader of the church, Parker still found time for writing. He was especially interested in writing for students who were preparing for the ministry. In addition to preaching at his own church on Sunday, he delivered sermons throughout England and Scotland. Every Thursday at noon he addressed a large congregation at City Temple. Only his boundless energy and marvelous intellectual gifts explain his ability to do so many things so well.

In addition to pastoring and writing, Joseph Parker found time to be active in the life of the Congregationalist denomination. He demonstrated his affection for his denomination by serving three times as chairman of the London Congregational Board and twice as chairman of the Congregational Union of England and Wales. He believed intently in the freedom provided by the Congregational structure and abhorred any kind of enforced church structure or creedal system. To him, the genius of Christianity was the liberty which the spirit of God provided.

Parker threw himself into the battle against secularism and agnosticism. A convinced evangelical, he crusaded for a conservative adherence to the Scripture. He not only tackled theological issues but also cared deeply about social concerns. Again and again he denounced the social evils of his day. He advocated a laymen's league of Christian laymen to elevate and purify the morals of London. Foreshadowing in some ways modern programs of urban renewal, he advocated reconstruction of parts of the city. He was a crusader against alcohol and a champion of the poor, the ignorant, and the underprivileged. Much of his income he gave to charity.

Not only did he speak against the evils of society, but he also was willing to become involved in the social structure in an effort to correct them. In 1880 he presented himself as a candidate for Parliament for the city of London. His platform advocated the disestablishment of the Church of England, the end of the liquor traffic, and the advancement of social and political reform. Upon the advice of several parishioners, he finally withdrew his candidacy. But he did not withdraw his concern and active support for the principles he believed in. He also turned his pen to social concerns; among his publications are those entitled *The Evils of Rum* and *Corrupt Politics.*

All that he did — writing, social reform, building of churches —

was centered in Christ. He said of preaching: "I have nothing to preach to my fellow men if it be not the gospel of Jesus Christ and the doctrine of the cross." This theme he followed faithfully until his death on November 28, 1902.

Preaching and Sermons

Joseph Parker's interest in preaching amounted almost to a preoccupation. A lady is said to have asked him once, "What is your hobby?" Parker replied instantly, "Preaching." "Yes, I know you love that, but I mean what is the hobby which occupies your time of leisure?" Parker replied, "Preaching, I have no hobby but preparing for or delivering sermons; they occupy my whole time, and engage the energies of my whole soul."[2]

With the kind of schedule that he endured at London's City Temple, it is no wonder that his hobby was preaching: twice on Sunday and every Thursday noon he spoke to congregations of more than three thousand; only Spurgeon at Metropolitan Tabernacle exceeded him in attracting crowds. In addition to the three new sermons he prepared each week, he invariably spoke for special services during the week. It was not uncommon for him to speak in Edinburgh on Wednesday night and return to speak at Thursday noon in his own pulpit.

Those who heard Parker preach described him as a dramatic figure:

> He had, of course, unusual natural endowments. His massive figures, and his leonine head, with its shaggy locks, would have attracted attention anywhere. The gleaming eyes, the sweeping gestures, the constantly changing inflexion of his wonderful voice, at one moment like a roar of thunder and the next soft as a whisper, held any audience spellbound. And there was always the element of the unexpected in what he said and how he said it. Yet there was something more, very much more, than all that. He was a supreme interpreter of the Scriptures. . . .
>
> The preacher had every gift. He was mystical, poetical, ironical, rebuking, by turns. . . . The next moment you could not help smiling at some keen witicism. . . . Then tears sprang to your eyes as he pictured the failure

---

2. Ibid., p. 155.

of success, and told of the long triumphant struggle and the victory turned into mourning by the death of the only child. But what description can render, or what analysis explain, the visible inspiration, the touch of fire from heaven?[3]

Parker was a thoroughgoing evangelical who believed in a completely biblical approach to preaching. In one of his later books he gave his opinion as to the themes a minister should preach:

The Apostle Paul has laid down the subjects of his ministry, and I do not see why I should change them. They are great subjects. They are at once historical and prophetical. Let me slowly repeat them: Christ died, Christ was buried, Christ rose again, Christ was seen, Christ was seen of me. This is the true modernness. The element of personal experience and testimony is essential to true preaching. No matter who else has seen Christ, if I have not seen Him myself, I cannot preach Him.[4]

There is no doubt that Parker meant what he said. After he had announced to his congregation that he would preach through the entire Bible, he took seven years of his preaching to do it. The massive results of his work remain as *The Speaker's Bible*. He had nothing but scorn for those preachers who were enamored with modern themes:

The first preaching was religious, with an occasional intellectual outlook; to-day religion is intellectual with an occasional religious reference. In some places of worship people have to ask whether they are in a lyceum or in a church, in a hall of science or a house of prayer. Wherein the pulpit has lost religiousness it has lost power.[5]

---

3. Alexander Gammie, *Preachers I Have Heard* (London: Pickering & Inglis, n.d.), pp. 40–41.
4. John Edwards, *Nineteenth Century Preachers and Their Methods* (London: Charles H. Kelly, 1902), pp. 101–2.
5. Joseph Parker, *A Preacher's Life* (London: Hodder & Stoughton, 1903), pp. 360–61.

W. Robertson Nicoll frequently heard Parker preach and after his death wrote the most complete description which exists of Parker's methods of preparation:

> Every morning he was in his study at half-past seven, and spent his first half hour looking at the newspapers. After breakfast he retired to his study, and dealt immediately with his correspondence. He answered letters either at once or not at all. He reserved to himself the right to ignore unreasonable requests and complaints. . . . He then went on with reading or literary work for a couple of hours. Afterwards he walked, invariably alone. It was during his walks that he loved to meditate his sermons; and he might be seen any day on Hampstead Heath absorbed in contemplation, sometimes with his lips moving. In the evening he loved to be read to. Hour after hour he would listen, and if he liked a book he had it read over to him again. He retired to rest early after his simple meal, and this was the routine of his days. . . .
> His method of preparing his sermons was his own. He read much in the Bible, and texts started out of its pages. When he found a text he brooded over it in his solitary walks, in his study, and in his garden, till he reached the heart of it. Once that was discovered, illustrations crowded upon him, and his work was practically done.[6]

According to Nicoll, Parker was a diligent student. He first selected his text, then read it in the original language; and only after that did he consult various commentaries. Parker often read aloud his sermons in private in order to hear their effect. Early in his ministry he wrote out his sermons in full, but later he became impatient with the method. He was not successful when he preached from a full manuscript; Nicoll said that the only time that Parker failed miserably in his preaching was on an occasion when he read a sermon before the Union of Churches in Scotland, a sermon which he had prepared for months and written out with meticulous revision.

In his London lectures on preaching, *Ad Clerum*, delivered early in his career, he advised young ministers to write out

---

6. W. Robertson Nicoll, *Princes of the Church* (London: Hodder & Stoughton, 1921), pp. 171–74.

their sermons for the first five to seven years. Parker warned these preachers against extravagant oratorical language and urged them to cross out all long words and elegant phrases such as "meandering rills," "crystal battlements of heaven," and "glinting stars." In those lectures he urged his students to write and rewrite their sermons; nevertheless, he vigorously opposed their reading from manuscripts. He urged them to "preach the gospel rather than read it." In his own preparation Parker was considerably more casual. In an interview he said:

> I feel more and more, when preaching, that I have next to nothing to do with the holy exercise. When I stand up to preach I hardly ever know the sentence I am going to utter. The subject itself I endeavor to know well. I mark out two or three main lines of exposition. As for words or sentences, I am not only the speaker, I am also one of the audience. I could honestly tell you at the end of the discourse that I have enjoyed it, and that I have profited by it as much as if it had been spoken by another man.
>
> Under such circumstances, I take no credit whatever for the sermon. I feel Christ's words have been true for me, "In that hour it shall be given you what you shall speak." I never think of it as my own. . . . This is the only answer I can give to your very plain question; this is a very brief note, as it were, out of what to me is a very deep and sacred experience.[7]

All of these remarks seem to indicate that Parker believed in careful preparation and study, even to the point of oral preparation, as well as written preparation; but when the moment came to preach he did not depend upon any manuscript or notes but spoke freely, drawing inspiration from the moment.

More specific suggestions concerning the preparation of his sermons can be deduced from *Ad Clerum*. Although the brilliant and erratic Parker himself may have varied somewhat from these careful suggestions which he delivered to the students, they do reveal his philosophy of preaching.

In the first place, Parker suggested that discipline of thought and intellectual study were necessary for the preacher. He believed that any preacher could train his intellect to a satis-

---

7. Edwards, p. 102.

factory level for his ministry. He warned the young preacher not to become so absorbed in intellectual pursuits as to look with contempt on the practical men and women who worked at ordinary occupations.

Parker recommended a regular program of preparation for the young preacher: take a text from the Scripture, read it carefully in the original languages if possible; trace the various meanings attached to the words in other parts of the New Testament; understand the meaning and grammar of the passage; commit these opinions to writing; and only then take the opinion of two or three of the most critical expositors.

With this background study completed, write in regular order the principal thoughts which the passage suggests to the mind; these thoughts then become the skeleton of the sermon. Proceed next to elaborate these thoughts, writing on wide lines so as to leave room for erasure and interlining. Strike out all the long words and "superfine expressions," such as "Methinks I see," "the stellar heavens," and so on. Rewrite the message with particular care, so that no one could doubt the meaning; write as if every line "might save a life." Then put the manuscript away and return to pastoral duties with assurance.

Parker exhorted young preachers to avoid what he called *clever* sermons — sermons built on detached expressions, broken sentences, or perverted accommodations of text. The preacher must take care not to "handle the Word of God deceitfully," but to remember that his duty is to declare the whole counsel of God. The text should not be regarded by itself but in its scriptural setting. No sermon should be started until the particular truth of the text had been discovered; then, and only then, should the preacher decide upon the treatment of the text.

As dramatic as Parker was, it is not surprising to hear him warn his students against being *sensationless* as well as sensational. He reminded the young preacher to avoid the temptation to play a role or perform grotesque tricks in the pulpit, but to remember also that he must make an impression. He should be as sensation-creating as the apostles. Therefore the plan of the sermon should show variety; it should not follow one pattern. If possible, all commonplace division should be avoided. Parker's sermons themselves were marked by freshness and originality.

Parker believed in simplicity of style rather than eloquence, and he urged students to remember that their business was not to impress but to bring men to the Savior. Every sermon must be prepared with that end in view. He also believed in the power of illustration:

> Most unquestionably, the use of figures is to be highly commended; and it is because of a strong belief that a good deal can be done to improve what I may (for want of a better name) call the metaphorical faculty, that I urge you to insist upon your mind giving you something in the way of illustration. Look for figures; work for them; take them in their rudest outline, and improve them. It is hardly necessary to remind you that figures are not to be expected to meet all the points of a subject; let it suffice to have one main line of application, and to shed light on one particular point.[8]

Parker counseled the preacher to cultivate to the fullest extent his gifts of mental composition. He believed that eventually a minister could develop the ability to compose his sermons mentally without the help of written material. He believed that such preparation was an indispensable part of extemporary preaching.

Parker's splendid sermons are marked by simplicity and dignity, but there is a great deal of color in every line. All of these qualities are evident in a striking passage from his sermon "Back to God":

> At the beginning of the creation what was man's relation to the lower animals? Providential, divine, priestly, educative. There were no wild beasts until there were wild men. We do not heed this. You might have had the wolf on your hearthstone as a gentle, trusting creature. You might have had the nightingale perched on your shoulder, singing you songs of heaven in the dark night. The dog meant and wanted to love you more: you are the dog's god; when his god fell, he became savage. Oh, foolish souls! There is a time coming when the Saviour of the seven spirits, the Prince of the four names, shall rule the earth, and then the wolf shall dwell with the lamb, the little child shall play at the den of the cockatrice, and there shall be none to hurt or to destroy in my mountain; for it is holy. The man that would

8. Ibid., pp. 110–11.

civilise by destruction is a poor man; he takes the very meanest, vulgarest way of making gardens. Being fallen, he must needs have a gun; having made of himself a savage, he must go into the jungle and shoot the noblest beasts that the divine hand ever formed; being himself dehumanised, he must be cruel to his own dog, to his own horse, ay, sometimes to his own children!

The scorching heat of his irony can be felt in another passage:

It will be very old-fashioned doctrine, and very unacceptable to the young and budding genius of the century, when I say that we must get back to prayer, in its real, true, deep, eternal signification, before we can get back to any real prosperity. . . . Here is the great call to young preachers, to missionaries of the Cross, to Christian leaders of society. I know you have your altruism and your socialism, and your schemes for making yourselves longer holidays; I know you have your battlings and your strikes and your lock-outs and your various social confusions and misunderstandings: but unless the Lord hath forsaken my soul, and left that soul as an empty tenement, I will say that the only way out of all personal sin and social trouble is by getting back to the divine intention in the making of men and in the construction of society.

The same kind of irony is used in the sermon "Destruction and Construction":

There is nothing so easy as destruction. That is a simple doctrine which is often forgotten. The unbeliever is not in any need of genius. The fool, the withered heart, hath said, "There is no God." I want to smite and humiliate and expel if I can the notion that it requires a very great genius to be an infidel. Christian ministers and Christian believers labour under a great disadvantage in this matter. They are supposed to be fanatics, well-meaning but weak; accountable, but wanting in brain force. Infidels are geniuses; to be heterodox is to be popular; to publish a book against Christ is to get a circulation.

There is, I repeat as my starting-point, nothing so easy as destruction, what is called iconoclasm, image-breaking, a man going round the temple with an iron rod in his hand and smiting all images of beauty and purity and dignity. How much genius does it require to break a vase?

Parker could also write with descriptive beauty:

Grow where you are; gather moss where you are at present place. The young sapling looks beautiful, yet after all there is something about the great mossy old tree, something that you cannot find upon a mushroom. It has religious looks; nobody knows how many generations it has seen go to their burial. And still upon its ever-young branches it bears the latest spring and summer seal of God: it is the root that is old: the little leaf that trembles on the tree is the child born yesterday.

Each of these sermons proves that Joseph Parker possessed all of the variety and versatility that he suggested to his students.

Sermons

THE THEOLOGY OF MONEY

> "Thou shalt remember the Lord thy God: for it is He that
> giveth thee power to get wealth" (Deuteronomy 8:18).
> "Upon the first day of the week let every one of you lay by him
> in store, as God hath prospered him" (1 Corinthians 16:2).

AFORETIME I have addressed those who are advanced in life upon the
dedication of property: some believed, "some mocked, and others said,
we will hear thee again of this matter." I propose at this time to turn
away from the old, the prejudiced and the unimpressible, and to
address those who are just beginning to understand their relations to
money – the young, whose hand is about to be laid on the property of
the world, and who are open to conviction as to the uses and responsibilities of their stewardship. They, I presume, are willing to be instructed as to the theology of money.

The word "stewardship" involves the vital principle of the whole
question. It brings us at once to the first text, "Thou shalt remember
the Lord thy God: for *it is He that giveth thee power to get wealth.*"
Remember *that,* and industry is turned into a sacrament. Remember
that, and you will feel yourself working side by side with God, in the
field, the warehouse, the bank, the shop, the office, the pulpit. What a
blow this text strikes at one of the most popular and mischievous fal-
lacies in secular life. That fallacy is, that *man is the maker of his own
money.* Men who can see God moulding worlds, and circling through
the heavens with a comet in His right hand, cannot see Him sug-
gesting an idea in business, smiling on the plough, guiding the merchant's pen, and bringing summer into a brain long winter-bound and
barren. We have dethroned the Most High in the realm of commerce;
and in place of the heavenly Majesty have erected unclean and pestif-
erous idols: we have put into the holy place the foul little gods named
Trick and Cunning; and over our completed fortunes have prepared

Reprinted from Joseph Parker, *Hidden Springs* (London: Frederick Pitman,
1864), pp. 254–65.

incense for our own nostril. We have locked God up in the *church;* we have crushed Him into the *Bible* like a faded rose-leaf; we have shut upon Him the iron gate of the market-place; we have forced commerce into widowhood, and compelled trade to babble the idiotic creed of atheism.

There is always a danger of becoming entangled in the intricacies of second causes. The element of mediation enters so largely into God's government: one world lighting another; one man depending on another; and one influence diffusing itself in a thousand directions, and entering into the most subtle and complicated combinations; all this, I say, intercepts our vision of the absolute and divine. We have a difficulty in understanding anything but straight lines. If money fell from the firmament like rain, or snow, or sunshine, we could, perhaps, more readily concede that it came from God; but because it comes through circuitous, and sometimes obscure channels, we feel not upon it the warmth of the divine touch, and see on it no nobler image than Caesar's. We are guilty as the ancient harlot, on whose giddy head God poured out His wrath. "She said, I will go after my lovers that give me my bread and my water, my wool and my flax, mine oil and my drink." But God hedged up her way with thorns, He caused her to lose her paths, and said, in a tone which combined complaint and anger, "For she did not know that I gave her corn, and wine, and oil, and multiplied her silver and gold, which they prepared for Baal." He who pours down the light of the sun, pours out the oil. He who arrays Lebanon and Bashan in all the pomp of summer foliage, gives wool and flax to cover the nakedness of man. The great world is one sky-domed church, and there is nothing common or unclean.

God wishes this fact to be treasured in the memory of His saints. "Thou shalt *remember.*" It is to be ever present in our recollections; it is to be a star, beaming on the troubled waters, by which we are to strike our course; it is to be a cloud, a fire, for the day and night of our long pilgrimage. Mark the happy consequences of this grateful recollection. First of all, God and wealth are ever to be associated. "The silver and the gold are mine." There is but one absolute proprietor. We hold our treasures on loan; we occupy a stewardship. Consequent upon this is a natural and most beautiful *humility.* "What hast thou that thou hast not received?" When the merchant sits down in the evening light to count his day's gains, he is to remember that the Lord his God gave him power to get wealth. When the workman throws down the instrument of his labour, that he may receive the reward of his toil, he is to remember that the Lord his God gave him power to get wealth. When the young man receives the first recognition of his remunerative industry, he is to remember that the Lord his God gave him power to get wealth. Thus the getting of money becomes a sacred thing. Money is a mighty power; wealth occupies a proud position in the parliament of action. Trade thus becomes a means of grace, and commerce an ally of religion. In one word, every act of life is restored to its direct and vital relation to the centre of the universe. There are men who assert that the voice of the pulpit should never be heard in the emporium of commerce. Fools, and blind. They forget that they could not move a muscle but for the grace of God. They could not originate or apply an idea but for the mercy of heaven. They have no objection to hear a short sermon once a week, and with that they rock their conscience into a six days repose. I hold, in opposition to this atheistic commerce, that every ledger should be a Bible, true as if written by the finger of God; that every place of business should be made sacred by the presence of righteousness, verity, honour and justice. The man who can be atheistic in business could be atheistic in heaven itself. The man who never turns his warehouse into a church will never fail to turn the church into a warehouse. Even christian men are anxious that too much of what they call religion should not be introduced into places of trade. They speak about God with a quivering whisper, as if they were speaking about a ghost, whose hollow eye was fixed upon them. When they refer to Him it is with a backward motion of a trembling finger or a jerk of the voice, which indicates anything but moral repose. There is no filial jubilance of spirit; no leaping of the heart, as if it would go straight up to God. They will come once on a Sunday to the sanctuary; they will snarl because there are so many collections; they will sing a hymn, but must sit down before finishing the last line of the last verse. Men who make money with both hands, who run greedily after gain, and serve Mammon with uncooling zeal, are not likely to remember that the Lord their God gave them power to get wealth. Memory is occupied with other subjects. The heart is foreclosed. The whole nature has signed, sealed and delivered a bond to entertain no such recollections. In enumerating the happy consequences arising from a grateful recognition of God's relation to wealth, the check upon all wastefulness and extravagance might be mentioned. Christianity enjoins frugality upon its disciples; its command is, "Gather up the fragments." The man who *wastes* money would also waste his moral dowry. An extravagant Christian — that is, a man who outruns his resources — is dishonest, and his life is a continual felony. Money is one of the limitations of power, and to overstep *that* is a practical blasphemy, an unpronounced but most terrible reproach upon divine arrangements.

This, then, is our basis principle — viz., that God giveth man power to get wealth, and, consequently, that God sustains an immediate relation to the property of the world. Take the case of a young man just entering business. If his heart is uneducated and unwatched, he will regard business as a species of gambling; if his heart be pivoted on right principles, he will esteem business a moral service, as the practical side of his prayers, a public embodiment of many aspirations and convictions. In course of time, the young man realizes money on his own account. Looking at his gold and silver, he says, "I *made* that." There is a glow of honest pride on his cheek. He looks upon the reward of his industry, and the light of joy kindles in his eye. While he looks upon his first-earned gold, I wish to speak to him, gently and persua- sively, these words – "Thou shalt remember the Lord thy God: for *it is He that giveth thee power to get wealth.*" Instantly his view of the property is elevated, enlarged, sanctified. He was just about to say that his own arm had gotten him the victory, and to forget that though the image is Caesar's, yet the gold is God's. What is the natural line of thought through which the young man would run under such cir- cumstances? It would lie in some such direction as this, I venture to suggest: – "What can be the meaning of this word 'remember'? Does it not call me to *gratitude*? Is it not intended to turn my heart and my eye *heavenward*? As God has given me 'power to get wealth,' am I not bound to return some recognition of His goodness and mercy?" While these questions are agitating his mind, the apostle Paul says to him, "On the first day of the week let every one of you lay by him in store, *as God hath prospered him.*" Thus the principle is turned to practical account. A time is named, a measure is fixed. The time, *God's elect day;* the measure, *God's gift of power.* Can anything be more beautiful? anything, presumptively, more like God? The sab- bath is emphatically a day of *remembrance;* memory is called to the awakening of the most sacred associations; the *recollective faculty* is to be engaged, from the rising of the sun until the going down of the same. Among the subjects of recollection is this of getting wealth, and Paul says that recollection is to be associated with distribution and sanctification.

I will assume that up to this point of the inquiry I have the full con- sent of the young man's mind and heart: the question now occurs, How *much* shall he "lay by him in store"? The young man is anxious to acknowledge God's goodness, and all he waits for is to ascertain the *measure* of his dedication. The answer is, "As God hath prospered him." There is not a word about tenth, or fifth, or twentieth. The whole New Testament arithmetic of the case is purely *moral.* The student is at liberty, indeed, to go back into the oldest biblical records, and to discover what grateful men did in dividing and dedicating property, yet, so far as the New Testament is concerned, not a word is spoken as to an arbitrary and unchangeable proportion. The spiritual law is, "as God hath prospered him." When the week has been unusually productive, the young man will "lay by" with unusual liberality; when the gains have been small, the "store" will be small; when there has been no gain there will be no dedication. All the details of work- ing must be left to the individual conscience. It is a service of love, of gratitude, of memorial; and the *heart* will soon arrange the best methods of marshalling details. A thousand difficulties might be sug- gested by *speculation* which would never be seen by *love.* I cannot pause to enumerate detailed methods of dealing with a weekly account; all I venture to say is this — Man derives from God power to get wealth; that he should consequently make some recognition of his obligation; and that the most clear intimation of doing this is given by Paul — "On the first day of the week let every one of you lay by him in store, as God hath prospered him." It is replied that this "order" was given in relation to a *particular* case of benevolence. What then? An *object* may be particular, when a *method* is universal. It is urged that this is the *only* instance in which the method is prescribed. What then? How *often* must a word be spoken in order to make it true? It is contended that there are difficulties in carrying out such an arrangement. What then? Point out any duty in life which is unattended with difficulty? If we work this plan up to the point that occasions insuperable difficulty, God will accept our service, and enrich the heart which renders it.

Let it be assumed that the plan of the Apostle is carried out with all willingness and diligence, what results would mark its adoption?

1st. The fickleness and fitfulness of benevolence would be terminated. Benevolence is now very largely a question of impulse. Little or no preparation is made for the regular and constant administration of God's bounty.

2nd. The benevolent operations of the church would be immensely facilitated. If I have a case which calls for sympathy and substantial support, I should find no difficulty with men who systematically store a portion for God. They know exactly what they have in their treasury; they know how they determine the relative merits of cases; and in a moment their answer, always genial and kind, even when not affirmative, may be returned. As it is *now*, persons who go a-begging, as it is termed, are sometimes actually affronted as if they were public nuisances; they make up their minds to be snapped at as if they were committing a species of masked felony.

3rd. The gratitude of the individual Christian would be kept in lively exercise. On the morning of every Lord's day he offers God a portion of his week's proceeds. Not only does he *pray* for the kingdom, he shows the reality of his word by the practical value of his *deed.* You may suggest that it is troublesome to be dividing every week; I answer, Is it troublesome to be *receiving* every week?

We speak of the "exceeding great and precious promises" abounding in God's word, but *often* overlook those which apply to our so-called *secular* life. Do you imagine that Almighty God is an unconcerned spectator of this service of dedication? Hear His word! "Honour the Lord with thy substance and with the firstfruits of all thine increase." What then? what result will follow? "*So* shall thy barns be filled with plenty, and thy presses shall burst out with new wine." We imagine that all God's benefactions are spiritual; we have shut Him out from the field and the vineyard; but hear His word! "The Lord shall command the blessing upon thee in thy storehouses, and in all that thou settest thine hand unto; and He shall bless thee in the land which the Lord thy God giveth thee."

We have cause and effect even in the religious administration of our worldly affairs: – "He which soweth sparingly shall reap also sparingly; and he which soweth bountifully shall reap also bountifully." Yet our "sowing" must be done with a good motive, or the harvest will be scanty and worthless. "Take heed that ye do not your alms before men, to be seen of them: otherwise ye have no reward of your Father which is in heaven." Thus the *hidden* influences the *revealed!* What is the true motive? "The love of Christ constraineth us." "Ye know the grace of our Lord Jesus Christ." "Whosoever shall give to drink unto one of these little ones a cup of cold water only *in the name of a disciple,* verily I say unto you, he shall in no wise lose his reward."

If you remember the Lord your God, He will remember *you,* for "God is not unrighteous to forget your work and labour of love."

BACK TO GOD

"But from the beginning of the creation God" (Mark 10:6).

THAT IS WHAT WE WANT to get at. We are perplexed, divided, and confused by things intermediate and transient. We have had enough of them. We want to get back to the beginning, back to the divine intent – back behind the beginning, back into the council-chamber of the Eternal. The context is graphic and beautiful. The Pharisees came to Jesus and asked him, "Is it lawful for a man to put away his wife?" They tempted the Teacher; they were inwardly mocking him, and secretly endeavouring to entrap him. "And he answered and said unto them, What did Moses command you?" You profess to be devoted to the law of Moses, how does that law read upon the question which you have put to me? "And they said, Moses suffered to write a bill of divorcement, and to put her away." Jesus answered: So far, so good; you are scholars of the letter, very poor scholars, or you would have

Reprinted from Joseph Parker, *Studies in Texts: For Family, Church, and School,* 2d ed., 6 vols., (London: Horace Marshall & Son, 1905), 1:84–94.

known that "For the hardness of your heart he wrote you this precept" — something to be going on with, a piece of paper you can handle and use under limited circumstances. "But from the beginning of the creation God." He did not stop at Moses or the prophets. This Teacher, as prophesied by Isaiah, drew his breath in the fear of God. He was not the disciple of any man: he brought messages directly from the mind and heart of God. We feel, therefore, that we are in company with the right Teacher now. Moses accommodated himself to the hardness of your heart; "but from the beginning of the creation God" made two, man and wife, one: whom, therefore, God hath joined together, let not man put asunder!

Thus all the little card-box legislation of all the great teachers that ever invented new schemes of society — all these inventions, suggestions, legislations — are rolled over by this Man whose breath was drawn in the fear of God, and who spake from the steps of the palace of the Eternal. That is what we want to get at. Not what Moses said, not what the Greeks philosophised, not what the Spartans turned into discipline; all this is more or less dignified gossip and conjecture — foolish, or useful for the moment. What we want to get at is God — what he meant when he said, "Let us make." If I could convey this thought to you as it is in my own mind, you would be inspired souls, you would take a new view of society and all its arrangements and divers trumperies.

In the context we are face to face with Moses and Christ. Moses, for the hardness of the hearts of the people, made a certain temporary arrangement, but it was aside from the eternal thought; permissible, but not perpetual. So we need minor providences — little bye-laws, small schedules, parliamentary enactments, things to be going on with — to restrain the wanton and the willful; but all these are playthings comparatively. If we could get back to "the beginning of the creation," and, like Christ, draw our breath in the fear of God, legislation itself would be natural breathing, Socialism would be deepest and truest life: "Behold, I make all things new." It is in the nature of a fallen curiosity and debased ingenuity to be making more wordy laws. Jesus Christ brought laws to a minimum. He said, All that the prophets and the law have been trying to say may be summed up in two words: "Thou shalt love the Lord thy God, and thy neighbour as thyself." Any society that is rich in schedules and bye-laws and subtle arrangements and difficult interpretations of the law is in a bad way. This is the condition of society to-day: the lawmakers divided, the bench cleft in two. We want to hear the sweet woman-voice of the Man who calls us away from all these things into fellowship with God, union with the Spirit, oneness with the eternal right. Every bolt on your door is a witness against society; every time you turn the key and lock a drawer, you indict human nature. Society is organised scepticism.

What we want to get at, then, is the divine thought, the divine intention "from the beginning of the creation." From the beginning of the creation what was man's personal relation to God? He was the under-god, the companion-god, the visible god, a partaker of the divine nature. What is man now according to our Catechism? A fallen and depraved being. True. "But from the beginning of the creation God" made man in his own image and his own likeness. We are not to be stopped by the law of Moses or by the catechism of theology; we must get back to God's own purpose in setting up man, to whom he could speak, and with whom he could hold communion of heart. How do you describe man? Small, few in days, his breath is in his nostrils, there is none abiding; one dieth in his full strength, another dieth in his youth and never eateth with pleasure; the earth is a graveyard; man is a sinner; man is of small account, he is as a wind that cometh for a little time and then vanisheth away.

Quite right up to a given point; but remember, "in the beginning of the creation God" made man in his own image and in his own likeness – made man immortal, gave him what is called an immortal soul; the soul being the true self. We must get back to that divine standard if we would set a right value upon any human creature that has debased humanity and brought discredit upon the very earth he treads. At present we are looking into reports, into the reports of royal commissions, forsooth! into reports of committees and councils, into examinations and cross-examinations; and we are basing our judgment of mankind or of society upon such reports. We have had enough. The reports are perfectly correct; the reports are useful within given limits; we cannot conduct society as it is at present, debased and degraded, without the assistance of such reports; "but at the beginning of the creation God" made man upright. When you hear of man, you ought to hear of uprightness; but "they have sought out many inventions," and the proudest of their "inventions" is a falsehood. There is great difficulty in some quarters as to the immortality of the soul. If you start the discussion of the immortality of man from a period after his historical apostasy, you will be wrong; starting from the wrong point, you will come to a false conclusion. What you must do is to get back to "the beginning of the creation." What did God make man when he made him in his own image? – a thing of clay, a thing that could be rusted by time, a thing that would be the sport of the centuries? Never! He made him immortal: the breath that warmed his nostrils came from the mouth of God.

What was man's relation to man "from the beginning of the creation"? Man was man's "keeper." A sweet thought – a divine socialism! – the socialism that is utterly forgotten to-day amid a thousand pamphlets that are snowed into the gutter. This man hath a dream, and that man a prophecy, concerning altruism, and another man hath a proposition to make. These may be good, they may suit a certain period of time and a certain definition of territory, they may be exceedingly useful within a limited period; "but from the beginning of the creation God"! That is what we want to know. God said, "Where is thy brother?"

This is not a doctrine that can be taught by pamphlets; this is not the issue of some very learned dissertation read before some very somnolent audience: this belongs to the "beginning" of things, this is the *a priori* condition. We thus get back and back to God's thought: no reformation can ever take the place of regeneration; no socialism can ever overtake the divine idea of man filled with solicitude about man, not happy until the other man is found, not at rest whilst there is one poor little drenched creature wandering about in the wilderness of the midnight. Not a mechanical law. God has no poor-law. We, being made in his image and likeness, should love one another, not by commandment of the letter, but by commandment of the Spirit, by the pressure of an infinite and ineffable necessity – the rush of God upon all the springs and motions of the soul. Man hath sought out many inventions: he tinkers and patches; he legislates and amends and enlarges and undoes; he is, before God, a fool! He doth not hold large commerce with God. When the spirit is right, all literal schedules may be discarded. We shall not be right until we cannot help doing good – until we breathe it, until we are transformed by it. That is the divine idea. God is love. He does not legislate himself into a momentary and evanescent affection; in his soul he is love: that is how he made man at "the beginning of the creation."

At the beginning of the creation what was man's relation to the lower animals? Providential, divine, priestly, educative. There were no wild beasts until there were wild men. We do not heed this. You might have had the wolf on your hearthstone as a gentle, trusting creature. You might have had the nightingale perched on your shoulder, singing you songs of heaven in the dark night. The dog meant and wanted to love you more: you are the dog's god; when his god fell, he became savage. Oh, foolish souls! There is a time coming when the Saviour of the seven spirits, the Prince of the four names, shall rule the earth, and then the wolf shall dwell with the lamb, the little child shall play at the den of the cockatrice, and there shall be none to hurt or to destroy in my mountain; for it is holy. The man that would civilise by destruction is a poor man; he takes the very meanest, vulgarest way of making gardens. Being fallen, he must needs have a gun; having made of himself a savage, he must go into the jungle and shoot the noblest beasts that the divine hand ever formed; being himself dehumanised, he must be cruel to his own dog, to his own horse, ay, sometimes to his own children!

When the Lord made all the animals to pass before man that he might name them, it means in the deepest spiritual significance that he might hug them, pet them, endear himself to them, so that the voice of man should be the voice of domination, not in the sense of fear, but in a very subtle sense of acquiescence. God gave man all the animals on the earth, in the air, whatsoever passeth through the paths of the sea; yet man has gone to the devil's side, and wants to civilise by pitiless extirpation. The poor fool has now no remedy but to destroy the aborigines! He would shoot down the blacks; he would evangelise them by laceration. And as for the beasts of the field, he makes weapons on purpose for their destruction, and traps for the purpose of catching them, that he may wound and disable and destroy. "At the beginning of the creation" God meant all the animals to be gentle, beautiful, serviceable, cooperative; but now the little bird, the little redbreast, the little lark, is afraid when man, who should be to him as god and providence and priest, comes near. That is our reputation! To that we have brought things! The very birds are frightened of us.

In the beginning of the creation what was man's relation to productive nature? God gave him all the green things, all the trees, all the herbs; they should be to man for seed and for fruit; and when man tilled the ground, it should laugh in bountifulness of harvest. All the seasons were handed over to man; all nature was to be as man's providing mother; she should say to him, "I am now ready, gather me into the garner, because winter snows are coming; here is thy bread; here is the anticipative answer to all thy winter's necessities." Man has spoiled the harvest; the earth does not hear him. From the beginning of the creation God meant that the earth was to hear the heavens, and the heavens were to hear himself, and there was to be a great interplay of ministry and action; the result being that man was to be knee-deep in flowers, and to have bread enough all the winter long. That was the divine idea "from the beginning of the creation"; that idea is yet to be realised in gospel times. There is a specific pledge or promise to this effect: "Let the people praise, O God, yea, let all the people praise thee; then shall the earth yield her increase." But man, foolish man, undertakes the agricultural question; the nation appoints a Minister of Agriculture!

Was there ever such a living haystack found on all the meadows of time? The agricultural question is pressed upon the attention of Parliament. That may be necessary just now – man may have brought himself into that condition; but the only ultimate and lasting way out of it is to get back "to the beginning of the creation," the divine idea: and when the people praise God, and all the people praise him, a choir large as humanity, an orchestra large as creation, then shall the earth yield her increase, and all garners will be poor to accommodate God's infinite reply.

This is the reason the Church exists; this is the reason that a religious ministry must be kept up. We must get man back to the *a priori* position, to the divine notion, to what God himself meant when he made man and constructed society. I know that this will get rid of all our intermediaries, all our social ameliorations, all our second causes, all our patchings and tinkerings. Men now read essays upon the poverty of the age – and print them – and forget them; in divers ways they beat the air and take the darkness home. It is very pitiful, but it looks legislative, inventive, clever. Now we are boastfully bringing to bear upon the poverty, the necessity, and the bad condition of society "a statesman-like capacity." O my Father, pity us! Thou didst make us upright, and we have made ourselves "statesmen"!

It will be very old-fashioned doctrine, and very unacceptable to the young and budding genius of the century, when I say that we must get back to prayer, in its real, true, deep, eternal signification, before we can get back to any real prosperity. From the beginning of the creation God provided for sin. Sin is no surprise to Omniscience: the Lamb was slain from before the foundation of the world; before the sin was done the atonement was rendered. Alas! we make our little plans and our infinite mistakes, and then we say we are as God made us. That is the chief of lies. When you made that statement, that you are as God made you, you told all lies in one black falsehood. Here is the foundation of the Evangelical ministry, here is the beginning of the divine regeneration. Men take all things into their own hand, and, having wrought out the problem, as they would call it, into all manner of confusion and disappointment, they say, "Where is Providence?" You should have asked that question ages ago; you should have got into a right relation to Providence before you made your first mistake. That which is bad from the beginning can never, saith the Roman law, be made right by any lapse of time. We are wrong at the start, we are wrong fundamentally, and no resolution-mongering will ever be permitted to usurp the throne of the Eternal and to direct the centuries in their moral and spiritual legislation. Back to prayer, to faith, to yourself, as God meant you to be!

The great lesson is to get back to God, get back to "the beginning of the creation." The cry of the day is, "Get back to Christ!" That was never Christ's own cry; his cry was, "Back to the Father, back to God!" We go to Christ that we may get to the Father; we go to the atoning Christ that we may pass on to the pardoning God. Then cometh the end, when Christ shall have delivered up the kingdom to God and his Father, and God shall be all in all. It is a weary way, to hang ourselves on the trees of our own invention. We make suicides of ourselves (notwithstanding the verbal paradox) every day we live; for we will not have God to reign over us.

That is, suggestively, without any attempt at exhaustive elaboration, how the case stands; and until we all get back to fundamental conceptions, and to a realisation of the divine intention, we shall be only making new plans in order to discard them; for man's inventions are shorter-lived than himself. Here is the great call to young preachers, to missionaries of the Cross, to Christian leaders of society. I know you have your altruism and your socialism, and your schemes for making yourselves longer holidays; I know you have your battlings and your strikes and your lock-outs and your various social confusions and misunderstandings: but unless the Lord hath forsaken my soul, and left that soul as an empty tenement, I will say that the only way out of all personal sin and social trouble is by getting back to the divine intention in the making of men and in the construction of society. Who can give us the information and the wisdom that we need? Jesus Christ. He dwelt in the bosom of the Father; he draws his breath in the fear of the Lord. Get audience of him, and he will show you how to build your house upon a rock.

DESTRUCTION AND CONSTRUCTION

"The thief cometh not, but for to steal, and to kill, and to destroy: I am come that they might have life" (John 10:10).

THERE is nothing so easy as destruction. That is a simple doctrine which is often forgotten. The unbeliever is not in any need of genius. The fool, the withered heart, hath said, "There is no God." I want to smite and humiliate and expel if I can the notion that it requires a very great genius to be an infidel.

Christian ministers and Christian believers labour under a great disadvantage in this matter. They are supposed to be fanatics, well-meaning but weak; accountable, but wanting in brain force. Infidels are geniuses; to be heterodox is to be popular; to publish a book against Christ is to get a circulation. There is, I repeat as my starting-point, nothing so easy as destruction, what is called iconoclasm, image-breaking, a man going round the temple with an iron rod in his hand and smiting all images of beauty and purity and dignity. How much genius does it require to break a vase? Look at Nature, and the same lesson is taught us. Any beast can crush a flower: who can put it in joint again? No angel; it takes God to make a flower, it takes God to repair it when it is broken. I am dwelling upon the ease of destruction.

Reprinted from Joseph Parker, *The Gospel of Jesus Christ: Sermons,* new ed. (London: Arthur H. Stockwell, n.d.), pp. 162–71.

It is an offhanded trick. Young men, there is nothing in it. Why are you befooled by it? Why do you allow yourselves to be taken away from the old altar and the old book and the old faith because somebody has said "No"?

Give me an hour to do what I please in before the Royal Academy is opened, and it will never be opened; I could destroy the pictures by the dozen. Am I then great? deserving of popularity? Will you cry out for me, "Let us have freedom of thought, freedom of action"? You will not allow that in the Academy. Show me the President's fairest painting, and with one dash it is out of sight. It took the President long months to make it; he dreamed about it, he conversed with fellow-artists respecting it, it grew upon him like a dawn; but as an iconoclast I went in, and with my pailful of inartistic colour I dashed it out of existence. Am I therefore to be memorialised, and to have my name written on monumental brass, and to be looked upon, if I am arrested, as a martyr and a hero? I think not.

You are building a bridge. I have a proper respect for all bridges; but, after the engineer has said, "It is finished," give me two hours, and I will blow it into atoms. It has taken years to build, it is a monument of engineering skill, the people who have had to do with its construction are justly proud of it; and yet, with an appropriate supply of dynamite, I will rend it in an hour, and the work of which you are so proud shall be a hideous ruin.

Young man, why do you follow so largely and enthusiastically men who have nothing to say to you but words of destruction, men who try to rob you? He who takes from you one tender and inspiring association is a thief. You are not the young man you were before that depletion took place. It was a tender association; some called it superstitious, but no association or uplifting of the soul is superstitious that sends a man back again into the market-place to keep honestly his scales and measures. Our religion might be charged as a religion of fanaticism and superstition, vision and contemplation and cloud-beating, but it sends us back to heal the sick, to nurse childhood, to take the blind pilgrim over the road out of danger's way; and it makes us, when we have spread our banquet, send a portion to him that is hungry. Associations, I care not how far they go upward among clouds and stars, if they send me back again a sturdier citizen, an honester, more chivalrous man, are true; they prove their truth by their moral effect.

Yet, what a great noise a little infidelity makes. One infidel will make more noise than a thousand Christians, and noise is thought to be prosperity and success and the utter uprooting and total routing of the Church. It is always so that the destructive becomes, I will not say more popular, but in the first instance more notorious, than the constructive. Did any of you hear that the Scotch express arrived safely in Edinburgh last night? If it had broken down between London and Edinburgh, the world would have heard of it. "Accident to the Flyman

Scotchman. Terrific Panic on the Great Northern. Awful Consternation among the Passengers." They report destructions; who cares to
hear that the train got in safely, and everybody went home, and there
was rest all round about? So if one little infidel a few inches high
should get up in this church and make a noise, we should all hear
about it. Do not mistake the importance of the event; it is not without
significance; even the noise of an infidel should attract some attention
finely adjusted to the occasion. But "Behold he prayeth." Ah, then the
whole church should turn round, and with tearful eyes gaze on the
beauteous spectacle, and with swelling, ennobled heart should praise
God that another soul had been saved.

So there is a common law in operation here. It applies to people, to
teachers, to hearers, to religious relationships, and to all the commercial economy of the world, and to everything that touches life at
any point. It is the destructive that is reported. Not a soul will hear of
this meeting to-night on the other side of the street, but if the roof fell
in all the city would talk about nothing else to-morrow. So when men
come and destroy, or attempt to destroy, our religious associations and
faiths and hopes, let us know that nothing uncommon has happened,
because there is much uproar and tumult about it; after all, the case
is not serious necessarily. Where one man has gone back, lapsed into
apostasy, a dozen hearts may have been quickened, stimulated, and
cheered by visitations from the unseen Spirit of the Almighty.

Jesus Christ contrasts Himself with this destroying power. He
comes to save. If He comes to save He will want time. Salvation is not
to be wrought out in a moment. The development of human history is
not an instantaneous act. Christ is building night and day; Christ is
advancing "with the process of the suns." Yet sometimes in the advance there appears to be a singular and discouraging recession. But
that recession is but like a refluent wave; it has gone back that it may
come forward again with a mightier energy and exceed the line where
the last wave fell. If Jesus Christ has come to save, He will require
patience. Men may be in a sense saved in a day, but they are not educated, instructed, edified, consolidated in a day. And what rude scholars
we are! how inapt, how reluctant of heart, how soon wearied, how disposed to gravitate to the centre of the earth!

But Jesus Christ is patient with us; when the hill is very steep He
takes us up in His arms that we may get our breath again. But all this
means expenditure of time, thought, care, solicitude; and all this
means the exercise of a patience that cannot be fluttered, because it
has its centre in eternity. You can make a wax flower to order; you can
say, "This flower shall be ready to-morrow at three o'clock." Who can
promise to grow one of these sweet bluebells that are on the hillsides,
and have it ready this day week? The little thing comes up out of eternity; it is a child of the solar system, it is a blossom upon rocks infinite.
You can order a coat to-morrow for your child, but you cannot order a

character. Jesus Christ is the Constructor, the Builder-up, and all the line of God's challenges is a line calling us to this view of His character and purpose. "Where wast thou when I laid the foundations of the earth?" He is always laying foundations here, is the Constructor, the Creator, the Builder. "Who hath laid the measures thereof, if thou knowest? or who hath stretched the line upon it? And as for thee, man of words and fretful spirit, canst thou bind the sweet influences of the Pleiades or loose the bands of Orion? Canst thou bring forth Mazzaroth in his season? or canst thou guide Arcturus with his sons?" This is not the voice of the destroyer, a little god with a great flail smiting and destroying things. He guides, rules, calls forth, keeps in order.

It is a greater miracle to have things preserved than to have them destroyed. We cannot be made to think this; we are curiously disposed to see more in the stroke of anger than in the smile of love. Did the sun rise and set to-day? – to use popular language. To this inquiry you return an instant "Yes." In that circumstance find the true miracle. A universe preserved is a universe created. If we could impart this conviction to the Church, we should have a new state of things. So you see ministers have hard work to do; Christianity is the grandly audacious religion, because it comes not to destroy men's lives but to save them. What other religion soever proposed to save the world, every one in it, and to save the world by a Cross, by the mystery of Crucifixion, by the great mystery of sacrifice and atonement, by the wondrous economy of blood? All this requires time, patience, long-suffering love. O wait for the Lord, yea, wait patiently for Him; when His economy is completed all Heaven will be filled with the music of thankful joy. But Christianity is audacious in its beneficence. Christianity will do nothing perfunctorily; it will make clean, clear, complete, exact, and permanent work along all the line. It does not rough-hew its subjects and allow them to finish; it continues all its operations until the very last is as the strongest, and the least is counted one of the mightiest in the kingdom. This is the Lord's doing, and it is marvellous in our eyes.

Give the Church more time, give ministers more time. An infidel might rush into your family, and in five minutes ask questions which all the philosophers in creation could not answer in five centuries. The minister goes in, asks where the sick one is, walks quietly to the bedside, and prays through tears. Who can measure the issue? The fool came in as upon the wings of a tempest; he went out with a noise destitute of music. The servant of God did not lift up his voice and cry and cause his voice to be heard in the street, but patiently, gently, lovingly, sympathetically, he passed through all the ministry of Christian priesthood, that sweet, gracious gradation of office which is permitted to Christian believers and fellow-pilgrims; and nothing was known of that tender miracle. What a prayer it was! The sick man threw off his sickness as the weird words went up in silence and brought back Divine

benedictions as replies. O ministers of Christ, to whatsoever communion attached, ours is the hard work; but it is enough for the servant that
he be as his Lord. If they have refused the Lord, they will refuse the
servant. We are to prove the divinity of our vocation by our persistence.
The time will come when all the other people will drop away. Time
tries all. So long as there is health, prosperity, rioting, and power of
imparting joy, you will have round about you all manner of speculators
and destroyers, but when the clouds gather, and the winds cool, and
the night deepens, you will say, "Where are they?" and echo will
answer "Where?" But there will be One left, and when you ask the
name of that One who remains, it will be the name of the Son of Man.
He may be represented by some poor, humble member of the flock, but
Christianity never leaves the soul. Yea, though I pass through the
valley of the shadow of death I will fear no evil; Thy rod and Thy staff
shall comfort me.

We have to be upon our guard in one direction, for it is possible for a
man to destroy his own life. Nothing is so easy as destruction there
as well as elsewhere, and no other destruction is possible, if you will
it to be so. No man can hurt you but yourself; you have nothing to do
with your reputation, with public criticism; you have nothing to do
with traduction and slander. "To thine own self be true," to Christ
be true. No man can murder thee; no weapon that is formed against
thee shall prosper. There is only one form of destruction possible, and
that is suicide, and suicide is easy. There is but a step between thee
and all kinds of death. Do not narrow that passage to one little meaning.
There is but a step between thee and social death, moral death, family
death, spiritual death – but a step. The road lies along a very high and
dangerous precipice – one step, and all is over. "Hold Thou me up, and
I shall be safe." O Thou God, who dost lay foundations and build uni-
verses, Thou who art the Builder, give me the edification of Thy grace
lest I stumble and fall and die.

Here again the doctrine holds good. Nothing is so easy as destruction. Here is a man who has been living forty years in the great city,
honoured by all, trusted of all. How long would it take that man to
destroy his character? One moment, and nothing could redeem it but
God the Father, God the Son, and God the Holy Ghost. Forty years has
this merchantman been in building the tower of a high and honoured
reputation; in one action he levels the tower to the dust. He has but to
forge a signature, he has but to utter one sentence, and let it be known
that he has uttered it, and his prayers are forgotten, his professions
are looked upon as unmasked hypocrisies, and the Church cries shame
and puts him into the wilderness. When some kind witness comes
forward to testify as to his good character, the old judge says he will
take note of the suggestion, but he adds that this only aggravates the
charge that is brought against the man. We need continual watchfulness. "Let him that thinketh he standeth take heed lest he fall." O
blessed are the dead that die in the Lord. "Call no man happy until he

is dead," says the proverb, "for at the last he may perish." Blessed day when I am permitted to put my foot within the door. So near is death, so easy is destruction, so broad the gate that opens upon perdition. Do not despair; let God work His miracles here. You are in process of salvation; that is to say, you are in process of education and edification. Yield to God; have no will but His. The tempter will be hard upon thee, O friend. He does not like to see that tower of a noble life rising course by course in fine, exquisite masonry, as if touched with an angel's finger, and if he can fight thee and win, he will do it. Through much tribulation we must enter the gate. Christ has not chosen the easy work. The thief has come to thieve and to kill and destroy—the easiest of all work, a coward's work. "I am come that they might have life"—that is the hard work, the noble work, the blessed work. Ministers, teachers, office-bearers, professing Christians, you are feeding the life of the world; that is the positive. You will often be discouraged and disappointed. When I began my ministry I said, Surely the people will only need to hear that Jesus Christ the Son of God loved them and gave Himself for them, and they will man by man fall down and hail Him Saviour, King. It has not been so. Some of you have outlived three ministries. You can mention the pastors one by one, and characterise them, and describe them, and eulogise them. But you eluded them all. When they speak of you, your name is as a wound, your memory is a stinging disappointment. Yet even now you may fall down broken-heartedly, you may be found at the Cross, the one way to Heaven, the only way to Heaven, the infinitely secure way to Heaven; and even now you may be, not destroyed, but saved.

THE INTERPRETER

"Which being interpreted is" (Matthew 1:23).

"WHICH BEING INTERPRETED"—that is what we need: a man to tell us the meaning of hard words and difficult things and mysteries which press too heavily upon our staggering faith. This expression occurs

Reprinted from Joseph Parker, *The City Temple Pulpit* (London: Hodder & Stoughton, 1899), pp. 40–47.

quite frequently in the New Testament: "Emmanuel, which being interpreted is, God with us"; "Siloam, which is by interpretation, Sent"; "Golgotha, which being interpreted is, The place of a skull"; "Barnabas, which being interpreted is, A son of consolation." If we were left with the hard, unknown words we should be left in darkness; the interpretation comes to us as a lamp, we instantly feel the comfort and the liberty of illumination. When we heard that word Emmanuel we were staggered; it was a foreign word to us, it brought with it no home associations, it did not speak to anything that was within us; but when the interpreter came, when he placed his finger upon the word and said to us, The meaning of this word is God with us, then we came into the liberty and into the wealth of a new possession.

So we need the interpreter. We shall always need him. The great reader will always have his day, come and go who may. We want men who can turn foreign words, difficult languages, into our mother tongue; then how simple they are and how beautiful, and that which was a difficulty before becomes a gate opening upon a wide liberty. We need a man who can interpret to us the meaning of confused and confusing and bewildering events; some man with a key from heaven, some man with divine insight, the vision that sees the poetry and the reality of things, and a man with a clear, simple, strong, penetrating voice who will tell us that all this confusion will one day be shaped into order, and all this uproar will fall into the cadences of a celestial and endless music. We shall know that man when we meet him; there is no mistaking the prophet; he does not speak as other men speak, he is not in difficulty or in trouble as other men are; on his girdle hangs the key, the golden key, that can open the most difficult gates in providence and in history, and in the daily events that make up our rough life from week to week. How distressing is the possibility that a prophet may have been amongst us, and we may have mistaken him for a common man! How much more we might have elicited from him if we had listened more intently to his wonderful voice! What miracles of music he might have wrought in our nature; but we take the prophet sometimes as a mere matter of course: he is a man in a crowd, his speciality we overlook, and we know not that he is talking to us from the mountain of the heavens, from the altar of the temple unseen.

We want the same prophet to put all the unbuilt and chaotic material of life into shapeliness and into statuesque music. What masses of material are lying about us without shape and without purpose, and we are not strong enough or wise enough to handle them and bring them to right uses and issues. The interpreter must see the soul of things; he must not be easily discomposed, he must live away from the tumult of appearances: the battle is not fought by the great general mixing in the fray, but away yonder, it may be, in some little canvas tent, it is there that the whole idea is seen, and the whole apparatus brought to bear and the whole issue first revealed. "I will lift up mine eyes unto the hills, whence cometh my help," I will ask some godly prophet to assure me that God is in the tent yonder, far away beyond the stars, and that He is watching the whole fight, and that He will bring His own cause, which is the cause of righteousness and purity and beneficence, to honour and enthronement and coronation.

In life there is a great place for the interpreter; in all life there is a sanctuary in which such a man can exercise his ghostly ministry. This house called Nature needs an interpreter. The grass is more than grass, herbage is more than herbage; it is beauty, it is fruit, it has a mission to man and beast, and nature needs a man who can understand her mutable appearances, her ever-changing voices, her silent but progressive and inevitable processions, so that she never halts long at one place, but is continually moving on to the old age of completion and the youth of a new beginning. We want some men who can read nature to us religiously, who can find tongues in trees, books in the running brooks, sermons in stones, good in everything—a wondrous parable interwrought with all that is visible and mutable and measurable. Understand that the present uproar does not exhaust the purpose of God. The uproar is on the way to music; the tumult neither begins nor ends the circuit of God. He means to subdue all things unto Himself; the Saviour is on the mediatorial throne, interesting Himself in all the struggling, pathetic prayers of earth, and working up these prayers into great prevalent supplications; and when He has completed His mediation He shall rise from His throne and deliver up the kingdom to God and His Father, and God shall be all in all. Do not interrupt Divine Providence; do not stop the literature of God at a comma or at a semicolon; let the massive paragraphs roll on until they have come to the full meaning of the heart of God; then say, What think ye of the temple which God has been building in the night-time and in the fury of the gale? Let us pray for patience; good waiting is good praying.

The interpreter is the sent of God. Interpretation is not a universal gift. Nearly every man can go to the dictionary for the meaning of words, but the dictionary is always poorest when we want it most. The dictionary cannot explain any word right into the heart. It can give you equivalent words, or words that grade into one another, or words that help one another to some higher definition than themselves; but interpretation is a divine gift: it is genius, it is a divine trust. Few men can read. All men within the compass of practical civilisation can read words, but that is not reading in the true and deep sense. We must read the soul out of the words, and read the soul into our souls, and catch the higher meanings and be struck dumb with rapture and with ecstasy. The speaker is often mightiest when he is silent; the apostle is an apostle reordained when he is caught up into the third heaven and the seventh heaven, and when he comes back dumb with intelligence, having seen so much that lies beyond the word-line, beyond the verbal horizon, and which he says he cannot put into the words of common time and common space, for in very deed they were not lawful to be uttered.

Who can express ecstasy? who can give the full range in expressive words to the rapture of his love and to the satisfaction of his answered prayer? We need the poet. The poet is not a rhymster: the poet is a reader; he knows what words to emphasise, what colour to throw into every tone, and he stops our vulgarity as he would stop blasphemy, that he himself may read to us the great words of the love of God. Of course the poet has often a sorry time of it in a world so rough, so unrefined, and so irreligious. The idealist is scorned out of the way. The age has come to love a certain little idol which is called practicalness. Men call out for something practical; they rebuke things that are supposedly academic and ideal and transcendental; not knowing that if a thing is wrong metaphysically it never can be right practically. The bridge that ignores mathematics allows its passengers to fall into the river. We need the idealist, the man who tells us to go back to our principles and our first and deepest conceptions of things if we would realise tranquility and enjoy a really intelligent and profound rest.

At present we are taken up with details; we are managers, not statesmen; we arrange and calculate things, we do not cause our souls to go back into the temple of the Logos, the innermost house of the Divine philosophy, and to work from that centre through all the noise and upheaval and tumult of a most unruly life. If I were to tell certain men to live their principles, they would smile at the innocent suggestion. If I were to say to a certain type of soul, Do not longer be perplexing and vexing yourself with arrangements and calculations and new disposals of circumstances and crumbling and dilapidated environments, but go back and live in God, I would be speaking in a tongue that in very deed needs an interpreter. But until we do get back to that state of living, moving, having our being in God, we shall be troubled by every new infidel, we shall be at the mercy of the thief and of the moth which break through and corrupt our spiritual treasures, we shall be building our little house upon a swamp, or we shall be putting up some little ornamental villa on the slopes of a volcano ready to explode; we shall, as the apostle says, be driven about by every wind of doctrine. What we have to do is to go into the innermost soul of things, and that innermost soul is God. Have we God in our hearts? do we live in God? or are we trying to checkmate some poor struggling rival? Shall one little sect try to get ahead of another little sect by some fantastic suggestion and movement of the pieces upon the board? and shall we try to bring in the kingdom of heaven by endless and verbose resolutions? Or shall we get back to the simple, primitive, but alluseful and all-potent idea of living in God, and leaving God to show us how the world is to be ruled and directed, converted and sanctified and brought back, a wandering star and prodigal no more, set in the family of heaven?

We need more poetic, ideal reading of things. Herein the preacher ought to serve a great purpose in the intellectual and social and religious life of the nation. The preacher as an interpreter will never lose his place; the preacher as a rival will often be second or tenth in the list. The preacher as an interpreter must keep his first place because he is ordained of God to retain the primacy. Preaching, in the parabolic, ideal, and spiritual sense, includes everything; it carries its baskets filled with fragments, carries by the grace and authority of God its fiat to rule confusion into order and speak clouds into stars. But the preacher must keep to his function; the preacher must remember that it is his business to find out the meaning of the Divine Word and to deliver it in the mother tongue. The preacher must know that he will become a mighty man in the degree in which he is mighty in prayer, mighty in sympathy, and mighty in the Word of God. Woe, woe! to the Church when a Scriptural ministry is undervalued! The Word of God is the strength of the Church, the strength of the ministry, the strength of the individual heart. Therefore let the preacher live with God; let him study history; let him not be a man given to alarmist and panic feelings; let the minister be quiet, let the preacher be tranquil, whoever else be excited. The greatest conception of preaching is that the only tranquil man in the audience is the preacher; he is the centre of rest so far as that assembly and that religious exercise may be concerned. So the pulpit is not a little panic-stricken invention and momentary timidity, looking peepingly out of the church-window to see how it can best save itself when the flood rises and when the wolves are in full pack and run. The pulpit of God has nothing to fear; the pulpit cannot be suppressed; the pulpit, when properly used, cannot be subdued or outrun or outshone. If the points in human life are a thousand, the pulpit speaks to the whole thousand to-day and to-morrow and next year and over the whole area of the ministry, and there is nothing left in human life that has not had its chance of being redeemed, restored, and sanctified.

It is the prophet's business to interpret things to us, to tell us that everything has been from the beginning, to assure us that there are no surprises in Providence, to calm our hearts with the deep conviction that God has seen the end from the beginning, and that nothing has occurred on all this theatre of time which God did not foresee and which God cannot control. The devil is but a black servant in the kitchen of God; the devil has limited chains; he counts the links, he would like to make seven eight, he strives to strain the links into greater length, he cannot do it, he was chained at the first, he has been chained ever since, he will be chained for ever — hallelujah! the Lord reigneth! There is but one throne, and all hell is subject to the governance and the authority of that throne.

Now always remember in following the interpretation of things that a flower may be looked at poetically as well as botanically. For want of knowing that, we have fallen into all kinds of bewilderment and confusion. Hear the botanist: he has a long name for nearly every leaf; he takes all the leaves out of their places, and the stamen and the pistils and all the various parts; he labels them all, and all in foreign languages without any hint at interpretation; and when he has murdered the flower and labelled the murdered pieces, he calls it botany! The poet never takes the flower to pieces; the poet looks at the flower as a whole, inhales the fragrance, interprets the colour, hears the silent music, turns the whole flower into a parable and a picture and a dream, and multiplies the summer seventyfold, yea, an hundredfold, by his faculty of idealisation and interpretation. But the poet, not the botanist, sees the flower. The child may be interpreted physiologically and made nothing of, or he may be interpreted religiously, ideally, and spiritually, and in the process may stand up a man, almost an angel.

When the interpreter abuses his gift he loses it. That is the law of God, that is the law of righteousness. When does the interpreter abuse his gift? When he becomes offensive in his interpretations, when he ceases to be philosophical and becomes fantastical, and wants to find meanings where there is none, and turn that which is inanimate into that which is only galvanically vital; then the man has begun to fritter away his gift, and God will soon see that he loses it altogether. When does the interpreter abuse his gift? When he turns it to self-seeking purposes, when he would make a livelihood by it, when he would keep the secret of God to himself and sell it to some Simon Magus; then God will see that his gift is soon lost, and lost for ever. We have nothing that we are to keep in our own hearts; we have to give our very souls away, and as for our livelihood, God must see after that, and He will do so. I have been young, and now am old, and I have not seen the prophet forsaken or the seer of God begging bread. Distrust all those masonries for which you have to pay. If a man shall say that he can cure you by this process or by that, by a secret which nobody knows but himself, I should allow him the solitary possession of the mean thing. No man can have the true Gospel and keep it, whether it is a gospel of law, a gospel of medicine, or a gospel of salvation. The Gospel sees to it that it must have an utterance, an outrance, an outgoing; because the Gospel will have the whole world know the goodness which it has to proclaim.

When does the interpreter abuse his power? When he panders to his clients, patrons, or admirers; when he says, "How shall I please these people? How shall I avoid giving them offence upon social or public questions? How can I get round the very strait and narrow places without being offensive to any man?" He is losing his power fast when he asks such base questions. It is not for the man to invent his sermon, but to preach it; not to invent a message, but to declare it; not to concoct a gospel, but to reveal it—come, go, who may; and as for the heathen and those who set themselves in opposition to God, He will dash them in pieces like a potter's vessel.

"Which being interpreted." We need the interpreter every day. We say, Affliction, and he says, I will interpret that word to you; it needs interpretation, it is a very bitter word, but affliction being interpreted is chastening, refining, sanctifying, making meet for the Master's use. The Cross being interpreted is law, righteousness, pardon, redemption, atonement, salvation. Being misinterpreted, it is to one class a sneer, to another an offence, to another foolishness; but to believe its interpretation at its best, it is the power of God and the salvation of God. Man being interpreted is child of God, son of the Eternal, a creature made in the image and likeness of God, and meant to live with God and to glorify Him for ever. The Church being interpreted is the most vital centre of the most blessed influence, an association of souls, a kinship of loving spirits, a gathering together of souls that love the Cross, that live in Christ, that are saved by Christ, and that have no joy that is not consonant with the purposes of God. God being interpreted is Love.

FOR ADDITIONAL INFORMATION ABOUT JOSEPH PARKER:

Adamson, William. *The Life of Joseph Parker*. New York: Fleming H. Revell Co., 1902.
Calkins, Harold L. "Joseph Parker." *Master Preachers*. Washington, D.C.: Review & Herald Publishing Assoc., 1960.
Edwards, John. "Dr. Joseph Parker." *Nineteenth Century Preachers and Their Methods*. London: Charles H. Kelly, 1902.
Jeffs, Ernest H. "Joseph Parker." *Princes of the Modern Pulpit*. Nashville: Cokesbury Press, n.d.
Nicoll, W. Robertson. "Dr. Parker." *Princes of the Church*. London: Hodder & Stoughton, 1921.
Parker, Joseph. *A Preacher's Life: An Autobiography and an Album*. London: Hodder & Stoughton, 1899.

FOR OTHER SERMONS BY JOSEPH PARKER:

The City Temple Pulpit. London: Hodder & Stoughton, 1899.
Hidden Springs. London: Frederick Pitman, 1864.
Also: *The Gospel of Jesus Christ* (1908), *The Inner Life of Christ* (1890–92), *Questions of the Day* (1860).

T. DeWITT TALMAGE

1832-1902

T. DeWitt Talmage, photograph from Thomas DeWitt
Talmage, *T. DeWitt Talmage As I Knew Him* (New
York: E. P. Dutton & Co., 1912), frontispiece.

THOMAS DeWITT TALMAGE

1832   *Born near Bound Brook, New Jersey, January 7*
1856   *Received B.D. from New Brunswick Theological Seminary; ordained; entered first pastorate at Belleville, New Jersey, Dutch Reformed Church*
1859   *Became pastor in Syracuse, New York*
1862   *Called to Second Reformed Church, Philadelphia*
1869   *Became a Presbyterian; answered call from Central Presbyterian Church, Brooklyn, New York*
1895   *Became pastor of the First Presbyterian Church, Washington, D.C.*
1899   *Retired from active ministry*
1902   *Died April 12*

"THE WHOLE HUMAN RACE was his congregation." That was the epitaph of the *New York Times* upon the death of Thomas DeWitt Talmage. His regular congregations numbered 5,000 or more. Each week an estimated 20 million persons read his sermons which were published in 3,000 newspapers throughout the world. Considered a rival of Henry Ward Beecher, Talmage was one of the most colorful and flamboyant preachers in American history.

LIFE AND TIMES

Thomas DeWitt Talmage was born on January 7, 1832, near Bound Brook, New Jersey. His father deeply inspired all of his children with Christian values; four of his sons became ministers. He read a chapter from the Bible every morning with the whole family on their knees. His mother was equally devout. Her usual prayer was, "O Lord, I ask not for my children

277

wealth or honor, but I do ask that they all may be the subjects of thy converting grace."[1]

With such a deeply Christian home Talmage felt a definite leaning toward the ministry. At first, however, he studied law at the University of the City of New York. Ultimately he turned to theology and studied at the New Brunswick Theological Seminary of the Dutch Reformed Church. From this seminary he received the B.D. degree in 1856. That same year he was ordained and entered his first pastorate at Belleville, New Jersey, in a Dutch Reformed church. In 1859 he moved to a pastorate in Syracuse, New York, and then in 1862 was called to the Second Reformed Church in Philadelphia. While in Philadelphia he helped fortify the city against expected attacks from the Confederate army. During the war he also served as a chaplain in the Union army. After the war he traveled in the South, speaking on the need for reconciliation.

The most significant era of his life came when he was called to become pastor of the Central Presbyterian Church, Brooklyn, New York, in 1869. Having left the Dutch Reformed church, Talmage remained a Presbyterian for the rest of his life. The church which greeted him in Brooklyn met in a large building but claimed only seventeen communicant members. Under his leadership the congregation grew rapidly. New buildings had to be constructed to care for the crowds which gathered to hear the famous orator preach. In 1870 a building seating 3,000 persons was built; after it burned in 1872, another church, seating 5,000 people, was constructed. This church burned seventeen years later and a building costing almost half a million dollars took its place. Amazingly, this building also burned five years later in the midst of a huge fire which engulfed the entire surrounding area.

These fires might well have been set by the enemies of Talmage. He attacked openly and often the vice of New York City. Sometimes he toured New York after dark with members of his congregation and of the police force. He used these expeditions to gather material for his sermons on the evils of the city. From his pulpit Talmage spoke out against corruption in civil government and denounced specific cases of fraud. In addition to these attacks on corrupt government, he also leveled his homiletical guns at the personal vices of his era such as

---

1. Louis Albert Banks, ed., *T. DeWitt Talmage: His Life and Work* (Philadelphia: J. C. Winston Co., 1902), p. 29.

dancing, card-playing, gambling, and drinking alcoholic beverages.

Always the crusader, Talmage attacked the atheists of his day, especially the famous Robert Ingersoll. Once he compared Ingersoll to a grasshopper on the rail trying to destroy an approaching locomotive. He also fought what he considered to be liberal tendencies in Christian theology. He despised evolution and pled for a literal interpretation of the Bible. He cared nothing for higher criticism and claimed that a copy of the Bible existed in heaven.

His verbal crusades excited all classes of society. The common man felt that Talmage spoke to him in ways he could understand. On daily walks the preacher chatted with workers in the city, and they responded with affection. Current events provided the subjects for many of his sermons. He was always informed on local and world affairs. As he grew in fame, he traveled throughout the world and used the experience from these travels to embellish his sermons.

His showmanship attracted crowds and his sermon subjects attracted criticism. Often police surrounded the church when he was preaching on controversial issues. In 1879 Talmage was tried by his presbytery because of alleged inaccuracies in some statements he had made.

Mark Twain took notice of him in his writings; in a short story about heaven Twain ridiculed Talmage, as he put these words in the mouth of an angel:

"Oh, there are a lot of such things that people expect and don't get. For instance, there's a Brooklyn preacher by the name of Talmage, who is laying up a considerable disappointment for himself. He says, every now and then in his sermons, that the first thing he does when he gets to heaven, will be to fling his arms around Abraham, Isaac and Jacob, and kiss them and weep on them. There's millions of people down there on earth that are promising themselves the same thing. As many as sixty thousand people arrive here every single day, that want to run straight to Abraham, Isaac and Jacob, and hug them and weep on them. Now mind you, sixty thousand a day is a pretty heavy contract for those old people. If they were a mind to allow it, they wouldn't ever have anything to do, year in and year out, but stand up and be hugged and wept on thirty-two hours in the twenty-four. They would be tired out and as wet as

muskrats all the time. What would heaven be, to *them*?
It would be a mighty good place to get out of – you know
that, yourself. Those are kind and gentle old Jews,
but they ain't any fonder of kissing the emotional
high-lights of Brooklyn than you be. You mark my
words, Mr. T.'s endearments are going to be declined,
with thanks. There are limits to the privileges of the
elect, even in heaven. Why, if Adam was to show himself
to every new comer that wants to call and gaze at him
and strike him for his autograph, he would never have
time to do anything else but just that. Talmage has
said he is going to give Adam some of his attentions,
as well as A., I. and J. But he will have to change his
mind about that."

"Do you think Talmage will really come here?"

"Why, certainly, he will; but don't you be alarmed;
he will run with his own kind, and there's plenty of
them. That is the main charm of heaven – there's all
kinds here – which wouldn't be the case if you let the
preachers tell it."[2]

Talmage's ministry was more than one of words. At one time,
during a severe famine in Russia, he sent a shipload of food to
help ease the famine. When subsequently he traveled to Russia,
the people received him enthusiastically.

He was also concerned about his own city. Talmage lived
in New York during an era of tremendous growth in the city.
Enormous wealth had accumulated in the hands of the rich,
and the poor experienced widespread suffering. The ghetto
and slum areas of New York expanded rapidly during this
time. The skyrocketing population, the growing number of
poor, and the general atmosphere of the times stimulated
crime and vice. Talmage vigorously attacked all of these problems. In the world as a whole, it was a time of rapidly developing thought in many areas: Darwin, Marx, and Freud became
household words. In the movements of these men Talmage
also found targets for his popular pulpit orations.

More negative than positive, more shallow than profound,
more controversial than creative, Talmage left little lasting
impression. His books and sermon volumes were favored

2. Charles Neider, ed., *The Complete Short Stories of Mark Twain* (Garden
City, N.Y.: Doubleday & Co., 1957), pp. 583–84. Reprinted by permission of
Harper & Row.

only for a short time. His editorial endeavors on several magazines, among them the *Christian Herald,* also resulted in no lasting impact. Like a falling star which blazes for a moment and then is gone, Talmage shot across the American pulpit scene.

Preaching and Sermons

DeWitt Talmage was the prototype of flamboyant oratorical preaching. He never used a pulpit. He paced up and down his long platform with theatrical gestures, scowling or smiling, pouring out a perfect stream of words. He was never accused of the crude displays of chair-breaking and aisle-sliding of Billy Sunday; Talmage was more the Shakespearean actor. Nevertheless, he was widely criticized for his theatrics.

His popularity was unquestionable. Thousands packed into auditoriums all over the world to hear him preach. Gammie described such an occasion:

> As a boy I heard Talmage's sermons read and discussed week after week, as they were at that time in many a home. Then I had the opportunity of hearing him on one of his last visits to this country. No church could accommodate the crowd, and the largest hall in the city was packed to overflowing. With fervent and dramatic power, he poured forth his torrent of oratory, piling up adjectives, heaping metaphor on metaphor, using a big brush to paint glowing word-pictures in vivid colours, now declaiming with tremendous vigour and the next moment, on a tender note, touching deep chords of emotion.[3]

In *The Masque Torn Off,* a collection of sermons about the sins of the city, a contemporary listener described his impression of Talmage:

> He presses the eyes, hands, his entire body, into the service of the illustrative truth. As he stands out before the immense throng, without a scrap of notes or manuscript before him, the effect produced cannot be understood by those who have never seen it.

---

3. Alexander Gammie, *Preachers I Have Heard* (London: Pickering & Inglis, n.d.), p. 72.

Clarence Macartney also described his memories of Talmage:

> He stood well back from the edge of the platform. . . .
> He commenced speaking with his eyes closed. The
> voice, although not melodious like Bryan's, was power-
> ful, arresting and stirring. He began with a descrip-
> tion of a man riding. . . . It was a vivid picture. . . . This
> went on for a minute or two. Then, opening his eyes,
> he leaped forward to the front of the platform, and
> with a mighty voice pronounced a sentence which I
> have not forgotten. There was something about the
> man that at once appealed to you. He had the air of
> friendliness, and also of complete command of the
> situation, as if there were no doubt at all that he would
> carry his audience with him, which of course he did.[4]

Talmage claimed to have developed his voice by speaking
in the forest. He claimed he could speak with ease to five thousand people, even outdoors. Whether or not that was true,
everyone who heard him admired his powerful voice.

Common men loved him for the directness of his language.
His style was pictorial; illustrations came naturally to him.
He said, "It has always been the question with me how to get
rid of illustrations. I naturally think in metaphor."[5] He was
wordy, colorful, and brilliant in his use of language. Sophisti-
cated people ridiculed him for his extravagant statements, but
his appeal was world-wide. In some respects he revolutionized
preaching:

> His style was unique because he imitated no one, and
> was not held in bondage by any fear of violating custom.
> He did not follow the fashion; he made it. He was him-
> self. He did more to set preachers free from slavish imi-
> tation of traditional pulpit style than any other man of
> his day.[6]

Talmage memorized his speeches word for word. They were
usually dictated several weeks in advance of delivery so that
the papers could carry them on the Monday after delivery. His

---

4. Clarence Edward Macartney, *Six Kings of the American Pulpit* (Grand
Rapids: Baker Book House, 1956), pp. 157–58.
5. Ibid., p. 169.
6. Banks, p. 69.

style made the memorized sermons seem extemporaneous. He did occasionally insert paragraphs extemporaneously, but he was so voluble that he had to resist the temptation to expand his sermons or he would never have finished at all. He said of his method of preparation, "I jot down my notes in a little book. . . . Then I take all available sources of information at that point and sift them thoroughly, avoiding beaten tracks."

Talmage leaned heavily upon illustration and application in his preaching; rarely did he devote much time to exposition, word studies, or background materials. He believed in proclamation, not argumentation:

> A lawyer who went to hear Talmage regularly in Philadelphia said he had never heard him attempt to prove any proposition except once, when he adduced four passages of Scripture to prove that Christ died for sinners. The next day he said to him, "Dr. Talmage, are you going to change your style? You argued yesterday for the first time." Talmage replied: "I have not been very well, and had to fall back on an old essay that I wrote in the Theological Hall to be criticized by the professors. If you will excuse me this time, I promise you I will never do it again." And he never did. He did not bother his hearers with problems or seek to demonstrate any propositions.[7]

And yet he must have done some arguing to have preached so frequently on the veracity of the Bible, evolution, and atheism.

Many have condemned Talmage for his theatrical preaching, but not as many have appreciated him for his practical approach to everyday human problems. When asked the secret of his great success in attracting crowds, he replied:

> If I had to give one reason I think it would be this. In my sermons I always aim at helpfulness. Show me a congregation of five hundred people, I do not care where or when, and I will tell you how many of them want help. Every man today, no matter how successful he may appear, notwithstanding that his face is always smiling and the cheery word always on his lips, finds a craving for sympathy, strength and encouragement. You may take it that every man and every woman

7. Gammie, pp. 73–74.

needs help. My one aim in preaching my sermons is
to be helpful. I want to encourage every one of my
hearers in the battle of life, to help them to get fresh
strength for their conflict.[8]

No one has ever classified Talmage as a life-situation preacher,
but perhaps that approach was more involved in his technique
than has been generally understood; if so, it would explain
much of his popular appeal.

The descriptive genius of Talmage is well illustrated in the
following sermons. His opposition to argument and his belief in
the value of emotional appeal is stated in the sermon "The
Broken Pitchers":

For instance, here is a man all armed on the doctrine
of election; all his troops of argument and prejudice
are at that particular gate. You may batter away at that
side of the castle for fifty years and you will not take it;
but just wheel your troops to the side gate of the heart's
affections, and in five minutes you capture him. I never
knew a man to be saved through a brilliant argument.
You cannot hook men into the kingdom of God by the
horns of a dilemma. There is no grace in syllogisms. . . .

In other words, you never can capture a man's soul
at the point at which he is especially intrenched. But
there is in every man's heart a bolt that can be easily
withdrawn. A little child four years old may touch that
bolt and it will spring back and the door will swing open
and Christ will come in.

The content of this sermon disproves the notion that Talmage
was nothing more than a fake or a cheap actor. Many of his
ideas in this sermon are profoundly Christian.

"Question of Questions," a sermon on Acts 16:30, "Good
sirs, what must I do to be saved?" is an extended dramatic
narrative, full of elegant prose and pointed, terse applications.
While reading this sermon, it is easy to imagine the rapt attention of a vast congregation as Talmage stalked the stage.

Talmage preached his sermon "The Ministry of Tears" on
June 15, 1879, in London. It was Talmage's first sermon in
England. An English newspaper described the scene:

---

8. Ibid., p. 74.

The members of the congregation and their friends who had obtained tickets of admission, entered at the side door. At 6:15 p.m., notwithstanding the crowded state of the church, the front doors at which considerable clamor for some time had been heard, were thrown open, and part of the large crowd which had by that time assembled, rushed in. Notwithstanding the edifice was full to overflowing the crowd continued to press forward into the aisles and the galleries.

Immediately began a scene of confusion and uproar, which, we think it is safe to assert, has never been seen in this church before, and amid cries of "crush! crush!" "No room! No room!" "We cannot move here!", Dr. Davidson ascended the pulpit and appealed to the people for quiet. Having given out the hymn, "Jesus Shall Reign Where'er the Sun," Dr. Davidson said of Dr. Talmage: "His inexhaustible originality, his fearless plainness of speech, and his unmatched pictorial power, have not only got around him the largest congregation in America, but have secured in all parts of the world, from week to week through the press, his hundreds of thousands of interested and profited hearers."

After this sermon Dr. Talmage went through the basement and out of the back door so as to get to his carriage unobserved; but no sooner did he step into the carriage, than the people gathered around and thousands shook hands, and as the driver attempted to start, the people lifted the carriage by the wheels, and it was necessary for the police to clear the way.[9]

Imagine that setting as you read the verbatim transcription of that sermon on Revelation 7:17.

Imagine also the impression Talmage must have made in the introduction to his sermon on Robert Ingersoll, as he quoted — entirely without notes — from numerous famous persons on the worth of the Bible. The entire sermon is one of the best examples of Talmage's many scornful denunciations of the noted atheist. And even though Talmage opposed evolution, it is interesting to see his openness at one point:

"In the beginning." There you can roll in ten million years if you want to. There is no particular date given —

---

9. Thomas DeWitt Talmage, *The Brooklyn Tabernacle: A Collection of 104 Sermons* (New York, London: Funk & Wagnalls Co., 1884), p. 11.

no contest between science and revelation. You may roll
in there ten million years, if you want to. Though the
world may have been in process of creation for millions
of years, suddenly and quickly, and in one week, it may
have been fitted up for man's residence. . . .

You are not compelled to believe that the world was
made in our six days; you are not compelled to believe
that. It may not have been a day of twenty-four hours,
the day spoken of in the first chapter; it may have been
God's day, and a thousand years with Him are as one day.

The little sermon "The Spider in Palaces" is a jewel of descriptive genius based upon Proverbs 30:28, "The spider
taketh hold with her hands, and is in king's palaces."

Had Talmage disciplined his erratic genius and approached
his subjects more carefully, more thoughtfully—in short, more
as a Christian minister than a platform elocutionist—his contributions to Christian preaching would have been more solid
and creative and his impact upon American Christianity more
lasting.

Sermons

THE BROKEN PITCHERS

"And the three companies blew the trumpets, and brake the pitchers, and held the lamps in their left hands, and the trumpets in their right hands to blow withal. . . . And they stood every man in his place round about the camp: and all the host ran, and cried, and fled" (Judges 7:20–21).

THAT IS the strangest battle ever fought. God had told Gideon to go down and drive out of the land the Midianites, but his army is too large; for the glory must be given to God, and not to man. And so proclamation is made that all those of the troops who are afraid, and want to go home, may go; and twenty-two thousand of them scampered away, leaving only ten thousand men.

But God says the army is too large yet; and so he orders these ten thousand remaining to march down to a stream, and commands Gideon to notice in what manner these men drink of the water as they come to it. If they get down on all-fours and drink, then they are to be pronounced lazy and incompetent for the campaign; but if, in passing through the stream, they scoop up the water in the palm of their hands and drink, and pass on, they are to be the men selected for the battle. Well, the ten thousand men march down to the stream and most of them go down on all-fours and plunge their mouths, like a horse or an ox, into the water and drink; but there are three hundred men who, instead of stooping, just dip the palm of their hands in the water and bring it to their lips, "lapping it as a dog lappeth." Those three hundred brisk, rapid, enthusiastic men are chosen for the campaign. They are each to take a trumpet in the right hand and a pitcher in the left hand, and there must be a lamp inside the pitcher, and then at a given signal they are to blow the trumpets and throw down the pitchers and hold up the lamps. So it was done.

It is night. I see a great host of Midianites, sound asleep in the valley of Jezreel. Gideon comes up with his three hundred picked men and surrounds the camp on all sides, and when everything is ready, the

Reprinted from Thomas DeWitt Talmage, *500 Sermons,* 20 vols. (New York: Christian Herald, 1900), 12:317–29.

signal is given and they blow the trumpets and they throw down the pitchers and hold up the lamps, and the great host of Midianites, waking out of a sound sleep, take the crash of the crockery and the glare of the lamps for the coming on of an overwhelming foe; and they run and cut themselves to pieces and horribly perish.

The lessons of this subject are very spirited and impressive. This seemingly valueless lump of quartz has the pure gold in it. The smallest dew-drop on the meadow at night has a star sleeping in its bosom, and the most insignificant passage of Scripture has in it a shining truth. God's mint coins no small change.

I learn in the first place, from this subject, the lawfulness of Christian stratagem. You know very well that the greatest victories ever gained by Washington or Napoleon were gained through the fact that they came when and in a way they were not expected—sometimes falling back to draw out the foe, sometimes breaking out from ambush, sometimes crossing a river on unheard-of rafts; all the time keeping the opposing forces in wonderment as to what would be done next. The northern troops beat their life out in the straightforward fight at Fredericksburg, but it was through strategy they got the victory at Lookout Mountain.

You all know what strategy is in military affairs. Now I think it is high time we had this art sanctified and spiritualized. In the church, when we are about to make a Christian assault, we send word to the opposing force when we expect to come, how many troops we have, and how many rounds of shot, and whether we will come with artillery, infantry, or cavalry, and of course we are defeated. There are thousands of men who might be surprised into the kingdom of God. We need more tact and ingenuity in Christian work. It is in spiritual affairs, as in military, that success depends in attacking that part of the castle which is not armed and intrenched.

For instance, here is a man all armed on the doctrine of election; all his troops of argument and prejudice are at that particular gate. You may batter away at that side of the castle for fifty years and you will not take it; but just wheel your troops to the side gate of the heart's affections, and in five minutes you capture him. I never knew a man to be saved through a brilliant argument. You cannot hook men into the kingdom of God by the horns of a dilemma. There is no grace in syllogisms. Here is a man armed upon the subject of the perseverance of the saints; he does not believe in it. Attack him at that point, and he will persevere to the very last in not believing it. Here is a man armed on the subject of baptism; he believes in sprinkling or immersion. All your discussion of ecclesiastical hydropathy will not change him. I remember, when I was a boy, that with other boys I went into the river on a summer day to bathe, and we used to dash the water on each other, but never got any result except that our eyes were blinded; and all this splashing of water between Baptists and Pedobaptists never results in any thing but the blurring of the spiritual eyesight. In other words, you never can capture a man's soul at the point at which he is especially intrenched. But there is in every man's heart a bolt that can be easily withdrawn. A little child four years old may touch that bolt and it will spring back and the door will swing open and Christ will come in.

I think that the finest of all the fine arts is the art of doing good, and yet this art is the least cultivated. We have in the kingdom of God to-day enough troops to conquer the whole earth for Christ if we only had skillful maneuvering. I would rather have the three hundred lamps and pitchers of Christian stratagem than one hundred thousand drawn swords of literary and ecclesiastical combat.

I learn from this subject, also, that a small part of the army of God will have to do all the hard fighting. Gideon's army was originally composed of thirty-two thousand men, but they went off until there were only ten thousand left, and that was subtracted from until there were only three hundred. It is the same in all ages of the Christian church; a few men have to do the hard fighting. Take a membership of a thousand, and you generally find that fifty people do the work. Take a membership of five hundred, and you generally find that ten people do the work. There are scores of churches where two or three people do the work.

We have to mourn that there is so much useless lumber in the mountains of Lebanon. I think, of the ten million membership of the Christian church to-day, if five millions of the names were taken off the books, the church would be stronger. You know that the more cowards and drones there are in any army the weaker it is. I would rather have the three hundred picked men of Gideon than the twenty-two thousand unsifted host. How many Christians there are standing in the way of all progress! I think it is the duty of the church of God to ride over them, and the quicker it does it, the quicker it does its duty.

Do not worry, O Christian, if you have to do more than your share of the work. You had better thank God that he has called you to be one of the picked men, rather than to belong to the host of stragglers. Would not you rather be one of the three hundred that fight, than the twenty-two thousand that desert? I suppose those cowardly Gideonites who went off congratulated themselves. They said, "We got rid of all that fighting, did not we? How lucky we have been; that battle costs us nothing at all." But they got none of the spoils of the victory. After the battle the three hundred men went down and took the wealth of the Midianites, and out of the cups and platters of their enemies they feasted. And the time will come, my dear brethren, when the hosts of darkness will be routed, and Christ will say to his troops, "Well done, my brave men, go up and take the spoils! Be more than conquerors forever!" and in that day all deserters will be shot!

Again: I learn from this subject, that God's way is different from man's, but is always the best way. If we had the planning of that battle, we would have taken those thirty-two thousand men that originally belonged to the army, and we would have drilled them, and marched them up and down by the day and week and month, and we would have them equipped with swords or spears, according to the way of arming in those times; and then we would have marched them down in solid column upon the foe. But that is not the way. God depletes the army, and takes away all their weapons, and gives them a lamp and a pitcher and a trumpet, and tells them to go down and drive out the Midianites. I suppose some wiseacres were there who said, "That is not military tactics. The idea of three hundred men, unarmed, conquering such a great host of Midianites!" It was the best way. What sword, spear, or cannon ever accomplished such a victory as the lamp, pitcher, and trumpet?

God's way is different from man's way, but it is always best! Take, for instance, the composition of the Bible. If we had the writing of the Bible, we would have said, "Let one man write it. If you have twenty or thirty men to write a poem or make a statute or write a history or make an argument there will be flaws and contradictions." But God says, "Let not one man do it, but forty men shall do it." And they did, differing enough to show there had been no collusion between them, but not contradicting each other on any important point, while they all wrote from their own standpoint and temperament; so that the matter-of-fact man has his Moses; the romantic nature his Ezekiel; the epigrammatic his Solomon; the warrior his Joshua; the sailor his Jonah; the loving his John; the logician his Paul. Instead of this Bible, which now I can lift in my hand; instead of the Bible that the child can carry to school this afternoon; instead of the little Bible the sailor can put in his jacket pocket when he goes to sea—if it had been left to men to write, it would have been a thousand volumes, judging from the amount of ecclesiastical controversy which has arisen. God's way is different from man's, but it is best, infinitely best.

So it is in regard to the Christian's life. If we had had the planning of a Christian's life we would have said, "Let him have eighty years of sunshine, a fine house to live in; let his surroundings all be agreeable; let him have sound health; let no chill shiver through his limbs, no pain furrow his brow, or trouble shadow his soul." I enjoy the prosperity of others so much, I would let every man have as much money as he wants, and roses for his children's cheeks, and fountains of gladness glancing in their large round eyes. But that is not God's way. It seems as if a man must be cut and hit and pounded just in proportion as he is useful. His child falls from a third-story window and has its life dashed out; his most confident investment tumbles him into bankruptcy; his friends, upon whom he depended, aid the natural force of gravitation in taking him down; his life is a Bull Run defeat.

Instead of twenty-two thousand advantages, he has only ten thousand —ay, only three hundred—ay, none at all. How many good people there are who are at their wits' end about their livelihood, about their health, about their reputation. But they will find out it is the best way after a while; God will show them that he depletes their advantages just for the same reason he depleted the army of Gideon—that they may be induced to throw themselves on his mercy.

A grape-vine says, in the early spring, "How glad I am to get through the winter! I shall have no more trouble now! Summer weather will come, and the garden will be very beautiful!" But the gardener comes, and cuts the vine here and there with his knife. The twigs begin to fall, and the grape-vine calls out, "Murder! what are you cutting me for?" "Ah," says the gardener, "I don't mean to kill you. If I did not do this you would be the laughing-stock of all the other vines before the season is over." Months go on, and one day the gardener comes under the trellis, where great clusters of grapes hang, and the grape-vine says, "Thank you, sir; you could not have done anything so kind as to have cut me with that knife." "Whom the Lord loveth he chasteneth." "Every branch that beareth fruit he purgeth that it may bring forth more fruit." No pruning, no grapes; no grinding-mill, no flour; no battle, no victory; no cross, no crown!

So God's way, in the redemption of the world, is different from ours. If we had our way, we would have had Jesus stand in the door of heaven and beckon the nations up to light, or we would have had angels flying around the earth proclaiming the unsearchable riches of Christ. Why is it that the cause goes on so slowly? Why is it that the chains stay on, when God could knock them off? Why do thrones of despotism stand, when God could so easily demolish them? It is his way, in order that all generations may co-operate, and that all men may know they cannot do the work themselves. Just in proportion as these pyramids of sin get up in height will they come down in ghastliness of ruin.

O thou father of all iniquity! If thou canst hear my voice above the crackling of the flames, drive on thy projects, dispatch thy emissaries, build thy temples, and forge thy claims; but know that thy fall from heaven was not greater than thy final overthrow shall be when thou shalt be driven disarmed into thy fiery den; and for every lie thou hast framed upon earth thou shalt have an additional hell of fury poured into thine anguish by the vengeance of our God; and all heaven shall shout at the overthrow, as from the ransomed earth the song breaks through the skies, "Hallelujah! for the Lord God omnipotent reigneth! Hallelujah! for the kingdoms of this world are become the kingdoms of our Lord Jesus Christ!" God's way in the composition of the Bible, God's way in the Christian's life, God's way in the redemption of the world, God's way in everything—different from man's way, but the best.

I learn from this subject, that the overthrow of God's enemies will be sudden and terrific. There is the army of the Midianites down in the valley of Jezreel. I suppose their mighty men are dreaming of victory. Mount Gilboa never stood sentinel for so large a host. The spears and the shields of the Midianites gleam in the moonlight, and glance on the eye of the Israelites, who hover like a battle of eagles, ready to swoop from the cliff. Sleep on, oh, army of the Midianites! With the night to hide them and the mountain to guard them and strong arms to defend them let no slumbering foeman dream of disaster! Peace to the captains and the spearmen!

Crash go the pitchers! up flare the lamps! To the mountains! fly! fly! Troop running against troop, thousands trampling upon thousands. A wild stampede! Hark to the scream and groan of the routed foe, with the Lord God Almighty after them! How sudden the onset, how wild the consternation, how utter the defeat! I do not care so much what is against me, if God is not. You want a better sword or carbine than I have ever seen, to go out and fight against the Lord omnipotent. Give me God for my ally, and you may have all the battlements and battalions.

I saw the defrauder in his splendid house. It seemed as if he had conquered God, as he stood amidst the blaze of chandeliers and pier mirrors. In the diamonds of the wardrobe I saw the tears of the widows whom he had robbed, and in the snowy satin the pallor of the white-cheeked orphans whom he had wronged. The blood of the oppressed glowed in the deep crimson of the imported chair. The music trembled with the sorrow of unrequited toil. But the wave of mirth dashed higher on reefs of coral and pearl. The days and the nights went merrily. No sick child dared pull that silver door-bell. No beggar dared sit on that marble step. No voice of prayer floated amidst that tapestry. No shadow of a judgment-day darkened that fresco. No tear of human sympathy dropped upon that upholstery. Pomp strutted through the hall, and Dissipation filled her cup and all seemed safe as the Midianites in the valley of Jezreel. But God came. Calamity smote the money-market. The partridge left its eggs unhatched. Crash went all the porcelain pitchers! Ruin, rout, dismay, and woe in the valley of Jezreel!

Alas for those who fight against God! Only two sides. Man immortal, which side are you on? Woman immortal, which side are you on? Do you belong to the three hundred that are going to win the day, or to the great host of Midianites asleep in the valley, only to be roused up in consternation and ruin? Suddenly the golden bowl of life will be broken, and the trumpet blown that will startle our souls into eternity. The day of the Lord cometh as a thief in the night, and as the God-armed Israelites upon the sleeping foe. Ha! canst thou pluck up courage for the day when the trumpet which hath never been blown shall speak the roll-call of the dead; and the earth, dashing against a lost meteor, have its mountains scattered to the stars and oceans emptied in the air? Oh, then, what will become of you? What will become of me?

If those Midianites had only given up their swords the day before the disaster, all would have been well; and if you will now surrender the sins with which you have been fighting against God, you will be safe. Oh, make peace with him now, through Jesus Christ the Lord. With the clutch of a drowning man seize the cross. Oh, surrender! Surrender! Christ, with his hand on his pierced side, asks you to.

THE MINISTRY OF TEARS

"God shall wipe away all tears from their eyes" (Revelation 7:17).

RIDING ACROSS A WESTERN PRAIRIE, wild flowers up to the hub of the carriage wheel, and while a long distance from any shelter, there came a sudden shower, and while the rain was falling in torrents, the sun was shining as brightly as ever I saw it shine; and I thought, What a beautiful spectacle this is! So the tears of the Bible are not midnight storm, but rain on pansied prairies in God's sweet and golden sunlight. You remember that bottle which David labelled as containing tears, and Mary's tears, and Paul's tears, and Christ's tears, and the harvest of joy that is to spring from the sowing of tears. God mixes them. God rounds them. God shows them where to fall. God exhales them. A census is taken of them, and there is a record as to the moment when they are born, and as to the place of their grave. Tears of bad men are not kept. Alexander, in his sorrow, had the hair clipped from his horses and mules, and made a great ado about his grief; but in all the vases of heaven there is not one of Alexander's tears. I speak of the tears of the good. Alas, me! they are falling all the time. In summer, you sometimes hear the growling thunder, and you see there is a storm miles away; but you know from the drift of the clouds that it will not come

Reprinted from Thomas DeWitt Talmage, *The Brooklyn Tabernacle: A Collection of 104 Sermons* (New York, London: Funk & Wagnalls Co., 1884), pp. 11–15.

anywhere near you. So, though it may be all bright around about us, there is a shower of trouble somewhere all the time. You think it is the cannonading that you hear along the banks of the Danube. No. It is the thunder of clouds of trouble over the groaning hospitals, and over the desolated Russian and Turkish homes. Tears! Tears!

What is the use of them anyhow? Why not substitute laughter? Why not make this a world where all the people are well, and eternal strangers to pain and aches? What is the use of an eastern storm when we might have a perpetual nor'-wester? Why, when a family is put together, not have them all stay, or if they must be transplanted to make other homes, then have them all live? the family record telling a story of marriages and births, but of no deaths. Why not have the harvests chase each other without fatiguing toil, and all our homes afflicted? Why the hard pillow, the hard crust, the hard struggle? It is easy enough to explain a smile, or a success, or a congratulation; but, come now, and bring all your dictionaries and all your philosophies and all your religions, and help me this evening to explain a tear. A chemist will tell you that it is made up of salt and lime, and other component parts; but he misses the chief ingredients – the acid of a soured life, the viperan sting of a bitter memory, the fragments of a broken heart. I will tell you what a tear is; it is agony in solution.

Hear me, then, while I discourse to you of the ministry of tears, and of the ending of that ministry when God shall wipe them all away.

First. It is the ministry of tears *to keep this world from being too attractive.* Something must be done to make us willing to quit this existence. If it were not for trouble, this world would be a good enough heaven for me. You and I would be willing to take a lease of this life for a hundred million years, if there were no trouble. The earth cushioned and upholstered and pillared and chandeliered with such expense, no story of other worlds could enchant us. We would say: "Let well enough alone. If you want to die and have your body disintegrated in the dust, and your soul go out on a celestial adventure, then you can go; but this world is good enough for me." You might as well go to a man who has just entered the Louvre at Paris, and tell him to hasten off to the picture galleries of Venice or Florence. "Why," he would say, "what is the use of my going there? There are Rembrandts and Rubens and Raphaels here that I haven't looked at yet." No man wants to go out of this world, or out of any house until he has a better house.

To cure this wish to stay here, God must somehow create a disgust for our surroundings. How shall He do it? He cannot afford to deface His horizon, or to tear off a fiery panel from the sunset, or to subtract an anther from the water lily, or to banish the pungent aroma from the mignonette, or to drag the robes of the morning in the mire. You cannot expect a Christopher Wren to mar his own St. Paul's Cathedral, or a Michelangelo to dash out his own "Last Judgment," or a Handel to discord his "Israel in Egypt"; and you cannot expect God to spoil the architecture and music of His own world. How then are we to be made willing to leave? Here is where troubles comes in. After a man has had a good deal of trouble, he says, "Well, I am ready to go. If there is a house somewhere whose roof doesn't leak, I would like to live there. If there is an atmosphere somewhere that does not distress the lungs, I would like to breathe it. If there is a society somewhere where there is no tittle-tattle, I would like to live there. If there is a home-circle somewhere where I can find my lost friends, I would like to go there." He used to read the first part of the Bible chiefly, now he reads the last part of the Bible chiefly. Why has he changed Genesis for Revelation? Ah! he used to be anxious chiefly to know how this world was made, and all about its geological construction. Now he is chiefly anxious to know how the next world was made, and how it looks, and who live there, and how they dress. He reads Revelation ten times now where he reads Genesis once. The old story, "In the beginning God created the heavens and the earth," does not thrill him half as much as the other story, "I saw a new heaven and a new earth." The old man's hand trembles as he turns over this apocalyptic leaf, and he has to take out his handkerchief to wipe his spectacles. That book of Revelation is a prospectus now of the country into which he is to soon immigrate; the country in which he has lots already laid out, and avenues opened, and trees planted, and mansions built. The thought of that blessed place comes over me mightily, and I declare that if this house were a great ship, and you all were passengers on board it, and one hand could launch that ship into the glories of heaven, I should be tempted to take the responsibility, and launch you all into glory with one stroke, holding on to the side of the boat until I could get in myself! And yet there are people here to whom this world is brighter than heaven. Well, dear souls, I do not blame you. It is natural. But, after a while, you will be ready to go. It was not until Job had been worn out with bereavements and carbuncles and a pest of a wife that he wanted to see God. It was not until the prodigal got tired of living among the hogs that he wanted to go to his father's house. It is the ministry of trouble to make this world worth less, and heaven worth more.

Again: it is the ministry of trouble *to make us feel our complete dependence upon God.* King Alphonso said that if he had been present at the Creation, he could have made a better world than this. What a pity he was not present! I do not know what God will do when some men die. Men think they can do anything until God shows them they can do nothing at all. We lay out great plans, and we like to execute them. It looks big. God comes and takes us down. As Prometheus was assaulted by his enemy, when the lance struck him it opened a great swelling that had threatened his death, and he got well. So it is the arrow of trouble that lets out great swellings of pride. We never feel our dependence upon God until we get trouble. I was riding with my little child along a road, and she asked if she might drive. I said, "Certainly." I handed over the reins to her, and I had to admire the glee with which she drove. But after a while we met a team, and we had to turn out. The road was narrow, and it was sheer down on both sides. She handed the reins over to me, and said: "I think you had better take charge of the horse." So, we are all children; and on this road of life we like to drive. It gives one such an appearance of superiority and power. It looks big. But after a while, we meet some obstacle, and we have to turn out, and the road is narrow, and it is sheer down on both sides; and then we are willing that God should take the reins and drive. Ah! my friends, we get upset so often because we do not hand over the reins soon enough.

Can you not tell when you hear a man pray, whether he has ever had any trouble? I can. The cadence, the phraseology indicate it. Why do women pray better than men? Because they have had more trouble. Before a man has had any trouble, his prayers are poetic, and he begins away up among the sun, moon, and stars, and gives the Lord a great deal of astronomical information that must be highly gratifying. He then comes on down gradually over beautiful tablelands to "for ever and ever, amen." But after a man has had trouble, prayer is with him a taking hold of the arm of God and crying out for help. I have heard earnest prayers on two or three occasions that I remember. Once, on the Cincinnati express train going at forty miles the hour, and the train jumped the track, and we were near a chasm eighty feet deep; and the men who, a few minutes before, had been swearing and blaspheming God, began to pull and jerk at the bell-rope, and got up on the backs of the seats, and cried out: "O God, save us!" There was another time, about eight hundred miles out at sea, on a foundering steamer, after the last lifeboat had been split finer than kindling wood. They prayed then. Why is it you so often hear people, in reciting the last experience of some friend, say: "He made the most beautiful prayer I ever heard"? What makes it beautiful? It is the earnestness of it. Oh, I tell you a man is in earnest when his stripped and naked soul wades out in the soundless, shoreless, bottomless ocean of eternity.

It is trouble, my friends, that makes us feel our dependence upon God. We do not know our own weakness or God's strength until the last plank breaks. It is contemptible in us, when there is nothing else to take hold of, that we catch hold of God only. A man is unfortunate in business. He has to raise a great deal of money, and raise it quickly. He borrows on word and note all he can borrow. After a while, he puts a mortgage on his house. After a while he puts a second mortgage on his house. Then he puts a lien on his furniture. Then he makes over his life insurance. Then he assigns all his property. Then he goes to his father-in-law and asks for help! Well, having failed everywhere, completely failed, he gets down on his knees and says: "O Lord, I have tried everybody and everything, now help me out of this financial trouble." He makes God the last resort instead of the first resort. There are men who have paid ten cents on a dollar who could have paid a hundred cents on a dollar if they had gone to God in time. Why, you do not know who the Lord is. He is not an autocrat seated far up in a palace, from which He emerges once a year, preceded by heralds swinging swords to clear the way. No. But a Father willing, at our call, to stand by us in every crisis and predicament of life.

I tell you what some of you business men make me think of. A young man goes off from home to earn his fortune. He goes with his mother's consent and benediction. She has large wealth; but he wants to make his own fortune. He goes far away, falls sick, gets out of money. He sends to the hotel-keeper where he is staying, asking for lenience, and the answer he gets is, "If you don't pay up Saturday night you'll be removed to the hospital." The young man sends to a comrade in the same building. No help. He writes to a banker who was a friend of his deceased father. No relief. He writes to an old schoolmate, but gets no help. Saturday night comes, and he is moved to the hospital. Getting there he is frenzied with grief; and he borrows a sheet of paper and a postage stamp, and he sits down, and he writes home, saying: "Dear mother, I am sick unto death. Come." It is ten minutes of ten o'clock when she gets the letter. At ten o'clock the train starts. She is five minutes from the depot. She gets there in time to have five minutes to spare. She wonders why a train that can go thirty miles an hour cannot go sixty miles an hour. She rushes into the hospital. She says: "My son, what does all this mean? Why didn't you send for me? You sent to everybody but me. You knew I could and would help you. Is this the reward I get for my kindness to you always?" She bundles him up, takes him home, and gets him well very soon. Now, some of you treat God just as that young man treated his mother. When you get into a financial perplexity, you call on the banker, you call on the broker, you call on your creditors, you call on your lawyer for legal counsel, you call upon everybody, and when you cannot get any help then you go to God. You say: "O Lord, I come to Thee. Help me now out of my perplexity." And the Lord comes though it is the eleventh hour. He says: "Why did you not send for me before? As one whom his mother comforteth, so will I comfort you." It is to throw us back upon an all-comforting God that we have this ministry of tears.

Again: it is the ministry of tears *to capacitate us for the office of sympathy.* The priests under the old dispensation were set apart by having water sprinkled on their hands, feet, and head; and by the sprinkling of tears people are now set apart to the office of sympathy. When we are in prosperity, we like to have a great many young people around us, and we laugh when they laugh, and we romp when they romp, and we sing when they sing; but when we have trouble we like plenty of old folks around. Why? They know how to talk. Take an aged mother, seventy years of age, and she is almost omnipotent in comfort. Why? She has been through it all. At seven o'clock in the morning she goes over to comfort a young mother who has just lost her babe. Grandmother knows all about that trouble. Fifty years ago she felt it. At twelve o'clock of that day she goes over to comfort a widowed soul. She knows all about that. She has been walking in that dark valley twenty years. At four o'clock in the afternoon some one knocks at the door wanting bread. She knows all about that. Two or three times in her life she came to her last loaf. At ten o'clock that night she goes over to sit up with some one severely sick. She knows all about it. She knows all about fevers and pleurisies and broken bones. She has been doctoring all her life, spreading plasters and pouring out bitter drops, and shaking up hot pillows, and contriving things to tempt a poor appetite. Doctors Abernethy and Rush and Hosack and Harvey were great doctors; but the greatest doctor the world ever saw is an old Christian woman. Dear me! do we not remember her about the room when we were sick in our boyhood? Was there any one who could ever so touch a sore without hurting it? And when she lifted her spectacles against her wrinkled forehead so she could look closer at the wound, it was three fourths healed. And when the Lord took her home, although you may have been men and women thirty, forty, fifty years of age, you lay on the coffin lid and sobbed as though you were only five or ten years of age. O man, praise God, if, instead of looking back to one of these berouged and bespangled old people fixed up of the devil to look young, you have in your memory the picture of an honest, sympathetic, kind, self-sacrificing, Christ-like mother. Oh, it takes these people who have had trouble to comfort others in trouble. Where did Paul get the ink with which to write his comforting epistle? Where did David get the ink to write his comforting psalms? Where did John get the ink to write his comforting revelation? They got it out of their own tears. When a man has gone through the curriculum, and has taken a course of dungeons and imprisonments and shipwrecks, he is qualified for the work of sympathy.

When I began to preach, I used to write out all my sermons, and I sometimes have great curiosity to look at the sermons I used to preach on trouble. They were nearly all poetic and in semi-blank verse; but God knocked the blank verse out of me long ago; and I have found out that I cannot comfort people except as I myself have been troubled. God make me the son of consolation to the people. I would rather be the means of soothing one perturbed spirit to-day, than to play a tune that would set all the sons of mirth reeling in the dance. I am a herb doctor. I put in the caldron the Root out of dry ground without form or comeliness. Then I put in the Rose of Sharon and the Lily of the valley. Then I put into the caldron some of the leaves from the tree of life, and the branch that was thrown into the wilderness Marah. Then I pour in the tears of Bethany and Golgotha; then I stir them up. Then I kindle under the caldron a fire made out of the wood of the cross, and one drop of that potion will cure the worst sickness that ever afflicted a human soul. Mary and Martha shall receive their Lazarus from the tomb. The damsel *shall* rise. And on the darkness shall break the morning, and God will wipe all tears from their eyes.

You know on a well-spread table, the food becomes more delicate at the last. I have fed you to-day with the bread of consolation. Let the table now be cleared, and let us set on the chalice of heaven. Let the King's cup-bearers come in. Good morning, Heaven! "Oh," says some critic in the audience, "the Bible contradicts itself. It intimates again and again that there are to be no tears in heaven, and if there be no tears in heaven, how is it possible that God will wipe any away?" I answer, have you never seen a child crying one moment and laughing the next; and while she was laughing, you saw the tears still on its face? And, perhaps, you stopped her in the very midst of her resumed glee, and wiped off those delayed tears. So, I think, after the heavenly raptures have come upon us, there may be the mark of some earthly grief, and while those tears are glittering in the light of the jasper sea, God will wipe them away. How well He can do that.

Jesus had enough trial to make Him sympathetic with all trial. The shortest verse in the Bible tells the story: "Jesus wept." The scar on the back of either hand, the scar on the arch of either foot, the row of scars along the line of the hair, will keep all heaven thinking. Oh, that great weeper is just the one to silence all earthly trouble and wipe out all stains of earthly grief. Gentle! Why His step is softer than the step of the dew. It will not be a tyrant bidding you to hush up your crying. It will be a Father who will take you on His left arm, His face gleaming into yours, while with the soft tips of the fingers of the right hand, He shall wipe away all tears from your eyes. I have noticed when the children get hurt, and their mother is away from home, they always come to me for comfort and sympathy; but I have noticed that when the children get hurt, and their mother is at home, they go right past me and to her; I am of no account. So, when the soul comes up into heaven out of the wounds of this life, it will not stop to look for Paul, or Moses, or David, or John. These did very well once, but now the soul shall rush past, crying: "Where is Jesus? Where is Jesus?" Dear Lord, what a magnificent thing to die if Thou shalt thus wipe away our tears. Methink it will take us some time to get used to heaven; the fruits of God without one speck; the fresh pastures without one nettle; the orchestra without one snapped string; the river of gladness without one torn bank; the solferinos and the saffron of sunrise and sunset swallowed up in the eternal day that beams from God's countenance!

> Why should I wish to linger in the wild,
> When Thou art waiting, Father, to receive Thy child?

Sirs, if we could get any appreciation of what God has in reserve for us, it would make us so homesick we would be unfit for our every-day work. Professor Leonard, in Iowa University, put in my hands a meteoric stone, a stone thrown off from some other world to this. How suggestive it was to me. And I have to tell you the best representations we have of heaven are only aerolites flung off from that world which rolls on bearing the multitudes of the redeemed. We analyze these aerolites, and find them crystalizations of tears. No wonder, flung off from heaven. "God shall wipe away all tears from their eyes."

Have you any appreciation this evening of the good and glorious times your friends are having in heaven? How different it is when they get news there of a Christian's death from what it is here. It is the difference between embarkation and coming into port. Everything depends upon which side of the river you stand when you hear of a Christian's death. If you stand on this side of the river you mourn that they go. If you stand on the other side of the river, you rejoice that they come. Oh, the difference between a funeral on earth and a jubilee in heaven – between requiem here and triumphal march there – parting here and reunion there. Together! Have you thought of it? They are together. Not one of your departed friends in one land, and another in another land; but together in different rooms of the same house – the house of many mansions. Together! I never appreciated that thought so much as recently, when we laid away in her last slumber my sister Sarah. Standing there in the village cemetery, I looked around and said: "There is father, there is mother, there is grandfather, there is grandmother, there are whole circles of kindred"; and I thought to myself, "Together in the grave – together in glory." I am so impressed with the thought that I do not think it is any fanaticism when some one is going from this world to the next if you make them the bearer of despatches to your friends who are gone, saying: "Give my love to my parents, give my love to my children, give my love to my old comrades who are in glory, and tell them I am trying to fight the good fight of faith, and I will join them after a while." I believe the message will be delivered; and I believe it will increase the gladness of those who are before the throne. Together are they, all their tears gone. No trouble getting good society for them. All kings, queens, princes, and princesses. In 1751, there was a bill offered in your English Parliament, proposing to change the almanac so that the first of March should come immediately after the 18th of February. But, oh, what a glorious change in the calendar when all the years of your earthly existence are swallowed up in the eternal year of God!

My friends, take this good cheer home with you. Those tears of bereavement that course your cheek, and of persecution and of trial, are not always to be there. The motherly hand of God will wipe them all away. What is the use, on the way to such a consummation – what is the use of fretting about anything? Oh, what an exhilaration it ought to be in Christian work. See you the pinnacles against the sky? It is the city of our God; and we are approaching it. Oh, let us be busy in the few days that shall remain for us. The Saxons and the Britons went out to battle. The Saxons were all armed. The Britons had no weapons at all; and yet history tells us the Britons got the victory. Why? They went into battle shouting three times "hallelujah!" and at the third shout of "hallelujah" their enemies fled panicstruck; and so the Britons got the victory. And, my friends, if we could only appreciate the glories that are to come, we would be so filled with enthusiasm that no power of earth or hell could stand before us; and at our first shout the opposing forces would begin to tremble, and at our second shout they would begin to fall back, and at our third shout they would be routed forever. There is no power on earth or in hell that could stand before three such volleys of hallelujah.

I put this balsam on the recent wounds of your heart. Rejoice at the thought of what your departed friends have got rid of, and that you have a prospect of so soon making your own escape. Bear cheerfully the ministry of tears, and exult at the thought that soon it is to be ended.

> There we shall march up the heavenly street,
> And ground our arms at Jesus' feet.

THE SPIDER IN PALACES

"The spider taketh hold with her hand, and is in kings' palaces" (Proverbs 30:28).

WE ARE ALL WATCHING for phenomena. A sky full of stars shining from January to January calls out not so many remarks as the blazing of one meteor. A whole flock of robins take not so much of our attention as one blundering bat darting into the window on a summer-eve. Things of ordinary sound, and sight, and occurrence, fail to reach us,

Reprinted from Thomas DeWitt Talmage, *The Brooklyn Tabernacle: A Collection of 104 Sermons* (New York, London: Funk & Wagnalls Co., 1884), pp. 121–23.

and yet no grasshopper ever springs up in our path, no moth ever dashes into the evening candle, no mote ever floats in the sunbeam that pours through the crack of the window shutter, no barnacle on ships' hull, no bur on a chestnut, no limpet clinging to a rock, no rind of an artichoke but would teach us a lesson if we were not so stupid.

God in His Bible sets forth for our consideration the lily, and the snowflake, and the locust, and the stork's nest, and the hind's foot, and the aurora borealis, and the ant hills. One of the sacred writers, sitting amid the mountains, sees a hind skipping over the rocks. The hind has such a peculiarly shaped foot that it can go over the steepest places without falling, and as the prophet looks upon that marking of the hind's foot on the rocks, and thinks of the Divine care over him, he says: "Thou makest my feet like hinds' feet, that I may walk on high places." And another sacred writer sees the ostrich leaving its egg in the sand of the desert, and without any care of incubation, walk off; and the Scripture says, that is like some parents, leaving their children without any wing of protection or care. In my text inspiration opens before us the gate of a palace, and we are inducted amid the pomp of the throne and the courtier, and while we are looking around upon the magnificence, inspiration points us to a spider plying its shuttle and weaving its net on the wall. It does not call us to regard the grand surroundings of the palace, but to a solemn and earnest consideration of the fact that: "The spider taketh hold with her hands, and is in kings' palaces."

It is not very certain what was the particular species of insect spoken of in the text, but I shall proceed to learn from it *the exquisiteness of the Divine mechanism*. The king's chamberlain comes into the palace, and looks around and sees the spider on the wall, and says: "Away with that intruder," and the servant of Solomon's palace comes with his broom and dashes down the insect, saying: "What a loathsome thing it is." But under microscopic inspection I find it more wondrous of construction than the embroideries on the palace wall, and the upholstery about the windows. All the machinery of the earth could not make anything so delicate and beautiful as the prehensile with which that spider clutches its prey, or as any of its eight eyes. We do not have to go so far up to see the power of God in the tapestry hanging around the windows of heaven, or in the horses and chariots of fire with which the dying day departs, or to look at the mountain swinging out its sword-arm from under the mantle of darkness until it can strike with its scimitar of the lightning.

I love better to study God in the shape of a fly's wing, in the formation of a fish's scale, in the snowy whiteness of a pond lily. I love to track His footsteps in the mountain mass, and to hear His voice in the hum of the rye fields, and discover the rustle of His robe of light in the south wind. Oh, this wonder of Divine power that can build a habitation for God in an apple blossom, and tune a bee's voice until it is fit for the eternal orchestra, and can say to a firefly: "Let there be light"; and from holding an ocean in the hollow of His hand goes forth to find heights, and depths, and length, and breadth of omnipotency in a dewdrop, and dismounts from the chariot of midnight hurricane to cross over on the suspension bridge of a spider's web. You may take your telescope and sweep it across the heavens in order to behold the glory of God; but I shall take the leaf holding the spider, and the spider's web, and I shall bring the microscope to my eye, and while I gaze, and look, and study, and am confounded, I will kneel down in the grass and cry: "Great and marvellous are Thy works, Lord God Almighty!"

Again, my text teaches me that *insignificance is no excuse for inaction.* This spider that Solomon saw on the wall might have said: "I can't weave a web worthy of this great palace; what can I do amid all this gold and embroidery? I am not able to make anything fit for so grand a place, and so I will not work my spinning-jenny." Not so said the spider. "The spider taketh hold with her hands." Oh, what a lesson that is for you and me! You say if you had some great sermon to preach, if you only had a great audience to talk to, if you had a great army to marshal, if you only had a constitution to write, if there was some tremendous thing in the world for you to do – then you would show us. Yes, you would show us! What if the Levite in the ancient temple had refused to snuff the candle because he could not be a high priest? What if the humming-bird should refuse to sing its song into the ear of the honeysuckle because it cannot, like the eagle, dash its wing into the sun? What if the rain-drop should refuse to descend because it is not a Niagara? What if the spider of the text should refuse to move its shuttle because it cannot weave a Solomon's robe? Away with such folly. If you are lazy with the one talent, you would be lazy with the ten talents. If Milo cannot lift the calf he never will have strength to lift the ox. In the Lord's army there is order for promotion; but you cannot be a general until you have been a captain, a lieutenant, and a colonel. It is step by step, it is inch by inch, it is stroke by stroke that our Christian character is builded. Therefore be content to do what God commands you to do. God is not ashamed to do small things. He is not ashamed to be found chiselling a grain of sand, or helping a honey bee to construct its cell with mathematical accuracy, or tinging a shell in the surf, or shaping the bill of a chaffinch. What God does, He does well. What you do, do well, be it a great work or a small work. If ten talents, employ all the ten. If five talents, employ all the five. If one talent, employ the one. If only the thousandth part of a talent, employ that. "Be thou faithful unto death, and I will give thee the crown of life." I tell you if you are not faithful to God in a small sphere, you would be indolent and insignificant in a large sphere.

Again, my text teaches me that *repulsiveness and loathsomeness will sometimes climb up into very elevated places.* You would have tried to have killed the spider that Solomon saw. You would have said:

"This is no place for it. If that spider is determined to weave a web, let it do so down in the cellar of this palace, or in some dark dungeon." Ah! the spider of the text could not be discouraged. It clambered on, and climbed up, higher, and higher, and higher, until after awhile it reached the king's vision, and he said: "The spider taketh hold with her hands, and is in kings' palaces." And so it often is now that things that are loathsome and repulsive get up into very elevated places.

The Church of Christ, for instance, is a palace. The King of heaven and earth lives in it. According to the Bible, her beams are of cedar, and her rafters of fir, and her windows of agate, and the fountains of salvation dash a rain of light. It is a glorious palace — the Church of God is; and yet, sometimes, unseemly and loathsome things creep up into it — evil-speaking, and rancor, and slander, and backbiting, and abuse, crawling up on the walls of the Church, spinning a web from arch to arch, and from the top of one communion tankard to the top of another communion tankard. Glorious palace in which there ought only to be light, and love, and pardon, and grace; yet a spider in the palace!

Home ought to be a castle. It ought to be the residence of everything royal. Kindness, love, peace, patience, and forbearance ought to be the princes residing there; and yet sometimes dissipation crawls up into that home, and the jealous eye comes up, and the scene of peace and plenty becomes the scene of domestic jargon and dissonance. You say: "What is the matter with the home?" I will tell you what is the matter with it. A spider in the palace.

A well-developed *Christian character* is a grand thing to look at. You see some man with great intellectual and spiritual proportions. You say: "How useful that man must be!" But you find, amid all his splendor of faculties, there is some prejudice, some whim, some evil habit, that a great many people do not notice, but that you have happened to notice, and it is gradually spoiling that man's character — it is gradually going to injure his entire influence. Others may not see it, but you are anxious in regard to his welfare, and now you discover it. A dead fly in the ointment. A spider in the palace.

Again, my text teaches me that *perseverance will mount into the king's palace.* It must have seemed a long distance for that spider to climb in Solomon's splendid residence, but it started at the very foot of the wall and went up over the panels of Lebanon cedar, higher and higher, until it stood higher than the highest throne in all the nations — the throne of Solomon. And so God has decreed it that many of those who are down in the dust of sin and dishonor shall gradually attain to the King's palace. We see it in worldly things. Who is that banker in Philadelphia? Why, he used to be the boy that held the horses of Stephen Girard while the millionnaire went in to collect his dividends. Arkwright toils on up from a barber's shop until he gets into the palace of invention. Sextus V toils on up from the office of a swineherd until he gets into the palace of Rome. Fletcher toils on up from the most insignificant family position until he gets into the palace of Christian eloquence. Hogarth, engraving pewter pots for a living, toils on up until he reaches the palace of world-renowned art. And God hath decided that, though you may be weak of arm, and slow of tongue, and be struck through with a great many mental and moral deficits, by His almighty grace you shall yet arrive in the King's palace – not such an one as is spoken of in the text – not one of marble – not one adorned with pillars of alabaster and thrones of ivory, and flagons of burnished gold – but a palace in which God is the King and the angels of heaven are the cup-bearers. The spider crawling up the wall of Solomon's palace was not worth looking after or considering, as compared with the fact that we, who are worms of the dust, may at last ascend into the palace of the King Immortal. By the grace of God may we all reach it. Oh, heaven is not a dull place. It is not a worn-out mansion with faded curtains, and outlandish chairs, and cracked ware. No; it is as fresh, and fair, and beautiful as though it were completed but yesterday. The kings of the earth shall bring their honor and glory into it.

A palace means splendor of apartments. Now, I do not know where heaven is, and I do not know how it looks, but, if our bodies are to be resurrected in the last day, I think heaven must have a material splendor as well as a spiritual grandeur. Oh, what grandeur of apartments when that Divine hand which plunges the sea into blue, and the foliage into green, and sets the sunset on fire, shall gather all the beautiful colors of earth around His throne, and when that arm which lifted the pillars of Alpine rock, and bent the arch of the sky, shall raise before our soul the eternal architecture, and that hand which hung with loops of fire the curtains of morning shall prepare the upholstery of our kingly residence!

A palace also means splendor of associations. The poor man, the outcast, cannot get into the Tuileries, or Windsor Castle. The sentinel of the king or the queen stands there and cries "Halt!" as he tries to enter. But in that palace, we may all become residents, and we shall all be princes and kings. We may have been beggars, we may have been outcasts, we may have been wandering and lost as we all have been, but there we shall take our regal power. What companionship in heaven! To walk side by side with John, and James, and Peter, and Paul, and Moses, and Joshua, and Caleb, and Ezekiel, and Jeremiah, and Micah, and Zachariah, and Wilberforce, and Oliver Cromwell, and Philip Doddridge, and Edward Payson, and John Milton, and Elizabeth Fry, and Hannah More, and Charlotte Elizabeth, and all the other kings and queens of heaven. O my soul, what a companionship.

A palace means splendor of banquet. There will be no common ware on that table. There will be no unskilled musicians at that entertainment. There will be no scanty supply of fruit or beverage. There have been banquets spread that cost a million of dollars each; but who can tell the untold wealth of that banquet? I do not know whether

John's description of it is literal or figurative. A great many wise people tell me it is figurative; but prove it. I do not know but that it may be literal. I do not know but that there may be real fruits plucked from the tree of life. I do not know but that Christ referred to the real juice of the grape when He said that we should drink new wine in our Father's kingdom, but not the intoxicating stuff of this world's brewing. I do not say it is so; but I have as much right for thinking it is so as you have for thinking the other way. At any rate, it will be a glorious banquet. Hark! the chariots rumbling in the distance. I really believe the guests are coming now. The gates swing open, the guests dismount, the palace is filling, and all the chalices flashing with pearl and amethyst and carbuncle are lifted to the lip of the myriad banquetters, while standing in robes of snowy white they drink to the honor of our glorious King! "Oh," you say: "that is too grand a place for you and for me." No, it is not. If a spider, according to the text, could crawl up on the wall of Solomon's palace, shall not our poor souls, through the blood of Christ, mount up from the depths of its sin and shame, and finally reach the palace of the eternal King? "Where sin abounded, grace shall much more abound, that whereas sin reigned unto death, even so may grace reign through righteousness unto eternal life by Jesus Christ our Lord."

In the far East there is a bird called the Huma, about which is the beautiful superstition that upon whatever head the shadow of that bird rests, upon that head there shall be a crown. Oh, thou dove of the Spirit, floating above us, let the shadow of Thy wing fall upon this congregation, that each, at last, in heaven may wear upon his head a crown! a crown! and hold in his right hand a star! a star!

QUESTION OF QUESTIONS

"Sirs, what must I do to be saved?" (Acts 16:30).

IN A CELL of the Philippian dungeon, dark, damp, chill, unilluminated save by the torch of some official who comes to see whether they are

Reprinted from Thomas DeWitt Talmage, 500 Selected Sermons, 20 vols. (New York: Christian Herald, 1900), 4:379–91.

yet alive, are two ministers of Jesus Christ; their feet fast in instruments of torture, their shoulders dripping from the strokes of leathern thongs, their mouths hot with inflammation of thirst, their heads faint because they may not lie down. In another room of the same building is a man asleep on a comfortable couch. He is a supervisor, a paid officer of the government to look after that prison. I take him to have been a moral and an honorable man from the trust reposed in him. It is twelve o'clock at night. No sound in all the corridors and wards in that prison, save as some culprit turns over in his chains or there is the cough of a slow consumptive or some wanderer, far away from her father's house, cries out in her dream: "Mother! mother!"

At midnight, crash! go the prison walls, and the two ministers of religion, Paul and Silas, are free. The supervisor of the jail, although he had been accustomed to the shadows hovering around the dungeon, is startled beyond all bounds; and flambeau in hand he rushes through between the falling walls, and throws himself down at the feet of his apostolic prisoners, crying out in the memorable words of my text: "Sirs, what must I do to be saved?"

There are hundreds and thousands with more or less earnestness asking the same question, and in this severe crisis of your soul I meet you with a message from the throne of God. There may be some who could surpass me in skilfulness of argument, there may be many who could drink from deeper fountains of knowledge and science, there may be many before whom, in some respects, I would be willing to bow as the inferior to the superior; but I yield to no one in this presence in a wish to have all the people saved; and with an all-conquering desire that sometimes well-nigh overcomes my utterance, I beg you to accept the eternal life of the Gospel. Lord, help us! Lord, help us now!

I proceed to characterize this question of the jail warden, and I characterize it in the first place as a courteous question. He did not come up to these men and say: "You outragers of the law, you miscreants, you vagabonds against society, you have upturned the whole city with excitement, and now you are trying to break down the walls of our prison, destroying government property; let me put on you these handcuffs and hopples, or else get out beyond the confines of the city." He said no such thing. He addresses them with that one word, "Sirs," a synonym for lords—as much as to say: "I acknowledge the dignity of your mission, I acknowledge the honor of your manhood, and I am here to see what you can do for my soul." It was a courteous question.

But it is often the case when people begin to inquire about religion they become impertinent, and they denounce all Christians as hypocrites, and the Church of God as a cheat, and they criticise this and they denounce that and they complain of something else. Is that fair? Is that right? Is that courteous? Suppose I should come into an audience of lawyers and denounce them all as pettifoggers, or an audience of physicians and denounce them all as quacks? "Oh," you say, "that would not be fair." It would be just as fair as for you to denounce all

Christians as hypocrites. There are pettifoggers among lawyers, and there are quacks among physicians, and there are hypocrites among Christians; but that is not the character of all lawyers or all physicians or all Christians. It was a courteous question, it was a gentlemanly question, it was a polite question, it was a deferential question. "Sirs! sirs!"

I go further, and I characterize the question of the jail supervisor as a practical question. He did not ask why God let sin come into the world; he did not ask how the Christ about whom they were preaching could be God and man at the same time; he did not ask who Cain married; he did not ask who was Melchizedek; he did not ask the proportionate number of the finally saved and the finally lost. No; his question involved his present and his everlasting welfare. Was not that a practical question? Yet a great many people, when they begin to seek after religion, begin to find fault with the Bible, and they say, "If this is so, how can that be so?" And they complain of this and they complain of that and they go fishing after snapping turtles instead of fishing after the truth. They do not seem to be satisfied with the plain Gospel of the Son of God. Now, the question for you is not whether John Calvin or Arminius was right, not what will be the proportion of the finally saved and the finally lost, not who was Melchizedek, not who Cain married; the question for you is, "Where will I spend eternity?" It is a practical question.

I go further and I characterize this question of the jail supervisor as a question personal to himself. He may have had hundreds of friends; he is not asking about them. In that catastrophe of the falling prison some of those friends may have perished. He is not asking about them. He throws all the emphasis of his question upon the pronoun of the first person: "What shall *I* do to be saved?" When a man becomes a Christian, of course he is anxious to have everybody else saved. You are not a Christian if you are not anxious to have all the world saved; but until your own sins are pardoned, my brother, you must look at home. The difficulty is, we are so anxious about the lack of culture in our neighbor's yard that we let our own garden go to weeds; we are so anxious to get the people into the lifeboat of the Gospel that we ourselves drown in the wave. We cry, "Fire! fire!" because our neighbor's house is consuming; while ours is in a blaze. Now, let us blot out everything, let us obliterate all other considerations, let it be as though you were the only person present, the rest of the audience all gone. Your sin — is it pardoned? Your heaven — is it secure?

I come up to the door of your soul with a message from the throne of God — about your pardon, your repentance, your enthronement, your exile, your eternal residence. This man of the text knew that there was coming an earthquake mightier than that which shook down the Philippian dungeon. The foundations of the earth shall give way. At one tremor of the world, all the modern cities will fall into the dust. Temples and towers that have stood a thousand years will fall as quickly as a child's block-house. The waves of the sea will roll over the land, and the Atlantic and Pacific oceans will join hands above the Sierra Nevadas and the Alps and the Pyrenees. This man of the text was guarding not more against the falling of the prison than he was against the falling of a world.

I go further, and characterize this question of the jail supervisor as a question of incomparable importance. Perhaps he was anxious to have his salary raised as a supervisor; perhaps he wished to have better apartments; perhaps he was discussing some questions of prison reform, something about warmth, light, ventilation, medical treatment, discipline. Men are wonderfully alike, and I suppose he may have had a hundred questions to discuss; but all earthly questions are submerged, are hushed up, are annihilated by the one question: "Sirs, what must I do to be saved?" And what question have you, my brother, comparable with that in importance?

Is it a business question? Do you not realize that you will soon have to go out of that store, that you will soon have to resign that partnership, that soon among all the millions of dollars' worth of goods that are sold in New York you will not have the handling of a yard of cloth or a pound of sugar or a pennyworth of anything; that soon, if a conflagration should start at Central Park and sweep everything to the Battery, it would not disturb you; that soon if every cashier should abscond, and every bank should suspend payment, and every insurance company should fail, it would not affect you? What are all the questions that stop this side the grave compared with the questions that reach beyond it? Are you making losses that are to be everlasting? Are you making purchases for eternity? Are you retailing for time, when you might be wholesaling for eternity? What question of the store is so broad at the base, and so altitudinous, and so overwhelming as the question, "What must I do to be saved?"

Or is it a domestic question? Is it something about father or mother or companion or son or daughter that you think is comparable with this question in importance? Do you not realize that by universal and inexorable law all these relations will be broken up? Your father will be gone, your mother will be gone, your companion will be gone, your child will be gone, you will be gone; and then this supernal question will begin to harvest its chief gains or deplore its worst losses, roll up into its mightiest magnitude or sweep its vastest circles—a question deciding whether you will live unending ages with God, the blessed, or go into exile; whether you will take wing and fly, or chain and drop; whether you will forever be built up or pulled down; whether for all the future you will be praising or blaspheming, chanting or groaning, living the life that always lives, or dying the death that always dies. Is there any question comparable with that?

What difference now does it make to Napoleon III whether he triumphed or surrendered at Sedan? whether he lived at the Tuileries or at Chiselhurst? whether he was emperor or exile? They laid him out in his coffin in the dress of a field marshal. Did that give him any better chance for the next world than if he had been laid out in a plain shroud? Soon to us what will be the difference whether in this world we rode or walked, were bowed to or maltreated, were applauded or hissed at, were welcomed in or kicked out; while, grasping the great future, and burning in splendor or grief, and overarching and under-girding all time and all eternity, is the plain, simple, practical, thrilling, agonizing, overwhelming question: "What must I do to be saved?"

I go further, and I characterize this question of the jail supervisor as one pressed out by crushing misfortune. The penitentiary fallen, his business was gone. It was a financial loss. Besides that, the flight of a prisoner ordinarily in those times meant the death of the jailor. If the prison walls had stood solidly all that night, and the incarcerated had been quiet in the stocks, and the sunlight on the following morning had dropped on the calm pillow of the supervisor, would he have hurled the agitating words of my text into the ears of the apostles? You know as well as I, it was the earthquake that roused his anxieties. And is it not the shaking of misfortune and trouble, and the crashing down of earthly hopes that has driven many of you to the Gospel? Your dress is not so bright as once. Why have you come to more subdued garb? You like the saffron and the crimson and the bright colors as well as ever; but you say: "Things that were in harmony with my feelings when I was young and bright and prosperous and gay would be a discord now." And so you have gathered up and plaited the darkness into your apparel.

There have been dark days in your house. It does not seem any more like home. You once wished the house might be quiet. It is too quiet. Others say they would not bring their loved ones back to this trouble-some world if they could; but if you had the power, how soon those hushed voices would be back in the home circle; and it would be as it was in the Christmas or the Thanksgiving holiday so long gone by, never to come back with its hilarities. Oh! it is the earthquake of domestic trouble that has started one-half of you toward God. The grave is so cruel, so relentless, so devouring, that when our loved ones are swallowed up by it, we must have some one to whom we can take our torn and bleeding hearts.

It needs a balsam better than ever exuded from any earthly tree to stop the sharpness of the pang. It is pleasant at such times to have friends come in and try to break up the loneliness; but Jesus only can take the frenzied spirit on his bosom and hush it with the lullaby of Heaven. Ah! the heavy gravestone will never be lifted from your heart until Jesus lifts it. Has it not been the loss of your friends, has it not been the crushing down of your estate, has it not been the earthquake of misfortune that led you to ask the question spelled in tears and heart-breaks, the impassioned outcry: "Sirs, what must I do to be saved?"

I take one step further, and I characterize this question of the jail supervisor as an urgent, hasty, immediate question that demanded an immediate answer. It was a question put on the run. You can see by the torch the jailor holds in his hand the startled and anxious look. He had no time to prepare himself in especial apparel, no time to comb his hair, no time to fix himself up. He must have that question answered before the earthquake has stopped rocking, or never perhaps have it answered at all. Is that the way you propound the question of your salvation, or do you drawl it out as much as to say: "Any time within fifteen years I would like to have it answered"? Do you know that thousands of souls have been ruined because they did not ask the question in time? If the door of the lost world could be opened, and one word of warning could come forth, and they could utter only one word of warning, that word would come sounding up like the howl of the everlasting storm: "Now!" I open the gate of those there incarcerated. I find some of the young are there. What is their history? How did they lose their souls? By procrastinating to old age, or to mid-life; but the rail-train shot from the track and in an instant they were gone; or they slipped on the icy pavement and the skull was fractured; or the typhoid fever came down and drove them in delirium out of life. There are some of the middle-aged who have lost their souls. What was their history? They adjourned religion until they got more time, until they got their worldly affairs arranged, until they made a competency. In the attempt to win the world they lost their soul. All their government securities, all their certificates of stock, all their warehouses, all their bonds, all their daybooks and ledgers, all their worldly accumulations are of no service to them now. There are some of the aged who lost their souls—through what cause? Adjourning religion until their hearts were so hard when they tried to repent they could not repent, and when they tried to pray they could not pray; and they went tottering on leaning heavier and heavier on their staff until it broke, and they fell headlong into outer darkness.

Are you proposing the question of the text with an urgency such as this man of the text employed, or are you adjourning it to the last hour? Adjourning it to the last hour, are you? I suppose that out of the one hundred death-bed repentances, ninety-nine amount to nothing. Of the large number of people in this Bible who are represented as dying, how many of them are represented as repenting successfully in the last hour? Fifty? No. Thirty? No. Twenty? No. Ten? No. Five? No. Two? No. One? Just one. Only one. As much as to say: "It is possible that a man may repent in the last hour of his life, but it is improbable; it is a hundred chances to one against him."

Have you ever seen a man after living a life of sin and worldliness trying to repent in the last hour? I have seen that spectacle. If you had ever seen it you would not try to repeat it. Why, it is most inopportune. There is the physician standing with the medicine, and here is the lawyer standing with the half-written will; and the bells of eternity are tolling at the passage of the soul from the body; and all the past is surging upon us, and all the future; and angels are flying through the room, and devils are plotting for the overthrow. The man is a fool who adjourns repentance until the death-hour.

My text asks the question, but does not answer it. That comes on in the next verse, and strict rules of sermonizing would say that must come in some other sermon. But what are rules of sermonizing to me when I am after souls immortal? Wait until another time! I might be dead before that time, and many of you I confront only once.

After a friend in Philadelphia died, his children gave his church Bible to me, and I read it with much interest. I saw in the margin written in lead pencil: "Mr. Talmage said this morning that the most useless thing in God's universe is that any sinner should perish." I did not remember saying it; but it is true, and I say it now, whether I said it then or not – the most useless thing in all God's universe is that any sinner should perish. Twelve gates wide open. Have you not heard how Christ bore our sorrows, and how sympathetic he is with all our woes? Have you not heard how that with all the sorrows of heart and all the agonies of hell upon him he cried: "Father, forgive them; they know not what they do!" By his feet blistered of the mountain way; by his back whipped until the skin came off; by his death-couch of four spikes, two for the hands and two for the feet; by his sepulchre, in which for the first time for thirty-three years the cruel world let him alone; and by the heavens from which he this morning bends in compassion, offering pardon and peace and life eternal to all your souls, I beg of you put down your all at his feet.

> I saw one hanging on a tree
>   In agony and blood,
> Who put his languid eyes on me
>   As near his cross I stood.
>
> Oh, never till my latest breath,
>   Will I forget that look;
> It seemed to charge me with his death,
>   Though not a word he spoke.

In the troubled times of Scotland, Sir John Cochrane was condemned to death by the king. The death-warrant was on the way. Sir John Cochrane was bidding farewell to his daughter Grizelle at the prison door. He said: "Farewell, my darling child! I must die." His daughter said: "No father, you shall not die." "But," he said, "the king is against me, and the law is after me, and the death-warrant is on its way, and I must die; do not deceive yourself, my dear child." The daughter said: "Father, you shall not die," as she left the prison gate.

At night, on the moors of Scotland, a disguised wayfarer stood waiting for the horseman carrying the mail-bags containing the death-warrant. The disguised wayfarer, as the horse came by, clutched the bridle and shouted to the rider—to the man who carried the mail-bags: "Dismount!" He felt for his arms, and was about to shoot, but the wayfarer jerked him from his saddle and he fell flat. The wayfarer picked up the mail-bags, put them on his shoulder and vanished in the darkness; and fourteen days were thus gained for the prisoner's life, during which the father confessor was pleading for the pardon of Sir John Cochrane. The second time the death-warrant is on its way. The disguised wayfarer comes along, and asks for a little bread and a little wine, starts on across the moors, and they say: "Poor man, to have to go out such a stormy night; it is dark and you will lose yourself on the moors." "Oh, no," he says, "I will not." He trudged on and stopped amid the brambles and waited for the horseman to come carrying the mail-bags containing the death-warrant of Sir John Cochrane. The mail-carrier spurred on his steed, for he was fearful because of what had occurred on the former journey, spurred on his steed; when suddenly through the storm and through the darkness there was a flash of firearms, and the horse became unmanageable; and as the mail-carrier discharged his pistol in response, the horse flung him, and the disguised wayfarer put his foot on the breast of the overthrown rider, and said: "Surrender now!" The mail-carrier surrendered his arms, and the disguised wayfarer put upon his shoulders the mail-bags, leaped upon the horse, and sped away into the darkness, gaining fourteen more days for the poor prisoner, Sir John Cochrane; and before the fourteen days had expired pardon had come from the king. The door of the prison swung open, and Sir John Cochrane was free. One day when he was standing amid his friends, they congratulating him, the disguised wayfarer appeared at the gate, and he said: "Admit him right away." The disguised wayfarer came in and said: "Here are two letters; read them, sir, and cast them into the fire." Sir John Cochrane read them. They were his two death-warrants, and he threw them into the fire. Then said Sir John Cochrane: "To whom am I indebted? Who is the poor wayfarer that saved my life? Who is it?" And the wayfarer pulled aside and pulled off the jerkin and the cloak and the hat, and lo! it was Grizelle, the daughter of Sir John Cochrane. "Gracious Heaven!" he cried, "my child, my saviour, my own Grizelle!"

But a more thrilling story. The death-warrant had come forth from the King of heaven and earth. The death-warrant read: "The soul that sinneth, it shall die." The death-warrant coming on the black horse of eternal night. We must die! We must die! But breasting the storm and putting out through the darkness was a disguised wayfarer who gripped by the bridle the on-coming doom and flung it back, and put his wounded and bleeding foot on the overthrown rider. Meanwhile pardon flashed from the throne, and, "Go free! Open the gate! Strike off the chain! Go free!" And to-day your liberated soul stands in the presence of the disguised wayfarer, and as he pulls off the disguise of his earthly humiliation and the disguise of his thorns and the disguise of the seamless robe, you find he is bone of your bone, flesh of your flesh, your brother, your Christ, your pardon, your eternal life. Let all earth and heaven break forth in vociferation! Victory through our Lord Jesus Christ!

> A guilty, weak, and helpless worm,
>   On thy kind arms I fall;
> Be thou my strength and righteousness.
>   My Jesus and my all.

MR. INGERSOLL, THE CHAMPION
BLASPHEMER OF AMERICA, ANSWERED

"Having the understanding darkened, being alienated from the life of God through the ignorance that is in them" (Ephesians 4:18).

It seems from what we have recently heard that the Christian religion is a huge blunder; that the Mosaic account of the creation is an absurdity large enough to throw all nations into rollicking guffaw; that Adam and Eve never existed; that the ancient flood and Noah's Ark were impossibilities; that there never was a miracle; that the Bible is the friend of cruelty, of murder, of polygamy, of obscenity, of adultery, of all forms of base crime; that the Christian religion is woman's tyrant and man's stultification; that the Bible from lid to lid is a fable, an obscenity, a cruelty, a humbug, a sham, a lie; that the martyrs who died for its truth were miserable dupes; that the Church of Jesus Christ is properly gazetted as a fool; that when Thomas Carlyle, the

Reprinted from Thomas DeWitt Talmage, *The Brooklyn Tabernacle: A Collection of 104 Sermons* (New York, London: Funk & Wagnalls Co., 1884), pp. 93–98.

sceptic, said, "The Bible is a noble book," he was dropping into imbecility; that when Theodore Parker, the infidel, declared in Music Hall, Boston, "Never a boy or girl in all Christendom but was profited by that great book," he was becoming very weak-minded; that it is something to bring a blush to the cheek of every patriot, that John Adams, the father of American independence, declared "The Bible is the best book in all the world"; and that lion-hearted Andrew Jackson turned into a snivelling coward when he said, "That book, sir, is the rock on which our Republic rests"; and that Daniel Webster abdicated the throne of his intellectual power and resigned his logic, and from being the great expounder of the Constitution and the great lawyer of his age, turned into an idiot, when he said, "My heart assures and reassures me that the Gospel of Jesus Christ must be a divine reality. From the time that at my mother's feet, or on my father's knee, I first learned to lisp verses from the sacred writings, they have been my daily study and vigilant contemplation, and if there is anything in my style or thought to be commended, the credit is due to my kind parents in instilling into my mind an early love of the Scriptures"; and that William H. Seward, the diplomatist of the century, only showed his puerility when he declared, "The whole hope of human progress is suspended on the ever-growing influences of the Bible"; and that it is wisest for us to take that book from the throne in the affections of uncounted multitudes, and put it under our feet to be trampled upon by hatred and hissing contempt; and that your old father was hoodwinked, and cajoled, and cheated, and befooled, when he leaned on this as a staff after his hair grew gray, and his hands were tremulous, and his steps shortened as he came up to the verge of the grave; and that your mother sat with a pack of lies on her lap while reading of the better country, and of the ending of all her aches and pains, and reunion not only with those of you who stood around her but with the children she had buried with infinite heartache, so that she could read no more until she took off her spectacles, and wiped from them the heavy mist of many tears.

Alas! that for forty and fifty years they should have walked under this delusion and had it under their pillow when they lay a-dying in the back room, and asked that some words from the vile page might be cut upon the tombstone under the shadow of the old country meeting-house where they sleep this morning waiting for a resurrection that will never come. This book, having deceived them, and having deceived the mighty intellects of the past, must not be allowed to deceive our larger, mightier, vaster, more stupendous intellects. And so out with the book from the court-room, where it is used in the solemnization of testimony. Out with it from under the foundation of Church and asylum. Out with it from the domestic circle. Gather together all the Bibles—the children's Bibles, the family Bibles, those newly bound, and those with lid nearly worn out and pages almost obliterated by the fingers long ago turned to dust—bring them all together, and let us make a bonfire of them, and by it warm our cold criticism, and after that turn under with the ploughshare of public indignation the polluted ashes of that loathsome, adulterous, obscene, cruel and deathful book which is so antagonistic to man's liberty, and woman's honor, and the world's happiness.

"Stop!" says some silly old man. "Stop!" says some weak-minded woman. "Stop!" says some small-brained child. "Perhaps you had better give the Bible a trial before you condemn it." Well, we will give it a trial. I empanel this whole audience as a jury to render their verdict in this case—Infidelity, the plaintiff, *versus* Christianity, the defendant. Twelve jurors are ordinarily enough in a case, but in this case, vaster in importance than any other, I this morning empanel all the thousands of people here gathered as a jury, and I ask them silently to affirm that they will well and truly try this issue of traverse joined between Infidelity, the plaintiff, and Christianity, the defendant, so help you God.

The jury empanelled, call *your first witness*. Robert G. Ingersoll! "Here!" Swear the witness. But how are you to swear the witness? I know of only two ways of taking an oath in a court-room. The one is by kissing the Bible, and the other is by lifting the hand. I cannot ask him to swear by the Bible, because he considers that a pack of lies, and therefore it could give no solemnity to his oath. I cannot ask him to lift the hand, for that seems to imply the existence of a God, and that is a fact in dispute. So I swear him by the rings of Saturn, and the spots on the sun, and the caverns in the moon, and the Milky Way, and the nebular hypothesis, that he will tell the truth, the whole truth, and nothing but the truth in this case between Infidelity, the plaintiff, and Christianity, the defendant.

Let me say that I know nothing of the private character of that person, neither do I want to know. I have no taste for exploring private character. I shall deal with him as a public teacher. I shall not be diverted from this by the fact that he has again and again in lectures and in interviews assailed my name. I have no personal animosity. I invite him the Sabbath after he has changed his views in regard to the Christian religion to stand here where I stand and preach his first sermon. I deal with him only as a public teacher.

You say: Why preach these three or four sermons which I intend to preach in answering the champion blasphemer of America? Am I afraid that Christianity will be overborne by this scoffing harlequinade? Oh, no. Do you know how near he has come to stopping Christianity? I will tell you how near he has come to impeding the progress of Christianity in the world. About as much as one snowflake on the track will impede the half-past three o'clock Chicago lightning express train. Perhaps not so much as that. It is more like a Switzerland insect floating through the air impeding an Alpine avalanche.

The Sabbath after Mr. Ingersoll in this region extinguished Christianity, we received in this church over four hundred souls in public and beautiful consecration of themselves to Christ, and that only a small illustration of the universal advance. Within ten years Mr. Ingersoll has done his most conspicuous stopping of Christianity, and he has stopped it at the following rate: In the first fifty years of this century, there were three million people who professed the faith of Christ. In the last ten years, there have been three million people connecting themselves by profession with the Church of Christ. In other words, the last ten years have accomplished as much as the first fifty years of this century. My fear is not that he will arrest Christianity. I preach these sermons *for the benefit of individuals.* There are young men who through his teachings have given up their religion and soon after gave up their morals. Ingersoll's teachings triumphant would fill all the penitentiaries, and the gambling hells and houses of shame on the continent—on the planet. No divine system of morals, and in twenty years we would have a hell on earth eclipsing in abomination the hell that Mr. Ingersoll has so much laughed at. My fear is not that Christianity in general shall be impeded, but I want to persuade these young men to get aboard the train, instead of throwing themselves across the track. God is going to save this world anyhow, and the only question is whether you and I will refuse to get into the lifeboat. Besides that, I want to put into the mouths of these young men arguments by which they can defend themselves in the profession of their faith in Christ when they are bombarded.

But that trial comes on. The jury has been empanelled. The first witness has been called. In the opening sentences of my sermon, I gave Mr. Ingersoll's charges against Christianity. Now, my friends, it is a principle settled in all court-rooms, and among all intelligent people, *"false in part, false in all."* If a witness is found to be making a misrepresentation on the stand, it does not make any difference what he testifies to after; it all goes overboard. The judge, the jury, every common-sense man says, "False in part, false in all." Now, if I can show you, and I will show you, the Lord helping me, that Mr. Ingersoll makes misrepresentations in one respect, or two respects, or three respects, I will demand that, as intelligent men and as fair-minded women, you throw overboard his entire testimony. If he will misrepresent in one thing, he will misrepresent all the way through. "False in one, false in all."

In the first place, he raises a roystering laugh against the Bible by saying: "Is this book true? the gentleman who wrote it said that the world was made out of nothing; I cannot imagine nothing being made into something." In nearly all his lectures he begins with that gigantic misrepresentation. I offer a thousand dollars reward to any man who will show me any passage in the Bible that tells me that the world was made out of nothing. The very first passage says it was *made out of*

God's omnipotence. "In the beginning God created the heaven and the earth." I do not ask you to refer to your Bible. Refer to your memory that you may see it is an *Ingersollian misstatement* – a misstatement from stem to stern, and from cutwater to taffrail, and from the top of the mainmast down to the barnacles on the bottom. If he had taken some obscure passage, he would not have been so soon found out; but he has taken the most conspicuous, the most memorable, the most magnificent passage, all geological and astronomical discovery only adding to its grandeur. "In the beginning." There you can roll in ten million years if you want to. There is no particular date given – no contest between science and revelation. You may roll in there ten million years, if you want to. Though the world may have been in process of creation for millions of years, suddenly and quickly, and in one week, it may have been fitted up for man's residence. Just as a great mansion may have been many years in building, and yet in one week it may be curtained and chandeliered and cushioned and upholstered for a bride and groom.

You are not compelled to believe that the world was made in our six days; you are not compelled to believe that. It may not have been a day of twenty-four hours, the day spoken of in the first chapter; it may have been God's day, and a thousand years with Him are as one day. "And the evening and the morning were the first day" – God's day. "And the evening and the morning were the second day" – God's day. "And the evening and the morning were the sixth day" – God's day. You and I are living in the seventh day, the Sabbath of the world, the day of Gospel redemption, the grandest day of all the week in which each day may have been made up of thousands of years. Can you tell me how a man can get his mind and soul into such a blasphemous twist as to scoff at that first chapter of Genesis, its verses billows of light surging up from sapphire seas of glory! Come now and let Mr. Ingersoll laugh at the fact that the world is made out of nothing. He rings his charges on that word nothing. He has gone all through the cities telling what every man, woman, and child of common-sense knows is a misrepresentation. There is as much difference between Mr. Ingersoll's statement and the truth as between nothing and omnipotence. Now I will take Mr. Ingersoll's first misrepresentation, and I nail it so high that North, South, East, and West may see it and remember it. Wilful misrepresentation! I repeat, there is as much difference between his statement and the Bible statement as between nothing and omnipotence. Now I demand, gentlemen of the jury, that you throw overboard his entire testimony. False in part, false in all – all that he has testified to in the past, all that he will testify to in the future – all overboard, by the common rules of evidence.

I take a step further in the impeachment of this witness. One would have thought that after misrepresenting the first passage he would have rested from his labors and given us some honest exposition. Oh, no! He rolls from side to side with laughter. He runs up and down the whole gamut of cachination. He can hardly contain his mirthfulness. He swoops upon the third and fourth verses of the same chapter in caricature and says: "Ha, ha! the Bible represents that light was created on Monday, and the sun was not created until Thursday. Just think of it! a book declaring that light was created three days before the sun shone!" Here Mr. Ingersoll shows his geological and chemical and astronomical ignorance. If Mr. Ingersoll had asked any schoolboy on his way home from one of our high schools, "My lad, can there be any light without the shining of the sun?" the lad would have said, "Yes, sir; heat and electricity emit light independent of the sun. Beside that, when the earth was in process of condensation, it was surrounded by thick vapors and the discharge of many volcanoes in the primary period, and all this obscuration may have hindered the light of the sun from falling on the earth until that Thursday morning." Beside that, he would say: "Mr. Ingersoll, don't you know that David Brewster and Herschel, the astronomer, and all the modern men of their class, agree in the fact that the sun is not light, that it is an opaque mass, that it is only the candlestick that holds the light, a phosphorescent atmosphere floating around it, changing and changing, so it is not to be at all wondered at that not until that Thursday morning its light fell on the earth? Beside that, Mr. Ingersoll," the lad of the high school would say, "the rocks in crystalization emit light. There is light from a thousand surfaces, the alkalies, for instance." The lad would have gone on to say "The metallic bases emit light." The lad would have gone on still further to say: "Mr. Ingersoll, don't you know there was a time in the history of the world when there were thousands of miles of liquid granite flaming with light?" The lad would have gone on and told Mr. Ingersoll that by observation it has been found that there are burned-out volcanoes in other worlds which, when they were in explosion and activity, must have cast forth an insufferable light, throwing a glare all over our earth. And the boy would have asked him also if he had ever heard of the Aurora Borealis or the Aurora Anchalis. And then the boy would have unbuckled the strap from his bundle of books, and read from one, entitled "Connection of the Physical Sciences," this paragraph:

"Captain Bonnycastle, coming up the Gulf of St. Lawrence on the 17th of September, 1826, was aroused by the mate of the vessel in great alarm from an unusual appearance. It was a starlight night, when suddenly the sky became overcast. In the direction of the high land of Cornwallis County an instantaneous and intensely vivid light, resembling the aurora, shot out on the hitherto gloomy and dark sea, on the lee bow that was so brilliant, it lighted everything distinctly, even to the masthead. The light spread over the whole sea between the two shores, and the waves, which before had been tranquil, became agitated. Captain Bonnycastle describes the scene as that of a blazing sheet of awful and most brilliant light—a long and vivid line of light that showed the face of the high frowning land abreast. The sky became lowering and more intensely obscure. Long, tortuous lines of light showed immense numbers of large fish darting about as if in consternation. The topsail yard and mizzen-boom were lighted by the glare as if gaslights had been burned directly below them, and until just before day-break, at four o'clock, the most minute objects were distinctly visible."

Mr. Ingersoll has only to go to one of our high schools to learn there are ten thousand sources of light besides the light of the sun. But if he had been in one of the classes in our high schools, a class in astronomy, or geology, or chemistry, the impatient teacher would have said to him: "Robert, go down to the foot and be in disgrace—be in disgrace for your stupidity!" This is not wilful misrepresentation in this case on the part of Mr. Ingersoll. He does not know any better. It is the most profound and most disgusting ignorance ever exhibited on a lecturer's platform in America, when he says there cannot be any light, or implies there cannot be any light, except that which comes from the sun.

In the first case which I showed you it was wilful misrepresentation. In this case it is ignorance, geological, and astronomical, and chemical. But whether wilful or ignorant misrepresentation, either and both will impeach Robert G. Ingersoll as incompetent to give testimony in this case between Infidelity, the plaintiff, and Christianity, the defendant. I nail on the top of the temple of scepticism this misrepresentation by the champion blasphemer of America. He misrepresented in the first case. He has misrepresented in the second case. Now I demand, gentlemen of the jury, that you throw overboard his testimony. "False in part, false in all."

I take a step further in impeaching this witness against Christianity. He sharpens all his witticisms to destroy our belief in the ancient deluge and Noah's Ark. He says that from the account there, it must have rained eight hundred feet of water each day in order that it might be fifteen cubits above the hills. He says that the ark could not have been large enough to contain "two of every sort," for there would have been hundreds of thousands and hundreds of thousands of creatures! He says that these creatures would have come from all lands and all zones! He says there was only one small window in the ark, and that would not have given fresh air to keep the animals inside the ark from suffocation! Then he winds up that part of the story by saying that the ark finally landed on a mountain seventeen thousand feet high. He says he does not believe the story. Neither do I! There is no such story in the Bible. I will tell you what the Bible story is. I must say that I have changed my mind in regard to some matters which once were to me very mysterious. They are no more mysterious. This is the key to the facts. This is the story of an eye-witness, Noah, his story incorporated afterward by Moses in the account. Noah described the scene just as it appeared to him. He saw the flood and he fathomed its depth. As far as eye could reach everything was covered up, from horizon to horizon, or as it says, "under the whole heaven." He did not refer to the Sierra Nevadas, or to Mount Washington, for America had not been discovered, or, if it had been discovered, he could not have seen so far off. He is giving the testimony of an eye-witness. God speaks after the manner of men when He says everything went under, and Noah speaks after the manner of men when he says everything did go under. An eye-witness. There is no need of thinking that the kangaroo leaped the ocean, or that the polar bear came down from the ice.

Why did the deluge come? It came for the purpose of destroying the outrageous inhabitants of the then thinly populated earth, nearly all the population probably very near the ark before it was launched. What would have been the use of submerging North and South America, or Europe, or Africa when they were not inhabited? Mr. Ingersoll most grossly misrepresents, when he says that in order to have that depth of water it must have rained eight hundred feet every day. The Bible distinctly declares that the most of the flood rose instead of falling. Before the account where it says "the windows of heaven were opened," it says, "all the fountains of the great deep were broken up." All geologists agree in saying that there are caverns in the earth filled with water, and they rushed forth, and all the lakes and rivers forsook their bed. What am I to think, and what are you to think of a man who, ignoring this earthquake spoken of in the Bible as preceding the falling of the rain, and for the purpose of making a laugh at the Bible, will say it must have rained over eight hundred feet every day? Taking the last half instead of the first half. The fountains of the great deep were broken up, and then the windows of heaven were opened. Is it a strange thing that we should be asked to believe in this flood of the Bible, when geologists tell us that again and again and again the dry earth has been drowned out? Just open your geology, and you will read of twenty floods. Is it not a strange thing that the infidel scientist wanting us to believe in the twenty floods of geological discovery, should, as soon as we believe in the one flood of the Bible, pronounce us asinine and *non compos mentis*?

Well, then, another thing, in regard to the size of the ark. Instead of being a mud-scow, as some of these infidels would have us understand, it was a magnificent ship, nearly as large as our Great Eastern, three times the size of an ordinary man-of-war. At the time in the world when shipbuilding was unknown, God had this vessel constructed, which turned out to be almost in the same proportions as our stanchest modern vessels. After thousands of years of experimenting in naval architecture and in ship-carpentery, we have at last got up to Noah's ark, that ship leading all the fleets of the world on all the oceans. Well, Noah saw the animal creation going into this ark. He gave the account of an eye-witness. They were the animals from the region where he lived; for the most part they were animals useful to man, and if noxious insects or poisonous reptiles went in, it was only to discipline the patience and to keep alert the generations after the flood. He saw them going in. There were a great number of them, and he gives the account of an eye-witness. They went in two and two of all flesh.

Two or three years ago I was on a steamer on the river Tay, and I came to Perth, Scotland. I got off, and I saw the most wonderful agricultural show that I had ever witnessed. There were horses and cattle such as Rosa Bonheur never sketched, and there were dogs such as the loving pencil of Edwin Landseer never portrayed, and there were sheep and fowl and creatures of all sorts. Suppose that "two and two" of all the creatures of that agricultural show were put upon the Tay steamer to be transported to Dundee, and the next day I should be writing home to America and giving an account of the occurrence, I would have used the same general phraseology that Noah used in regard to the embarkation of the brute creation in the ark — I would have said that they went in two and two of every sort. I would not have meant six hundred thousand. A common-sense man myself, I would suppose that the people who read the letter were common sense people.

"But how could you get them into the ark?" says Mr. Ingersoll with a great sneer. "How could they be induced to go into the ark? He would have to pick them out and drive them in, and coax them in." Could not the same God who gave instinct to the animal inspire that instinct to seek for shelter from the storm? However, nothing more than ordinary animal instinct was necessary. Have you never been in the country when an August thunder-storm was coming up and heard the cattle moan at the bars to get in? and seen the affrighted fowl go upon the perch at noonday, and heard the affrighted dog and cat calling at the door, supplicating entrance? And are you surprised that in that age of the world, when there were fewer places of shelter for dumb beasts, at the muttering and rumbling and flashing and quaking and darkening of an approaching deluge, the animal creation came moaning and bleating to the sloping embankment reaching up to the ancient Great Eastern, and passed in? I have owned horses and cattle and sheep and dogs, but I never had a horse, or a cow, or a sheep, or a dog that was so stupid it did not know enough to come in when it rained! Yet Mr. Ingersoll cannot understand how they could get in. It is amazing to him. And then, that one window in the ark which afforded such poor ventilation to the creatures there assembled — that small window in the ark which excites so much mirthfulness on the part of the great infidel. If he had known as much Hebrew as you could put on your little finger nail, he would have known that the word translated window there means *window course*, a whole range of lights. This ignorant infidel does not know a window pane from twenty windows. So, if there is any criticism of the ark, there seems to be too much window for such a long storm. If he had studied Hebrew two weeks he would have been saved the display of that appalling ignorance, that most disgraceful ignorance, when he scoffs and scoffs and scoffs, and chuckles and chuckles and chuckles over the small window in the ark. This infidel says that during the long storm the window must have been kept shut, and hence no air. There are people in this house to-day who, all the way from Liverpool to Barnegat lighthouse, and for two weeks, were kept under deck, the hatches battened down because of the storm. Some of you, in the old-time sailing vessels, were kept nearly a month with the hatches down because of some long storm.

For the tenth or the fifteenth misrepresentation by Mr. Ingersoll, he says that the ark landed on a mountain seventeen thousand feet high, and that, of course, as soon as the animals came forth they would all be frozen in the ice! Here comes in Mr. Ingersoll's geographical ignorance. He does not seem to know that Ararat is not merely the name for a mountain, but for a *hilly district*, and that it may have been a hill one hundred feet high, or five hundred, or a thousand feet high on which the ark alighted. Noah measured the depth of the water above the hill, and it is fifteen cubits or twenty-seven feet. But in order to raise a laugh against the Holy Scriptures, Mr. Ingersoll lifts the ark seventeen thousand feet high, showing an ignorance of just that altitude!

Ah! my friends, this story of the ark is no more incredible than if you should say to me: "Last summer I was among the hills of New England, and there came on the most terrific storm I ever saw, and the whole country was flooded. The waters came up over the hills, and to save our lives we got in a boat on the river, and even the dumb creatures were so affrighted, they came moaning and bleating until we let them in the same boat." The flood that Ingersoll describes is not Noah's flood; it is Ingersoll's flood of hatred against God. It is not Noah's ark that Ingersoll describes; it is Ingersoll's ark with a whole flock of hooting owls of the midnight of Infidelity, whole nests of viperine and adderine venom against God, whole lairs of panthers which, with spotted claw, if they could, would maul the eternal God to pieces. And there is only one small window in that ark, and it opens into the blackness of darkness described by my text, "having the understanding darkened, being alienated from the life of God through the ignorance that is in them." The first misrepresentation of Mr. Ingersoll was wilful, the second was geological and astronomical ignorance, the third was geographical ignorance.

We are not dependent on the Bible for the story of the flood, entirely. All ages and all literatures have traditions, broken traditions, indistinct traditions, but still traditions. The old books of the Persians tell about the flood at the time of Ahriman, who so polluted the earth that it had to be washed by a great storm. The traditions of the Chaldeans say that in the time when Xisuthrus was king there was a great flood, and he put his family and his friends in a large vessel and all outside of them were destroyed, and after a while the birds went forth and they came back and their claws were tinged with mud. Lucian and Ovid, celebrated writers, who had never seen the Bible, describe a flood in the time of Deucalion. He took his friends into a boat, and the animals came running to him in pairs. So, all lands, and all ages, and all literatures, seem to have a broken and indistinct tradition of a calamity which Moses, here incorporating Noah's account, so grandly, so beautifully, so accurately, so solemnly records.

But I must halt in this argument, as in a great trial sometimes an attorney will stop for lack of time to finish, and I must on other Sabbath mornings take up this subject. I have only opened the door of a subject it will take me other Sabbath mornings to explore. I have impeached Robert G. Ingersoll for having misrepresented once, twice, thrice. I demand that you put into execution the principle of every court-room, gentlemen of the jury, and throw overboard his entire testimony. "False in part, false in all." I have this morning only discussed the cleanest part of Mr. Ingersoll's infidelity – the best part of Mr. Ingersoll's infidelity. There are depths below depths, and I shall go on and say all I have to say on this subject.

My prayer is that the God who created the world, not out of nothing, but out of His own omnipotence, may create us anew in Christ Jesus; and that the God who made light three days before the sun shone, may kindle in our souls a light that will burn on long after the sun has expired; and that the God who ordered the ark built and kept open more than one hundred years that the antediluvians might enter it for shelter, may graciously incline us to accept the invitation which this morning rolls in music from the throne, saying: "Come thou and all thy house into the ark."

FOR ADDITIONAL INFORMATION ABOUT THOMAS DEWITT TALMAGE:

Banks, Charles Eugene. *Authorized and Authentic Life and Works of T. DeWitt Talmage.* Chicago: Bible House, 1902.

Macartney, Clarence Edward. "T. DeWitt Talmage." *Six Kings of the American Pulpit*. Philadelphia: Westminster Press, 1942.

Talmage, May, comp. *Wisdom and Wit of T. DeWitt Talmage*. New York: George H. Doran Co., 1922.

Talmage, T. DeWitt. *Life and Teachings of Rev. T. DeWitt Talmage*. Philadelphia: American Book & Bible House, 1902.

Wilkinson, William Cleaver. "Thomas DeWitt Talmage." *Modern Masters of Pulpit Discourse*. New York: Funk & Wagnalls Co., 1905.

FOR OTHER SERMONS BY THOMAS DEWITT TALMAGE:

The Brooklyn Tabernacle. New York: Funk & Wagnalls Co., 1884.

The Masque Torn Off. Chicago: Fairbanks, Palmer & Co., 1883.

Also: *Old Wells Dug Out* (1874), *Palestine Sermons* (1890), *Fifty Short Sermons* (1923), *New Tabernacle Sermons* (1886).